DEPENDENT AMERICA
HOW CANADA AND MEXICO CONSTRUCT US POWER

Following the acclaimed *Uncle Sam and Us* and the influential *Does North America Exist?* Stephen Clarkson – Canada's pre-eminent analyst of North America's political economy – and Matto Mildenberger turn continental scholarship on its head by showing how Canada and Mexico contribute to the United States' wealth, security, and global power.

This provocative work documents how Canada and Mexico offer the United States open markets for its investments and exports, massive flows of skilled and unskilled labour, and vast resource inputs – all of which boost its size and competitiveness – more than does any other US partner. They are also Uncle Sam's most important allies in supporting its anti-terrorist and anti-narcotics security. Clarkson and Mildenberger explain the paradox of these two countries' simultaneous importance and powerlessness by showing how the US government has systematically neutralized their potential influence.

Detailing the dynamics of North America's power relations, *Dependent America?* is a fitting conclusion to Clarkson's celebrated trilogy on the contradictory qualities of its regionalism – asymmetrical economic integration, thickened borders, and emasculated governance.

STEPHEN CLARKSON is a professor of political economy at the University of Toronto, a senior fellow at the Centre for International Governance Innovation, and a fellow of the Royal Society of Canada. He was recently invested with the Order of Canada.

MATTO MILDENBERGER is a PhD student in the School of Forestry and Environmental Studies at Yale University.

STEPHEN CLARKSON AND
MATTO MILDENBERGER

Dependent America?

How Canada and Mexico Construct US Power

UNIVERSITY OF TORONTO PRESS
Toronto Buffalo London

and

WOODROW WILSON CENTER PRESS
Washington, DC

© University of Toronto Press 2011
Toronto Buffalo London
www.utppublishing.com
Printed in Canada

ISBN 978-1-4426-4463-2 (cloth)
ISBN 978-1-4426-1277-8 (paper)

Printed on acid-free, 100% post-consumer recycled paper with
vegetable-based inks.

Library and Archives Canada Cataloguing in Publication

Clarkson, Stephen, 1937–
Dependent America? : how Canada and Mexico construct US power /
Stephen Clarkson and Matto Mildenberger.

Includes bibliographical references and index.
Also issued in electronic format.
ISBN 978-1-4426-4463-2 (bound). – ISBN 978-1-4426-1277-8 (pbk.)

1. United States – Relations – Canada.   2. Canada – Relations – United
States.   3. United States – Relations – Mexico.   4. Mexico – Relations –
United States.   5. United States – Economic conditions.   6. National
security – United States.   7. United States – Foreign relations.
8. Hegemony – United States.   I. Mildenberger, Matto   II. Title.

E183.8.C2C53 2011   327.73071   C2011-905261-X

University of Toronto Press acknowledges the financial assistance to its
publishing program of the Canada Council for the Arts and the Ontario
Arts Council.

University of Toronto Press acknowledges the financial support of the
Government of Canada through the Canada Book Fund for its publishing
activities.

to
Nora
and
Leah
our partners in life and love
for
their insights and inspiration

Contents

DEPENDENT AMERICA?
HOW CANADA AND MEXICO CONSTRUCT US POWER

Introduction: Is America 'Dependent'?

With its financial implosion, its military withdrawal from the Middle East, and its intermittent sparring with a resurgent China, the United States' falterings on the world stage have opened the latest in a series of intellectual debates that have accompanied the ups and downs of its hegemony over the last half-century. Back in the 1970s, Europe's recovery, the emergence of the Organization of Petroleum Exporting Countries (OPEC), and Japan's then-spectacular rise were allegedly tolling the bell for US global dominance. Yet, by the time the dust had settled from the Soviet Union's 1991 collapse, the United States had actually risen to an apparently incontestable supremacy on the global stage.

The academic research community has played a central role in detailing the vicissitudes of the United States' power trajectory as Keynesian liberal internationalism gave way to a more conservative neorealism. But whether laudatory or critical, scholars have seldom questioned that the United States is the largest economic, military, diplomatic, and cultural power in the world, even as they have debated whether America is in decline or, in Paul Kennedy's words, has just been getting back to 'normalcy.'[1]

Throughout, analysts have treated US power as self-determined. It would have elicited a blank stare from most professional observers if one asked from where the United States obtained its extraordinary wealth, or its impregnable defences, or its structural power in the world's institutions. Even scholars who wrote matter-of-factly about the United States as 'empire' did not use the word to suggest that the country became rich and powerful by pressing colonies to contribute money to its mint or men to its military. Quite the contrary, the United

States' power tended to be viewed as autonomously determined by its own citizens' industriousness, by their beliefs in individual freedom, by their capitalist system's inherent dynamic, and by their coast-to-coast territory's bounteous endowments in soil, water, and resources.

Beyond being compared quantitatively with that of actual or potential rivals, the power of the United States is generally assessed instrumentally in terms of whether American decision makers exercise that power wisely and effectively – that is, whether they act unilaterally on the world stage or work cooperatively within international organizations. Either way, US power is typically taken as given. The United States' massive physical assets and mission for leadership are assumed as the material and normative starting points for explaining the country's capacity to shape events around the entire globe. Understanding Washington as master of its own house, analysts routinely present its problem as how to flex its muscles: Should it exercise its will by imposing its hard power or should it work collaboratively by using its soft power – or should it try some blend of the two? At the receiving end of American might, intellectuals and policy makers in other countries normally focus on analysing the myriad ways in which the United States influences them rather than on their own governments' generally minor influence on it.

In this book we engage with another problematic. Our initial presumption is that it is not just their own human and material resources that make Great Powers great. If they have more strength abroad than can be explained by their domestic assets alone, this is because their capacity to foster economic wealth, to build military muscle, and to promote their international influence is also generated through their relationships with other states. A century ago, an imperial state enhanced its geopolitical clout by exploiting its colonies' economic resources, pressing their youth into its armed forces, and managing their international actions. But, even if it does not formally control another country, a state can become a Great Power by extending its economic reach through trade and investment relations, securing greater military heft through alliances, and building coalitions with like-minded counterparts to achieve its foreign-policy goals.

From this starting point we can imagine a matrix that identifies for any Great Power how other states in the international system contribute to its international efficacy by building its economy, by supporting its military positions, and by cooperating with it internationally. For historians of empire, it is obvious that Spain achieved its global dominance in large part through having extracted hoards of gold from its colonies in the New World, that the reach of France's military depended on recruiting soldiers from its African colonies, and that much of Great Britain's clout, when negotiating the terms of peace at Versailles in 1919, came from speaking for an empire of colonies and a commonwealth of dominions on which the sun never set.

In this spirit, our study questions the presumption that the United States' power is entirely self-determined. Even if it does not have an empire in the European tradition, its industry requires more resources than can be found within its borders, its exporters must find markets, its transnational corporations seek host economies in which to set up their branches or outsource their suppliers, the Pentagon needs allies, and its soft-power legitimacy stems largely from overseas subscribers to the American dream.

Whereas much of the existing thinking about global politics has concentrated on the United States as the international order's *prime actor*, whose economic and military heft explains its consequent capacity to shape the world outside its borders, we are initially approaching the United States as an *object*. To do this we explore the extent to which its power is a function both of the benefit it has derived from other states' resources in the past and of its capacity to mobilize their material and moral support in the present. To reframe this issue in terms of our ambiguous title, we want to find out how *dependent* on foreign sources is US power. Once we establish that a significant portion depends on another country's assets, we will ask to what extent Washington, as *agent*, has attempted to neutralize its dependence on, or vulnerability to, interruptions of the flow of that power.

The United States' Power in Its Continental Context

We are not so much scholars of global international relations as analysts of North America's political economy. Accordingly, this inquiry applies our general interest in Great Powers' dependence on their external relationships to a territorially narrower field by asking how much of its power the United States draws from its two continental neighbours.

Restating the logic of our enquiry, we are asking:

• to what extent Canada and Mexico as *agents* contribute to US power;
• whether any of these contributions create a *dependency* that makes

the United States vulnerable to its neighbours' withdrawal of their support; and

- in what ways Washington has taken the initiative, as *agent* itself, to neutralize the autonomy-reducing consequence of such dependence.

This book is the last of three studies in which Stephen Clarkson has engaged with North America's post-Cold War evolution. In 2002 his *Uncle Sam and Us* explored the significance of two paradigm-shifting transformations for Canada. At issue was how a radically new conservative ideology and its continentally (the North American Free Trade Agreement, NAFTA) and globally (the World Trade Organization, WTO) institutionalized rules had affected the Canadian state's ability to promote its citizens' social welfare, its economy's development, its culture's integrity, and its external capacity to operate effectively on the global stage. Although provincial and federal governments had cut back their programs supporting social justice, industrial promotion, and cultural expression, the book argued that Canada still enjoyed substantial domestic autonomy and continued to demonstrate a capacity for collaborating multilaterally to achieve such goals as the 1997 treaty banning the deployment of anti-personnel landmines.

In 2008 Clarkson's *Does North America Exist?* asked to what extent NAFTA's new rules and the United States' attempts to create a continental security perimeter after September 11, 2001 ('9/11') had developed an integrated North American economy and a meaningful transnational governance within the three-state North American region. The volume established that North America had no trilateral governance institutions of any importance, that its principal economic sectors were becoming globalized rather than regionalized, but that the three countries had been reconstituted into an increasingly integrated security zone driven by Washington's wars on drugs and terrorism.

It is obvious to all that the United States is the overwhelmingly dominant state in North America, with the greatest population (307 million compared to 107 million in Mexico and 34 million in Canada) and the largest economy ($14.1 trillion compared to $1.3 trillion for Canada and $0.88 trillion for Mexico).[2] Nevertheless, in this third volume, Matto Mildenberger joins Stephen Clarkson in asking to what extent this discrepancy in size and wealth is itself due to the benefits that the continental hegemon has derived from its two smaller neighbours. Simply put, our question is: How much have Canada and Mexico contributed to building the United States' wealth and security?

This Introduction's remaining tasks are to explain why it is not frivolous to ask how Canada and Mexico construct US power and then to outline how we propose to find answers to our query.

An Unfrivolous Question

There are many reasons why it is worthwhile to ask about the components of US strength. For one thing, with the United States having driven the world's development for almost a century, its multiple powers remain a valid and vital object for study. Its economic dynamism has for decades been the capitalist world's prime growth engine as a market for other countries' exports, as a client for their resources, as an investor in their economies, and as a financial centre where international investors could confidently place or exchange their own capital.

At the same time, US muscle has determined the security parameters of almost every other country – be it friendly and to be recruited, hostile and to be contained, or neutral and to be courted. The United States has done this by leading alliances like the North Atlantic Treaty Organization (NATO), by establishing bases around the world, by sending operatives to support its allies in other states' civil conflicts, or by openly waging wars to overthrow hostile regimes.

Also, US foreign policy has long set the agenda for the rest of the world both in designing global institutions and in making crucial decisions – whether to intervene (between the two Koreas in the 1950s) or not (in the Rwanda genocide in the 1990s). The United States put its former enemies Japan and Germany back on their feet in the late 1940s by overseeing their constitutions' reforms and guiding their economies' recoveries. It supported the consolidation of Europe's formerly fratricidal states when they worked towards reconfiguring the continent as a zone of peace, a common market, and a transnational governance community. It pushed for the decolonization of its collapsing empires and provided substantial aid for the South's new states. It wore down the Socialist bloc's leaders with its relentless pressure, all the while offering their publics an alternative vision of life, liberty, and the pursuit of happiness. It maintained its Jekyll and Hyde role in the Western hemisphere, presenting itself both as a model for those seeking a market-driven development path and as a monster for those who feared its Marines' intervention in their politics.

Finally, American culture helped build soft-power legitimacy for the United States abroad. Whether it was the soulful jazz that emanated from New Orleans' brothels, or Hollywood's fantasy of America-the-beautiful-and-bountiful, or the rock 'n' roll that blasted out the eardrums of adolescents around the world, or the risqué shenanigans of *Dallas* or *Sex in the City*'s many TV episodes, or hip-hop's provocative rapping, or Facebook's globalized intimacies, the American entertainment machine propagated the United States' appeal as the model of what (almost) everyone on the planet wanted to emulate. US mass media exports were not just hugely profitable; they helped offset the United States' coercive, hard-power face in the world's consciousness. Meanwhile, American news services refracted international affairs through the lens of US interests, and American universities set the global standards for academic research.

We are interested in understanding what built this power that fundamentally shaped the twentieth century, but we are raising our question at a moment when US dominance is itself in question. What even recently was considered the United States' unchallengeable military superiority has failed to prevail in the face of local resistance to its first two twenty-first-century ventures. Its economic pre-eminence has been jeopardized by a financial collapse of its own making. At a historical watershed when the country's relative power may be on the cusp of a permanent decline and when analysts and scholars are trying to recalibrate their understanding of its position in the global balance of forces, it is far from frivolous to deconstruct this phenomenon.

With the United States' economic strength, military might, and even values being openly challenged, it becomes even more important to determine how the sources of its power have derived from the relations it has sustained over time with its international partners. This done, we will better understand the factors that may condition its future prospects.

Our Proposed Approach

To explain our approach, we will first outline how our thinking developed. This will lead us to detail our methodology, specify our use of key concepts, note some of the special characteristics of our analysis, and set out the book's plan.

This study was sparked by a simple curiosity about how the United States benefits from its relationship with Canada and Mexico. Having long worked in a continental scholarly tradition that positions the United States as the dynamo to which Canada and Mexico react, we started to wonder about reversing the causal arrows. At first, our interests in this inverted question were purely material. Could we establish in dollars-and-cents terms how much the United States had become richer because of its relationships with Canada and Mexico? The obvious fields of research for such an inquiry were economic: trade and investment in general, resources and labour in particular.

It did not take us long to realize that we could not simply discuss the extra jobs Americans gained when Canadian consumers buy their products, or the extra profits that US transnational corporations (TNCs) reap from investing in Mexico, as if these questions were separate from the domain of public policy. The cross-border flows of goods and services may seem to be objectively determined by market forces, but they are not solely so. Markets are political constructions in the sense that their parameters are established by government policies. For instance, US exporters' access to Canadian consumers is related in good part to Canadian trade policy, and US TNCs' ability to expand south of the Rio Grande depends on the Mexican government's policy towards foreign direct investment (FDI). Questions of policy became central as soon as our analysis bore on the determinants of the continental periphery's contributions to US power.

'Power' is a term so ubiquitous in the social sciences that it has acquired a legion of meanings. We use two. First, we view power as an *attribute* that describes a country's material assets. In this respect, we focus on such measurable foundations of US power as its economic size, material resources, and population.

National capacity does not influence outcomes if it is not actively leveraged vis-à-vis other states. For this reason, we also speak of power as a *relation*. To win the Cold War, the United States not only needed a bigger economy and armaments strong enough to deter those of the USSR. It also had to deploy those capabilities strategically to wear down the Soviet state. Within North America, we will therefore consider how Canada and Mexico have contributed to (or sometimes limited) the United States' material assets and how they have strengthened (or on occasion weakened) its capacity to realize its strategic objectives.

We will use the notions of *construction* and *constraint* to distinguish these two dynamics. To construct US power means to provide material and/or moral resources in a way that boosts the United States' strength and supports its interests. To constrain US power means to withhold moral and material resources in a way that opposes Uncle Sam's interests.

From these first reflections, our thinking spread horizontally in terms of scope and became more nuanced in its approach to causality.

Scope

Once we framed the United States' material wealth as an aspect of its global power, we naturally asked whether there were other facets of US strength to which Canada and Mexico contributed. Of course, security issues could not be calibrated as quantitatively as could economic indicators but they became no less necessary for a study that had morphed into an effort to rethink the North American continent's power realities. Questions also occurred to us about issues that were unrelated to Canada's and Mexico's geographical proximity to the United States. Did these two middle powers play any special role in determining US power on the global stage, whether in building institutions of global governance or pursuing particular foreign-policy objectives?

Causality

As our interests expanded thematically, they became more complicated causally. Although our original goal was simply to document how much the United States *gained* from its relationships with Canada and Mexico, we recognized that there might be some ways in which US power was *constrained* by the periphery. The most obvious example was Mexico's nationalization of American oil companies in 1938. More recently, Canada successfully led the world community's effort to establish at the United Nations Educational, Scientific and Cultural Organization (UNESCO) rules authorizing countries to protect their cultures against the import of foreign media products. This was an initiative to which the United States strenuously objected, because UNESCO's 2005 Convention for the Protection and Promotion of the Diversity of Cultural Expression gave signatory governments a legal norm to justify restricting the distribution of such US mass media products as movies.

It was not just the question of the periphery as *agent* that was causally complex. So was the issue of the United States as *object*. We recognized that it is absurd to think of the world's most powerful state as passive vis-à-vis the way its neighbours impinge on its own interests. Indeed, from its original Declaration of Independence, the United States has shown itself acutely conscious of the way that its adjacent territories affect its well-being. Positively, it has persuaded its neighbours to take measures that contribute to its power. Negatively, it has tried to deter them from pursuing initiatives overseas that limit the sway of its foreign policies.

The United States has vigorously sought to induce its periphery to promote its own economic, military, and international interests. It has encouraged its two neighbours to increase their supplies of energy. It has pressed them to bulk up their defences against its enemies, whether these were hostile states or drug cartels. It sought Mexico's support at the UN Security Council for its invasion of Iraq and it urged Canada to send troops to Afghanistan.

Pre-emptively, Washington has often striven to prevent Canada and Mexico from leveraging its dependence on them into significant influence over its policies and has attempted to have them change foreign policies it finds injurious. It has resisted past efforts by the Mexican and Canadian governments to restrict American TNCs' operations in their economies and has tried to dissuade them from trading with and offering other supports to Fidel Castro's Cuba.

Our conundrums with causality are not restricted to the relationships among America's three members which are so interwoven that none can be presented solely as agent or as object. We must also be sensitive to the contested quality of most public policy and we must recognize that many governmental or private-sector actions have unintended consequences. The United States' real or imagined impact on Mexico or Canada has on occasion incited domestic voices to push their government to take actions that, in turn, rebound against US interests. When, for instance, American TNCs (as *agents*) were deemed to exploit the Mexican economy or stifle Canadian culture, the periphery governments introduced measures to protect their domestic enterprises and so constrict either the actual or potential income of the affected US investors (once more the *object* in the interlocked relationship).

We do not view North American power relations through a zero-sum lens. It may be the case that Canadian integration into the US security perimeter is inherently a win-win situation that serves both Canadian and US national interests, as earlier efforts jointly to manage continental security during the Second World War would suggest. Just as important, the ways in which the three North American governments perceive their self-interests matter a great deal. When Ottawa and Mexico City passionately adopted the US trade-liberalization agenda in the mid-1980s, the continent's periphery in effect redefined its national interests in a way that resonated with the economic preferences of many Washington elites.

Taking energy as a simple case of one of these causal chains, we know from the official data that Canada is the largest foreign supplier of oil to the US market. From this fact we could infer that Canada is the agent and the United States is the object of Canadian agency. But we also know that much of that oil had been discovered and developed by US corporations in response to Washington's tax incentives. This means that the United States must be considered as much the causal *agent*, which generated the supply it sought, as it was the causal *object*, whose power was enhanced by Canada exporting the fuel. Uncle Sam nevertheless remained vulnerable to Canada appropriating its energy output for its own use. When Ottawa attempted to do just that during the late 1970s and early 1980s, it showed that the United States was vulnerable to its neighbour's actions. How Washington partnered with domestic Canadian interests to neutralize this vulnerability to Canadian policy autonomy became the next episode in the complex causal chronology of the continent's trinational energy-power relationship.

Another way to present our inquiry's rationale is to pose the question counterfactually: In what ways and to what degree would US power be reduced (or enhanced) if Canada and Mexico did *not* exist on its northern and southern borders? This hypothetical question can be raised in a number of ways. The simplest is to ask this question: If Canada and Mexico disappeared, would the United States be more prosperous or less so? safer or less secure? globally more effective or ineffective? For instance, if the landmass called Canada had sunk into the sea during the Cold War, the United States would have been more directly threatened by the Soviet Union's military machine and would have had to bear all the costs of its own defence without Canada's financial contribution and military support. Equally, if Mexico's terrain was all ocean, Uncle Sam would have an easier time controlling the smuggling of narcotics from Colombia.

Throughout this manuscript, our main objective is to document the extent to which Canada and Mexico matter to the United States – whether helping it to achieve its economic, security, or diplomatic goals or hindering it in these pursuits. In short, we hope to demonstrate the actual impact that Canada and Mexico have on US material, military, and international power. To sum up our causal approach, we are primarily looking at Canada and Mexico as the *agents* and the United States as the *object*. In our nine chapters our primary aim is to find out how much Canada and Mexico make the United States richer or poorer, more secure or less, globally effective or ineffective. If we determine that US power is significantly based on an input from the periphery, we are then interested in establishing any ways in which US agency has played a part: To what extent did American actions create the relationship in the first place? How did Washington act to reduce its subsequent vulnerability to its neighbours' potential power over it?

Extensive Canadian and Mexican research has been devoted to the degree to which each country has itself been affected by the United States. Whether the United States makes Canada and Mexico economically richer or poorer, militarily more or less secure, and internationally stronger or weaker concerns us in this book only when these effects, in turn, significantly affect US interests.

Describing the United States' Continental Relationships

Although our purpose is more empirical than theoretical, our study has required us – as did *Uncle Sam and Us* and *Does North America Exist?* – to reflect on the conceptual challenges involved in describing the United States' bilateral relationships with its two neighbours.

Scholars have long struggled over how to describe the connection between a giant power and its smaller neighbours. Even when there is no formal relationship, a larger state exerts a gravitational pull on smaller neighbours in its region by offering greater opportunities for their people or larger markets for their entrepreneurs. Resisting this attraction in the name of national survival leads smaller states to generate policies oriented towards autonomous development. The hegemonic state will attempt to exploit its advantages of size by discouraging lesser powers' protectionism at the same time as it protects its own space. In the North American case, the relationships are so multifarious that finding a single conceptualization for them has defied academic efforts for decades.

'Alliance' is sporadically used to describe the periphery-centre relationship in North America, but the word's application is generally restricted to security matters. Although the United States' strategic documents and political rhetoric still employ the concept when recognizing the historic participation of its Second World War military 'allies' or

Cold War containment partners, it now applies the word increasingly to its partners in its current 'wars' on terrorism and narcotics. Canada and Mexico have strengthened their anti-terrorist and anti-narcotics measures out of their governing elites' agreement to collaborate in these same two causes. Even when their publics' conviction was lacking, the periphery governments believed that, to prevent their economic relationships with the United States from being further disrupted, they had no choice but to conform to its security-policy demands for a continental security perimeter. These realities notwithstanding, 'alliance' still remains a predominantly military concept which sits uneasily on the North American reality.

'Partnership' is too broad a category for describing most aspects of these relationships because they are rarely formalized and are even more rarely symmetrical. When one side is in a balanced relationship with the other, the two parties may well approach their common problems in a partnership-like way, as occurred when the ten American Great Lakes states, Ontario, Quebec, and the two federal governments negotiated a protocol defining conditions for diverting water from this aquatic ecosystem, a development recounted in *Does North America Exist?*[3]

But the United States' relations with its neighbours rarely involve dealings among equals. It is in the US interest not to appear to dominate its neighbours, and it is in the Mexican and Canadian governments' interests to appear to have retained their autonomy. So NAFTA's language framed its provisions in a legal discourse which presumes that the 'parties' are sovereign states which are solemnly and equally committing themselves to precisely demarcated undertakings. The North American Aerospace Defence Command (NORAD), the Canada-US Free Trade Agreement (CUFTA), and the North American Free Trade Agreement may have been presented in legalistic discourse and for public consumption as balanced treaties between equally sovereign countries, but there has rarely been much doubt about who calls the shots in the relationships between the United States and the two neighbours who implement these agreements.

'Junior partnership' would be a more appropriate designation in most cases, but the implication of inferiority makes the phrase unacceptably invidious for public officials' discourse. While it is true that the United States formally binds itself by the same norms when signing and ratifying agreements, two geopolitical realities modify this image of nominal partnership. Though universal in their scope, free-trade principles express American interests. For instance, 'national treatment' prohibits Canada and Mexico from effectively competing with the United States by employing the kinds of national-development policies that it used itself in the nineteenth century to promote domestic entrepreneurs as they were building the American economy. Neoconservative principles lock in the continent's asymmetries, but Washington is so powerful it can refuse to comply with unpopular rulings generated by the very same global governance it has taken the lead in establishing. In short, the continent's relationships among unequals are more like junior partnerships, since its formal declarations of equality among the three nations have rarely passed from rhetoric to reality.

'Empire' is not just politically unacceptable but is too historically identified with earlier regimes of territorial control to be helpful in describing the United States' more sophisticated relations of dominance with its two neighbours. The economic benefits it receives are on the whole generated without political coercion, since the marketplace in which US capital is typically dominant produces US profits and jobs thanks, in large part, to laws and regulatory measures which were put in place autonomously by Canada and Mexico as they pursued what the respective governments considered their own interests. This is not to say that Washington has never dictated Canada's or Mexico's measures. While preferring to clothe its fist in a velvet glove, it has, when aroused, exerted such coercive pressure to enforce compliance with its wishes that its behaviour can on these occasions be properly described as 'imperial.'

Perimeter

Rather than considering Mexico or Canada to be US 'colonies' – a word that connotes direct control from the imperial centre – we found it more descriptively accurate to employ the metaphor of 'perimeter,' which carries fewer historically distracting connotations but conveys the notion of unencumbered US access to particular parts of Mexican or Canadian markets, mineral sectors, and regulatory spaces.

Extending the United States' immigration-control perimeter into Canadian space formally began when 'pre-clearance' measures allowed US customs and immigration officials in a few Canadian airport hubs to process passengers flying from Canada to the United States. This model was conceptually extended to include the whole of Canada – and later the whole of Mexico – when the United States radically tightened its anti-terrorism border measures after 9/11. At that time, the idea of a 'continental defence perimeter' was greatly favoured by business spokespersons in the periphery, who believed that the United States would demilitarize its land borders if, and only if, it could be assured that Canada's and Mexico's own external borders met its standards for heightened security.

Focusing as we have in this study on how much the United States gains or loses from its relations with Canada and Mexico, we found it helpful to extend our use of 'perimeter' beyond security issues to encompass economic sectors and policy-making domains. In markets, we can consider the US auto industry as having once extended its perimeter to Canada's external borders because it had acquired virtually complete control of the Canadian automobile industry through the 1965 Auto Pact. Later, it was to see that perimeter pushed back by its overseas competitors' encroachment on the continental market. We may also talk of a partially extended perimeter. For instance, US banks have a relatively small share of the market in the north, which is dominated by the Canadian banking oligopoly, but, to the south, such US financial institutions as Citibank extended their perimeter into Mexico when they made huge inroads into its banking system.

Alberta's oil and natural gas sector is so seamlessly integrated in the United States' economy that the US energy *market's* perimeter can be seen to include this province. Whether the US energy *policy* perimeter embraces Alberta is another matter. If Edmonton imposes regulations on the corporations operating in its oil industry that are different from those in the United States, Alberta could be considered to be inside the United States' energy-market perimeter but outside its energy-policy perimeter.

These categories are not mutually exclusive. Hollywood's success in extending its perimeter to include the whole of Canada is graphically demonstrated by the US film industry, whose marketing data distinguish between foreign or overseas sales but do not break down the figures for the United States *and Canada*. Hollywood's near-complete dominance of the Canadian film market resulted in markedly coercive – in other words, imperial – behaviour by Washington, which threatened direct retaliation on those occasions when the government of Canada proposed to carve out space within its film market for domestic distributors so that Canadians could watch Canadian movies.

Having a continental policy perimeter may not be in what all Americans consider their best interests. Far from supporting a continental labour perimeter, for example, the United States has reinforced its borders to constrict the ingress of Mexican workers. Opening the US borders to unrestricted inflows of Canadian and Mexican labour generally suits business lobbies but outrages socio-cultural groups who feel threatened by losing their jobs or their identity.

The Periphery

We must also make a disavowal about a word which we are simply using in its geographical connotation. In this book, the United States' two immediate territorial neighbours to the north and south constitute North America's periphery. We are not using the concept in the normative sense employed in world-systems theory to describe the most destitute and powerless states which languish at the bottom of the global power hierarchy. Nor are we using the word pejoratively to cast aspersions on Canada's and Mexico's importance. These two states are situated on the United States' geographical edges but they are not necessarily 'peripheral' in the sense of 'unimportant.' Their significance for Washington may in many issues be marginal – a research question we will address particularly in Part Three – but this is not an assumption that we make a priori.

To talk about North America's periphery presents another pitfall since it suggests that Mexico and Canada *together* constitute a meaningful economic, political, or even military entity. This, too, is an issue to be researched, not assumed. For their first two centuries as colonizing European societies taking root in the New World, Canada and Mexico had almost no connection with one another. Then, for almost half a century after they established formal diplomatic relations, neither government paid much attention to the other, despite experiencing similar challenges when trying to coexist with their overbearing common neighbour. It was only in the early 1990s, when Mexico sat down to negotiate an economic-integration agreement with Washington, that Ottawa took serious cognizance of the United States' southern neighbour, although less as a potential comrade-in-arms dealing with a mutual problem than as a rival economy competing for privileged access to the world's greatest market.

Prime Minister Brian Mulroney was so worried that Mexico might pull off a better deal than the little he had got from the Canada-US Free Trade Agreement that he persuaded President George H.W. Bush

– in return for a Canadian naval contribution to the Gulf War – to trilateralize these bilateral palavers. Behind closed doors, Mexico's elite discovered that it had much to learn from its Canadian counterpart's prior experience when negotiating economic-integration measures with Washington and then dealing with the resulting treaty's impact. The Canadian negotiators, in turn, came to understand that Mexico now meant more to Canada than just a place where Canadian tourists could cavort on its beaches and quaff its tequila. There were economic advantages to be gained for Canadian business from the fact that President Carlos Salinas de Gortari had recanted his party's decades-long protectionism and committed Mexico to exploiting the advantages of living next to Uncle Sam. The prospect of Mexico integrating in an expanded North American marketplace meant that Canadian firms in auto parts (Magna), steel (Dofasco), and transportation (Bombardier) could extend their productive capacity. In a short period, Mexico became a serious political and economic interlocutor for Canada.

Subsequently, NAFTA made the North American periphery an actual political-economic reality because many of its new rules applied equally to the two countries. With Mexican labourers contracting themselves under the aegis of both governments to work on Canadian farms and with Canadian companies locating plants in Mexico to take advantage of its low wages and weak social regulations, the two governments gradually developed a more substantial relationship. In 2000, when the Vicente Fox and the Partido Acción Nacional (PAN) brought seventy-one years of one-party rule to an end, his foreign minister, Jorge Castañeda, who wanted to involve Mexico more fully in international affairs, found in Canada a model middle power which shared many of his views about multilateralism. Following Washington's drastic border-tightening responses to the al-Qaeda attacks of 9/11, North America's 'third bilateral' came into its own, because the two governments found they needed to make common cause in pressing Washington not to let its obsession with security against terrorism jeopardize the continent's economic well-being by excessively inhibiting cross-border flows of commercial goods and travellers.

In this book, in contrast to the approach taken in *Does North America Exist?* we do not focus on the North American periphery in terms of the Mexico-Canada relationship. We are reporting on how Mexico and Canada affect the United States' economic strength, security, and global power. Whether they do this together or separately, consciously or unconsciously, supporting or opposing each other depends on the issue under consideration. Even if their actions are not deliberately coordinated, they still form part of the North American political economy whose dynamic we are analysing. For instance, Canada exports huge volumes of natural gas *to* the United States, while Mexico imports natural gas *from* the United States. Nevertheless, the two countries are linked by the world market's energy prices and they are connected organizationally through such little-known institutions as the now moribund North American Energy Working Group.

US Interests

A further complication arises when trying to determine just what America's 'interests' are. US interests can change markedly over time. From the nineteenth to the twentieth centuries, the US interest in guarding against a British threat coming through Canada became a need to incorporate Canada as its closest military ally in the defence of Great Britain. This is an example of long-term change, but US interests can also change very rapidly. Overnight, an incoming administration whose beliefs about what is best for the United States contradict those of the outgoing administration can reverse the official US position. Such political reversals can have serious repercussions for the periphery. As we will see, Ottawa's diplomatic effort to create an International Criminal Court (ICC) was largely in line with the Clinton administration's soft-power approach to multilateral affairs and so was seen to support US global power. When the George W. Bush administration made it clear that it considered the ICC a dangerous limit on the Pentagon's freedom of action around the world, the very same Canadian policy suddenly turned out to be a constraint on US power.

Inside the 'Beltway,' political discourse unavoidably includes the question of means: Should the United States impose its control in distant parts of the world by unilaterally deploying its coercive 'hard power' or is its long-term interest in peace and prosperity better served by exercising its persuasive 'soft power' and working cooperatively on the international stage? The point is that the United States' interests are not objectively given. Rather, they are politically defined.

Diplomatic tensions may arise when Canada's or Mexico's definition of its interests in a given issue does not coincide with the way that the US administration views the same matter. In such situations, the periphery may constrain US power in the short term. But, if their analysis is sound and if they are effective in executing their own policies, the two US neighbours may end up promoting US power in the longer term. Mexico and Canada faced this conundrum in the 1980s when they opposed the Reagan administration's active support for the 'contras' in Central America's civil wars. Mexico's diplomacy favoured incorporating the insurgency movements in a political process that ultimately reestablished a measure of peaceful and largely democratic governance in the region and served later US administrations' sense of their best interests there.

Other Necessary Simplifications

The concepts of 'Washington,' 'Ottawa,' or 'Mexico City' present another analytical stumbling block. As shorthand for the actions of a nation-state, its capital is commonly anthropomorphized as if it were itself a player on the global scene interacting with other governments. But a capital has neither a mind nor a will. Treating a country's capital as an actor is a literary device we use, knowing full well that it is an over-simplification which always obscures the complexities that roil within any government, none more than in the United States where partisan battles and inter-agency turf wars can make it very difficult to know what 'Washington' really wants.

Even to write the words 'US government,' 'Canadian government,' or 'Mexican government' is to collapse many complicated domestic political processes into one artificially homogeneous entity. The branches of the US government rarely speak with one voice, and, even within Congress, it is often difficult to isolate a dominant set of interests that can be said to represent the United States. The formulation and implementation of any government's policy emerge from the interplay of multiple actors, not all of whom are governmental or located in the federal capital. In the case of this study's three countries, many positions taken by the American, Mexican, or Canadian executives can be overruled or stymied respectively by the US Congress, the Mexican Senate, or a Canadian province exercising its sovereign jurisdiction. What may be seen by foreign eyes as 'American' actions may be less what the US government does than the product of US corporations pursuing profits in the marketplace or American non-governmental organizations acting in civil society. The political contestation of US interests and the fashion in which Canada and Mexico insert themselves into these debates can thus become matters for our study.

The Book's Plan

The book's three parts address the major vectors of US power – economic strength, military security, and global influence. These subjects are so vast that we do not attempt to engage with all their dimensions as might be done in a more traditional international relations study. Rather, we will in each case address only Canada's and Mexico's specific impact on, for example, the American labour market or Washington's foreign economic policy. While our general purpose is to identify the external sources of US power, our illustrative material comes exclusively from the United States' immediate periphery. Our next interest lies in understanding how the United States has worked to maximize these external sources while minimizing the constraints that its resulting dependence may generate.

Our nine chapters are less individual case studies than probes set up as open-ended explorations of our research question: To what extent do Canada and Mexico construct and/or constrain US power? In Parts One and Two, we selected what we saw a priori as the highest-profile .issues within North American economic and security debates. In Part Three, we limited ourselves to three quite disparate issues in order to investigate aspects of Canada's and Mexico's international relevance for the United States. These probes were not intended as encyclopedic accounts of North America's power dynamics. Nor were they chosen with an eye to emphasize the periphery's importance, either positive or negative. Not surprisingly, in some of this research, we end up reporting little evidence of Canada's or Mexico's impact. Still, we believe that the range and diversity of our probes are sufficient to illustrate the broader significance of Canada and Mexico to US power by highlighting some major contributions while also showing the limits of the periphery's influence.

Part One: Growing the United States' Economy

We start the book by engaging with the three principal facets of US material power. Chapter 1 marshals aggregate trade and investment data to identify how much Canada and Mexico contribute to the United States' prosperity by expanding its market, creating jobs, and so raising its economy's size and productivity along with American citizens' standard of living. Examples from some key sectors illustrate how the North American periphery has bolstered and/or limited US corporations' scope and success. Natural resources form a sector that is given special treatment in chapter 2, which focuses on the contribution to US resource security of oil and natural gas flows from Canada and, to a lesser extent, from Mexico. In chapter 3, migration data document how Mexican unskilled workers and highly trained Canadian workers meet various US economic sectors' labour needs.

Part Two: Reinforcing the United States' Security

Since the United States' global power is intimately related to its defence capacity, this part of our study will consider the periphery's participation in (or abstention from) three aspects of US security. Chapter 4 considers traditional military defence. Canada supported US continental defence in the Second World War, cooperated with the United States inside NATO and NORAD during the Cold War, and has worked with the Pentagon's Northern Command since 2001. After the Second World War, Mexico refused to participate in this kind of partnership and actually took the lead in opposing US interventionist proclivities in the Western hemisphere, thereby constraining US power in the region. Chapter 5 acknowledges that Mexico's and Canada's vast territories can make the United States vulnerable to terrorists penetrating its territory. At the same time, the two governments have bolstered US security with a wide range of anti-terrorist initiatives. Similarly contradictory are the considerable role of Canada and the even greater role of Mexico in supplying narcotics to the enormous American consumer market. While drug gangs and cartels based in the periphery can be seen to undermine US social power, chapter 6 shows how the two governments have cooperated with Washington to interdict these suppliers, thereby buttressing US security.

Part Three: Constructing and Constraining the United States' Global Power

Since the Second World War, Canada and Mexico have participated as middle powers in developing transnational governance regimes, some of which expand the United States' global influence. Chapter 7 shows how Canada's and Mexico's negotiations of trade and investment treaties propagated economic norms that supported the enhancement of US power in global economic governance. In contrast, by leading the effort to create an International Criminal Court, Canada was helping forge governance norms that could potentially constrain the US military internationally, as chapter 8 discusses. Finally, in chapter 9 we look at how Mexico was Latin America's leader in resisting US intervention in Fidel Castro's Cuba, while, as its major foreign investor and source of hard-currency from its tourists, Canada contributed to Castro's survival.

The ambiguity implied in our title, *Dependent America?* suggests the paradox which is our principal finding. On the one hand, our analysis shows that Uncle Sam does 'depend' on the periphery in the sense that it derives a considerable amount of its wealth, security, and global clout from its intense relationships with Canada and Mexico. On the other hand, Washington has managed to neutralize its vulnerabilities. It does not 'depend' on these two neighbours because it has forestalled their wielding significant influence over it. We will develop this theme in the volume's Conclusion.

An Issue of Readers, Dates, and Language

This work is directed – as was *Uncle Sam and Us* and *Does North America Exist?* – at two distinct sets of readers. On one level, we have written for colleagues who are experts in the field – whether as scholars in the academy, analysts in think tanks, or policy makers in government. But we are also addressing our study to members of the general public who are interested in current issues – either as citizens or as students. This dual objective has required us to be meticulous in seeking factual accuracy and conceptual rigour. It also pushed us to strive for clarity in our exposition and to avoid technical jargon.

These two objectives conflict when we come to the concept of neoconservatism. Social scientists generally apply the notion of 'neoliberal' to such thinkers as Milton Friedman, whose rejection of mid-twentieth-century Keynesianism harkened back to the purer liberalism of the nineteenth-century British political economists. But 'neoliberal' can be confusing in common discourse, because 'liberal' is strongly associated in the United States with politically progressive thinking and, even in Canada, suggests positions that are centrist or slightly left-leaning on the political spectrum. As a result, this text eschews the concept of 'neoliberal,' because it can be misread as 'newly progressive.' Instead, we use 'neoconservative' broadly to describe the ideas that pushed out the Keynesian paradigm and came to animate the thinking of most political, economic, and media elites around the capitalist world following the election of the movement's two most powerful political exponents,

Margaret Thatcher in Great Britain (1979) and Ronald Reagan in the United States (1980).

The last several years have seen major upheavals in North America's political economy, changes that have only accelerated since the publication of *Does North America Exist?* We have endeavoured to keep our figures as recent as possible and have updated all figures through to the most recent data available to us in the summer of 2011.

In each of our nine separate probes, little of what we have presented about the United States' relationships with Canada or Mexico is unknown to individual American, Canadian, or Mexican policy experts knowledgeable about their subject. But rarely does an analyst's knowledge about one of North America's two main bilateral relationships extend to expertise about the other. Nor is this material generally analysed by framing Canada and Mexico together as the continental periphery. Even more rarely is this kind of information presented in the context of the periphery's *agency* in relating to the United States as the *object*. And never has it been assembled to paint a comprehensive picture of the periphery's contribution to the three basic vertices of US power – its economy, its security, and its structural presence on the global stage. Here conceived from the perspective of how much the United States derives its power from Canada and Mexico, this information gives us the chance to refresh our understanding of North America's political and economic dynamics – even if US global strategic interests involve the country in all other regions of the world to the point of ignoring its own continental neighbours.

We will argue in the Epilogue that, if the United States wants to slow down, arrest, or even reverse its global decline, it can no longer afford to take these two neighbours for granted. Their contributions have been crucial components in the construction of US power historically. While they remain key components of the United States' present strength, Canada's and Mexico's capacity to maintain their contributions is being jeopardized. How the United States rethinks its dependency on its neighbours and reactivates its relationships with them will, we believe, help determine whether it emerges weaker or stronger from its present travails.

PART ONE

Growing the United States' Economy

Assuming that the United States' power in the world is a function of its economic size and vitality, we start our book by asking to what extent this material strength is derived from the country's links with other economies in general and its two nearest neighbours in particular.

For the United States, Canada and Mexico are vast markets for exports, huge sources of imports, major sites of investment by US transnational corporations, large suppliers of natural resources, and significant providers of human capital. In chapter 1 we marshal trade and investment statistics to document the degree to which Canada and Mexico contribute to the overall size of the US economy by expanding its market size, bulking up its GDP, creating jobs for Americans, and raising their productivity. Beyond its quantitative inputs to the US economy, the periphery's material contributions produce such important qualitative benefits as making the US economy more competitive. Within an increasingly integrated continental economy, trade and investment flows with Canada and Mexico have indirectly shifted production patterns to the United States' advantage by fostering more specialized and efficient production, greater economies of scale, and the faster diffusion of technology and ideas.

Chapter 2 documents the continental periphery's contribution to the US energy base. With generous incentives from Washington, US investments in energy and resource extraction, along with considerable domestic investment, developed the largest and most reliable foreign sources of natural gas and petroleum products for the US market. Concerned about its resulting vulnerability to supply interruptions caused by nationalist political pressures, Washington partnered with Canadian business interests to constitutionalize the Canadian petroleum industry's incorporation within its effective perimeter through the Canada-US Free Trade Agreement. The United States' energy relationship with Mexico has been far more tumultuous not just because of US corporate assets being nationalized there in 1938 but because Mexico had, until NAFTA, resisted US lobbying to open its energy sector to foreign participation.

Chapter 3 shows how the continental periphery has extended the reach and flexibility of the US labour market. Migration data make clear how, before the Mexican border's recent thickening made passage to and fro much more difficult, low-wage Mexicans provided a readily available labour supply that flexibly responded to the US market's needs for both skilled and manual labour. Canada's parallel contribution of high-skilled workers to the United States is less obvious, but Canadian labour flows also help fill key US labour-market needs.

While Canada's and Mexico's economic spaces retain considerable public sectors and domestic business communities, the United States has managed over the last century and a half to extend its economic perimeter continentally by expanding its access to its neighbours' markets and inhibiting their governments' capacity for a self-directed development path that might have competed with, rather than complemented, its own economic needs.

1 Making the US Economy Stronger and More Competitive[1]

"Our prosperity provides a foundation for our power," Barack Obama told cadets at West Point. "It pays for our military. It underwrites our diplomacy. It taps the potential of our people, and allows investment in new industry."

– New York Times, February 2, 2010[2]

The United States' economy does not just provide the American people their much envied high standard of living: it is the sine qua non for US global power, the indispensable base for the American state's global military and diplomatic dominance. Given this fact, we start our study by asking to what extent the US economy's size and vitality derive from its trading and investment links with Canada and Mexico.

The United States has economic relations with almost every national economy. As the world's eleventh- and thirteenth-largest economies, Canada and Mexico are far from being the most economically powerful of the United States' commercial partners.[3] Nevertheless, their geographical proximity and their shared history have embedded the two North American countries within such multiple and productive sets of interlocked social, cultural, and business structures that, when taken together, they turn out to comprise the United States' largest economic partnership, with sustained trade flows exceeding $1 trillion per annum. Analysing aggregate economic data and then discussing specific industrial sectors, we argue that the North American periphery has critically boosted US economic strength, increased its GDP, and raised its employment levels, all the while significantly augmenting the economy's competitiveness.

This situation did not evolve of its own accord. Reacting against Mexico's major efforts and Canada's more half-hearted attempts to give priority to their own industrial enterprises, Washington has successfully managed to induce its neighbours to reorient their policies and economic ideologies from competitively promoting their self-directed development to pursuing growth through an integration whose complementarity promises mutual economic benefits. Compared to its other economic partners, the Canadian and Mexican markets respond faster and more flexibly to the United States' economic needs. As a result, its trade and investment relations with Canada and Mexico are not just crucial to its prosperity; they are responsive and reliable. Furthermore, the continental periphery's extreme dependence on the US economy for its own domestic prosperity makes it costly for either neighbour to reorient its principal trade and investment relationship so as *not* to contribute to US economic strength.

We begin by tracing the evolution of the continent's economic integration. Highlighting instances where Mexico consistently and Canada spasmodically tried to resist the development of a dependently integrated trade and investment regime, we show how Canada and Mexico came to support a strong, binding, neoconservative architecture by negotiating the Canada-US and North American free-trade agreements. Drawing from mainstream economic theory, the chapter then assesses the aggregate effects of first trade and then investment relationships on American GDP and employment. Finally, examples from a number of sectoral studies illustrate how the United States' investment and trade relationships with Canada and Mexico enhance various components of US economic competitiveness.

From Autonomy to Integration: The Economic-Policy Trajectory of the US Periphery

Although Canada and Mexico had barely any connections with each other in their first century as sovereign states, their economic-policy trajectories were remarkably similar.

Canada

With adjacent provincial markets easily accessible owing to the absence of significant border or cultural barriers, Canada served as the natural nursery for successful US companies which were learning to export and invest transnationally in the late nineteenth century.[4] Once the Anglo-American entente of 1906 erased US anxieties that Canada could be a vehicle for British imperial designs, Washington clarified what it expected of its northern neighbour: a source of the raw materials necessary to fuel its own industrial machine and a manufacturing capability that was complementary to – but not competitive with – its domestic producers.[5] For their part, most Canadians perceived their economic ties with the United States as a mutually beneficial arrangement despite suffering from the high import tariffs imposed by the US Congress during the Great Depression. Following the trade shutdown provoked by the draconian Smoot-Hawley tariff, Canadian-US economic tariffs were reduced by the executive branch as a result of the 1934 Reciprocal Trade Agreements Act. Revived economic cooperation surged during the Second World War when the 1941 United States-Canada Hyde Park Agreement created a temporarily integrated military economy, which was a harbinger for post-war developments.

After the war, when it became clear that Canada's once-productive economic relationship with Great Britain had eroded to the point of no-return, Ottawa encouraged US investment in the mining and manufacturing sectors, paying little attention to the possible political consequences of the economy's strengthening north-south ties. As a result, the process of economic integration continued both unobtrusively (with the steady, large-scale inflow of US capital) and officially (with such sectoral landmarks as the 1958 Defence Production Sharing Agreement and the much celebrated 1965 Automotive Products Trade Agreement, which extended the United States' economic perimeter to include Canada's military and automotive sectors). As host to high levels of US foreign direct investment by the mid-1960s – comparable to total US direct investment in the entire European Community – Canada remained a proving ground for the expansion abroad of US transnational corporations, which profited handsomely by establishing dominant positions in the country's resource, chemical, electrical-machinery, and automobile industries.

Only when the horrors of its futile war in Vietnam turned the United States from friendly neighbour to ugly imperialist in the eyes of many did Canadians take issue with their country's high degree of economic, cultural, and political dependency on the United States. With North America's assertive hegemon now in control of large segments of the Canadian economy – a development that one economist at the time called Canada's *Silent Surrender*[6] – concerns were raised that the country's putatively unlimited resources were actually non-renewable, becoming scarce, and yielding less value than what they would produce were they processed and used as industrial inputs to develop the domestic economy. In the words of a lapel button of the period playing on the distrust of the US president and a popular ginger ale brand, 'Nixon drinks Canada Dry.' New research in the early 1970s revealed that some 9,000 branch plants dominating Canada's most technologically advanced industries in fact truncated the country's capacity for innovation and entrepreneurial management.[7] Foreign direct investment now seemed to present a zero-sum dilemma: what contributed to greater profits for the US economy left Canada with less revenue and poorer jobs than it would have had were Canadian capitalists in control.

Political and public pressure to create more space for domestic enterprise (and so to restrict US-Canadian economic linkages) peaked during the Trudeau era. A Canada Development Corporation was founded in 1971 to buy back control over companies previously acquired by Americans. New strategies were announced in 1972 to diversify Canada's trade and investment patterns across the Atlantic with Europe and across the Pacific with Japan. And a Foreign Investment Review Agency (FIRA) was created in 1973 to screen acquisitions of Canadian companies, thereby slowing down the acceleration of US corporate takeovers.

That Washington also saw economic relations in zero-sum terms was clear from its angry reactions to these initiatives, which it understood as threatening Canada's construction of US wealth. Washington pressed Ottawa to weaken FIRA's ability to extract commitments from American TNCs when they took over Canadian firms, including those involving technology transfers, export development, domestic sourcing of components, and local job creation. It retaliated against federal or provincial subsidies that improved Canadian companies' export competitiveness in the US market and it complained that so much of the retail banking system in Canada was out of bounds to US financial institutions.

In 1980 Canada's new economic nationalism reached its policy zenith in the form of a short-lived National Energy Program (NEP) that mandated greater Canadian ownership and control of the oil and natural gas industries. Virulent opposition to the NEP by American TNCs and politicians made the point that, as a site for investment and a source of raw materials, Canada was making a valued contribution to the United

States' wealth creation, a support they did not want to sacrifice on the altar of greater Canadian economic self-sufficiency and prosperity.

When the post-Second World War policy paradigm associated with the Keynesian welfare state came under attack in the early 1980s from ever more persuasive neoconservative arguments, the Canadian economic elite came to believe that their activist, mixed-economy state was in a crisis from which it could be rescued only by market-liberating policies. In a reaffirmation of earlier beliefs that what was good for the United States was also good for Canada, free trade with the United States became the watchword for Canada's economic salvation.

Mexico

In sharp distinction from Canada, Mexico's stance was largely antagonistic towards the United States for most of the twentieth century. Following the long turmoil of its 1910–17 Revolution, economic ties with the United States were understood in starkly zero-sum terms. What was good for the 'gringos' was perceived as decidedly bad for Mexicans, as exemplified by the prototypical case of petroleum. On March 18, 1938, a day still celebrated as a virtual declaration of independence, Mexico nationalized all foreign subsidiaries operating in the oil and natural gas sector. The United States took the equal, but opposite, position. Losing ownership and control of Mexican oil was a blow to its economic interests. The corporate parents of expropriated companies retaliated swiftly, refusing to buy petroleum from the new public company, Petróleos Mexicanos (Pemex).

Mexican nationalism did not preclude subsequent cooperation with Washington. Mexico and the United States created the 'Bracero' program, a formal guest-worker initiative to alleviate US labour shortages during the Second World War that lasted through the mid-1960s. This very partial labour market integration notwithstanding, the Mexican government's overriding post-war economic priority was centred on reducing its dependence on the US economy. It developed an explicit development strategy known as import-substitution industrialization (ISI) that was designed to constrain imports and foreign investment from the north in order to carve out space within which an autonomous, self-contained domestic market could grow and prosper.

ISI resonated well with the Mexican elite, both in government and in the private sector. In power since 1929, the Partido Revolucionario Institucional (PRI) aspired to transform Mexico's backward campesino economy into a hemispheric powerhouse through the magic of industrialization.[8] Under ISI, the Mexican government enacted high tariffs and other trade barriers to limit the entrance of foreign goods into Mexican markets, particularly from the United States. Among other measures, it fixed a high exchange rate for the peso, imposed stringent licensing requirements on imports, restricted FDI, and provided significant tax exemptions and incentives to develop new Mexican enterprise in such strategic sectors as steel.

ISI was controversial. Some considered it to be an uplifting economic success. In 1940, 68 per cent of the Mexican labour force was employed in the agriculture sector but by 1980 that proportion had declined to 37 per cent.[9] The Mexican economy was also buoyed by government income from the appropriated oil and gas industries. By some accounts, ISI helped generate a period of sustained 6 per cent growth known as the 'Mexican miracle.'[10]

For others, ISI was a claustrophobic economic detour that doomed Mexico to remaining isolated and uncompetitive. Even though exports rose, ISI could not provide Mexican industry the goods and services it needed to modernize, nor could it generate the productivity increases necessary for competing internationally. Worse, rising interest rates and crashing world oil prices brought the Mexican economy to its knees in 1982. As the government found itself unable to service its international debt, the administration of José López Portillo devalued the peso and nationalized key sectors of the Mexican economy, including banking and steel. These drastic measures triggered destabilizing domestic inflation and throttled international investment flows into what was by then deemed a risky economic space.

Throughout the period, Mexico still had important ties with the American economy. Bracero's demise in the 1960s prompted the two governments to establish a policy that would let US firms appropriate the benefits of low Mexican wages by exporting components to plants south of the border without paying duties. When reimporting the assembled machinery, they were liable only for US import duties on the value added to the finished products during their assembly. First located in the country's impoverished northern zones and then spreading throughout Mexico, these *maquiladora* (screwdriver) facilities allowed US firms to take advantage not just of Mexico's cheap labour but of its lax social and environmental practices.

The Bracero and maquiladora programs were not the only evidence of the Mexican government's inconsistency. By the 1970s, Mexicans were experiencing a growing ambivalence about their role in the international order. The government still refused to join the General Agreement on Tariffs on Trade (GATT), which would have required it to reduce its barriers to US exports and direct investment, but it participated actively in the GATT's Tokyo Round from 1973 to 1979.[11]

From Regime Crisis to Continental Integration

By the mid-1980s, both of Washington's neighbours were experiencing political/economic crises, whether imagined or real. Adopting neoconservative thinking as their own, their political and economic elites came to believe that the way out of their respective impasses lay in domestic political deregulation and – assuming they could negotiate free access to the American market – export-driven, trade and investment liberalization. This policy trajectory proved a perfect complement to Washington's own economic strategy for North America – increased integration of Canada and Mexico to consolidate the US economy's access to its periphery's markets at a time when the United States' global economic dominance seemed threatened.

Canada took the lead in putting this new thinking into practice. The defeat of the Liberal government by Brian Mulroney in 1984 set the stage for Ottawa to adopt US-friendlier economic policies and support Washington's push at the GATT to liberate the global market through lowering trade and investment barriers. Responding to the Canadian business community's discontent with the previous Trudeau government's rhetorically nationalist policies and heeding the 1985 Macdonald Royal Commission's alarmist declaration that Canada's economic future was at risk unless a free-trade agreement was made with a dangerously protectionist US Congress, Prime Minister Mulroney proposed to President Ronald Reagan that the two countries work out a comprehensive bilateral agreement. With the pre-negotiations for a new GATT round still unresolved, the US administration decided to invest political capital in reconstituting an economic relationship already so open and with such low average tariffs that most American businesses already took their access to it for granted.

Given the ensuing negotiations' asymmetrical power relationship, the Canadian government failed to achieve its prime negotiating objective, a genuine free-trade relationship. However integrated the two economies might already be, Congress would not allow its trade-policy jurisdiction to be constrained by giving Canada an exemption from its carefully constructed battery of measures such as anti-dumping and countervailing duties with which US manufacturers could obtain protection against imports that threatened their domestic position. Still less would US politicians forego any of their carefully constructed legislative capacity to retaliate against foreign governments' trade-promoting policies.

Notwithstanding the impossibility of achieving free access, Ottawa proved a willing negotiating partner. It agreed to guarantee the stable supply of its petroleum exports and to extend 'national treatment' to American corporations, a concession it had always resisted on the grounds that offering powerful US TNCs the same policy treatment as Canadian companies received meant abandoning efforts to boost the competitiveness of domestic enterprise. Because the Canadian public strongly supported maintaining a vibrant generic drug industry, Mulroney was reluctant to incorporate intellectual property rights in the controversial bilateral agreement. Instead, he used his majority-party control of Parliament to quietly push through legislation that wrote into Canadian law the major US demands favouring Big Pharma.

By January 1, 1989, when CUFTA came into force, Mexico's government was well on its way towards its own trade agreement with its historical nemesis. The PRI had carried out a self-administered counter-revolution following its 1982 currency crisis, when it was compelled to adopt the structural-adjustment measures that the International Monetary Fund (IMF), the World Bank, and the US Treasury had insisted upon as conditions for their financial rescue. Joining the GATT in 1986 required Mexico to dismantle its protectionist barriers still further – it had to change its import-licensing system into tariff quotas, to cut its minimum tariffs (between 1982 and 1989 from 16.4 to 9.8 per cent[12]), to harmonize its customs evaluation practices, and to bring its anti-dumping provisions and subsidies code up to international standards. The PRI went on in 1989 to pass a new law that promoted rather than restricted foreign investment and proceeded to privatize many state-owned enterprises including those in the steel and sugar sectors, as well as the same banks it had nationalized in 1982.

Mexico's abrupt shift from market protectionism to market liberalization was not only prompted by the United States' direct pressure. The devastating currency crisis had triggered bitter ideological debates within its ruling party. The PRI's older leaders, who remained rooted in practical politics, wanted to stick with the import-substitution policies that had performed well until the crisis and whose anti-American premise remained broadly popular. Challenging these 'dinosaurs' was a new guard who had learned the language of state deregulation and market liberalization at such leading US graduate schools as Chicago and MIT. This younger elite, which found positions in the government's economic bureaucracy, saw the United States as a model to emulate, not an enemy to resist. For these Americanophile technocrats, Washington's demands that Mexico mend its ways were politically helpful, requiring the government to follow the deregulated economic-development path and adopt the multiple democratic reforms which they were themselves advocating.

As Washington saw it, the PRI's overthrow of state-centred social democracy and adoption of market-centred neoconservatism were the necessary preconditions for a formal economic-integration treaty that would lock in the rules needed to prevent Mexicans from ever again choosing a nationalist route.While discussed in public using the idealistic rhetoric of democracy and liberalization, the Mexico agenda of the United States Trade Representative (USTR) was compiled from the wish list of major American industries. Having lost its rich market in the Soviet Union, for instance, the US farm lobby eyed Mexico as a market for its large surpluses of corn. Wal-Mart and other retail chains wanted unfettered access to the growing Mexican consumer market. The automobile and textile industries sought rules of origin that would give them greater market share in Canada and Mexico while protecting their North American production chains from overseas competition. Frustrated by the multilateral stalemate in the Uruguay Round of talks, Big Pharma pressed Mexico to adopt the powerful intellectual property rights that were languishing in the GATT's Dunkel Draft.

Fed up with the legal imbroglios encountered when trying to resolve commercial disputes within the Mexican judicial system, the USTR – supported by Canada – insisted that Mexico incorporate US administrative law holus-bolus into its legal system, so that American and Canadian firms could feel legally at home in their Mexican business dealings. As it had with Ottawa, Washington also insisted that the Mexican government grant national treatment for US investors. This time it proposed an unprecedentedly comprehensive definition of investment that Canada, as the guest at the negotiating table and by then one of the world's largest exporters of mining capital, was also happy to endorse. In short, while further deepening and securing American access to Canada's economy, NAFTA did not just open Mexico's door for US exporters and investors; it took that door off its hinges.

While unfettered access to Mexico's economy would benefit the competitive sectors of the US economy, lowering its protections threatened less competitive American businesses. When the US executive requested fast-track authorization from Congress to negotiate NAFTA, it roused the vocal opposition of agricultural producers, companies anticipating they would lose market share to lower-cost Mexican competitors, and the US labour movement, which feared that its members' jobs would disappear as US plants shut down and moved to Mexico. The further mobilization of environmental and human-rights organizations made NAFTA a highly contentious political issue. Faced with the possibility of the agreement's political defeat in Congress, Mexico opened a Washington office whose staff lobbied US representatives on more than 320 occasions during the fast-track process.[13] Mexico also secured the US Hispanic community's support for the agreement and encouraged the American business community to influence Congress members' grass-roots supporters. Having ingested the same neoconservative paradigm that the United States had proclaimed, the Mexican government was intervening in US politics to help Washington achieve its official economic goal.

With NAFTA, the United States had finally put the trade and investment policies of its largest economic relationship into a constitutionalized form that entrenched Canada and Mexico's continental integration while pre-empting their capacity to reassert their autonomy in the future. With this historical context in mind, we can proceed to examine the size and significance for the United States of its economic relationship with its continental periphery.

Taking the Trade Measure of the US-Periphery Relationship

There are good reasons to be wary of the information we derive from statistics. What can be counted is not necessarily what we want to know. Nevertheless, we will see that the United States' economic relationship with its continental periphery, as expressed in official trade and investment data, is significant in both absolute and relative terms. Having laid out the impressive quantitative dimensions of the relationship, we will turn in our final section to the implications of this relationship for enhancing the competitiveness of the US economy.

Before proceeding with our analysis, we need to make a further caveat. The inferences that are drawn from the masses of data that governments produce are often based on highly contestable assumptions. The increase of an economy's gross national product (GNP), for example, is generally assumed to be a good thing, but if that country's revenues are not equitably distributed, the well-being of the majority may deteriorate even as the wealth of the minority grows. Even economists' analysis of an issue as apparently straightforward as foreign trade is laced with lasting, actually unresolvable, disputes. For two centuries, economic liberals have taken the position that both exports and imports benefit the economy, if in different ways, and the more, the better. For even longer, mercantilists have maintained the opposite view, insisting that a country's exports were good because they generated jobs for its citizens, while imports were to be discouraged because they represented jobs lost to other economies. We will abstain from discussing in this chapter what ought to be the American economic interest. An ethical argument can be made, for instance, that it is in the United States' own soft-power interest to become a society boasting high levels of individual equality. But in this study we will discuss economic gains flowing from the United States' relations with other countries in light of the mainstream US viewpoint which is more concerned about increasing material wealth than in decreasing economic disparities.

The North American Periphery as the United States' Largest Trading Partner

With first CUFTA and then NAFTA, the intensity of continental trade and investment deepened. As seen in Figure 1.1, US-Canadian trade flows have increased steadily since 1960, with only a small decline in the aftermath of the 9/11 attacks, likely a function of US border restrictions, and a much more abrupt decline as a result of the 2008 global financial crisis. In 2010 the United States exported $301 billion worth of goods and services to Canada, while importing $308 billion of Canadian goods and services.[14]

Across its southern border, US-Mexican trade expanded even more rapidly after 1986. Figure 1.2 shows a minor reduction in US exports to Mexico in the aftermath of the 1994 peso crisis, the result of Mexicans' decreased purchasing power for American goods. There was also a post-9/11 stall and a recessionary crash. With the relationship recovering quickly from the financial crisis, the United States exported $188 billion of goods and services to Mexico in 2010, while importing $247 billion.

Placed within the context of global US trade flows, the North Ameri-

Figure 1.1: Canada-US trade flows, 1960–2010[15]

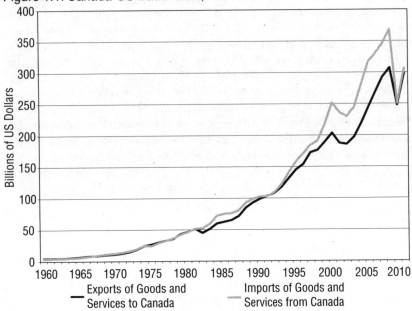

Exports of Goods and
Services to Canada

Imports of Goods and
Services from Canada

Figure 1.2: Mexican-US trade flows, 1986–2010

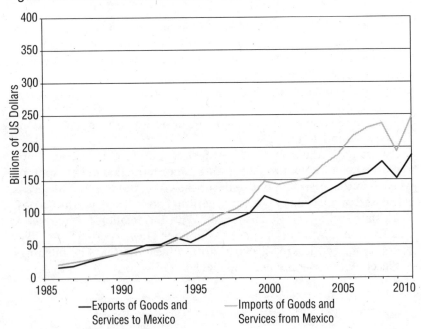

Exports of Goods and
Services to Mexico

Imports of Goods and
Services from Mexico

Figure 1.3: US exports to select countries

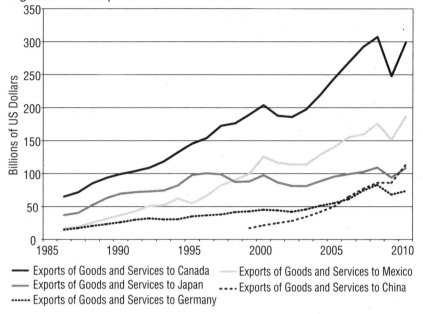

Exports of Goods and Services to Canada
Exports of Goods and Services to Japan
Exports of Goods and Services to Germany
Exports of Goods and Services to Mexico
Exports of Goods and Services to China

can trading relationship is colossal. Canada has been the largest export market for US goods for decades, as can be seen in Figure 1.3. The Mexican market for US goods grew so significantly that it supplanted Japan in the late 1990s as the United States' second-largest export market. Much of this commerce represented a direct extension of the US economic perimeter into Mexico, with unfinished US goods being sent for assembly there and reimportation into the United States.

Although Canada has been the most important source of imports to the United States for decades (Figure 1.4), by 2008 China was vying with it for first place and the eonomic giant surpassed Canada in the aftermath of the financial crisis. Mexico remained well ahead of Japan as the third-largest source of US imports.[16]

Table 1.1 provides a snapshot of US trade with select countries and regions and shows that, taken together, Canada and Mexico accounted for almost 27 per cent of total US exports and about 24 per cent of total US imports in 2010 – slightly more than the United States' trade relationship with all twenty-seven countries in the European Union and still considerably more than its much discussed trading relationship with China.

Figure 1.4: US imports from select countries

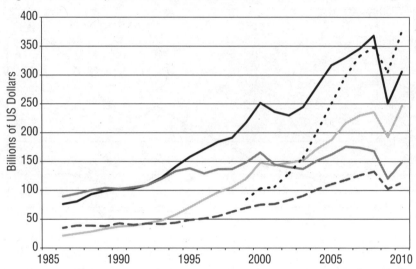

— Imports of Goods and Services from Canada ——— Imports of Goods and Services from Mexico
———Imports of Goods and Services from Japan - - -Imports of Goods and Services from China
- - Imports of Goods and Services from Germany

Table 1.1
US trade flows to select international economies, 2010

	US Exports (billions of USD)	Percentage of Total US Exports (%)	US Imports (billions of USD)	Percentage of Total US Imports (%)
Canada	300.9	16.4	308.0	13.2
Mexico	187.6	10.2	246.6	10.5
Canada and Mexico	**488.5**	**26.6**	**554.6**	**23.7**
EU	412.8	22.5	460.8	19.7
China	114.2	6.2	376.1	16.1
Japan	106.7	5.8	148.8	6.4
India	29.7	1.6	43.4	1.9
Latin America (excluding Mexico)	222.2	12.1	204.8	8.8
Middle East	69.9	3.8	93.8	4.0
Africa	40.2	2.2	93.0	4.0
World	**1837.6**		**2337.6**	

Building a Bigger US Economy: Trade Effects on Income

Liberal economists' belief that the United States gains much from trade and international economic openness has long constituted a cornerstone of US trade policy. Surprisingly few estimates quantify the actual benefits that the United States derives from its trade, however, largely because of disputes over how to interpret the often inadequate data that are published. It is difficult, for instance, to make reliable inferences about how much exports and/or imports have increased the size of the economy's GDP, whether in any particular year or over a longer period of time. Nor is it easy to calculate how many jobs are produced by exports or even whether jobs are lost by imports whose indirect effects, some argue, are more creative than destructive.

One of the few comprehensive surveys suggests that trade has had a significant positive benefit for the American economy, though its estimates remain mostly silent as to the distribution of these benefits within the country. Between 1950 and 2003, trade is conservatively thought to have increased US GDP in the order of $1 trillion annually, with specific estimates ranging from $800 billion to $1.45 trillion depending on the assumptions used. These figures suggest that the American economy was, in 2003, between 7 and 13 per cent larger than it would have been without its international economic linkages, meaning that the income of the 'average American' was raised by between $2,800 and $5,000. This suggests in turn that US trade has made the average American household richer by between $7,100 and $12,900 (in 2003 US dollars).[17]

Because of these calculations' relatively crude nature and because of significant data gaps, many of the methods used to estimate the overall pay-off from trade for the United States are difficult to apply to its trade relationship with Mexico and Canada.[18] One of the few methods generating estimates of benefits at the regional level relies on the concept of *trade exposure* – the value of an economy's exports plus the value of its imports divided by the size of its GDP. The Organization for Economic Co-operation and Development (OECD) calculates that every 10 per cent rise in a developed country's trade exposure yields a 2 per cent increase in its national income or GDP per capita.[19] Assessing US trade exposure produces the estimate that the United States gains $1.45 trillion annually from its total international trade.[20]

This finding allows us to estimate the share of this benefit that is attributable to the United States' trade exposure to Canada and Mexico. Extrapolating from work done by Scott Bradford, Paul L.E. Grieco, and Gary Hufbauer, we calculate that increases from 1970 to 2003 in its trade exposure with Canada have raised the United States' annual GDP by 17 per cent of the total US gains from trade during the period or by about $245 billion. For 2003, this $245-billion annual increment represented a 2.2 per cent contribution to overall US GDP and translated into additional annual income gains for the same 'average American' of just under $850.[21]

In the Mexican case, calculations are most meaningful from 1990, when the liberalization of trade between the two countries hit its stride. Extrapolating from the same work, we estimate that, between 1990 and 2003, increases in trade exposure between Mexico and the United States increased the latter's annual GDP by an additional $42 billion and increased the annual income of the 'average American' by some $150. While the Mexican contribution to the US economy's strength is more modest than Canada's, these data capture the benefits to the United States over a shorter time period. Between 1990 and 2003, Mexico became an increasingly significant determinant of US economic strength. The increase in US GDP by $42 billion amounted to 0.4 per cent of total US GDP in 2003, and increases in US GDP associated with Mexican trade exposure accounted for just over 14 per cent of the estimated total gains in US GDP from trade over the 1990–2003 period. Increases in US trade exposure to Canada before 1970 and Mexico before 1990 are not captured by these estimates, so the North American periphery's cumulative economic contribution to the United States over a longer historical period is potentially understated.

Other economists have produced even higher figures which increase the overall magnitude of this benefit. One estimate suggests that up to 14 per cent of US GDP is attributable to trade. Since US commerce with the North American periphery represents between one-fifth and one-quarter of this total pay-off, the estimate implies that Mexico and Canada contribute about $500 billion annually to US GDP, or some $1,650 annually in per-capita income.[22]

Even more dramatic gains from trade are reported in a study commissioned by the Canadian government in 2008 to assess the counterfactual 'impact on U.S. output and employment of a cessation of trade with Canada.'[23] Using a general computable equilibrium model that includes both direct and indirect effects of trade, the authors concluded that trade with Canada *alone* increased US output by over $470 billion in 2008, equivalent to about 3.3 per cent of annual GDP. These gains were shared across sectors but concentrated in services, including components of the service sector that support the domestic production of export goods. This concentration of benefits in the service sector was linked to the general profile of services in the US economy, including the service-intensity of its manufacturing. Trade with Canada was equally important when broken down to the state level, with every US state significantly benefiting from Canadian trade. Overall, benefits from trade appeared to be spread evenly across the country, with most states benefiting from just over a 3 per cent increase in output as a result of Canadian trade linkages.

The same study also considered the impacts of US-Canadian trade on the US job market, assessing the number of American jobs that 'depend' on US economic linkages with Canada and 'would not exist if not for trade.'[24] Slightly over 8 million US jobs were found to derive from US-Canadian trade, with the majority in the service sector but about 450,000 jobs in manufacturing. This reflected between 4 and 5 per cent of the labour market in each state, and 4.4 per cent of the national labour market.

These estimates corroborate our presumption about the general importance of trade to the US economy and the specific importance of Canada and Mexico. If we take our more modest estimate of the annual income gains of $1,000 for the average US citizen and cumulate them over a lifetime, they suggest that US trade with Canada and Mexico currently increases the income of the putative 'average American' by $78,000 over the course of a seventy-eight-year life. This would mean that the average American household is some $200,000 better off because of the United States' continental trade links. Other estimates would suggest even greater gains. Were the income effects of the huge American direct and portfolio investments in Canada to be included, the estimated benefits would surely be higher.

It is, of course, not possible to determine the actual distribution of this incremental wealth. While some Americans prosper under economic openness, others get caught in the maelstrom of a changing economic environment. Given the vast discrepancies between very rich and very poor Americans, the actual benefits received by low-income and unemployed Americans from their country's economic relations with Canada and Mexico can be assumed to be very modest compared to the much larger benefits received by the wealthier.

This general line of analysis can be challenged. One can begin by noting the simplifying assumptions underlying any statistical calculations that distil extremely complex economic relationships into a single figure. The results from this approach are also contested by economists who consider the relative factor endowments of Canada and the United States to be quite similar in profile. It follows that the comparative advantages offered through trade would be modest, at least with respect to the United States' northern neighbour.[25] From this vantage point, the primary benefits to the United States of the economic relationship would come through investment flows, in particular returns on investments in Canada for US companies.

Although these calculations give a sense of the periphery's contributions to the United States' economic size and to individual Americans' wealth, it is also clear that they cannot take account of many related issues. The deregulation of investment boosts multinational corporations' profits but undermines the wages received by their workers. The statistical calculation of trade benefits takes no account of the environmental costs engendered by participating in a deregulated global economy. From a more holistic perspective, the United States' expanded trade relationship with Mexico may actually have had an adverse impact on the American public's welfare, reducing its social and environmental security while liberating TNCs from much regulatory control and so undermining its democratic system. Focusing on aggregate economic benefits also glosses over the social costs generated by the economic displacement resulting from domestic enterprises relocating to Mexico or work being outsourced to a maquiladora.

Whatever the merits of these viewpoints, many of which are espoused within the US Congress (though more rarely within the US executive branch), we cannot here resolve this bitter and complex debate. Instead, we are assessing Canada's and Mexico's role in building the United States' wealth from the perspective of mainstream economics.

Building a Bigger US Economy: Direct Investment Flows across North America's Borders

In classical political economy, capital was seen as immobile, and thus trade and investment were analysed as substitutes. If entrepreneurs invested in another country, they were thought not to trade with it; conversely, if they traded with another economy, they did not invest there. Even in the Keynesian era, when national economies enjoyed some tariff protection, foreign investment in manufacturing represented a corporate decentralization that typically created branch plants. These miniature replicas of the parent companies were set up to produce for the local market. They imported components from the parent company but were not allowed to compete with it in other markets by exporting.[26] Of course, foreign investment in such resources as iron ore, pulp and paper, or oil is generally made in order to export the raw materials to the home economy, whereas foreign investment in services, which are not tradable, generates exports but not imports.[27]

Direct investment abroad creates jobs for workers, software engineers, advertisers, lawyers, and local managers in the host country. This investment may cost jobs at home if a plant closes down in order to relocate abroad, but if the corporation is expanding rather than moving it may also create more work for executives, researchers, and back-office workers in the home economy. The subsidiary may pay taxes to the host state but will also send profits, royalties, management fees, and other charges back to headquarters to the ultimate benefit of the TNC's shareholders and ultimately the general public through the tax system. As a result, the economic benefits to the United States of both inbound and outbound FDI are high.

Contiguous geography, similar histories, and their relative underdevelopment turned the United States' immediate neighbours into important investment locales for American businesses. Some expanded vertically by integrating various stages in a production chain under one corporate roof to capture the profits at each stage of the production process – for instance, Exxon extracting oil, refining it into gasoline, and distributing it. Others grew horizontally by combining plants in Mexico and Canada that produced the same product under the same corporate roof to gain economies of scale.

Canada was the first foreign site for US investment abroad and remained centrally important through the twentieth century, US FDI being largely focused on the mining, manufacturing, finance/insurance, and information-technology sectors.[28] The northern neighbour was still the single largest site for US FDI in the early 1980s, receiving flows of $43.5 billion (over 20 per cent of total US FDI) in 1982. At that point, US investment in other jurisdictions was increasing at a faster pace, so that, by 2009, when US investment flows in Canada had increased to $260 billion, this significant sum represented only 7.4 per cent of US direct investment abroad. By then, Canada was the third-largest destination for US investment.[29]

To the degree that prosperous US businesses help strengthen the American economy, high levels of US FDI in Canada and Mexico produce direct benefits for the United States. US investments in Canada in

Figure 1.5: The US direct investment position in Canada, 1982–2009[30]

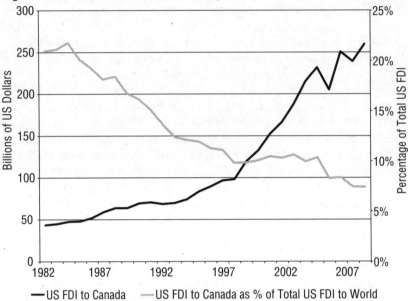

US FDI to Canada   US FDI to Canada as % of Total US FDI to World

2008 generated just over $25 billion in direct investment income for US businesses, second only to US FDI registered in the Netherlands.[31] US direct investment in Canada and Mexico also creates a virtuous feedback cycle that stimulates the import of even more goods and services from the United States. Figure 1.5 charts the US investment position in Canada over the past three decades.

Since the mid-1970s, when Canadian direct investment abroad first exceeded incoming FDI, Canada has also been an important source of capital investments for the United States. After declining abruptly in the early 1980s, Canadian investments in the United States remained constant in relative terms over the course of the 1990s and 2000s, as we can see in Figure 1.6. In 2009 Canadian foreign direct investment in the United States – which was concentrated in the finance/insurance, manufacturing, and banking sectors[32] – totalled $226 billion or just under 10 per cent of total inbound foreign investment.[33]

Mexico has played a far less significant role in continental investment flows. In 2008 it was the site of $96 billion in US foreign direct investment, just over 3 per cent of total US FDI abroad.[34] These investments were largely in the manufacturing, non-bank holding company,

Figure 1.6: Canadian FDI in the United States, 1982–2009

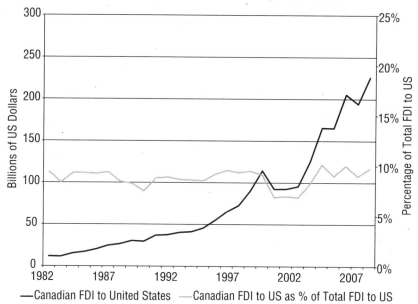

—Canadian FDI to United States   ——Canadian FDI to US as % of Total FDI to US

and finance/insurance sectors.[35] Investment income in Mexico by US-based multinationals was $10.2 billion.[36] Flows of investment from Mexico into the US economy have been negligible. In 2008 Mexican FDI in US manufacturing, wholesale trade, and banking[37] was just under $8 billion, a mere 0.4 per cent of global FDI in the United States.[38]

Generally, the United States saw NAFTA as a way to become a more attractive site for capital investment from overseas.[39] The United States experienced an eightfold increase in FDI from abroad when we compare pre-1992 and post-1992 levels and a fivefold increase in the ratio of inward FDI to GDP assessed over similar time frames.[40] Theoretically, integrated continental production systems could have encouraged foreign firms to divert investments to Canada and Mexico, using these markets as platforms from which to penetrate the United States. Instead, offshore firms' desire to locate close to end markets, along with such other considerations as the available inputs and skills, policies towards foreign investment, US business harassment of Canadian and Mexican exports with anti-dumping and countervailing duties, and the high subsidies offered by some US states, led to greater than expected Asian and European investment in the United States, for example, in the auto industry.[41] Like the overall trade with Canada and Mexico, foreign investment from the periphery supported valuable ancillary economic activities and favoured investment in the United States by other foreign TNCs servicing the same industry.[42]

We can see that the continental periphery provides a fertile field for US capital investment abroad as well as a considerable source of capital inflows that directly fund the US economy's expansion. The inadequacy of detailed data on FDI makes it impossible to estimate in dollar terms the aggregate contribution to US GDP of revenues accruing from US foreign investments in Canada and Mexico or from these economies' direct investment in the United States.

Interpreting the Data: Improving the US Economy's Competitiveness

To develop a more textured understanding of the continental periphery's contribution to US economic strength, we will shift from discussing the quantitative data to considering the qualitative impacts of continental trade and investment on US economic competitiveness. We illustrate our observations using examples from three sectors that represent a diverse set of North American industrial sectors: textiles and apparel (light consumer products), steel (heavy industry), and automobiles (consumer durables), each of which has a long history of cross-border integration. We postpone the consideration of two crucial topics. We give the natural-resources sector, particularly oil and natural gas, separate treatment in chapter 2 because of its unique role in quite literally fuelling US power. And we leave to chapter 3 the question of the periphery's supply of astonishingly large numbers of skilled and unskilled workers to the US labour market.

From Economies of Scale to Specialization of Production

At the most basic level, a larger market for sales enables firms to capture economies of scale which reduce costs by allowing their plants to operate at optimum levels and by permitting the industry to achieve efficiency-creating specialization. For example, if the United States fully enclosed the rest of North America within its economic perimeter, Canada would add a market of some thirty-four-million citizens with a per-capita income of $37,590. By the same token, Mexico would add almost 113 million consumers to the US market, albeit with the much lower per-capita income of $14,110.[43] If fully integrated, Canada's economy of $1.5 trillion and Mexico's of $1.1 trillion would increase the United States' $14.6-trillion economy by about 17 per cent to create a $17- trillion market.[44]

Larger production runs also allow machinery to be used to its optimum capacity for production efficiency and engender specialization, as individual processes are spun off by innovating entrepreneurs. In turn, external economies of scale may develop when the clustering of industries lowers input costs through enhanced labour training and specialization, production coordination, and other spillover effects. Together, economies of scale and specialization of production will attract other foreign direct investors to exploit the benefits of economic integration and agglomeration.[45] This new investment then introduces innovative technologies that further increase productivity as they are diffused from one firm to another. Through these mechanisms, increases in both trade and investment linkages expand not just the US economy's size but its vitality, with foreign investment having twice the spillover effect on productivity than does trade.[46]

The massive North American auto industry presents the most dramatic example of such rationalization of production processes. Its specialization facilitated major gains from economies of scale,[47] while the expanded continental market stimulated the total demand for automobiles.[48] High-value-added, high-wage processes such as research, design, and development tended to gravitate towards the United States[49] while Mexico became an important location for the labour-intensive assembly of components:[50] more than half of the value of Mexican vehicles exported to the United States are made up of US-made components.[51]

Continental reorganization had the opposite effect in the steel industry, where US trade harassment belied the promise of free trade. US anti-dumping and countervailing-duty measures blocked expanded imports of steel products from more efficient Canadian competitors to the point that the major Canadian steel companies located their new investments in the United States. In this way, the US steel industry's aggressive protectionism yielded unusually high FDI flows from the periphery. The Canadian Steel Producers Association estimated that, for every dollar of Canadian steel exports to the United States, Canadian steel mills invested $1.2 to $1.4 in that country.[52] Consolidations in the steel industry improved its efficiency,[53] and the $1.3 billion invested by Canadian steel producers in the American industry had by 2006 created over 8,000 jobs[54] in a sector that employed roughly 192,000 American workers.[55] More generally, the periphery's investments contributed to the US steel industry's improved profit and productivity levels through economies of scale in management and investments in maintenance, new equipment, and automation processes.[56]

The Flexibility of a Continentally Structured Economy

Continentally differentiated production also created economic flexibility for US-based steel producers. Thus, for example, US Steel Corp. purchased Canada's largest smelter, Stelco, in a period of industry consolidation in 2007. During the ensuing recession, it shut down its newly acquired Canadian capacity and laid off most of its Canadian workforce while maintaining near full employment within its US operations.[57] In this way, continental consolidation allowed some US businesses to maximize their profits by offloading the costs of economic downturns onto the periphery.

More generally, because NAFTA's Chapter 11 forbade Canada and Mexico from imposing performance requirements on US corporations' branch operations, American TNCs were freed to manage their operations without having to provide specified benefits to the periphery economy. The resulting 'hollowing out' of branch-plant operations in Canada suggests that American TNC head offices benefited substantially from eliminating the periphery's ability to require their foreign subsidiaries to transfer technology, train and employ host-country labour, carry out research, buy components locally, or increase exports.[58]

Mexico's maquiladora program presents another example of the flexibility offered to US economic interests through production-process specialization. Consolidated in 2007 with such other Mexican industrial programs as IMMEX, manufacturing zones were set up within Mexico to assemble goods from US components for re-export to the US market. These low-wage industrial enclaves in Mexico generate cheaper goods for US consumers. By 2009, over 5,200 IMMEX factories employed 1.6 million Mexicans and accounted for over 60 per cent of Mexican exports.[59] While other countries have taken advantage of the maquila rules to locate manufacturing facilities within Mexico, between 85 and 90 per cent of foreign direct investment in these export-industries since 1994 has come from the United States. Total FDI in maquiladoras more than tripled from $895 million in 1994 to $3.0 billion in 2006.[60]

In the short term, maquiladoras provide low-cost economic inputs for US corporations and offload to Mexico the environmental, social, and human costs of these facilities' poorly regulated activities. But what may be a short-term benefit to the United States may result in longer-term costs. The increased density of industrial plants discharging dangerous toxic waste exacerbates the severe water problems caused by population growth and seriously worsens environmental conditions in the fragile, semi-arid topography south of the US border.[61] Mounting deficiencies in housing, urban services, transportation facilities, and communications infrastructure in these urbanized zones add serious social deficits with grave health implications to the already deplorable environmental ledger.[62] The consequences of the Mexican labour movement's repression are inhuman working conditions for very young women and men who toil bereft of human rights and with no possibility for training or improving their job situations.[63] While advocates point to the equally difficult living conditions in a pre-maquiladora campesino economy, this environmental, social, and human degradation south of the US border has longer-term consequences in the north. Wretched social and labour conditions induce poorly remunerated Mexican workers to join the northward flow of undocumented immigration. The moral cost of profiting from the maquiladora workers' physical and mental misery, which would not be tolerated in the homeland, is incalculable.[64]

Competition and Productivity

Though competition from Canadian or Mexican imports can threaten some US businesses and the jobs of some workers, the American standard of living may increase because of this competition. At one level, US consumers benefit directly when increased competition drives down prices. At another level, US productivity grows when the foreign competition forces unproductive firms out of business and allows productive firms to flourish. In general, imports drive a reallocation of resources to higher productivity uses. Such survival-of-the-fittest selection is seen by some as a key long-term driver of economic strength.[65]

It is inherently difficult to single out the precise role that Canada and Mexico play in this Darwinian struggle, but in the short term continental trade can provide an important strategic support for beleaguered, uncompetitive US enterprises. This is because, to a degree much greater than other international competitors, Canada and Mexico make their products from US inputs, so that competing imports from the periphery are themselves providing jobs for US exporters. The periphery can also act as a short-term buffer for sectoral restructuring in the United

States, balancing competitive pressures through a continental demand for US inputs. The value of this buffering is ambiguous. To the extent that the periphery buffers US industry from restructuring in response to international competition, it may weaken the US economy's long-term capacity to compete in the face of rapid global economic change.

US-Mexican trade in textiles and apparel in the late 1990s presents a clear example of such benefits and risks. North American trade flows in the sector left the United States a net importer. Beginning with the maquiladora program and continuing under NAFTA, Mexican apparel production expanded the market for US textile exports, replacing sales to East Asian and other exporters who used fewer American-made inputs. In NAFTA, continentally integrated production was protected by complex rules of origin. 'Fibre forward' and 'yarn forward' provisions required that textile and apparel goods exchanged in the free-trade area use North American components at each of the three transformation stages (fibre to yarn, yarn to fabric, and fabric to finished garments). These rules favoured the highly mechanized US textile industry which made yarn and fabric efficiently.[66]

After the WTO's 1994 Agreement on Textiles and Clothing set a time frame for the phasing-out of industrialized states' tariffs on the imports of textiles and apparel from developing economies, the United States began a 'managed liberalization' of the industry[67] which protected *textiles* while sacrificing US *apparel* production (which relocated to Mexico). American *textile* exports, which were produced by an industry with significant barriers to entry for competitors, showed a strong increase under NAFTA. These exports helped to offset industry losses from competing East Asian *apparel* producers who used fewer American inputs and enjoyed the cost advantages deriving from overcapacity and currencies devalued after the 1997 Asian crisis.[68] In some cases, American companies relocated their operations to preserve their own profits. Among the handful of US textile firms to move to Mexico were Burlington Industries and the Dixie Group,[69] both of which invested in capital-intensive plants near the US border, directly replacing previous American production.[70]

In the longer term, this buffering function may decline as Mexican and Canadian producers develop into more self-sustaining, direct competitors. Since the late 1990s, Mexico's complementary support for US output was weakened by its industrial upgrading and the rise of overseas, lower-cost textile and apparel exporters. As Mexican textile producers adjusted to a new environment, they reduced the amount of textiles they imported from the United States.[71] Along with imports from non-American suppliers, this expansion quickly decreased the use of US fabrics in Mexican apparel manufacturing. Subsequent Mexican growth in the sector was slowed by rising labour costs[72] and an appreciating peso.[73] These challenges had a significant impact on the US industry, which shed approximately 60,000 jobs in a sector-wide shock in 2001.[74] Thus, the short-term support that Mexico provided ultimately failed to foster the American textile industry's long-term interests. Mexico's maquiladora program may have let it remain less agile, ultimately contributing to the industry's steep decline.

Conclusion

From the vantage point of mainstream economic analysis, Canada and Mexico make significant contributions to the United States' economic strength, increasing the size of its market and enhancing its competitiveness. At the same time, although the ultimate trajectory of North American economic relations has been towards lowering border barriers to the free flow of all trade and investment, the periphery has offered some obstacles to US economic demands. By resisting economic integration during certain periods and in certain sectors, Canada and Mexico have protected some sectors of their economies from American competition, thus preventing the United States from embracing the whole continent within its economic perimeter and hampering the realization of its full economic potential at a regional scale. At the same time, however, by signing CUFTA and NAFTA, the periphery severely restricted its ability to revert to protectionist, self-directed policies and so created not just the largest but the most reliable trading partner for the United States. These policies arose from the neoconservative turn in continental economic policy that, while championed by US elites, was equally influential in the periphery. Both Canadian and Mexican elites endorsed an economic reorientation that defined their national interests as complementary rather than competitive with those of the United States.

Practically speaking, the periphery's asymmetrical dependence on the US economy limits the capacity of either state to disrupt its economic relations with the United States. Neither Canada nor Mexico can initiate a trade war without risking its own prosperity. As a result, the United States' own policy dependence on the periphery is neutralized by Canada's and Mexico's even greater vulnerability to the United

States' retaliation against any move that they might make to reduce the benefits that it extracts from their economies.

While the United States has secured its highly profitable relationship with the periphery against actions by Canada or Mexico that might diminish these benefits, it is free to take its own initiatives which may jeopardize the gains it receives from the periphery. The border-thickening measures adopted after 9/11 and strengthened over the ensuing decade constricted the growth of the United States' economic relations with its periphery. The 2008–9 economic crisis further up-ended much of the economic status quo, and the Buy America stipulations of the Obama administration's stimulus package caused some US TNCs to break their production chains, replacing Mexican- and Canadian-sourced inputs with purchases from higher-cost American producers.

We will return to questions of economic relations in chapter 7, where we consider Canada's and Mexico's contribution to the development of a US-friendly multilateral economic architecture by supporting US international trade positions. Meanwhile, we turn to the role that Canada and Mexico play in supplying the US economy the resources it needs, with special emphasis on petroleum products.

2 Supporting US Energy Security[1]

Q: Do you consider Canadian oil to be "foreign" oil?
A: No. I consider Canadian oil part of America's energy independent strategy. I consider Canadian oil to be a reliable, safe, and secure source ... To me, this is an extension of the United States' energy independence – by growing our ability to receive oil from Canada.

> – Lindsey Graham quoted in 'US Senator Sold on the
> Oil Sands,' *Globe and Mail*, September 17, 2010

Obviously we've got to look at neighbors like Canada and Mexico who are steady and stable ... And when it comes to the oil we import from other nations, we can partner with neighbors like Canada, Mexico, and Brazil, which recently discovered significant new oil reserves, and with whom we can share American technology and know-how.

> – US President Barack Obama, March 30, 2011

Countries that depend on foreign sources for an essential commodity have a number of basic options. Most governments rely on the whims of the global marketplace, placing their national economies at the mercy of delivery interruptions and volatile international prices, because they cannot shape international markets to guarantee stable supply chains. If it fears that another state may try to manipulate the global supply, an imperial state with the requisite military means can go further, intervening coercively either to occupy the resource-bearing lands or to exert sufficient political control over a foreign government that the latter ensures access to its resources. If the political, economic, or strategic costs of such overt intervention are prohibitive, the resource-deficient state may more subtly influence resource-rich states so that they deem it in their own interests to make their raw materials available for purchase.

A decisive factor contributing to the United States' spectacular rise as the world's largest and most dynamic economy was the abundance of the raw materials necessary for its industrial machine that were found within the confines of its own territories. Vast reserves of coal and iron ore provided easily accessible and completely secure sources for the economy's industrialization in the second half of the nineteenth century, when steam-engine technology drove both manufacturing and railroad transportation.

With the development of the internal-combustion engine, liquid forms of hydrocarbons became essential inputs to every industrial economy. At first it seemed that its expansion to the Pacific had provided the United States with the considerable reserves it needed. Oil was discovered in Texas and California, territories that had been annexed in 1848 following the Mexican War. But even these bounteous petroleum supplies could not keep pace with the demands of an expanding economy. The United States' need for foreign oil increased in proportion to its growing petroleum deficiency. The discovery of huge reserves in South America and the Middle East posed the foreign- and even military-policy question of securing the supply of a fuel that had become an essential component of US power. When oil and natural gas were found in Canada and Mexico, American corporations eagerly moved in to develop these resources, supply local markets, and then meet their home demand.

Canada and Mexico were of interest for other energy sources as well. The large uranium reserves in Saskatchewan made Canada a major source for the United States' nuclear-arms production and nuclear-generated electricity. Canada's direct contribution to US electricity needs came from a number of provinces' large-scale exports of their hydro-generated excess capacity. With growing demands for low-carbon energy in the face of global climate change and the gradual integration of its electricity markets, North America's energy markets span a wide range of commodities and governance structures.

This chapter will nevertheless limit its focus to oil and natural gas, which continue to be critical components of the US energy supply mix. Petroleum has been the single most important source of energy in the United States since 1951. By 2009, oil made up 36 quadrillion British thermal units (BTUs) of energy, or 37 per cent of total US energy consumption. Almost three-quarters of this amount provided 95 per cent of US transportation energy demand. About 22 per cent supplied industrial needs, with only small amounts directed at commercial and residential uses. Natural gas, the second most important energy source, provided 23 quadrillion BTUs of energy, about 25 per cent of total US energy consumption split evenly between industrial, commercial/residential, and electricity-generation needs.[2]

We will start by quantifying Canada's and Mexico's material contribution to American energy security as sources of oil and natural gas. Absent Canadian or Mexican energy supplies, the United States could well supply its energy demands from other jurisdictions and, in fact, the American appetite for these resources is so large that US demand alone can influence global supply patterns. However, we are interested less in international energy economics and more in the intricate political relationships that complement the complex energy flows within North America. Here we will discuss how Canada and Mexico became strategically preferable sources of material resources and, in turn, how the United States managed its political relationships with its two neighbours to minimize its vulnerability to their interrupting the supply of these strategic commodities.

Logistics: North America's Oil and Natural-Gas Supplies

Oil and natural gas share some physical qualities and differ in others. In its various grades, oil can be transported large distances overland by pipeline or can be transported by tanker across oceans. The associated, cleaner energy form of natural gas can also be piped across land or, less commonly, shipped in liquefied form. Because of its durability and fungibility as a commodity, a single global market for oil has developed with a single global price. By contrast, natural-gas markets remain regionalized and display differentiated global prices rooted in regional variations in supply and demand. These alternatives in transportation modes and economic contexts offer us a way to clarify how geographical contiguity distinguishes Canada and Mexico from overseas suppliers of these two resources that helped construct the twentieth-century US economy and remain vital to sustaining its power in the twenty-first. From being almost insignificant energy partners in the 1950s, Canada and Mexico have emerged as the premier suppliers of oil and natural gas to the United States.

Figure 2.1: US imports of crude oil and petroleum products from
Canada and Mexico by volume, 1973–2010

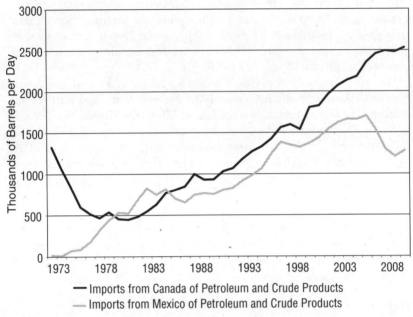

Source: US Energy Information Administration (2011).[3]

Oil

Economically, it is worth distinguishing two broad categories of oil
products: crude oil, which is a raw unprocessed material, and processed
petroleum products, which can include anything from gasoline and
heating oil to chemical products and asphalt. In 2010 the United States
consumed 19.1 million barrels of petroleum products per day (MMbd),
more than any other country.[4] While the United States is the world's
third-largest crude oil producer, its domestic production satisfies only
51 per cent of its petroleum thirst.[5]

Figure 2.1 shows how US imports of oil and petroleum products
from Canada and Mexico have grown massively since 1973. Canadian
exports increased steadily to a high of over 2.5 million barrels per day in
2010. Imports from Mexico are smaller both in absolute and in relative
terms but still account for a noteworthy share of total US supply from
abroad. Having been insignificant until the mid-1970s, Mexican energy

Figure 2.2: Relative contributions of Canada and Mexico to US imports of crude oil and petroleum products, 1973–2010

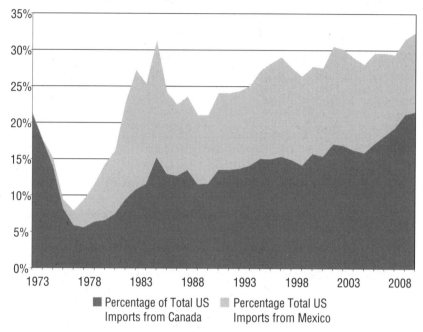

Source: US Energy Information Administration (2011).[6]

exports increased until 2006, after which they declined owing in large part to the exhaustion of Mexico's principal reserves.

Figure 2.2 demonstrates that the relative contribution of Canadian oil and petroleum products to the United States has increased every decade since 1980. By 2010, Canadian and Mexican exports accounted for over 32 per cent of US imports.

Table 2.1 shows that in 2010 Canada and Mexico were the largest foreign suppliers of crude oil and petroleum products to their mutual neighbour. Only the sixth-largest producer of crude oil in the world, Canada was nevertheless the United States' largest single source of crude and petroleum products.[7]

The relative importance of Mexico and Saudi Arabia has varied over the past few years. Until 2007, Saudi Arabia was the second-largest exporter of crude oil to the United States, but its oil sales dropped precipitously in 2008, allowing Mexico to overtake it. The seventh-largest

Table 2.1
US imports of crude oil and petroleum products from select countries, 2010 (thousand barrels per day)

	Crude Oil Imports	Percentage of Total Imports (%)	Petroleum Product Imports	Percentage of Total Imports (%)
Canada	1,972	21.5	561	21.7
Mexico	1,140	12.4	140	5.4
Saudi Arabia	1,080	11.8	14	0.5
Venezuela	912	10.0	75	2.9
Nigeria	986	10.8	40	1.5
World	**9,163**		**2,590**	

Source: US Energy Information Administration (2011).[8]

producer of crude oil internationally in 2009, Mexico was the second most important supplier of crude oil to the United States, although it exported only a modest amount of refined petroleum products.

The net figures in Table 2.1 obscure oil exports from the United States to the periphery. For example, Canada is the only country in the world to which the US exports crude oil, but this trade is a marginal 44,000 barrels per day. By contrast, both Canada and Mexico import significant quantities of petroleum products from their shared neighbour. For example, in 2008 Canada imported about 180,000 barrels per day of various refined products, 34 per cent the size of its export flow. Mexico, by contrast, actually imported from the United States more than twice the amount of petroleum products that it exported, about 322,000 barrels per day. Presented in terms of net imports, Canada is still the largest supplier of oil to the United States (25 per cent of all imports), but Mexico drops to fifth place (9 per cent), behind Saudi Arabia (12 per cent), Nigeria (11 per cent), and Venezuela (10 per cent).

Potential Reserves

Acknowledging that the periphery currently provides the United States with one-third of its petroleum imports – thereby bolstering its economic power and political security – does not tell us whether this will be the case twenty years ahead. Whether the periphery remains the United States' major supplier role depends not just on the quantities Canada and Mexico have available, but on the costs involved in bringing them to market, the world price of oil, and the decisions involved in determining which market they will supply. Indeed, there is one fungible global

Table 2.2
Estimated oil resources for select groups, January 1, 2010

	Proven Reserves (billions of barrels)	Percentage of World Reserves (%)
United States	19.2	1.42
Canada	175.2	12.94
Mexico	10.4	0.77
North America	**204.8**	**15.12**
OPEC	939.8	69.40
Other Non-OPEC	209.1	15.45
World	**1353.7**	**100**

Source: US Energy Information Administration (2010).[9]

oil market, and the United States will ultimately purchase the cheapest oil as long as there are no political obstacles to doing so.

Predicting future scenarios is complicated by the notorious difficulty of measuring resources. The most basic indicator of future oil capacity is 'proven reserves,' an estimate of the oil that can be recovered with more than 90 per cent certainty within the existing political, economic, and technological climate. Given the sophistication of their available scientific techniques, geologists and economists make increasingly fine distinctions between *proven* reserves that are recoverable using existing technologies, *known* reserves that cannot yet be extracted, and *undiscovered* reserves that they have reason to believe exist but have yet to be located. Even within the latter category, experts distinguish between the more likely *probable* and the less likely *possible* reserves which they believe are waiting to be discovered. Published figures are in turn vulnerable to political and corporate manipulation.

Table 2.2 shows that North America accounts for just over 15 per cent of total proven oil reserves worldwide. Of these, over 85 per cent is located in Canada, which has the second-largest proven oil reserves after Saudi Arabia, with 19 per cent of the global total. Much of Canada's oil is trapped within the oil sands – also known as 'tar sands' – in northern Alberta and Saskatchewan. Without counting this unconventional oil, Canada would drop to twenty-first in terms of global oil reserves.[10]

Unlike conventional reserves, oil from tar sands is more difficult to extract and process since the bitumen-impregnated earth has to be heated to such high temperatures that the bitumen liquefies, enabling it to be drained away. The further development of oil-sands reserves will necessitate costly techniques that remain under development.[11]

The huge financial costs of oil-sands development constitute only one factor that may limit Canada's construction of US energy power. The extraction process is a significant culprit in global warming and has led to the resource being deemed 'dirty' both in Europe and in the United States where environmentalists have endeavoured to legislate constraints on its importation from Canada. The upgrading involved in its production also requires very large amounts of natural gas, which is not only an expensive input but ultimately a cleaner source of energy than the oil it helps extrude. In addition, the refining process requires large supplies of fresh water, creating further problems both because the availability of water is declining in relatively arid Alberta, with farmers competing for its use, and because the discharged water contaminates downstream rivers and thereby increases disease rates among Aboriginal communities. Framed in this way, by exporting petroleum derived from oil sands, Canada assumes the ancillary environmental and resource costs while the United States secures more oil supplies without bearing the externalities left behind in their production.

Outside Alberta, Canada has increasingly viable sources including the offshore oil reserves of Newfoundland and Labrador as well as the conventional heavy oil in the Bakken reserve of southeastern Saskatchewan and Manitoba. In 2008 the US Geological Survey announced that up to 4.3 billion barrels of oil could be recovered from this shale – almost a thirtyfold increase from its 1995 assessment, which reported that up to 150 million barrels were to be found in a formation that crosses into North Dakota and Montana.[12]

This story of growth in reserves is reversed in Mexico where proven reserves in the Gulf of Mexico and in the country's northeast are rapidly declining.[13] The Cantarell oilfield was one of the world's biggest oil wells from 1979, when it came on stream, until 2004, when its impending exhaustion became evident. Its decline in output has reduced the country's total production by over 19 per cent – a loss worth some $13 billion in 2007. The Chicontepec field in the northeast state of Tamaulipas contains 39 per cent of the country's present total reserves, including some 18 billion barrels of crude, extending 16,000 square kilometres off the coast of the northeast state of Campeche.

Of the country's 15 billion barrels of probable reserves, 60 per cent are in Chicontepec and 28 per cent off the coasts of Tabasco and Campeche. Given the unexpectedly rapid depletion of Cantarell's reserves, Ku Maloob Zaap was, by 2009, the country's most important production site for crude oil. The deep waters in the Gulf of Mexico offer the potential to reverse this trend.[14] Recent oil finds in the Gulf of Mexico, including British Petroleum's 'Tiber' discovery in US waters, suggest the potential for millions of economically recoverable barrels, a possibility whose realization may be jeopardized by BP's own 2010 disastrous oil spill in the Gulf.

Natural Gas

Natural gas, for which the United States has a voracious appetite, is expected to be the fastest-growing component of worldwide energy consumption over the coming decades.[15] It is cleaner and more convenient than oil for heating, transportation, and electricity generation,[16] and, by 2007, US consumption of 23 trillion cubic feet accounted for just under 21 per cent of global consumption.[17] With US natural-gas production of 19 trillion cubic feet falling short of domestic needs, the United States imported between 13 and 16 per cent of its natural-gas needs between 2003 and 2008.[18]

Unlike oil, which is traded in a largely identical form irrespective of the geographical distances involved, the form of natural gas depends on the means used to transport it. Natural gas extracted within North America can be transported in its naturally occurring gaseous form. By contrast, to ship gas from overseas to the United States, it must be liquified and then transported by tankers to specialized liquefied natural-gas (LNG) terminals. Given the technical difficulties, costs, and dangers of catastrophic explosions involved in this type of transport, only 1 to 3 per cent of American natural-gas needs were met by LNG between 2003 and 2008. Because of these challenges, the future for LNG imports in North America is unclear. Recent massive shale-gas finds may lead to the United States exporting, rather than importing, natural gas in its liquefied form.

As Figures 2.3 and 2.4 make clear, Canada has long been the United States' primary foreign natural-gas supplier.[19]

From 1990 to 2007, Canada increased its natural-gas production by about 5 per cent. Since domestic consumption increased only marginally, the excess production was exported to the United States. By contrast, Mexico has a deficit in its production and consumption of gasoline, natural gas, liquefied natural gas, and petrochemicals[20] and so is a net importer of these products, having quadrupled its natural-gas imports from the United States since the 1990s.[21] Mexico's natural-gas reserves are estimated to be less than half of Canada's, although up to 65 tril-

Figure 2.3: US imports of natural gas from Canada and Mexico by volume, 1973–2010

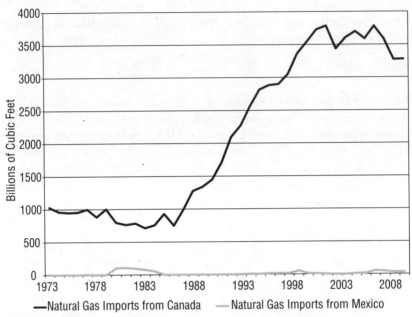

—Natural Gas Imports from Canada   — Natural Gas Imports from Mexico

Source: US Energy Information Administration (2011).[22]

lion cubic feet of gas may be located in the Burgos Basin of northeastern Mexico.[23] To compound the problem, although Mexico's known natural-gas reserves have declined, its consumption is expected to increase as the country moves from oil- and coal-generated electricity to natural-gas generation. In 2010 Mexico produced 3.6 billion cubic metres a day (MMpcd), imported 536 MMpcd, and exported 19 MMpcd.[24]

The prospects for large-scale extraction of natural gas from shale in various parts of the continental United States could dramatically reshape the US domestic energy sector. Shale-gas extraction is an intensive process, requiring the fracturing of underground rock formations with a combination of high-pressure water, chemicals, and sand. Large shale-gas reserves holding huge natural-gas supplies have been known to exist for several decades. Cost-reducing improvements in extraction technology coupled with rising demand for natural gas have accelerated the development of these shale 'plays.' Since the fracturing process creates significant contaminated waste-water problems, however, the

Figure 2.4: Percentage of total US natural-gas imports from Canada and Mexico by volume, 1973–2010

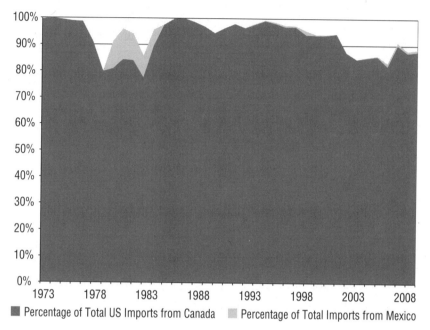

■ Percentage of Total US Imports from Canada   ▨ Percentage of Total Imports from Mexico

Source: US Energy Information Administration (2011).[25]

production of shale gas could be blocked because of environmental concerns. Late in 2010, for example, New York State lawmakers declared a moratorium on shale-gas exploration until environmental regulations were drafted.

Shale gas may ultimately upend the existing continental energy dynamic. A recent US government study estimated that domestic shale reserves could meet 110 years of domestic gas demand.[26] Canada also has significant shale-gas reserves, particularly in the St Lawrence area, but, given the United States' new-found energy wealth, these reserves may prove less important for American energy security. While Canada may still be a major supplier of natural gas, we can expect this role to diminish over the coming decade as conventional Canadian sources are depleted and as more shale-gas reserves come on stream. Official US estimates already predict significant declines in natural-gas imports

Table 2.3
FDI in the US petroleum and natural-gas industry, 1998–2000 (billions of US dollars)

	1998	1999	2000	Percentage of World FDI in 2000 (%)	Percentage of World GDP in 2000 (%)
Canada	2.5	2.9	4.5	4.9	2.4
Europe	43.8	45.8	82.6	88.9	29.1
Netherlands	10.4	10.7	13.2	14.2	1.3
United Kingdom	29.4	32.4	66.1	71.2	4.9
Asia and Pacific	1	0	0.6	0.6	25.3
World	**49**	**51.9**	**92.9**	**100**	**100**

Source: US Energy Information Administration (2000).[27]

from both Canada and Mexico by 2035.[28] The United States is accelerating the production of its own natural gas so rapidly that some analysts believe it will become a major exporter while Canada joins Mexico as a natural-gas importer. Since natural-gas markets are more regionally constrained than oil markets, US shale reserves will almost certainly reduce Canada's importance to US energy security.

The Periphery's Investments in US Energy Sectors

In addition to providing its own energy supplies, the periphery bolsters US economic power with its own foreign direct investment in the United States. In 2000 the United Kingdom and the Netherlands (the head-office location of many non-Dutch transnational corporations) were the leading foreign investors in the US petroleum and natural-gas industry. Although investing only one-tenth as much as Britain and one-quarter as much as corporations registered in Holland, Table 2.3 shows that Canada was nevertheless the US oil and gas industry's third-largest foreign investor. A number of Canadian companies, such as Talisman and Encana, are making sizeable investments in the development of US energy resources, indicating the increasing activity of the Canadian-owned energy industry in promoting the integrated Canadian-American energy market.[29]

The Policy Construction of North America's Energy Markets

So far, our exposition of the United States' petroleum logistics has shown its energy security to be substantially enhanced by its two geographical neighbours' pipeline-delivered oil and natural-gas exports. Were the continental periphery suddenly to disappear from the face of the globe, US economic strength and security would be considerably compromised. While analysts debate the nature of US energy dependence,[30] without the periphery's oil and natural gas, the United States would – at the very least – have to pay higher prices to import oil and natural gas from a smaller global pool of resources, and these shipments from overseas would make it more vulnerable to supply interruption resulting from hostile action (al-Qaeda), unfriendly governments (Venezuela), or cartels (OPEC). But this energy-supply counterfactual does not take us far enough in understanding the complex political dynamics that drive the energy relationship between the United States and its periphery in North America's petroleum sector.

As the data describing the United States' energy predicament reveal, the geographical distribution of petroleum resources on the continent placed Canada and Mexico in the mixed position of being, primarily, suppliers which could meet their neighbour's resource demands with pipeline-delivered reliability and, secondarily, customers buying from it. Other things being equal, the material dependence of a country on such a large proportion of the material assets needed for the generation of its economic strength at home and the consequent projection of its military power abroad might be expected to make that country vulnerable to its suppliers' pressure politics and leverage.

But other things have not been equal. Confronting the gravity of its supply needs, Washington has not been passive. Far from simply being an object in the face of foreign suppliers' agency, it has actively pursued a dual approach to securing external supplies. On the one hand, it has worked to expand supply abroad by offering its own energy transnationals incentives to discover and develop oilfields around the world and by encouraging friendly foreign governments to do the same. On the other hand, it has striven to prevent these same governments from favouring their own economic or political priorities or exerting pressure on the United States by manipulating the supply or pricing of their petroleum exports to the US market.

Because Mexico and Canada have on occasion demonstrated their capacity to redeploy their own hydrocarbon resources from supplying the US market to satisfying their own needs, this section will explain how Washington has worked over the decades not just to encourage its neighbours to expand their productive capacity but to limit both governments' ability to constrain it by reducing their exports.

However important for the US economy the periphery's assets may potentially be, they cannot be supplied unless the political conditions in Canada or Mexico are propitious. Energy is particularly interesting in this regard since the two countries have followed different policy trajectories with significant implications for their resources' development and export. The rest of this chapter will explain how this dynamic has played out in the two bilateral relationships.

Keynesian National Capitalism

Consistent with its staple-driven history since the sixteenth century, when Newfoundland first entered the world market as a cod-exporting colony, Canada has mainly favoured maximizing its energy exports with only spasmodic interruptions during periods of public concern for its energy self-sufficiency or economic autonomy. Because the Canadian energy sector's growth was in good part driven from its inception by large US corporate investments, it has remained intimately connected with the US oil sector. At the highest corporate echelons, the CEOs of Canadian resource giants are often American; for instance, Rick George of Suncor is a US emigrant. The cultural cohesion derived from shared social circles blurs distinctions between Canadian and American national interests within this resource community and stimulates the cooperative development of an integrated system.

Driven by a nationalist imperative devoted to its autonomous economic development, Mexico was far more culturally and physically isolated throughout most of the twentieth century. Mexico put a burr under the American saddle with its nationalization of foreign oil companies at the beginning of the Keynesian period, although more was at stake in principle than in practice. Canada, having at first enthusiastically supported the Americans' petroleum plans after the Second World War , caused them some alarm in the 1970s and early 1980s when it gave priority to its own energy security. With the subsequent shift to neoconservatism, Washington succeeded in reintegrating Canada within its continental energy perimeter but only managed to push its ideological allies within Mexico to move gingerly towards the same goal. We will first discuss Washington's dual role as object and agent in Mexico.

Mexico

From its emergence as a strategic raw material, oil has provided a symbolic focus for Mexico's deeply conflicted relationship with the United

States. The civil bloodletting that culminated in the 1910 Revolution marked an abrupt end to the long period identified with Porfirio Díaz's presidency, when British and American direct investment in raw-material extraction for export determined the form of Mexico's economic development. In the light of popular Mexican feeling that the country's patrimony had been stolen by foreigners, Articles 27 and 28 of the 1917 constitution proclaimed the Mexican people's sovereignty over the country's natural resources, precluding their exploitation by private, still less foreign, ownership. In fact, this constitutional constraint on US companies' control of Mexican reserves remained inoperative at first, since Washington exerted such strong pressures on Mexico that US oil interests were left to operate there for two more decades.

When President Lázaro Cárdenas nationalized all foreign subsidiaries operating in the oil and natural-gas sector in 1938, he created Petróleos Mexicanos (Pemex) to run the petroleum industry as a state monopoly. Having asserted exclusive ownership of its oil and gas resources, Mexico prevented foreign companies from either buying oil or investing in such downstream operations as distribution and marketing. Yet Mexico's assertion of sovereignty over its oil sector constrained US power more symbolically than substantially.

Demonstrating that losing ownership, control, and the resulting supply of Mexican oil had dealt a blow to their economic interests, the US parents of the expropriated companies retaliated swiftly, refusing to deal with their new socialized rival. For the US government, however, the Mexican government's dramatic oil nationalization was more objectionable in principle than in practice. In 1938 the 3.8 million barrels of oil[31] that Mexico exported were not quantitatively significant, but the nationalization of any US transnational corporation by any foreign country was a provocation that Washington could not accept – unless some higher priority such as national security prevailed.

The Mexican government was indeed able to capitalize on Mexico's geostrategic importance to the United States in light of the looming world war. When faced with the US oil companies' boycott of its exports, Mexico turned to selling oil to the Axis countries. This countermove pressured Washington to settle the oil dispute in order to secure its cooperation in a bilateral defence agreement. By 1941, President Manuel Ávila Camacho had negotiated an accord that resolved this dispute on very favourable terms.[32] Faced with a conflict between its strategic security and its economic power, the US government made a trade-off. It was willing to sacrifice its oil companies' interests in favour of the broader national interest by obtaining – as we explain more fully in chapter 4 – Mexico's contribution to its military security against Germany and Japan. Mexico did not again take on significance for US energy security until the late 1970s, when its large Cantarell oilfield began production.

Canada

Given the centrality of petroleum to its military power, the United States has vigorously flexed its muscles to address global supply challenges. Indeed, energy security has been a major factor driving its foreign policy towards both the Middle East and the Western hemisphere since the Second World War. Within the North American continent, Washington has made repeated – although not always successful – efforts to promote its foreign partners' energy-sector development and to curtail their ability to withhold their supply. When the Soviet bloc's threat became acute in the Korean War, President Harry Truman established the Paley Commission to study the problem of American access to strategically important raw materials where domestic production could not meet the demand.[33]

The commission's report was based on the assumption that interdependence was the best approach to supplying material shortages.[34] It recognized the role of private enterprise as the driver of US raw-material security and recommended that the Western hemisphere should be recognized as the country's prime supplier. By 1950, of the $13.5 billion in US private direct investment abroad in mining, petroleum, and related industries, over 65 per cent was in Canada and Latin America.[35] Of twenty-two key resources then available in the non-communist world, Canada produced ten and accounted for over 10 per cent of all free-world production of five: nickel, copper, lead, zinc, and asbestos.[36] Mexico also produced ten of these resources and generated over 10 per cent of free-world production for three: lead, zinc, and antimony.[37]

Energy, including oil and natural gas, was at the centre of the Paley Commission's focus. The commission was most concerned that US crude-oil production would taper off despite rising demand,[38] but it adopted a positive outlook towards the United States' ability to source petroleum abroad. The North American periphery did not feature prominently in its report since Canada was then a minor player and Mexico was not even mentioned as a potential source of imported oil.

Concerning natural gas, the commission felt that the United States would have to rely on both conservation and foreign imports to meet demand.[39] It regarded the import of Canada's growing natural-gas production as 'assured' and noted that the possibility existed for future imports from Mexico.[40] Overall, the potential for either Mexico or Canada to supply US natural-gas demand would likely be small relative to future US demand.[41]

To enhance the availability of foreign oil, the US government provided tax breaks for American transnational corporations to encourage them to explore and develop foreign oil wherever it could be found. Consequently, when large petroleum reserves were discovered in Alberta, American TNCs provided investment capital, technology, managerial expertise, and public-policy models for its exploration, development, refining, transportation, and marketing.[42]

In addition to offering these incentives to its own private sector, the US government worked to consolidate its energy industry's access to the Canadian market by relaxing some of its protectionist measures and by trying to influence Canadian government policy. Not only did the US oil majors participate in the discussions of Prime Minister John Diefenbaker's government regarding the development of a national petroleum strategy, but the US State Department also weighed in to lobby against Canada piping Alberta's new-found oil riches eastwards to its industrial heartland in Ontario and Quebec.

Uncle Sam's persuasion built upon Alberta's own preference to serve the adjacent midwestern market, thus prompting Diefenbaker's 1961 National Oil Policy to split the Canadian market into two. Out west, the bulk of Alberta's oil and natural gas would be exported southwards. Instead of being fuelled by prairie oil, central and eastern Canada would be supplied by American TNCs shipping oil from their overseas subsidiaries in unstable countries like Venezuela where there was some urgency to pump out the oil in case their assets were nationalized.[43] In return for Diefenbaker's consent to halt an Edmonton-Montreal pipeline, the United States exempted Canada from its oil-import quotas. Washington had effectively teamed up with Albertan interests to redirect Ottawa's policy from ensuring domestic energy security to mitigating US energy insecurity. While central and eastern Canada remained dependent on the supply and price vagaries of the world market, the United States had extended its energy perimeter to include Alberta's petroleum economy.[44]

Almost two decades after Paley, President Richard Nixon commissioned George Shultz to propose how the United States should meet its rising energy demand in the face of volatile world energy conditions.

The resulting Shultz Report warned that the oil-producing nations in the Middle East and north Africa, along with Venezuela, might band together and 'economically exploit' the United States.[45] Unlike the 1952 Paley Report's somewhat casual treatment of North American energy relations, Shultz paid them careful attention, noting that 'the ties between Canada and the United States are close, and the two countries have already recognized their energy interdependence, in, for example, electrical interconnections.'[46] Canada also featured prominently in his report's discussion of future import sources. Recognizing the potential for the Alberta tar sands, he went so far as to suggest that their successful development could lead one day to 'continental self-sufficiency.'[47]

In postulating US vulnerability to several supply-interruption scenarios, Shultz clearly considered Canadian energy reserves already to be within the American perimeter. American and Canadian energy production capacity was a single whole 'because of the existence of an integrated transport network and the likelihood that the two countries would consult closely during a crisis.'[48] Canada was deemed the safest oil source: 'The risk of political instability or animosity is generally considered to be very low in Canada. The risk of physical interruption or diversion of Canadian oil to other export markets in an emergency is also minimal.' The Shultz Report proposed a harmonized 'continental resources policy' to expand the coordination of the two countries' energy policy, provided that Canada accept the premise of a common resource policy.[49]

Talk of a continental energy policy came at an inopportune moment for Canadians, who were just beginning to realize that their putatively limitless petroleum resources were actually turning out to be finite and, alas, non-renewable. As Shultz had predicted, an international cartel soon formed to exploit the fact that oil was a diminishing resource in high demand. In 1973, when the new Organization of Petroleum Exporting Countries doubled, then re-doubled, its price for oil, the Canadian government belatedly attempted to construct a national energy economy by limiting energy exports going south and redirecting Alberta's petroleum output to central Canada via a pipeline[50] – actions that were perceived in Washington as offensive and a dangerous constraint on US power. In 1975 Pierre Trudeau's government created Petro-Canada as an integrated public-sector energy company that received federal subsidies and special exploration rights. Ottawa also introduced a two-tiered pricing system whose domestic, 'made in Canada' price for oil was substantially lower than the escalating world price which Americans would have to pay for their imports from Canada.[51] Oil imported to supply the eastern Canadian market was to be financed by a tax levied on Alberta's exports to the United States.

While these steps caused concern among US officials, the Trudeau government's 1980 National Energy Program provoked outright consternation. Conceived in the fallout from the second OPEC crisis in 1979, when the world price of oil again doubled, the NEP promoted Canadian energy ownership and self-sufficiency by measures that encouraged the diversion of western Canadian oil to supply the central and Atlantic provinces.[52] In keeping domestic oil prices below world-market prices, the program effectively subsidized the price of energy for the eastern provinces which still relied on insecure overseas imports. Since the NEP also curtailed oil and natural-gas exports, the policy generated acute tensions with the United States and also in Canada itself.

Under the Canadian constitution, the provinces have jurisdiction over their own natural resources. Intensely conscious of their sovereignty in this domain, Albertans were incensed by the federal government's intervention in their petroleum economy. Supported by a storm of popular indignation, the Albertan government successfully challenged the constitutionality of the export tax in the Supreme Court of Canada.[53] Alberta's virulent opposition directly limited the federal government's efforts to reorient the Canadian petroleum industry along an east-west axis and so supported the United States' continued energy security by defending the prairie market's integration in the US petroleum sector.

Although the NEP had been effectively eviscerated by 1982, US energy interests were determined to eliminate the possibility of Canadian politicians again threatening their continued full access to Alberta petroleum. George Shultz's vision of a continental energy policy materialized later in the 1980s when first Canada and then Mexico shifted from their Keynesian mode to a neoconservative approach and knocked on Washington's door asking for an economic-integration agreement.

Neoconservatism and the Continental Extension of the US Energy Perimeter

In their economic-liberalization negotiations with Ottawa in 1986 and 1987, US negotiators successfully sought provisions that would prevent the Canadian government from ever again adopting NEP-like policies. In its final text, CUFTA prohibited Canada from reintroducing a two-tiered pricing system through which it sold exported energy for more than the domestic price. This provision ensured that Canada would not use its abundance in energy supplies to give its own industries a competitive advantage over US manufacturers. In addition, CUFTA's 'proportionality clause' prevented the federal government from reducing exports of oil and gas to the United States unless also reducing domestic consumption by the same proportion. Through these new energy rules, Washington neutralized Ottawa's capacity to intervene in its domestic market in order to favour Canadian industry and consumers and so restrict exports to the United States. Thus insulated from the federal government's regulatory reach, Alberta's petroleum sector could be safely developed to serve the US market. CUFTA's negotiation was a pivotal move that constitutionalized Canada-US energy market integration, bringing into high relief the significance of Canada's contribution to US energy security and Washington's determination to lock in this reality. Making this point in more popular terms, the former premier of Alberta, Peter Lougheed, exulted that there could henceforth be 'no son of NEP.'

The Shultz Report had concluded that, after Canada, the United States' next most secure oil came from Mexico, with which energy relations could be more easily integrated than elsewhere in Latin America.[54] When the subsequent oil-price escalation made it profitable to develop its newly discovered offshore reserves in Cantarell, Mexico was able to produce far more than was necessary to satisfy its immediate needs. Even better, exporting surplus oil to the United States provided it with foreign currency that helped finance its own industrialization plans. From constraining US petroleum power, Mexico had turned to constructing it, and US energy interests were keen to work alongside their Mexican counterparts to secure that neighbour's supply role.

While Washington's CUFTA negotiators, with Edmonton's support, had succeeded in curtailing Ottawa's ability to interrupt the southward flow of Albertan oil and gas, they failed five years later to achieve a similar constraint on Mexico's energy autonomy. When negotiating NAFTA with the George H.W. Bush administration, Mexico refused to consider the pricing and supply restrictions that Canada had accepted with CUFTA. On the contrary, it insisted that the agreement explicitly acknowledge its constitution's declared sovereignty over Mexican resources. This meant in practice that Mexico retained its licensing system and reserved downstream petroleum and natural-gas operations for Pemex,[55] thus frustrating the US industry's efforts to expand its investment in a Mexican energy sector that, by then, had become a major source of US petroleum imports.

Beyond its attempt to achieve energy security by binding its neighbours with formal trade agreements, the United States uses various other channels in order to ensure secure and reliable continental energy flows. On an informal basis, top federal energy officials in the three countries frequently compared notes in order to develop 'parallel (though not identical) approaches' to energy challenges.[56] The US Federal Energy Regulatory Commission and Canada's National Energy Board shared a memorandum of understanding committing both countries to exchange information and to coordinate positions on energy projects. The United States later signed a letter of intent with Mexico's Comisión Reguladora de Energía (Energy Regulatory Commission) proposing the same arrangement as with Canada.

Towards Trinational Energy Governance

With the election in 2000 of two former petroleum industry executives, George W. Bush and Dick Cheney, the US government formally shifted its continental energy strategy to a trilateral level. Beyond recommending the maximization of the United States' own production, the 2001 Cheney Report advised the US government first to seek its foreign energy supplies within the Western hemisphere and only then to look overseas. It recommended the expansion of US-Canada natural-gas pipelines, particularly from Alaska and in the east. The report also discussed Canadian oil production,[57] particularly Alberta's oil sands, and the need to build new pipeline capacity to transport it to the United States.[58]

Cheney was far more circumspect about cooperation with its other neighbour, noting that 'Mexico will make its own sovereign decisions on the breadth, pace, and extent to which it will expand and reform its electricity and oil and gas capacities.'[59] Nonetheless, the report highlighted Mexico as a net importer of US refined oil products and a potential source of future crude oil production.[60] It identified Mexico's licensing practices as a potential bottleneck to the construction of cross-border pipeline and other energy developments, recommending that these be better coordinated.[61] From having been insignificant energy partners in the 1950s, Canada and Mexico had emerged as the United States' premier resource suppliers. Unlike many of the other facets of the North American periphery's contribution to US economic power, US policy makers had officially acknowledged its energy importance and recommended that Washington play an active part in fostering the periphery's contribution to US energy security.

Given that Canada and Mexico were now the United States' first-

and second-largest petroleum suppliers, the Cheney Report's principal international recommendation was to adopt a trilateral framework
to promote US energy security, one that could 'develop closer energy
integration among Canada, Mexico and the United States,' albeit with
due regard paid to its neighbours' sensitivity about their sovereignty.[62]
Anticipating this recommendation to spur on the cooperative development of an ever more integrated North American energy market, a
working group was struck to provide a comprehensive framework that
could promote greater coordination.[63] On March 8, 2001 the US energy
secretary met with his Canadian and Mexican counterparts in Mexico
City where they announced the creation of a North American Energy
Working Group (NAEWG) to promote communication and cooperation on mutual energy interests as well as to enhance energy trade on
the continent.[64] As its core mission, the working group was to change
the analytical framework for energy from three separate markets to one
integrated continental market.

The NAEWG became a partnership for information exchange on
common issues such as energy efficiency, harmonization of statistical
methods, transparency in the marketplace, and renewable energy. Its
official meetings of energy officials from each country were held twice a
year but were not open to the public. Much of the group's work was run
by mid-level officials who focused their attention on technical standards
and regulations.[65] Its discussions reportedly helped the three governments realize how integrated their energy markets were. For example,
energy planners struck a committee to identify opportunities for cooperation in research and development projects, and a computer model-
ling system was developed that framed the continent as one unit.[66] The
upshot of these structured and unstructured interactions among high-
level officials and mid-ranking bureaucrats from the three countries
suggested that progress was being made towards the implementation of
a continental vision which extended the US energy perimeter from the
Northwest Passage to Mexico's Guatemala border.

To this end, the NAEWG produced overview reports on the supply-
and-demand picture in each of the three countries, providing reliable,
comparable data even on the politically sensitive issue of Mexico's
depleting oil reserves. In 2005 *North American Natural Gas Vision*
acknowledged the challenge facing all three countries. Because Mexico
relies on the United States, because the United States relies, in turn, on
Canada as its premier foreign source of natural gas, and because Canada's gas reserves were depleting,[67] the document stressed the impor-

tance of making new investments in natural-gas pipelines from Canada and Alaska and of installing facilities for bringing liquefied natural gas from overseas.[68] Though these reports generally avoided specific recommendations, they recognized Canada's and Mexico's importance as primary contributors of energy resources to the United States.[69] By promoting coordination and open dialogue, the NAEWG provided the United States an instrument for pursuing its energy-security goals with its neighbouring governments.

On March 23, 2005 US President George W. Bush, Canadian Prime Minister Paul Martin, and Mexican President Vicente Fox announced the creation of a Security and Prosperity Partnership of North America (SPP) to improve collaboration on a broad range of issues, including the harmonization of energy regulations, the integration of the three energy markets, and the satisfaction of each country's energy needs.[70] In effect, the SPP incorporated the NAEWG under the umbrella of its anti-terrorism security agenda by maintaining its nine expert groups,[71] which were already working on energy efficiency, regulation, and technology in the oil, natural-gas, electricity, and nuclear-energy sectors.[72]

The SPP established a business wing, the North American Competitiveness Council (NACC), in 2006 to serve as a trinational private-sector forum and make recommendations to the SPP's working groups.[73] Among fifty-one recommendations presented in NACC's initial report in 2007 was the call for the Mexican energy sector's liberalization.[74] The text identified Mexico's restrictions on private investment and the government's budget constraints as obstacles to its discovering new energy sources and developing them.

Pemex suffered from an investment deficit, having been unable to develop its proven resources, access new ones, and invest in refineries for its downstream operations. In order to expand its oil and natural-gas sectors enough to have surpluses for export, Mexico would need colossal investments in exploration, production, and technology. In 2007 Pemex declared that it required $18 to $20 billion over the following five years for investment in physical infrastructure. Just to maintain production, it would have to complete the drilling of at least ten costly deep-water projects in the short and medium term, and it required an additional $10 billion to sustain existing operations.[75] Located in deep waters, its Lakach field alone would require investment of $190 billion between 2011 and 2025 to bring its resources to market.[76]

Since foreign and private investment in the petroleum sector is constitutionally prohibited, Pemex's only source of capital is its own government. With its tax revenue remaining at a low 12 per cent of GDP, the Mexican government has financed one-third of its own budget by taking more than 60 per cent of Pemex's gross revenue.[77] As a result of losing this revenue, Pemex has had to operate with very little capital, reinvesting its own revenue in long-term infrastructure projects only when the federal budget has allowed. It is also handicapped by such internal problems as overstaffing, poor management, waste, and reported corruption.

US participation through capital contributions and administrative assistance to Mexico's infrastructure is an indirect means of constructing its own energy sources by increasing capacity on its southern flank, and Washington has taken an active part in helping Mexico address its infrastructure needs. In partnership with the US Trade and Development Agency, the American embassy in Mexico City ranked 300 infrastructure projects in order of importance, helping Mexico generate a National Infrastructure Plan in 2007 which presented over $250 billion in business opportunities for American and Mexican firms through to 2012. Projects in ports, airports, highways, power, oil and gas, and the environment offered valuable openings for US contractors, subcontractors, and suppliers in these sectors. But even such gentle pressure from outside cannot induce the changes that are required to bring Mexico's state-directed energy sector fully within the United States' energy perimeter.

In 2008 Mexico brought in an energy reform designed to increase the flexibility of the public sector's contracting with private-sector enterprises. Along with the 2007 fiscal reform, that of energy should increase Pemex's capacity for reinvestment. More flexible contracting conditions may help Pemex modernize its productive plant, exploit new wells, and modernize its technology. If successful, this will assist US business through offering new investment opportunities and may boost US energy security by increasing Mexico's capacity to export energy. But, as the Ministry of Energy and Pemex itself put it, 'Pemex's challenge is not just a financial one but is basically operative, technological, and managerial.'[78]

Addressing the question of private investment, NACC had emphasized that 'expertise and resource contributions from Canada or the United States' could provide a supportive role for liberalization efforts. While it recognized that the reforms should be led by Mexican stakeholders, it advised Mexico to liberalize the trade, storage, and distribution of refined products and 'to maximize the storage and distribution capacity of multinational oil companies with distribution capabilities in the United States.'[79] NACC thus provided a forum through which the United States could push its agenda of increasing access to Mexico's energy reserves through expanding technical assistance and opportunities for its TNCs' investments. NACC's importance lay in its ability to shift Mexican energy policy discourse from defending the country's statist stance to envisaging more privatization.

The Cheney Report had recommended that, 'to the extent Mexico seeks to attract additional foreign investment consistent with its Constitution, which reserves exploration and production rights to the Mexican government, the United States should actively encourage the US private sector to consider market-based investments.'[80] Resolving Pemex's dilemmas opens up space for this kind of American involvement, particularly in providing new extraction technology, which could in turn lead to increased US access to Mexican reserves.

Mexico's energy sector has slowly but steadily moved in the direction of making the major fiscal and regulatory change that would welcome US investments. Retail gasoline sales are competitive, and the distribution of natural gas involves private franchising.[81] Other openings for US penetration of the oil sector include multiple service contracts (MSCs) through which Pemex grants foreign companies permission to explore and extract resources. The creation of MSCs has prompted little international interest, however, since prospective partners do not gain ownership of the oil they help produce. Oil companies want risk-related return, but Mexico still does not provide them the business climate they demand. Because US firms can only provide services instead of acquire supplies for their own use as they can in Canada, Mexico's constitutional limitations constrain efforts by American TNCs that would bolster US energy security.

To date, US participation in Mexico's oil development has been through contracts that do not concede ownership of any of the extracted oil to the contracting company. Data from its engineering and project-development division indicate that, between 2003 and 2010, Pemex had signed contracts for basic engineering, technical assistance, professional services, and legal assistance with thirteen US companies totalling $477 million.[82]

Reforming Mexico's nationalized model is a highly sensitive issue both culturally and politically. Public-opinion polls confirm that national ownership of energy reserves is entrenched in the Mexican people's social consciousness. Although the public has begun to accept the implications of economic globalization, energy remains the major excep-tion.[83] Issues that incite the greatest opposition in public opinion are foreign involvement in oil exploration, production, and distribution,[84] and political parties have helped cement these feelings.

Once deliberate, Mexico's constraint on US energy security has become inadvertent on account of the country's shortage not just of oil but of natural gas. In 1995 Mexico authorized foreign investment in downstream operations in the natural-gas sector, although drilling remained a public monopoly.[85] There is little potential for it to supply the United States with its own natural gas. Liquefied natural gas is another matter since it comes by ship. Because LNG does not originate in Mexico, it is not under Pemex control. This gap in its neighbour's con-stitutional constraints has enabled American enterprise to plan several LNG terminals south of the US border. Already one LNG project has begun connecting Baja California to US markets such as Phoenix and Las Vegas.

Although energy exports contribute to US energy security, the under-development and limited supply of Mexican oil and gas have put the country into an ambiguous position. Alternately, and sometimes simul-taneously, Mexico has both constructed US power by exporting petro-leum and constrained it by being unable to develop potential reserves over which it maintains national control.

Conclusion

With petroleum we have a literal example of how Canada and Mexico have fuelled US geopolitical power. As the United States' largest suppli-er of oil and natural gas, Canada significantly contributes to its energy security. As a corollary, the depletion of Canada's natural-gas reserves could constrain US power if the United States then has to search farther afield or find alternative domestic fuels to satisfy its needs. However, the prospective exploitation of vast shale-gas supplies may complete-ly reverse the energy relationship, with the United States contributing to Canadian energy security, rather than the opposite. For three dec-ades, Mexico also constructed US power as a substantial oil supplier, though its own needs made the country a net gas importer from the United States. In terms of potential supply, Canada's unconventional oil reserves present troubling trade-offs and Mexico's undiscovered reserves in the Gulf of Mexico remain a question mark.

While Canadian corporations have made significant investments in the US energy sector relative to their other US investments, Mexico does not construct US power through investment. At the same time, Mexican energy policy prevents the US energy TNCs, which generate much of Canada's energy supplies, from investing in Mexico's development projects. Without adequate capital and technology, Mexico will be unable to maintain even its current supply levels for domestic use into the next decade, a deficit that indirectly compromises US energy security.

Washington recognized the danger of the continental periphery limiting its energy power when it negotiated the proportionality and pricing clauses in the Canada-US Free Trade Agreement. But the Canadian constitution further limits the Canadian government's capacity to constrain US power. With jurisdiction over their natural resources, resource-rich provinces typically insist on selling their energy to the United States.

The three countries' mid-2000s effort to remediate NAFTA's institutional failure by setting up a modest form of trilateral governance came to naught. The NAEWG represented Washington's acknowledgment of Canada and Mexico as crucial contributors to its energy security. The significance of its incorporation within the SPP lay in energy being explicitly subsumed within the United States' security paradigm, and its energy committee was a trilateral effort to square the circle between security and prosperity. Canada considered the SPP another avenue through which to strengthen its already-close bilateral relationship with the United States, and Mexico relished the prospect of a more equal forum for interacting with Washington. Meanwhile, the United States saw benefits in having Canadians in the room when pressing the Mexican government to reform its energy policies, since Mexicans tend to perceive Canadians as more disinterested and so more credible than their generally overbearing American neighbours. But insiders were disappointed with the three governments' incapacity to get their own bureaucratic departments and agencies to cooperate in the process. The SPP may have established a US-defined framework within which energy-security issues could be discussed, but no actions of consequence resulted, and the Obama administration's 2009 decision to close it down suggests that Washington had lost interest in working with its neighbours to address their future energy dilemmas cooperatively. Instead, President Obama and Prime Minister Harper informally reinstitutionalized bilateralism in 2009 with the officials-level Clean Energy Dialogue.[86]

Possible policy counterfactuals add further uncertainties. Given the continuing severe polarization in the Mexican body politic, it is conceivable that a more radical party could come to power. Striking the chords of Mexico's still vibrant nationalism and denouncing continuing US deportations of undocumented immigrants, a left-wing government might attempt to re-establish autarchy for at least some parts of Mexico's energy sector, despite the economy's dependence on very significant imports from the north. Yet, without Mexico discovering and developing major new petroleum supplies, the impact on US energy security of such a return to the country's previous development strategy would be minimal.

In Canada a different power reversal might have more serious consequences. Should Alberta lose its stranglehold over Canadian energy policy in the aftermath of a national embrace of ecological consciousness, US energy security might be adversely affected. Remarkably, it was the US Congress that characterized Alberta tar-sands oil as 'dirty oil' and thus subject to import sanctions. While it seems unlikely that effective actions will be taken against Canadian oil imports, the flare-up of concern both domestically and in Washington about the proper role for Canadian energy resources in an environmentally conscious North America speaks to some deeper uncertainties that infuse continental energy politics. Were the exploitation of the oil sands to be halted until its refining no longer caused climate change or emitted greenhouse gases, Canada might wield considerable weight in discussions about the most appropriate balance among the conflicting goals of supply adequacy, environmental protection, and realistic timing of a move towards a more sustainable course. Complications would be considerable, even costly. Voluntary restraint in its oil-sands output could turn Canada into a net oil importer. But rediscovering its moral authority might help assure its long-term survival, particularly if it helped break the United States free of its oil addiction and increase its actual energy security.[87]

Giving up income in the pursuit of environmental objectives would provoke storms of opposition within both countries. In addition, being nudged by Canada might strain binational relations, since it would reaffirm American dependence and underline the extent to which overall US power is conditioned by the country's energy security. While oil imports from Canada could be replaced from other sources, this could not be done without the loss of the strategic benefits that reliable and flexible North American energy provides. Such an exercise of Canadian soft power that deliberately connected energy and environmental policy could help redirect US energy security along a new sustainable path. Whether Canada chooses to play such a far-sighted but tough role rests on its own political and constitutional considerations.

In the shorter term, conservation efforts and the development of sustainable energy sources could reduce the United States' consumption of petroleum, but, even if it were to lower its reliance on imports, it will still be unable to achieve petroleum autarchy. As long as it needs foreign oil, the value of the periphery's exports will remain high compared to other less stable sources of supply.[88]

Oil transportation across the high seas generates American security anxiety because of the volatile political situation in some oil-producing countries. Three-fifths of the top ten oil exporters to the United States rank among the world's most corrupt countries – an understandable cause for concern. Strained relations with the United States have caused Venezuela to threaten withholding its energy exports. Political turmoil across the Middle East jeopardizes the prospects for that region's energy exports.

In the context of this global instability, Canada and Mexico are not only two of the United States' three leading petroleum suppliers; they are its most reliable. We can thus conclude that, whether evaluated quantitatively or qualitatively, the United States has come to depend on its continental periphery. Yet, perfectly aware of the implications of this dependency, Washington has managed to neutralize its vulnerability to Canadian politics and has even made progress in opening up the Mexican energy system to its private sector's participation.

In the next chapter we tackle an even more complex subject, the question of whether and how emigrants from Mexico and Canada build US economic strength.

3 Supplying Workers for the US Labour Market[1]

Mexican migrants make a very important contribution to the economy of the United States, and the great majority do not compete with the local work force, but rather fill a critical gap in the US economy that cannot otherwise be met in a satisfactory way.

– Mexican President Zedillo, Tijuana, April 26, 1996[2]

Despite having the world's largest economy, the United States has only its third-largest labour force, estimated in 2009 at just over 154 million people.[3] US economic might is thus a function of the productivity it leverages not only from its capital and technology but from its workers. We have already assessed the contribution made by Canadian and Mexican markets and resources to American economic power. Here we evaluate labour as the third basic component of US economic competitiveness.

The endless flow of immigrants bringing their talents and aspirations to the United States has been one of its major assets, maintaining the demographic momentum that was a prerequisite for the economy's supremacy in the post-Second World War era. Other things being equal, a larger population increases the domestic demand for goods, opens new markets, increases consumption, and promotes the specialization of labour into more productive uses.[4] As with trade and investment, population growth builds the size of the domestic economy, reduces the per-capita cost of providing public goods,[5] helps the United States rejuvenate its aging workforce, and offsets its declining birthrate.[6] Although Canada and Mexico have long immigrant histories of their own, both countries have produced large flows of emigrants who, seeking better prospects for their ambitions and higher returns on their abilities, became important sources of labour to the United States over the past two centuries.

The diversity of Canadian and Mexican emigration to the United States almost defies analysis. While they were labourers in the nineteenth century, the bulk of emigrating Canadians are now highly skilled individuals, taking advantage of the greater opportunities offered by the larger, more dynamic marketplace next door. A significant number of highly educated Mexicans also leave for the United States, but these skilled emigrants are outnumbered by the hundreds of thousands of low-skilled economic migrants who, both legally and illegally, cross the Rio Grande each year in search of more remunerative work than they can find at home.

Many conservative Americans rail against both the Mexican immigrants who stay and the migrants who return home, maintaining that these aliens 'hispanicize' the United States' culture, steal jobs from Americans, and burden US taxpayers. Others welcome this immigration as an affirmation of America's promise to the world. Only rarely does the American immigration debate interrupt its ideological sparring in order to consider more soberly the impact of the migrants from next door on the country's economic and political power.

The recent economic contributions made by these migrants must be framed in the context of a changing US labour market that was under pressure from the forces of economic globalization at the turn of the twenty-first century. The manufacturing economy – on which post-war US economic prosperity had been built – was struggling to maintain its economic competitiveness in the face of rapid trade liberalization. In its stead, the US economy was refocusing its energies on knowledge-based information and service sectors that were perceived as constituting the new US comparative advantage, from software development to nanotechnology and from entertainment media to bioengineering.

At the same time, the US labour force has been aging. Driven by decreased fertility and the tendency to early retirement, demographic trends foreshadow significant reductions in the workforce's growth rate. While average growth was a robust 2.6 per cent in the 1970s, when it was buoyed by increases in female labour-market participation, it had declined to 1.1 per cent growth in the 1990s and 2000s on its way to a predicted scant 0.3 per cent by 2020.[7] To compound this dilemma, the same demographic trends that weaken labour-market supply create new demands for labour, as an aging retiree population generates new health, homecare, and other service-sector needs.

Considering these trends, forecasters suggest that two labour-market developments are necessary to promote a competitive US economy over the coming decades. First, to facilitate the transition away from manufacturing to the knowledge and service economy, there is a critical need for highly skilled workers who can navigate the human-capital-intensive demands of the twenty-first-century economy. Second, more untrained workers are needed to meet increased demands in the retail and service sectors.[8]

Evaluating the available evidence, we find that the periphery's labour flows have helped to mitigate both of these tensions by offering a flexible supply of labour that has serviced unmet demands in the US labour market, boosted the US economy's size, increased its productivity, and buffered some sectors from the shocks of global competition. In this chapter we will first present the data on Mexican and Canadian emigration to the United States, linking the quantities of immigrants to efforts by US immigration policy to control these flows of people. We will then assess the periphery's contribution of skilled and unskilled labour to the US economy's strength and competitiveness. Finally, we will ask to what extent the massive Mexican and modest Canadian diasporas in the United States give their respective governments any enhanced capacity to influence, and potentially constrain, US policy.

Quantifying North American Labour Flows

Early population movements in both directions across the Canadian-American border were virtually unrestricted.[9] Following the American Revolution, large numbers of 'Loyalist' refugees fled to the British colonies to the north. From the nineteenth century through the 1920s, Canadian migration to the United States grew substantially in response to work opportunities, often in regionally distinct patterns.[10] Although the 2.8 million Canadians who left for the United States between 1840 and 1930 constituted that period's third-largest immigrant group,[11] they have been generally ignored by American scholarship, apart from the subset of some 900,000 culturally homogeneous French Canadians[12] whose impact on New England was considered just as threatening at the turn of the nineteenth century as was the Mexican impact on the United States as a whole one hundred years later.

Canadian emigration reached its height in the 1920s, when an astonishing 2 per cent of the country's total population crossed the US border every year. Subsequently, emigration flows slowed until, by the 1990s, they amounted to a small fraction of 1 per cent of the Canadian population per annum, a portion that does not include the considerable number of Canadians working or studying in the US under temporary visa arrangements. Between about 1820 and 2009, just over 4.7 million Canadians legally emigrated to the United States, about 6 per cent of total US immigration over that period.[13] While the concept of illegal aliens is often associated with the Mexican border, data derived from the 2000 US census indicate that some 122,000 unauthorized Canadians were residing in the United States at the time.[14]

Throughout the second half of the nineteenth century, movement across the southern US border was equally unrestricted. Notwithstanding a temporary influx triggered by California's 1848 gold rush,[15] immigration remained minimal until the 1870s, when American employers began to recruit Mexicans for heavy farm labour and railroad construction. In the decade following the Mexican Revolution of 1910, over 700,000 emigrated legally, to be followed by a further 950,000 in the 1920s.[16] Since Washington did introduce immigration restrictions after the First World War, these legal immigrants were joined by large numbers of 'wetbacks,' Mexicans who swam or waded across the Rio Grande to evade the new border controls. The Great Depression revealed an important characteristic of Mexico's contribution to the US labour market – its flexibility. As job opportunities in the American southwest vanished, an estimated 400,000 Mexicans returned to their *pueblos*.[17]

Temporary Programs

Contracting foreign citizens to work on US soil was made illegal in 1885, but the Second World War's double manpower challenge eroded this ban. The American economy had to meet the government's urgent need for military equipment, supplies, and munitions at the same time as large numbers of working-age men were drafted to fight overseas. Faced with pressure from business – particularly in the southwest – which had been lobbying since the 1930s for regulatory changes to bring in more cheap labour, Washington negotiated a contract-labour program with Mexico. Under these arrangements, the first cohort of labourers to boost the wartime economy arrived in September 1942 to assist with the American beet harvest. By the end of the war, approximately 215,000 agricultural workers and 75,000 railroad workers had been authorized for contract employment in the United States under what became known as the Bracero program. While the arrangements for railroad workers collapsed at the end of the war, this guest-worker program for agriculture continued afterwards, with up to 200,000 'braceros' a year working in twenty-six states under government contracts.[18] Braceros constituted only 2 per cent of the United States' total farm-labour force during that period, but they comprised 20 per cent of its seasonal migrant workers.[19]

These legal employment opportunities had a demonstration effect, attracting others to cross the border illicitly. By the early 1950s, even many of the braceros were wetbacks who were subsequently legalized by US authorities to simplify the labour-recruitment process.[20] Wetback migration played an important role in the collapse of the Bracero system, which had guaranteed temporary workers certain social and financial supports and so was more expensive compared to what undocumented migrants cost. At the same time, US labour unions protested that the Bracero program was reducing American farm workers' wages. Unable to resolve the tension between business demanding low-cost foreign labour and American workers objecting to this wage competition, Washington closed down its guest-worker program in 1964.

Immigration Reform

Fears of job competition, political displacement, or cultural contamination have typically vied with pro-immigration idealism and economic interests, so that the United States' immigration policy has veered back and forth. On the one hand, it has self-interestedly opened its borders to the world's best and brightest or idealistically beckoned to the 'huddled masses yearning to breathe free.'[21] On the other hand, it has tightened controls in response to worries about foreign cultural contamination or fears that US prosperity is too fragile to be shared with newcomers. Amendments to the Immigration and Nationality Act in 1965 established a quota system for immigration, setting an annual limit of 120,000 for the Western hemisphere. These reforms moved the United States away from a country-specific quotas system towards one favouring family reunification. In 1976 annual per-country limits of 20,000 were added.[22] Mexican immigration numbers stabilized in the 1980s at between 10 and 15 per cent of total immigrants to the United States, but the family-centred priority subsequently multiplied the flow from Mexico.[23]

Reforms in the 1986 Immigration Reform and Control Act (IRCA) included legalization for permanent residents and some seasonal labourers. Over 70 per cent of the 2.7 million people who applied for legal status were Mexicans.[24] Mexican immigration numbers relative to other nationalities spiked in the late 1980s, cresting at an astonishing 52 per cent of all immigrants to the United States. These ratios reflected both an increase in domestic Mexican pressures to migrate to the United States and the relative decline of emigration from Europe after standards of living increased there. In spite of some highly racialized anti-immigrant rhetoric, most forcefully expressed by such conservatives as Patrick Buchanan,[25] the legal migration of Mexicans during the 1990s grew four times faster than that of other nationalities.[26] These figures increased again during the 2000s, when between 150,000 and 200,000 Mexicans immigrated legally each year. Between 1820 and 2009, over 7.6 million Mexicans had moved to the United States – almost 10 per cent of total immigration over that time. Putting Canada and Mexico together, over 16 per cent of all documented immigrants to the United States have come from the North American periphery.

Undocumented Immigration

Following the 1964 demise of the Bracero program and the associated policy changes that limited the types of applicants who could legally immigrate,[27] the number of undocumented migrants to the United States actually increased. IRCA's legalization program caused a temporary decline in undocumented flows, but these increased once more by the early 1990s[28] and by the middle of the decade were exceeding legal entries.[29]

Estimates of the total number of undocumented migrants entering the country, which are based on mathematical models extrapolated from apprehension rates, vary significantly. In the twenty-five years after 1965, 56 million undocumented workers are thought to have entered the United States, but 86 per cent of these are believed to have come on a temporary basis, so that there was a further net inflow of 5.2 million Mexicans.

Following the al-Qaeda attacks of September 11, 2001, anti-terrorist fears joined job concerns and cultural xenophobia to toughen US immigration measures and 'securitize' the US border. Citizen vigilantism and the construction of a wall to keep out both Mexicans and terrorists necessarily impeded cross-border immigration. These policy developments had paradoxical effects. Tightened border security increased the risk

Table 3.1
The foreign-born US labour force, 2009[30]

	Labour Force (millions)	Percentage of Total Labour Force (%)	Percentage of Foreign Born Labour Force (%)
Native Born	130.2	84.5	–
Foreign Born	23.9	15.5	–
Total	**154.1**	–	–
Country of Birth			
Mexico	7.7	5.0	32.2
Other Central American	2.0	1.3	12.3
Canada	0.3	0.2	1.5
European	2.5	1.6	10.3
Philippines	1.1	0.7	4.7
India	1.1	0.7	4.7·
China	0.9	0.6	3.6
Other Asia	3.0	1.9	12.9
Caribbean	2.2	1.4	9.3
South America	1.7	1.1	7.0
Other World	1.3	0.8	5.3

of being caught, so that individuals who managed to cross over chose not to return home even during periods of higher unemployment. As a result, although the number of Mexicans entering the United States has declined since the mid-2000s (by almost 40 per cent from an all-time high of 1 million in 2006–7 to about 630,000 in 2008–9), and although the 2008–9 recession dimmed their employment prospects, the number of migrants returning to Mexico remained quite steady, only falling from 480,000 to 430,000 over that period.[31] Because they are stuck in the United States, these migrants try to arrange for their families to join them. Policies designed to staunch incoming flows have thus had the opposite effect. In other words, US border militarization may now be the major factor driving increased Mexican migrant pressure.[32]

Mexican and Canadian Workers in the US Labour Market

The significant presence of undocumented Mexican workers through-out the US economy makes it difficult to arrive at precise estimates of the periphery's contributions to US labour markets. Nonetheless, while focusing predominantly on documented workers, the latest fig-ures reveal the huge contribution that Mexican immigrants make to the American workforce. As Table 3.1's data show, Mexican immigrants were by a large margin the single biggest foreign-born worker group in the United States in 2009. Some eight million Mexican immigrants comprise 30 per cent of the foreign-born workers in the United States, with the next two largest contributing countries – the Philippines and India – a distant second, at 5 per cent each. By contrast, only 300,000 Canadian immigrants are reported in the US workforce, a paltry 1.5 per cent of the foreign-born labour force.

Mexican and Central American migrants are also the fastest-growing segment of the US labour force, having grown 6 per cent on average in the decade from 1994 to 2004, and at 3 per cent in the half-decade since. These growth rates are considerably higher than the 0.7 per cent growth rate in the domestic labour force.[33] There is no doubt, then, that Mexican migrants are a massive presence in the US labour market. What remains to be seen is how this impressive pool of human capital benefits the US economy.

The Economic Impact of Periphery–United States Migration

Depending on which issues one chooses to emphasize, immigration can be analysed as having either positive or negative effects on an economy. We will start with the negative effects.

The argument that immigration from its periphery imposes a burden on the United States' economy has two main thrusts. One position suggests that the large-scale migration of unskilled labour, of which Mexico is the predominant source, can lower American wages, often with negative effects on the employability of less-educated Americans but with positive effects on the wages of educated Americans as a result of productivity gains.[34] Analysts who contradict this view find that only limited numbers of low-skilled Americans actually compete with unskilled immigrants for low-paying jobs.[35] More generally, there is a lack of robust evidence that immigrants to the United States, including Mexicans, affect domestic wage rates, except for a modest effect among the least-educated portion of the US population.[36] This appears true at both the national and the state level. Even in California, where dramatic numbers of migrants settle, recent analysis questions whether immigration has had any systematic effect on the employment prospects of American-born workers.[37]

A second position argues that the presence of these immigrants places 'a monumental burden on the public sector.'[38] Undocumented migrants are also thought to leech the fiscal system by extracting more in social services than they pay in taxes.[39] Actually, considerable uncertainty surrounds the net fiscal effect of Mexican migrants on American society. The counter-argument points out that many undocumented migrants are paid by company cheques, rather than with black-market cash, and so do have Social Security and payroll taxes deducted from their wages. Because they are ineligible to receive any rebates or benefits from these payments, such migrants actually contribute to the Social Security Administration's budgetary surplus by generating nearly $7 billion annually in the form of taxes collected by their employers,[40] a contribution that helps explain their tolerance by US politicians.[41] In addition, whether from ignorance, linguistic inability, or fear, many undocumented migrants are either unable or unwilling to risk applying for public services.[42]

Statistical estimates of the net annual effect that Mexican immigrants have on the American economy range from a drain of $43 billion to a contribution of $30 billion.[43] A major study commissioned by the US Congress ended up squarely in the middle of this dispute by showing that immigrants have no fiscal impact, except perhaps for a very modest one at the municipal level.[44] Domestic economic gains from immigration are concentrated in certain sectors and may amount to between $1 billion and $10 billion a year.[45] While these figures are not trivial, they pale in comparison with the United States' GDP in 2008 of almost $15 trillion.

Representing the policy community's consensus on the economic impact of all immigrants, this congressional study reported that immigration was a less important contributor to US GDP than other variables such as the American savings rate. The study maintained that the biggest gains come when highly skilled workers, such as Canadian immigrants, increase US productivity. Canadians living in the United States are better educated than Americans generally, with 28 per cent having a bachelor's degree compared to the US norm of 23 per cent. This helps explain why Canadians' salaries in the United States are on average 10 per cent higher than those of their American counterparts.[46] Canadian workers tend to outperform the average US worker economically and so pay higher taxes.[47] A parallel phenomenon is found among young adults, because those Canadians studying at US universities are among Canada's best minds.[48] If they subsequently settle in the United States, their contribution to its economy is more significant than their modest numbers would otherwise suggest. While it is not possible to quantify Canadian immigrants' impact on the US economy, they are dynamic,

innovative, and skilled individuals who constitute an impressive transfer of human capital to the United States.This positive impact also characterizes labour flows across the other US border. While the average
Mexican migrant is poorly educated, most are not as desperate as they
are often portrayed. Many are highly skilled, constituting a northwards
brain drain to the United States that parallels the Canadian experience.
Even when migrants and their children arrive unskilled, they may have
high-performing careers. Often to a greater degree than Canadian-born
Americans, first-generation Mexicans are a major source of professionals, from engineers to managers to administrators.[49]

Low-skilled Mexican households, which use migration as a ration-
al strategy to overcome the lack of economic opportunities at home,
are more than just a large supply of low-wage labour.[50] Through economic and cultural innovations in small-scale enterprise, many Mexican migrants become successful entrepreneurs, thus enhancing US
economic potential.[51] The growth of Hispanic business in the United
States is triple the national average[52] and is consistent with the record of
entrepreneurship that generally characterizes immigrants to the United
States.[53]

Unskilled Immigrants and US Economic Competitiveness

For 100 years, unskilled Mexican labourers have acted as an important
economic support for the US economy. Mexicans provided the manual labour that built much of the early infrastructure in the US southwest, laying railroad tracks, clearing ranch land, and digging irrigation
canals.[54] Between 1890 and 1930, US business considered Mexicans to
be a critical input.[55] By the 1920s, this argument had developed a racist
rationale. Industry officials found Mexicans suited 'both biologically
and psychologically for monotonous, backbreaking stoop labour in
desert heat ... [and] would spare whites the serious physical consequences of manual labour in the Southwest.'[56] Whatever the rationalization, Mexican labourers acted as a motor of US economic growth,
enabling more rapid development than would have occurred without
them in mining, railroad building, construction, and meat processing,
along with many agricultural and service sectors.[57]

Mexicans continue to account for a high proportions of the labour
force in several key sectors, including almost 33 per cent of farming,
fishing, and forestry and 20 per cent of industry and manufacturing.[58]
Undocumented Mexican workers alone account for 17 per cent of the

agricultural workforce, 17 per cent of cleaning jobs, 14 per cent of construction labour, 12 per cent of the food-preparation sector, 9 per cent of industry workers, and 7 per cent of transportation employees in the United States.[59] Mexicans are concentrated in the American southwest, where they make up an even larger portion of the workforce, with the agriculture, service, and clothing industries being largely dependent on these migrants.[60] In every way, Mexican labour is a critical component of the US labour market.[61] According to the Consejo Nacional de Población de México (National Population Council of Mexico), in 2007 there were 11 million Mexican-born residents over fifteen years of age residing in the United States, of whom two-thirds were employed and earning an average annual income of $24,270. Of these, 28 per cent were in construction, maintenance, and repair; 23 per cent in cleaning, building maintenance, and food preparation; 23 per cent in transport and manufacturing; 15 per cent in services, sales, and administration; 7 per cent in professional occupations; and 4 per cent in agriculture, fishing, and forestry.[62] Not surprisingly, Mexican migrants are significantly more likely to be employed in the service sectors than other migrants, particularly in production, building maintenance, transportation, and food services.[63]

By accepting jobs at very low wages, Mexican workers support many of the United States' most basic goods and services. This phenomenon was particularly important during the industrial restructuring at the end of the twentieth century. Driven by a shift from its declining manufacturing base to its rising service industries, the American economy is now dependent on millions of low-wage jobs that are unattractive to the US-born labour force.[64] Mexican migrants provide the key labour inputs for these important sectors, mainly as complements, not substitutes.[65] Put in general terms, immigrant workers increase the factor productivity of the US economy.[66]

In a complementary trend, recent evidence suggests that Mexican labour may lower the market prices of low-skill goods and services,[67] something of considerable benefit to middle-class US families and retirees alike. Since Mexican migrants tend to be younger than the average international labour migrant,[68] they also help counter the demographic pressures associated with an aging US population. At least for several decades, Mexico will not face the same demographic crunch as the United States, opening the door for Mexican migrants to help manage shifting US labour needs.[69]

The enabling reach of cheap labour penetrates beyond low-wage industries, since Mexican migrants bring with them skills that are lacking in such industries as shoe manufacturing and masonry.[70] This labour substructure at times supports the larger body of skilled labour. In parts of California, a two-tiered economic hierarchy has emerged, with an upper stratum of high-wage unionized workers providing the same services as a non-union, low-wage tier of firms which use largely immigrant labour. While some of these second-tier firms compete directly with the larger firms, many do subcontracting for them at very low prices. Through this exchange, the long-term resilience of high-wage union jobs in core economic sectors may be sustained by the low-wage buffer of immigrant-powered companies.[71] These processes suggest that the US economy has become dependent on migrant labour not only in the industries to which they are directly necessary but also in industries where they play key subsidiary roles. Entire production processes could become uncompetitive without having what one might call the Mexican labour subsidy at their base. To the extent that many US jobs depend on Mexican labour for their long-term survival,[72] Mexican labour has been unobtrusively institutionalized within the American economy.[73]

Some analysts dismissed the Bracero program's value because crops in the southwest did not rot in the fields when it was terminated, as some had warned. But the Bracero program helped US agriculture manage a radical transformation from a structure that relied on small family farms to one based on the industrialization of farming. Agriculture's high-volume practices were premised on having high-tech inputs but also low-wage labour.[74] If the US agricultural industry did not suffer after 1965, it was largely because of Mexican labour.

The general evidence on guest-worker schemes suggests they are rarely temporary. Whether in Europe or in North America, they lead to the guest workers' permanent settlement and attract further illegal arrivals, entrenching migration patterns that cannot easily be reversed.[75] The Bracero program laid the foundation for a series of economic and social networks in the United States that rooted Mexican workers' position in the US economy. Mexican labour's resulting structural embeddedness left employers in many parts of California's economy with few other options. In one survey of employers, who tried a number of alternatives from higher wages to technological innovations, only 11 per cent reported any success in reducing their need for Mexican migrants in their production processes.[76] As Senator John McCain argued before the Council on Foreign Relations in 2005, 'we couldn't round them all up and deport them even if we wanted to. It would be impossible to identify and apprehend everyone here illegally, and if we did, it would ground [*sic*] America's economy to a halt.'[77]

That said, an important counter-argument needs to be acknowledged. Far from increasing the US economy's competitiveness, cheap Mexican labour may have actually made it more brittle by allowing less mechanized sectors to postpone investing in technology that would enhance their productivity.[78] To the extent that agriculture in the US southwest is unable to survive without cheap labour,[79] Mexican workers have helped perpetuate a vicious circle by increasing the costs of transferring to a high-tech system while simultaneously weakening organized labour's position in the economy.

Unskilled Immigrants and US Economic Flexibility

Undocumented Mexican migrants not only boost the US economy's growth and competitiveness by their willingness to take low-wage jobs. They are of even greater value because of the flexibility with which they have responded to its ups and downs. When jobs became available, Mexicans quickly arrived; when work disappeared, they returned home. This unusual tidal effect outsources the costs of managing the American labour surplus to Mexico, where unemployed migrants return during US economic downturns.

Since the early twentieth century, Mexico's geographic proximity and lax regulations provided this cyclical labour supply – flowing in with demand but ebbing away when no longer needed.[80] The Bracero program consolidated the pattern for contract labourers typified by early-season immigration and late-season emigration.[81] Throughout the rest of the twentieth century, Mexican migrants remained a flexible supply of labour, streaming in and out of the United States as needed.[82] That Mexican labourers could cycle in and out of the United States every year to supply a portion of its need for seasonal agricultural workers was indispensable for a sector that did not offer year-round employment. US agriculture's increased investments in new technology reduced some of its need for seasonal migrants, but mechanization did not reduce the US market's overall demand for low-skilled workers, because other technological innovations created low-skilled assembly-line jobs that Mexican migrants continued to fill.[83] Demand for Mexican labour also rose with the expansion of the US service sector.[84]

But times have changed. The more the US-Mexico border thickened, the less flexible this informal labour market became. Despite the economic crisis that erupted in 2008, those Mexicans trapped without work in the United States were less inclined to go home, where they faced not only worse unemployment but also the prospect of being permanently marooned, without the ability to cross back and look for work again in the north.[85]

Beyond its seasonal flexibility, Mexican labour also acts as shock absorber for domestic US businesses in transition. Not having to provide for these workers' longer-term health-insurance needs and with very loose or even non-existent contractual obligations, companies needing to change their production processes can spread their transition costs over longer time horizons, and so adapt to changing economic conditions,[86] because Mexican labourers are more willing than other unemployed labour groups to accept precariousness and variability in their working hours.[87]

Counter-intuitively, this responsiveness can raise the demand for Mexican labour in periods of economic decline and turbulence. By integrating undocumented migrants into production processes with no job security and low wages, companies have enjoyed lower costs during difficult economic conditions. Put otherwise, employing Mexicans instead of unionized labour to produce many of their goods and services allows entrepreneurs to survive when global competitive pressures increase.[88]

Skilled Immigrants and US Innovation

In contrast with the Mexican brawn that has supported the low-wage side of the US economy, a very different pattern characterizes the skilled-labour flows authorized by the tightly controlled channels of government-issued visas. US immigration law did not at first require migrants to meet the economy's labour needs.[89] Nevertheless, the McCarren-Walter Act of 1952 legalized the entry of trained temporary workers with the H1-B visa, which began the official differentiation between skilled and unskilled immigrants.[90] As a rule, individual skilled workers could get visas only when US employers certified that no Americans were available to fill their specific job. The H1-B visa became the primary means for recruiting trained workers to come for periods of up to six years. By the turn of the century, strong demand for this visa meant that the annual quota was generally reached before the start of the fiscal year.[91] Canadians are the third most numerous group of foreigners receiving this visa.[92] A wide variety of more specialized visas are available but they have generated numerically less significant numbers of immigrants.[93]

Under CUFTA and NAFTA, an additional 'TN visa' became available to Canadians and Mexicans wishing to work in the United States. This visa is not limited by quotas for Canadians[94] and can be issued directly at a border crossing if the migrant can provide a passport, proof of a bachelor's degree, and a job offer from a US employer.[95] Although issued for a one-year period, the TN visa can be renewed an unlimited number of times if certain legal requirements are met,[96] thus enabling skilled labour from Canada and Mexico to move with few restrictions into the United States. Professionals can also move to the United States through the more recent WTO General Agreement on Trade in Services (GATS), but this is a more restrictive route.

The inflow of highly educated professionals increased by up to 30 per cent during the mid-1990s.[97] TN visas became ever more popular through 2000, growing 600 per cent in eight fiscal years[98] and reaching 91,082 in 2000, a figure greater than a quarter of the total H1-B visas issued to foreign workers in that year.[99]

TN visa bearers are skilled individuals working in the health-care professions; education; and such high-technology industries as engineering, scientific, and technical services.[100] Between 1997 and 2002, about 117,000 university-trained Canadians are estimated to have migrated to the United States, likely as a result of increased labour mobility under NAFTA.[101] By 2001, Canadian scientists were less likely to remain in Canada than at any time since the Second World War.[102] Similarly, economists, particularly those with PhDs, are now least likely to remain in Canada than at any time between 1929 and 2000.[103]

After 9/11, US immigration officers at border crossings were replaced by more security-driven personnel who were often untrained about immigration regulations. Because decisions about individuals requesting TN visas are often made arbitrarily by these border agents, rejection rates increased substantially[104] to over 50 per cent at high-traffic crossings.[105] This border rigidity, coupled with other new security measures, have pushed would-be labour migrants and their prospective employers to return to applying for H1-B visas.

Having declined significantly from 2002 through to 2004, TN visa use has since increased dramatically, with over 99,000 visas issued in 2009 to Canadians and Mexicans, representing about 10 per cent of total temporary workers admitted to the United States and just under a third of all highly skilled visa workers admitted in that year.[106] Between TN visas and H1-B visas, Canada has become a significant supplier of trained labour to the US economy. However, critics contend that TN visa statistics are flawed because they might include multiple entries and short, insignificant work stays. Numbers may also be inflated by changes in US regulations and statistical categories over the years.[107]

While these labour flows are historically large, they may seem small, given the relative ease with which they can be obtained and the greater financial returns available to Canadians if they move south.[108] On the other hand, the TN visa program's labour mobility is professionally more limited than that of the H1-B visa,[109] because NAFTA specifies only sixty-three occupations that qualify for this special cross-border liberalization.[110]

There is also a Mexican brain drain, although the absolute numbers are too small to have a specific impact on the US economy.[111] Mexican TN visas were limited to 5,500 annually until 2004, but this cap was never reached[112] because it is much more complicated for Mexicans to apply. Unlike Canadian applicants who simply need a letter from a prospective employer, Mexicans must wait three to five months while their application is vetted by the US government, so US employers tend to hire Mexicans under the H1-B program.[113]

Although Canada annually contributes a number of skilled workers to the US economy that rivals the flow of temporary skilled labour from all the other countries of the world combined, these 100,000 skilled workers[114] appear at first glance too modest in scale to have discernible economic effects. Yet a small number of highly skilled immigrants can have a disproportionate impact on economic growth if they are not only themselves productive but also increase the productivity of a large number of workers around them.[115] As people move to the United States, they bring with them knowledge and ideas that can help the country better manage and use its own resource base.[116] The costs of doing science and engineering degrees in US universities are so prohibitive that imported workers and students are needed to fill expertise shortages within the United States.[117] The availability of university-trained Canadians provides a highly flexible cadre that can help meet US needs in a number of high-tech and skill-dependent industries that have become dependent on foreigners.

During the debates about the 1990 Immigration Act, the House of Representatives' Judiciary Committee addressed both the growing need for highly specialized skilled labourers for some industries and how to meet a temporary skills gap in some professional fields.[118] The Independent Taskforce on Immigration and America's Future argued that there was some 'skills shortfall' that immigration could help to overcome.[119] Other analysts dismissed this position, asserting that no critical labour shortages existed within the United States.[120] Still others believed that the United States had become structurally dependent on these skilled-labour inputs. For instance, the American engineering sector expressed concern that the increased reliance on foreign workers was not a temporary shift but indicated a long-term weakness of the US economy. The Institute for Electrical and Electronics Engineers stated that it was 'apprehensive that current engineering workforce management practices are driven by cost savings that shorten the careers of US engineers, while increasing our nation's reliance on temporary foreign workers, [and] short-term contract employees.'[121] If the United States is to maintain its economic prosperity, the institute argued, attracting 'talented international students and professionals is crucial to its continued leadership.'[122] Foreign-born individuals have been involved in founding as many as 25 per cent of high-tech start-ups in the United States over the past two decades.[123]

If high-productivity, high-skilled sectors are central to US economic competitiveness, then those countries that are culturally and intellectually most compatible with the American system will play a greater role in providing the human capital needed to drive its economic innovation.[124] Canada distinguishes itself in this respect because of its close geographic ties and similar academic culture. Insofar as its skilled labour can boost American innovation and productivity and fill critical skills gaps in such key sectors as science and engineering, Canada can be seen to be making a positive contribution to US economic competitiveness.

Trying to Constrain US Power by Mobilizing the Diaspora

It is one thing to show that the North American periphery has played an unequalled role in constructing US economic power through the flexible supply of hundreds of thousands of trained and millions of unskilled workers, a contribution far greater than its economies' size would have led one to expect. It is another thing to establish whether US prosperity's 'dependence' on this constructive role gives Canada and Mexico any political leverage that might enable them to constrain US power by affecting US policy in other respects. The political power of the Cuban émigrés clustered in Miami and the redoubtable Jewish lobby's influence over US foreign policy might lead one to expect that the large numbers of Canadians and Mexicans residing in the United States give the governments of Canada and Mexico their own special political leverage over US politics. But that is not the case.

Canadian immigrants assimilate so undetectably and individualistically into American society that they do not form a coherent cultural block that can be mobilized by the Canadian government – although this prospect has on occasion been the subject of Ottawa's hopes. If anything, it is equally plausible that Canadians who have lived in the United States will bolster US power at home should they return to Canada where they may support US values and policy goals.

The government of Mexico has acted more determinedly than Canada to turn the United States' need for Mexican workers to its own advantage. During the Second World War, when it enjoyed a position of strength because of the United States' labour shortage, it was able to impose conditions – albeit only on the Bracero program, refusing to allow braceros to go to Texas because of that state's discriminatory practices.[125] With the coming of peace and the end of US labour dependence, the Mexican government lost this situationally determined capacity to influence US policy.

From the mid-1940s, US immigration and labour policies ignored Mexico's concerns. Uncle Sam's unilateral approach and general disregard for Mexican interests continued for half a century in which Mexico enjoyed little bargaining power.[126] If anything, growing levels of public hostility in many parts of the United States towards Mexican immigrants handicapped the Mexican government's attempts to influence US policy and public opinion. California's Proposition 187, which in 1994 denied undocumented immigrants access to such public services as education, soured the bilateral relationship and may have jeopardized Mexico's other foreign-policy objectives, showing that US agency could trump Mexican agency.[127]

Whether the huge numbers of more recently arrived Mexican immigrants constrain US power is an issue that has been little studied. An authoritative paper on US foreign policy and Mexican immigration, for instance, does not even consider the influence that Mexican-born Americans might give the Mexican government over US foreign policy.[128] Mexico's relationship with its own American diaspora has in any case been turbulent.[129] Historically, Mexican émigrés were perceived with distaste as 'deserters' who had abandoned the homeland.[130] Conversely, emigrants harboured considerable animosity towards the Mexican state for having failed to generate the opportunities they needed for pursuing a good life at home.[131]

In the early 1980s, the Mexican government adopted a new approach in the hope of engineering from its American diaspora a powerful force akin to the Jewish or Cuban lobbies.[132] It began to develop emigrant leadership and mobilize expatriate Mexicans by creating in 1990 the Program for Mexican Communities Abroad (Programa Para las Comunidades Mexicanas en el Exterior).[133] At the same time as it tried to generate support for NAFTA within the United States, the Salinas government attempted to organize Mexican Americans into a domestic political force[134] and expanded its US consular network to support both legal and undocumented Mexicans living in the United States.[135] In 1995 President Ernesto Zedillo affirmed his desire to 'develop a close relationship between [his] government and Mexican-Americans, one in which they could be called upon to lobby US policymakers on economic and political issues involving the United States and Mexico.'[136] It cannot be proven that these governmental efforts had any success in swinging American opinion in favour of the treaty.[137]

In 2000 Mexico established a presidential office for Mexicans abroad that later became the new Instituto de los Mexicanos en el Exterior (IME). Supported by staff in Mexican consulates in both Canada and the United States as well as by foreign ministry employees in Mexico City, the IME aimed to develop a Mexican diaspora elite who would remain sympathetic to the needs of their mother country.[138] One hundred individuals are elected from the Mexican foreign national community to an advisory council that meets several times a year and advises the IME on how better to engage Mexican American nationals.[139]

These institutional efforts have been complemented by a number of other Mexican initiatives. First is the long-standing practice of issuing consular identification cards to Mexican immigrants in the United States, whether undocumented or legal. These identity cards foster a sense of connection with the Mexican homeland and provide a practical way to assess the scope, composition, and distribution of the Mexican American community.[140] This government-émigré relationship became more concrete when Mexico legalized dual citizenship and gave Mexican Americans the right to vote in Mexican elections.[141] If this development increases the political efficacy of Mexican Americans in Mexico, it could make them feel more capable of acting politically in the United

States.[142] Dual citizenship also increases Mexico's responsibilities to protect the interests of its citizens residing in the United States.

These efforts notwithstanding, the United States' Mexican-born population has not evolved into a powerful lobby supporting Mexican interests in the United States. Although Mexican Americans may value and treasure Mexican lifestyle, customs, and language, these values do not appear to have remained embedded within a patriotic outlook.[143] Despite claims to the contrary, Mexican Americans have largely adopted prevailing US values.[144] Even when almost 5 million Hispanics mobilized on US city streets in the spring of 2006 to draw attention to the plight of immigrants and unauthorized migrants,[145] this protest emerged from the distinct interests and domestic experiences of Mexican Americans and other migrant communities, rather than from any direct agenda set by the Mexican government. The protest demonstrated that Mexican Americans were preoccupied more with their own personal issues than they were with the border-immigration or foreign-policy issues on Mexico's agenda.[146] The IME has become less an arm of the Mexican government for lobbying the US government and more a way for Mexico to try to insert specific Mexican-American concerns within the existing US Latino lobbying network.[147] Mexican government efforts to mobilize the US diaspora may ultimately have to focus on domestic political matters.

Even were their interests to coincide more completely with those of the Mexican government, Mexican Americans' political participation rates in US politics remain very low.[148] As a result, there is little evidence that the Mexican-origin population can help Mexico influence the US government, let alone constrain it.[149] However, the mistreatment of Mexican nationals in the United States tends to ghettoize Mexican Americans and, by increasing their identification with Mexico, enhances the Mexican government's leverage within migrant communities.[150]

Large-scale Mexican immigration may also work in the reverse direction by constructing US power inside Mexico. The Independent Taskforce on Immigration and America's Future stresses that 'immigration is an invaluable soft power resource that helps the United States win political influence around the world. Those who live, study, *or emigrate to* the United States often build up a reservoir of good will towards America and learn first-hand about the American values of individual rights, personal responsibility, opportunity, freedom, pluralism, the rule of law, democratic principles, and civil society. When they return to their home countries, they help spread these values.'[151] The Mexican diaspora's absorption of American values has spread these attitudes to Mexico itself, vitiating in turn the fierce anti-American nationalism that once characterized Mexican opinion.[152] Opinion research confirms that average Mexicans, some 60 per cent of whom have relatives living in the United States and some 20 per cent of whom receive remittances, do not share the anti-gringo views of the political elite and the Mexican media.[153]

The fact that more than a third of the Mexican population – over thirty million people – have been in the United States at some point may actually enhance US legitimacy in Mexico, including within its elites.[154] That both presidents Carlos Salinas de Gortari and Vicente Fox studied in the United States led the taskforce to infer that the United States was enjoying ever greater traction while interacting with their government.

Conclusion

The US labour market will continue to need more highly skilled workers to facilitate its transition to the new global economy, as well as more manual labourers to compensate for its ageing workforce. Canadian and Mexican workers, who have moved to the United States and back for over a century, will continue to help the US economy meet its requirements.

A significant component of the United States' population – over 16 per cent of total US immigration since 1820 – has come from its continental periphery. Canadians were an important source in the early since twentieth century, while Mexicans came to dominate immigration flows from the mid-1960s, helping to sustain US economic growth. Legal and undocumented Mexicans continue to constitute a sizeable portion of the US labour force's bottom end, supplying mainly low-skilled labour to the point that some sectors have become economically dependent on these migrants.

Unlike the flow of resources and material inputs into the United States, where US agency has been actively exerted to secure American supply needs, the country has hardly needed to lift a finger to promote the flow of migrants. Mexican and Canadian workers naturally gravitate to their north and south, attracted by the US economy's dynamism and the greater rewards it offers. In this sense, US economic abundance has become self-reinforcing, as the American economy magnetically draws the hardest-working and brightest human capital from its North American neighbours.

At the same time, neither the Mexican nor the Canadian diaspora offers the Mexican and Canadian governments additional lobbying resources with which they can constrain US power. Mexican Americans tend to respond to their own individual interests and identify more closely with American values than the Mexican government's needs. If anything, the United States is probably the soft-power winner, benefiting when workers and students from both Canada and Mexico return home and spread its core values.

Large migrant movements do not occur in a political vacuum. They prompt the governing process to balance competing economic and social pressures, so it is understandable that the US government has not been passive vis-à-vis the awesome flows of human beings crossing each of its borders. Except for its early days, when American political institutions were embryonic and US borders were uncontrolled, the country has been consumed by the issue of immigration, with politicians being forced to respond to highly emotional and often contradictory political demands.

The resulting immigration policies have tried to reconcile opposing domestic pressures in which businesses' need for workers and a belief in the United States as a refuge for the world's destitute have clashed with the fears of those fearing to lose their jobs or identities to alien hordes. As a result, US immigration policy has lurched between earlier, more generous admission policies and current, semi-militarized restrictions, thereby shaping the architecture within which the pull of economic opportunity and the push of economic need have animated the flows of Canadian and Mexican emigrants.

Under NAFTA, the TN visa signalled a partial recognition of North America as a single labour market, a vision that was supposedly institutionalized by the North American Commission for Labour Cooperation (NAALC), whose mission was to champion worker rights under the new trade paradigm. But the TN visa's impact was offset by Washington's subsequent border-security agenda, and the NAALC was quietly shut down in 2010 with little to show for its decade and a half of efforts.

Instead, continental labour flows have been shaped until recently by what amounts to a discretionary perimeter, with Mexico bearing the social costs of looking after excess labour during US economic downturns and the United States benefiting from these workers' endowments during periods of economic boom. Yet the United States appears to be in the process of devaluing the economic contribution that this unusually flexible source of human capital offers. If the Great Depression and other twentieth-century economic downturns sent waves of labour migrants back into Mexico, Washington's thickened border has muted this cyclicality. Since the recent financial meltdown, the opportunity costs of being caught at the border have risen so high and the border wall has become such an effective barricade that even undocumented Mexican migrants are settling in the US permanently, bringing their families and other dependants, and so increasing the social burden on the US state. At the same time, Mexico's southern border with Guatemala has seen increased undocumented migration coming into Mexico, with an estimated 400,000 Central Americans transiting through Mexico to the United States each year. Even as the United States tries to control migrant flows at its Mexican border, Mexico's apparent inability to control the southern flank of the North American labour-market perimeter amplifies the effects of undocumented migration on the US economy by increasing the pool of prospective migrants.

While the jobs and remittances that result from the US demand for Mexican labour may constitute a safety valve for potential political instability arising from mass unemployment in Mexico, these, in turn, could impinge on American interests.[155] More than ever, the United States will need to find creative ways to provide for the increasing permanence of the periphery's migrants while it struggles to reach a political balance that recognizes Mexican labour as a critical driver of US economic competitiveness.

Having now examined the material contributions that Canada and Mexico make to the American economy through their markets, their investment opportunities, their supplies of energy, and their expatriate workers, we now turn to a more abstract but more subjective and emotional aspect of the United States' power, its security.

PART TWO

Reinforcing the United States' Security

The paradox of North American security is that their geographical contiguity makes Canada and Mexico the United States' chief security threat while simultaneously making the Canadian and Mexican governments its most essential allies. This part of the study will consider the periphery's participation in (or abstention from) three facets of US security.

Even though they are not politically incorporated within the United States, Canada's and Mexico's territories can still offer a buffer area for US military security, a zone outside the front line of US fortifications where threats can be identified and warded off before they reach the homeland. During the Second World War, both members of the continental periphery had shared interests in resisting the Axis powers. Canada was the largest military contributor to the Allies' operations in Europe after the United States, the Soviet Union, and the United Kingdom. Chapter 4 goes on to show that Mexico's role was more defensive than aggressive, securing its air, land, and sea approaches against German or Japanese attacks on the United States. During the Cold War, Canada shared and Mexico opposed the Pentagon's anti-Soviet defence doctrine. Ottawa supported the extension of the Americans' defence perimeter to Canada's northern boundaries by merging its air forces under the US-controlled North American Aerospace Defence Command. This meant that approaching Soviet long-range bombers and missiles were to be detected, intercepted, and their nuclear payloads destroyed over Canadian territory before they reached the United States. Mexico resisted contributing to US continental defence and even took the lead in obstructing the Reagan administration's militarization of civil conflicts in Central America, thereby constraining Washington's anti-communist efficacy in the region.

The events of September 11, 2001 transformed the United States' understanding of its vulnerability and so its definition of its security needs. Whereas the Canadian government was the United States' unqualified supporter and shared its interest in the 'war on terror,' the Mexican government was a more reticent partner because it did not consider its own security to be threatened by militant Islamic anti-Americanism. Since Canada and Mexico have been conceptualized by US security policy as spaces where US-targeted threats can be identified and even eliminated, the periphery's role as an anti-terrorist buffer zone has taken the form of increased intelligence sharing and immigration-policy toughening. Chapter 5 explores how the US security perimeter has been extended in the anti-terrorist sphere to establish an increasingly integrated, continent-wide security zone. The extension of the US security perimeter also developed programmatically through the harmonization of the periphery's policies with those of the United States. Washington demanded that Mexico and Canada bring their many pertinent public policies up to a common US-deter-

mined standard, and these governments largely concurred when they could. The Anti-Terrorism Act was the clearest indication of Canada's willingness to harmonize its laws with American measures in the age of network terrorism, but harmonization also occurred when Ottawa made substantial changes to its immigration regime. Under both presidents Vicente Fox and Felipe Calderón, Mexican anti-terrorism policies increasingly adopted US models, but Washington had to provide assistance to enable the Mexican government to implement its commitments.

Mexico's greater and Canada's lesser roles as producers and conduits of narcotics for the enormous American drug market are equally contradictory. Chapter 6 explores how, while drug cartels based in the North American periphery can be seen to undermine US social power, the two governments have cooperated with Washington to restrict these suppliers and in that manner have constructed narcotics defences. At first, Mexico was ambivalent about Washington's efforts to expand its anti-narcotic security perimeter southward. Once growing domestic drug consumption and an unprecedented increase in cartel-generated violence began to pose a serious threat to its own domestic security, however, Mexico's sense of shared interests led it to engage more fully in supporting the United States' war on drugs.

To the extent that the periphery governments become de facto extensions of the US security apparatus, they expand the United States' security perimeter, thereby enlarging the amount of space that the United States controls beyond its national boundaries.

4 Extending the United States' Military Perimeter[1]

> The strategic partnerships and unique relationships we maintain with Canada and Mexico are critical to U.S. national security and have a direct effect on the security of our homeland. With billions of dollars in trade, shared critical infrastructure, and millions of our citizens moving across our common borders, no two countries are more directly connected to our daily lives.
>
> – US *National Security Strategy*, May 2010[2]

From its revolutionary war of independence to the present day, the United States has been preoccupied with its international influence, a disposition that ultimately resulted in its achieving a global military reach. In the Great War, US armed forces made a decisive contribution to the defeat of Kaiser Wilhelm's Germany, and the Second World War repeated the story more dramatically. The awesome detonation of atomic bombs over Hiroshima and Nagasaki proved the United States had the capacity for technological innovation to ensure that its military strength surpassed that of all potential rivals.

Analysing a nation's military power involves assessing its capacity for offence against its actual or potential enemies and its defensive ability to protect its territory and population from attack. Since the United States took over the Spanish empire at the turn of the twentieth century, its military strategy has often emphasized offence. Nevertheless, it remains vulnerable to attack in every major dimension of modern warfare – over land via its neighbours, by sea, or through the air. The oceans to its east and west function as direct routes to its coasts. Air assault was a defensive concern in the Cold War, first from Soviet bombers and then from intercontinental ballistic missiles.

The Periphery: From Military Targets to Military Perimeters

For over a century after they gained independence by force of arms, Americans' sense of their 'manifest destiny' turned the territories to their north, south, and west into candidates for conquest. To the north, Britain's maritime and Laurentian colonies represented extensions of an imperial threat best pre-empted by annexation. Two unsuccessful invasions of Canada, in 1775–6 and during the War of 1812, alongside continuing military tension through the American Civil War, prodded London to federate its principal North American colonies. Confederation in 1867 made the semi-autonomous Dominion of Canada more defensible and better tasked to colonize the territories from the west of the Great Lakes to the Pacific Ocean and north to the Arctic.

Lingering political tensions with Great Britain evaporated in the face of a common concern about the rearing threats from Germany and Japan. The resulting Anglo-American Entente of 1906 reframed the young Dominion of Canada from being a dangerous extension of the British empire to a valuable American ally. But the American dream of displacing Canada's imperial parent was slow to be realized. In the First World War the Dominion contributed massive numbers of men and materiel as a loyal member of the empire. Well before Washington joined the fray, Canadian soldiers fought and died by the tens of thousand on Flanders' fields and strengthened the young country's will to affirm its autonomy as a full nation-state.

To its south, the United States faced another European colony as an early neighbour. Although Mexico had started to shake off its Spanish yoke in 1810, its territories in the middle of the continent and on the Pacific coast lay on the westward path of the burgeoning American state whose horizons expanded as its citizen adventurers pushed their settlements towards the setting sun. The two power systems came into direct contact only after Washington's absorption of Florida made Mexico's territory an attractive target for occupation. With little industrial strength or governmental capacity to defend its farthest reaches, the young Hispanic republic collapsed, losing half its territory in the face of the aggressive political leadership, superior weaponry, greater economic muscle, and the ruthless diplomacy that the Americans deployed in the Mexican-American War of 1846–8 and its aftermath.

The irony of that American triumph is that the traumatic loss of what became the states of California, Nevada, and Utah along with portions of Texas, Arizona, New Mexico, and Wyoming left Mexico not just humiliated but deprived of the enormous mineral, agricultural, and industrial wealth which might have made the nascent country a secure and viable neighbour for the United States. Not only was Mexico condemned to poverty and instability. Its defeat rankled in the Mexican consciousness, making binational collaboration difficult, as conflicts over water and refugees were exacerbated by fresh incidents along the chronically troubled border.

When the United States intervened militarily in the Mexican Revolution to protect its investments against expropriation, resentment of American power even led Mexico to flirt with the idea of collaborating with Germany in the First World War in the hope of recovering its lost lands.[3] Thereafter, US-Mexico security relations have been marked by cycles of cooperation, withdrawal, and disagreement, all of which have largely inhibited the development of a stable mutual-defence framework.

Although their own military weakness and their economic dependence minimize their threats as potential enemies, Canada and the Mexico present the United States with a proxy threat, given the possibility that enemies from other continents might use their territories to stage land-based attacks. Beyond their unique roles as territorial neighbours, Canada and Mexico can support or frustrate US objectives abroad, and their contribution to American offensive capacity has occasionally been important. This integration, deep and mature with Canada, recent but now slowly solidifying with Mexico, has manifested itself in a wide variety of forms.

First, the continental periphery acts as an extension of the United States' security apparatus, extending its defence perimeter outwards and thereby expanding the amount of space that it directly controls beyond its formal territorial boundaries. Even when they are not formally incorporated within the United States' security perimeter, Canadian and Mexican territories still offer a buffer area for US security, a zone outside the homeland where threats can be identified and eliminated by the armed forces of its neighbours. When acting as buffers, Canada and Mexico autonomously provide a de facto support that reduces the economic, strategic, and political burden that the United States bears for defending itself, thereby freeing its military resources for offensive deployment elsewhere.

Canada and Mexico also enhance the United States' military security when they harmonize their military doctrines and equipment. When the periphery adopts US strategic thinking and tactical procedures, the United States increases the effectiveness of joint manoeuvres with its neighbours' military forces. Adopting US weapons systems strengthens this interoperability by eliminating incompatible techniques. It also boosts sales for the US armaments industry. Participating in US defence planning and negotiating arms purchases nourish bilateral human contacts at the command level that can generate support within the Canadian and Mexican military establishments for the Pentagon's objectives. Even Canada's and Mexico's autonomous security policies can have spillover effects on US security. Mexico's military suppression of its own insurgency movements may result in a more stable state on the United States' southern border. Conversely, either Mexico or Canada can create critical weaknesses in the Pentagon's security architecture.

Offshore, when Canada contributes to the United States' collective-security regimes by providing personnel and equipment, it directly augments US military capability. These supports do not only confer international legitimacy on Washington's military stance; they can even enhance its domestic palatability.[4] In contrast, a neighbouring state's disengagement from – or opposition to – a US military stance limits its practical effectiveness and can delegitimize the defence policy in question.

We will examine Canada and Mexico's relationship with US defence during warfare's three distinct stages over the past seventy-five years – the Second World War's fully mobilized industrial conflict with the Axis powers, the Cold War's nuclear deterrence vis-à-vis the Soviet bloc, and asymmetric warfare against terrorist networks. The chapter will focus on the shifting roles that Canada and Mexico have played – from near-complete integration in the Pentagon's fighting machine to outright opposition to its objectives – and will conclude by assessing the factors that promote the construction and constraint of US military power by the periphery.

Fully Mobilized Industrial Warfare in the Second World War

In the military paradigm that prevailed throughout the mid-twentieth century, the chief actors were states, which mobilized their human and physical assets by recruiting their manpower and pressing their industry to engage in trials of strength with their enemies in fights to the finish.[5]

Canada and the United States

As the cataclysm of the Second World War approached, the United States recast Canada in its strategic thinking to be a buffer against possible attacks from overseas. This role was heralded in 1938 when, in the face of the revived German and Japanese threats, US President Franklin Delano Roosevelt proposed a formal military understanding with Canada, pledging that America would not 'stand idly by' were the physical security of Canada to be threatened.[6] Prime Minister William Lyon Mackenzie King responded to this novel extension of the Munro Doctrine, affirming that 'as a good and friendly neighbour, Canada has a responsibility to see that it did not become an avenue of attack against the United States.'[7] This celebrated exchange was an acknowledgment of North America's new military reality: Canada had become both the United States' most necessary ally and its protectorate.

For almost two years after the war broke out in 1939, Canada mobilized its resources for the transatlantic struggle against Germany while the Roosevelt administration, hamstrung by Congress' refusal to loosen its neutrality laws, was limited to offering Canada and Great Britain war matériel. When the United States sold Canadians arms to help equip their land, sea, and air forces for the fighting in the North Atlantic, it was in effect helping them defend it at their expense.

While Canadian military thinking focused on supporting Great Britain, Roosevelt brokered joint initiatives designed to increase US military strength and strategic effectiveness. Since Britain could no longer play its traditional role as the Dominion's defender, Mackenzie King accepted the need to forge an intimate defence association with the United States, with which it shared the common goals of defending the continent, saving Britain, defeating Hitler, and warding off a Japanese attack.

By the summer of 1940, when few thought that Britain could survive, the defence of North America against both Nazi and Japanese aggression had become a pressing concern. That year, Roosevelt and King held discussions at Ogdensburg, New York, and created the Permanent Joint Board on Defence (PJBD) to address mutual military problems,[8] to make extensive plans for shielding the continent against possible attack, and thereby, in the president's words, to 'help secure the continent for the future.'[9] The PJBD proceeded to draw up plans to coordinate each country's military efforts in mobilizing troops and material resources to defend North America in the event of an attack,[10] thus bringing Canadian territory into the United States' direct defence-planning zone and expanding its effective security perimeter to the North Pole.

This military cooperation was deepened in April 1941 by the Hyde Park Declaration, which proposed to coordinate the two economies for war. In what was a limited form of free trade under government control, each country was to provide the other with the defence materials that it was 'best able to produce and above all produce quickly,'[11] thus committing the economic facilities of both countries to their most effective use.

There was also an imperial dimension to US-Canada defence cooperation. When negotiations to draft a Joint Canadian-United States Basic Defence Plan began in 1940, the United States sought outright control of Canadian forces should Britain be defeated. Canada reluctantly agreed, but, by the time the United States joined the war in response to the Japanese bombing of Pearl Harbor on December 7, 1941, the Royal Air Force had won the Battle of Britain and fended off Hitler's threat of invasion. When the United States again sought strategic control by proposing that eastern Canada be integrated within its Northeast Defence Command and British Columbia within its Northwest Defence Command, Prime Minister King worried that this extra step towards full wartime integration might precipitate Canada's absorption into the American union. He rejected Washington's demand.[12]

Notwithstanding this mild constraint on the forward exercise of US military power, Canada contributed more than any other country to augmenting US defensive capacity. After Germany invaded the Soviet Union, Canada permitted the construction of a secure land route across its territory east of the Rocky Mountains, so that American forces could better defend Alaska. By the end of the war, the United States had built airfields, an oil pipeline, weather stations, and a host of other installations on Canadian territory,[13] having mobilized Canadian space in the joint pursuit of its security.

Not only did Canada cooperate with Washington to create a continental defence perimeter, it made autonomous contributions to the offensive effort against the Axis powers during the Second World War. As the war progressed, the Canadian Navy protected convoys shipping supplies to England and the Soviet Union in the Battle of the Atlantic, the Canadian Army and Air Force fought in most major European theatres, and the Canadian economy made such concerted efforts that, at the end of hostilities, the country boasted the world's third-largest air force and fourth-largest navy.

Mexico and the United States

When Mexican leaders grasped the danger of Germany and Japan's global ambitions, military relations with United States improved markedly. In 1938, when President Lázaro Cárdenas expressed his willingness to collaborate on mutual defence, negotiations between both countries' military officials began, although in secret to preclude a nationalist backlash from the public. In 1940 a Joint Mexican-US Defence Commission was established in order to develop bilateral defence plans along three main fronts: defending the hemisphere, bilateral security relations, and protecting California.[14] Although this commission's scope was not nearly as large as the PJBD on which it was modelled, it helped move Mexico into Washington's orbit.

Well before its official declaration of war, Mexico had closed its ports to German ships, reducing the threat of disastrous assaults by German submarines on US shipping. That decision in May 1942 came some six months after the United States formally mobilized in the aftermath of the Japanese attack on Pearl Harbor. Responding to the sinking of the Mexican oil tankers *Potero del Llano* and *Faja de Oro* by German submarines,[15] President Manuel Avila Camacho emphasized that '[Mexico] shall ... respond to any aggressive intents of our adversaries, and shall at all times defend our country's integrity and *cooperate actively for the safety of the American continent*, within the limits of our abilities, our security, and the *coordination of hemispheric defence procedures.*'[16]

The Mexican Senate promptly accorded the United States full use of Mexican ports and airports. Installations were set up, principally in Baja California to detect Japanese ships and submarines, and transit airports were built to service US military aircraft shuttling to and from the Panama Canal. These efforts to build a bilateral defence system were part of a broader plan for hemispheric security, an effort that benefited markedly from Mexico's broad cooperation.[17]

Once Mexico entered the war, the Joint Defence Commission served as a mechanism for a more active cooperation between the two countries' military commanders.[18] Yet, unlike Canada, Mexico took no part in the offensive war in Europe, even if it did make a late and limited air contribution to the Pacific front in 1945, when its 201st fighter squadron fought alongside the US Air Force during the battles in the Philippines and Formosa. Insignificant offensively, Mexico's participation was defensively important for the United States, effectively extending its security perimeter far to its south and so freeing its defensive resources for use in its offensive operations. At the same time, Mexico's industrial and mineral production made a more material contribution to the US effort, as did the thousands of Bracero workers who went north – as explained in chapter 3 – to stand in for the Americans who had left their farms and factories to serve overseas.[19] A former nemesis, Mexico evolved over the course of the Second World War into a critical security partner.

Without a secure homeland, US power could not be fully projected abroad, and throughout the war the United States' neighbours' military support was a central buttress for its brilliant successes in Europe and in Asia. Not only was Canada essential to the Allies' war effort, it was crucial to the United States' defence in North America. By virtue of their contiguity, Canada and Mexico were in a position to secure their own territories and so provide buffers that extended a de facto US military periphery to cover the whole continent. The US periphery was willing to construct US power because it agreed with Washington's strategic goals and accepted its tactical imperatives, believing them to be in their mutual interest.

At the same time, the periphery's military contributions were not unlimited. Mexico's fixation on US interventionism continued to rule out any formal extension of the Pentagon's military perimeter to Mexico's southern border. Even Canada's sovereignty concerns limited the extent to which Washington could fully achieve its strategic goals in the north – that is, until the Cold War, when the two countries shared sufficient ideological consensus that Canada put its air defence forces under joint, but US-controlled, management.

The Cold War's Intercontinental Stand-Off

Prolonged confrontation between the capitalist and socialist blocs structured international relations during the Cold War when ideological alignment with one side or the other – or non-alignment – defined all countries' military, political, and strategic stances.

Canada

After Germany and Japan's defeat, the United States' containment of the Soviet Union was centred on the delivery of nuclear destruction. Once Moscow developed long-range bombers, Canada's strategic location on the flight path from the USSR to the United States gave it critical importance to the Pentagon. In material terms, Canada's weapons-manufacturing capacity, which largely took the form of US branch-plant production, was added to the United States' own armaments engine through the Canada-US Defence Production Sharing Agreement of 1956. This effective integration of the two defence industries had the further advantage of dispersing the Kremlin's targeting of US military production sites and thus shifting some of the dangers of the United States' defence onto Canadian shoulders.

The United States sought to defend itself against such air attacks by extending its defence perimeter northward so that Soviet bombers or missiles could be intercepted over Canada before they could reach its territory. Ottawa agreed to establish the North American Air Defence Command in 1957, putting the Royal Canadian Air Force (RCAF) under de facto Pentagon control. Soviet bombers, and later Soviet missiles, were to be detected and intercepted over Canada before they reached their targets in the United States.[20] Detection was provided by building radar stations in northern Canada along the Pinetree Line, the McGill Line, and the Distant Early Warning Line.[21] Interception was first provided by the RCAF's US-made aircraft, then later by US surface-to-air BOMARC missiles sited in Canada. The Canadian Army wrote that '[either] by accident or design, Canadian air defences contribute to the perimeter defence of the USA while using Canada as the killing area.'[22] Since the 'killing' would probably have been with a missile armed with a US nuclear warhead, Canada went beyond functioning as a defence buffer to becoming a geographical extension of the US military system, with the added political advantage to Washington that it would be the immediate receiving area for any resulting nuclear fallout. Because Ottawa accepted the Pentagon's defence doctrine of mutual assured destruction (MAD) to contain the Soviet threat, it willingly participated in a warning and defence system which assured that US bombers delivering nuclear retaliation would get off the ground before being hit.

Canadians' close cultural, social, and economic affinity with the United States and their consensus that the Soviet Union posed a mortal threat to the whole 'free world' explains Ottawa's sustained support of the United States' tactical doctrine and overall anti-communist strategy despite its periodic misgivings about certain US policies. Staunch support by a much-admired middle power also helped buttress the United States' legitimacy as military leader of the West.

While it generally subscribed to Washington's Cold War vision, Ottawa's occasional questioning of the Pentagon's technological and tactical positions imposed some limits on Washington's freedom of manoeuvre. In 1962 Prime Minister John Diefenbaker's initial refusal to join the United States in putting NORAD forces on high alert over the Soviet effort to instal missiles in Cuba has been generally interpreted as proof of Canada's capacity to constrain US military power.[23] But the fact that the Canadian military command put its air and naval forces on alert in defiance of its political superiors demonstrated the extent to which it constituted an actual extension of the United States' military machine.

As the threat of attack by transpolar Soviet bombers faded during the 1960s, the limited constraints that Canada posed to US military power were only underscored. By this point the two superpowers had perfected their capacity to launch not just intercontinental ballistic missiles but also submarine-launched ballistic missiles, which allowed them to deliver a nuclear strike from anywhere on the globe. This new threat prompted the US military to push for a ballistic-missile-defence (BMD) program, introducing the possibility that security against a nuclear-missile attack could be achieved not only through MAD's strong, second-strike deterrent capacity but also through strategic defence. While Canada agreed with the US framing of the communist threat, it did not support the BMD initiative, insisting on inserting a clause in the 1968 renewal of NORAD stipulating that it 'would not involve ... a Canadian commitment to participate in active ballistic missile defence.'[24]

As a result of Canada's opposition, the United States was unable to place BMD missile sites north of its border, which reduced the degree to which Canada bolstered US defensive capacity. However, in contrast with the previous air-defence realities, the United States no longer needed Canadian territory or air space for BMD, so it was easy for Washington to accept Canada's refusal to participate. The Pentagon dismissed Canada's stance as a case of its junior partner's periodical moralistic obstinacy, while Ottawa, believing that the United States did not understand its own best interest, thought that in opposing BMD it was constructing US security. Either way, the disagreement had few, if any, strategic repercussions for the US military, particularly once the contretemps was provisionally laid to rest in 1972 when the United States and the Soviet Union signed the Anti-Ballistic Missile (ABM) Treaty, which limited each country's defences against missile-delivered nuclear weapons and affirmed the need to conserve the nuclear balance of terror. Similarly, Ottawa's delay a decade later in permitting the Pentagon to test its cruise missiles over Canadian territory was little more than a short-lived constraint. Under heavy pressure from an aroused public opinion, the Trudeau government had deep misgivings that this new weapon would trigger another arms race with the Soviet Union, but it finally recognized the autonomy-constraining realities of its military integration and acceded to US demands in 1983.

The same year, US President Ronald Reagan launched the Strategic Defense Initiative (SDI) to design ground- and space-based systems to protect the United States from attack by ballistic missiles. In 1985 he invited all NATO members to participate in SDI research. Although it was not a party to the ABM Treaty, Canada was committed to its principles. The Mulroney government announced that Canada's 'own policies and priorities do not warrant a government-to-government effort in support of SDI research.'[25] But this No was really a Yes because, at the same time, 'Canadian firms could participate and compete for contracts under existing bilateral defence development and production-sharing agreements.'[26] Following NORAD's 1986 renewal, the United States announced the creation of the Air Defense Initiative (ADI), which was intended to work along with SDI in modernizing continental defences. While acknowledging that there was a certain degree of overlap between ADI and SDI, the Mulroney government nonetheless committed itself to participating in the modernization of its air defences and contributed financially to the initiative by pledging $47 million.[27] In short, from ballistic missiles to ballistic-misille defence, Canada's inconsistent opposition during the Cold War cannot be interpreted as more than a minor limitation to the Pentagon's defence capacity.

Mexico

Mexico's ideological orientation to the Cold War was vastly different from Canada's. It was less concerned with combating communism than with promoting a new international economic order in which the United States was neither so dominant nor so interventionist. Motivated by its historical fear of US military intervention, it based its foreign policy on the mutually reinforcing principles of national sovereignty and non-intervention in the affairs of other states.[28] Resisting pressure from the United States to join its crusade, Mexico City maintained its de facto neutrality. In its international diplomacy, it was so non-aligned that it refused to join the non-aligned movement of developing countries. It also strove to block the United States' efforts to enlist the Western hemisphere's major multilateral organizations in its struggle against communism.

In 1947 Mexico signed the Inter-American Treaty of Reciprocal Assistance (Rio Treaty), a pale complement of NATO's promise of 'collective defence' of the Western hemisphere in the face of communism's external threat.[29] Although not a military alliance like NATO, the Rio Treaty may have provided implicit ideological support for the United States' effort to neutralize leftist political movements considered threats to the internal stability of friendly governments. But Mexico distinguished between external threats and the hemisphere's domestic struggles with revolutionary movements, which had found some political support in Latin American countries.[30] Accordingly, Mexico interpreted the Rio Treaty in a way that prohibited incursions into Hispanic states' internal affairs: 'If ... the Inter-American Treaty of Reciprocal Assistance were to be used to intervene in the internal affairs of any State of the Americas, Mexico would have to give serious consideration to denouncing the Treaty and withdrawing from its commitments under it.'[31] By articulating an interpretation of the Rio Treaty that was diametrically opposed to the US view, Mexico effectively neutered the collective-defence mechanism that the United States sought to establish.

As the Cold War entered its final decade, the differences between Washington's and Mexico City's understandings of hemispheric security intensified. The dominant faction in the US foreign-policy community maintained that, if one country in a region came under communist control, then the surrounding countries would follow in a domino effect, perhaps even threatening the US homeland.[32] Impelled by fears that its southern border would be insecure if Latin American guerrilla activity moved into Mexico and then northward, successive US administrations used the domino theory to justify interventions in Central American states where leftist insurgencies were strong.

Apart from the Cuba question, which we analyse in chapter 9, the most significant Cold War differences over hemispheric security revolved around how to address the civil wars that erupted in Nicaragua, El Salvador, and Guatemala in the early 1980s and drew the ruling US Republicans into actively and materially supporting the anti-revolutionary ('Contra') forces. Although Mexico recognized that the wars could spill over its southern border if a solution was not reached, it still maintained its principle of non-interventionism.[33] Rear-Admiral Mario Santos Caamal stated: 'We seek to stabilize the area through a defence policy of détente, while the policy of the United States is to stabilize the area through deterrence and containment. While our goals may be the same, the means we are employing are different and this is producing sometimes violent disagreements, arguments, and opposition.'[34]

In other words, while Mexico and the United States shared the goal of achieving stability in Latin America, their diplomatic means to that end were diametrically opposed. Mexico withdrew diplomatic recognition from the US-supported Anastasio Somoza regime in Nicaragua in favour of the Sandinista insurgency and resisted the invocation of the Rio Treaty to justify US military action there.[35] In 1980, after the Sandinistas overthrew President Somoza, Mexico began shipping petroleum and goods to Nicaragua.[36] The Mexican government also recognized the Farabundo Martí National Liberation Front in El Salvador, another position that clashed with the United States' stance.[37] Mexico's moral and material support for these revolutionary movements deepened Washington's concerns about its neighbour's reliability as a buffer.

When Miguel de la Madrid became president, he mounted an active diplomatic campaign to defuse the Central American tinderbox. In January 1983 Mexico spearheaded with Venezuela, Panama, and Colombia the creation of the Contadora Group to negotiate solutions to the Central American states' internal conflicts.[38] The group's main opponent was the United States, which was still seeking to overthrow the Sandinista government and to crush guerrilla activity in El Salvador.[39] For its part, the Contadora Group wanted to include the Guatemalan and Salvadoran guerrillas in a democratization process in order to wean them from military action and convert them into a political force. Although the Contadora group failed to establish a durable peace with the backing of all parties, it laid the groundwork for the ultimate resolution of the Central American crisis through political means – internal democratization, elections, and negotiations between governments and insurgents. Washington perceived Mexico's opposition to US intervention and its support for some of the regimes it considered dangerous as a thorn in its side, if not as an outright hostile foreign policy. Unlike Canada, then, Mexico did not serve as a buffer against one of the United States' declared external threats, but rather as a potential conduit for this menace. In this way, Mexican opposition increased the short-term political and diplomatic costs for Washington's pursuit of its stated national interests. In the longer term, by diffusing the political crises in Central America, Mexico paved the way for the installation of more stable popular governments with which Washington has since established positive relations.

In another security dossier, the United States found its interests surprisingly in step with a major Mexican objective, nuclear non-proliferation. Mexico was the main promoter in 1967 of the Treaty of Tlatelolco, which sought Latin America's complete denuclearization. The United States supported the treaty from the beginning. For instance, Senator Robert F. Kennedy in 1965 declared to the US Congress: 'Nowadays, one of our main advantages is that there are no nuclear weapons in Africa nor Latin America. This situation can continue if the nuclear powers commit themselves to not introduce nuclear weapons in these areas, if the nations in those areas commit themselves not to acquire them, and if we establish the right machinery for the verification of those commitments. Some nations – particularly in Latin America – have already exchanged informal guarantees in the matter. We should encourage them to keep on with all our means.'[40] The treaty's strategic advantage to the United States was to preclude any nuclear competition in the hemisphere and to reduce the fear that nuclear proliferation could get out of hand. For these reasons, the United States signed both Protocol 1, which related to its territories in the area, and Protocol 2, which established the principle of nuclear-weapon-state responsibility.

The abrupt collapse of the East-West confrontation in 1990 and the concomitant reduction of Washington's concerns about Central America's revolutionary movements coincided with the Mexican elite's embrace of neoconservatism. But the non-institutionalized nature of Mexico's military relations with the Pentagon and persisting anti-gringo sentiment among the public left the Mexican military disconnected from the Pentagon's system well after the Cold War's tensions in the hemisphere had dissipated and a new type of war consumed the energies of Washington's defence community.

Canada, Mexico, and Hemispheric Security before 9/11

During the Cold War, politicians like John Diefenbaker were wary of supporting US objectives outright. However, Canada's ideological alignment with the United States essentially ensured that what supports Canada did provide would be geared towards the construction of US power. Even in cases where Canada disagreed with the United States over the means of maintaining continental security, its constraint on US action was arguably conceived as supporting America's *true* interests, as in the case of ballistic- missile defence. Mexico's ideological orientation, on the other hand, led the country to oppose US policy in some major aspects although it could also have argued persuasively that it was serving the United States' longer-term need for stability in the region. For both Mexico and Canada, then, their geographical location with respect to US defence needs, their military capacity, and their political orientation towards the East-West confrontation determined their impact on US power during the Cold War.

Asymmetrical Warfare

After the Cold War, new threats to international security appeared in such other forms as globally operating terrorist networks, civil wars, and genocide within weak states.[41] Nation-states were no longer the sole entities capable of mobilizing resources for large-scale fighting. Non-state actors could also strike across national borders in the new, globally coordinated asymmetric warfare.[42]

After al-Qaeda's devastating attacks of September 11, 2001 demonstrated this point, the Bush administration formally identified terrorism as the American homeland's greatest security danger. Rather than addressing global terrorism as an international intelligence and policing problem, it defined the issue in military terms. This was the meaning of President Bush's declaration of a 'war against terrorism,' a concept that was translated into the administration's *National Security Strategy* as a doctrine for pre-emptively fighting terrorists abroad so that they could not attack the United States at home.[43] Spurred on by this new conception of security, Washington launched a war on Afghanistan's Taliban government on the grounds that it was sheltering al-Qaeda.

While both its NAFTA partners revised their foreign-policy doctrine to include the struggle against terrorism, Mexico remained faithful to its non-interventionist principles and chose not to support the new US crusade abroad. The Mexican public favoured its country's greater participation in world affairs, but it was divided about involvement in the United States' wars. Some felt that Mexico could be called on to contribute its armed forces to military action abroad under the aegis of Article 43 of the United Nations Charter.[44] Others maintained that, even with a UN mandate, Mexico's principle of non-intervention required it to remain out of the fray unless it had itself been subject to an attack.

Unlike Mexico, Canada declared international terrorism to be a threat to its own national security. With NATO's invocation of Article V declaring that al-Qaeda's attack on the United States was an attack on all alliance members, Canada became automatically committed to supporting

American military operations in Afghanistan and volunteered its troops
to serve under US command. When the NATO International Security Assistance Force took over responsibility for combat operations in
Afghanistan in 2003, Canada sent more troops, helping to secure Kabul.
Not being a NATO member, Mexico remained on the sidelines.

Canada was one of the few NATO countries not to refuse the deployment of their troops in combat situations.[45] Since Afghanistan was an
'economy of force' mission for the Bush administration, meaning that
the Americans aimed to employ limited combat power, US forces handed over command of the dangerous Kandahar province to newly committed Canadian troops in the spring of 2006.

Canada's direct material and moral contribution to the United States'
war in Iraq was more ambiguous. Prime Minister Jean Chrétien lobbied the presidents of Mexico and Chile, which had temporary seats
on the UN Security Council, to resist Washington's pressure for the
United Nations to endorse its military intervention in Iraq. President
Vicente Fox's decision not to support the United States in the Security
Council and Canada's decision not to vote at the UN General Assembly
in favour of the US war constituted part of a broader-based international opposition that undermined the contested mission's legitimacy.
In March 2003 US Ambassador Paul Cellucci openly criticized Canada's official opposition to the invasion of Iraq, confirming how much
Washington had wanted Canada's moral support, even more than its
material contribution, to help legitimize its attack on Saddam Hussein's
regime.

Yet, even as Canada opted not to join the 'Coalition of the Willing,'
one hundred Canadian exchange officers still played technical-support
roles in Iraq and three Canadian frigates were integrated with the US
Navy in the Gulf of Aden.[46] These actual contributions to the American
war effort in Iraq exceeded those of most of the countries that formally
participated in the coalition.[47]

Continental Defence in the Twenty-First Century

Although traditional military defence still retained a place on the US
agenda after the Cold War, North America was the only region in the
world for which the Pentagon did not have an integrated command
structure to coordinate Army, Navy, Air Force, Marine Corps, and Coast
Guard operations. To correct this omission, the Pentagon established
US Northern Command (USNORTHCOM) in 2002 with a mandate

for defending US interests not just in the United States but in Canada, Mexico, and the Caribbean. The new command's principal responsibilities included the military defence of the United States' homeland, military coordination with Canada and Mexico, and the development of a ballistic-missile-defence system for North America.[48]

NORAD continued to have responsibility for warning and assessing aerospace attacks on the continent, but any activation of US missile-defence systems would take place under the unilateral authority of USNORTHCOM. Subsequently, NORAD's responsibility for warning and assessment was expanded from aerospace to include monitoring maritime traffic in both the Atlantic and Pacific oceans. To manage relations between the two structures and to investigate specific ways to strengthen North America's defences, Ottawa and Washington established a Binational Planning Group (BPG) in 2002.[49] The BPG considered how to deal with threats, attacks, or civil emergencies in either country, as well as to harmonize maritime surveillance and intelligence.

The BPG's work was well under way when the Canadian government announced that it would create a Canada Command to oversee 'six regional headquarters across the country that integrate land, sea, and air elements.'[50] Canada Command explicitly paralleled the structure and functions assigned to USNORTHCOM by uniting domestic operations under one chief commander. Although it might appear that Canada Command was a case of Canadian harmonization with the US model, Jean Chrétien's government developed Canada Command as an alternative to further binational integration.[51] Despite the intimate evolution of US and Canadian continental security architecture, the Canadian government was not yet prepared, echoing Mackenzie King's cautious rebuff of full wartime integration sixty years before, to delegate full control of military planning to its continental hegemon.

To the south, military integration remains nascent. While Canada Command and USNORTHCOM speak daily, Mexico lacks any such institutional entry point for combatant command-level engagement, thus reducing prospects for bilateral or continental defence cooperation.[52] Notwithstanding this vacuum, Mexico has become a somewhat more active neighbour, stationing naval and air force officers at the USNORTHCOM headquarters.[53]

Disagreements necessarily occur between Ottawa and Washington. In 2001 the issue of missile defence reared its head again when the Bush administration withdrew from the ABM Treaty to pursue its missile-defence program. Still wrapped up in its opposition to the weaponization of space, Canada refused to participate, except through allowing NORAD to relay information about ballistic-missile threats to USNORTHCOM. In doing so, Ottawa relinquished the slim prospect that it might have some say in the final design or the potential use of the missile-defence system, raising the uncomfortable prospect that Canada might learn of a major security threat only after the US military had shot down a missile over Canadian territory.[54] As with SDI, Ottawa's non-participation had little impact on the United States' pursuit of BMD, an indication that, with the disappearance of the Soviet threat, Canada's role in either constructing or constraining US defensive strength had continued to decline.

With Barack Obama's election as president, the United States' approach to its North American allies shifted in tone, specifically identifying collective action as the best means for defending American values at home and abroad. As the administration's new *National Security Strategy* stated: 'The belief that our own interests are bound to the interests of those beyond our borders will continue to guide our engagement with nations and peoples.'[55] Referring to its most important allies, it mentioned North America in terms of the 'strategic' and 'unique' value of its relations with Canada and Mexico for its territorial security. 'No two countries are more directly connected to our daily lives.'[56] Canada was described as the United States' 'closest trading partner, a steadfast security ally, and an important partner in regional and global efforts.'[57] Mexico was accorded priority on account of the country's stability and security being 'indispensable to building a strong economic partnership, fighting the illicit drug and arms trade, and promoting sound immigration policy.'[58]

In the face of new, asymmetrical security threats, the periphery has played a constructive but increasingly invisible role. As in earlier periods, Canada tended to construct US power when it perceived the two countries' goals to be aligned. Put differently, the United States was able to secure the periphery's support – thus increasing its power – when it was able to convince Canada and Mexico of their common stake in addressing new security threats.

Conclusion

When the United States has neighbours to its north and south who commit resources and provide political support for its military strategy, it can secure its home territory more effectively and project its power more easily in far-flung theatres. It is their intimate connection with US defensive concerns that makes Canada and Mexico unique among US allies. While both can be considered indispensable elements of the United States' buffer zone, they differ significantly in the material and moral support they have offered for its defence initiatives. Having been rebuffed in two earlier invasions of Canada, Washington paradoxically finds it much easier to enjoy enthusiastic cooperation with a strong, self-confident Canada than with Mexico, which still nurses the wounds and suffers the debilitating consequences of its earlier humiliations.

Congruent Canadian and American strategic doctrines and military practices have facilitated the smooth workings of their bilateral defence regime.[59] Having committed itself to preventing the passage of enemy troops to the United States over its territory or through its airspace and waters before the Second World War, Canada then provided a territorial platform for the US military to intercept a Soviet attack during the Cold War. Offensively, it contributed contingents to the Korean War, stationed Air Force and Army units in Europe, and deployed military forces to both the Afghan and Iraq theatres.

As alliance leader, Washington has always pressed its lesser partners to contribute more money and manpower to their common defence effort. In response to this pressure, Canadian defence spending rose steadily throughout the past half-century. Compared to Canada, Mexico's military spending is small; compared to the Pentagon's, it is tiny. In 2008 there were 202,000 poorly equipped and badly paid Mexicans in the Army and Air Force and 52,000 in the Navy – figures that represented a 50 per cent increase over twenty years. Mexico's military forces are used for maintaining internal security, whether in aiding the civil population in cases of natural disaster or in fighting such domestic insurrections as the 1994 Chiapas rebellion by the Zapatista National Liberation Army. However, the Mexican military budget has increased substantially since 2004 when the federal government intensified its war against the drug cartels, a topic to which we return in chapter 6.

Mexico has generally resisted the United States' strategic control of the hemisphere and worked hard during the Cold War to stymie its interventionist tendencies. For this reason, Mexican-American security relations have been marked by disagreements over regional and bilateral goals. On account of differing threat assessments, there have been few shared understandings upon which a workable defence regime could be built. In short, because the United States has generated a consensual hegemony with its northern neighbour but signifies coercive imperialism to the south, Canada has tended to construct US power while Mexico has tended to constrain it.

President Barack Obama's *National Security Strategy*'s repudiation of the Bush administration's doctrine of preventive aggression and his preference for international cooperation with allies over the unilateral use of military force has set the stage for better relations with Mexico. Yet tentative steps towards the establishment of closer cooperation with the Pentagon come up against the institutionalized fragmentation of the Mexican military, divided as it is between a more open-minded Navy and a more isolationist Army and Air Force, each with its own ministry and political culture.

If Canada and Mexico were to disappear into their respective seas, we can see that the United States would be more vulnerable to its north and south for lack of friendly territories buffering it from its military threats. If the territories currently occupied by Canada and Mexico on the continent were completely barren of resources and uninhabitable, the United States would be able to extend its military perimeter over the whole of North America but without profiting from the financial and military muscle provided by these two countries. The value of Canada and Mexico to US defence is not just material, however. When the two peripheral countries' foreign-policy objectives coincide with Washington's, they support the United States' global legitimacy – the importance of which for US military might was demonstrated, by its absence, during the US war in Iraq.

Our analysis reveals, then, that the periphery constructs US power when it perceives its goals to be aligned with those of the United States. On occasion, Canada and Mexico proved themselves willing to oppose American defence policy, but only if their goals conflicted in some fundamental way. While Washington could, for the most part, count on the support of its neighbours throughout the twentieth century and into the twenty-first, history dictates a clear lesson. For the United States to defend itself in North America and extend its military might overseas, it needs to build a continental consensus on the shared nature of its interests. American leadership cannot assume that Canada and Mexico will automatically march in step. Even like-minded Canada, which in 2008 set its own defence as the Armed Forces' top priority but maintained that Canadian security is best achieved through cooperation with the United States, must be convinced that it shares the United States' moral principles and material objectives.[60]

Hitler made it easy for Mexico and Canada to agree that fascism had to be destroyed and the continent defended at any cost. Communism failed to galvanize the two countries into supporting the United States equally but was threatening enough to sustain Canada's support with minor exceptions.

Terrorism presents the most ambiguous opponent and has already tested Washington's relations with its neighbours. Now, more than ever before, the United States' ability to count on its neighbours' valuable support will require a clear demonstration that they continue to share its goals, interests, and principles, the subject of the next chapter.

5 Building US Homeland Security against Terrorism[1]

America historically has relied heavily on two vast oceans and two friendly neighbors for border security ... [but] the increasing mobility and destructive potential of modern terrorism has required the United States to rethink and rearrange fundamentally its systems for border and transportation security.

– *US National Strategy for Homeland Security*, July 2002[2]

Following the establishment of the United States' unchallengeable supremacy in North America, land-border regulation on the continent consisted mostly of such non-military functions as controlling immigration, imposing tariffs on imports, and combating the smuggling of goods and people. Looking north after the Second World War, the United States had few security concerns along the almost 9,000 kilometres of its moderately policed borders owing to its intimate economic, social, and cultural ties with Canada. Crime was dealt with by the various US police agencies in cooperation with their Canadian counterparts, so that American and Canadian politicians could proclaim with good reason that they shared the world's longest undefended border.

Looking south, the United States could see a surprisingly similar situation for many decades. Despite Mexico's economic underdevelopment and social disparities, the intense human and commercial traffic across the shared border raised few security challenges until the 1960s. Then, with increasing numbers of undocumented Mexicans trying to cross over and with the US 'war on drugs' confronting a growing narcotics traffic coming from Central America, controls along the 3,000-kilometre-long border with Mexico were continually tightened. By the

1970s, the resulting increase in the Hispanic presence in their midst was causing conservative US border constituencies to target undocumented migration as a socio-cultural and, therefore, political issue. But this threat was generally downplayed by US authorities in favour of the trade-liberalization priority that dominated Washington's policy paradigm through the 1980s and into the 1990s.

Even while the United States struggled to shut its doors to drugs and migrants at the turn of the twenty-first century, it was actively pressuring its two neighbours to accelerate continental integration by lowering their economic barriers. In the wake of CUFTA, US-Canadian trade had doubled from about $250 billion in 1988 to just under $500 billion in 2000.[3] And, following NAFTA, US-Mexican trade had jumped from $90 billion in 1993 to $290 billion by 2000.[4] As the new millennium opened, trade clearly trumped security on the increasingly borderless continent's agenda.

The shock of September 11, 2011 abruptly inverted these priorities for Washington, recasting Canada and Mexico from valued economic partners to dangerous if unwitting conduits for Islamic terrorists. The new US default reflex was to stress security over all else. While debris from the World Trade Center's twin towers was still falling over Lower Manhattan, Washington shut down the continent's two busiest land crossings. The Ambassador Bridge linking Detroit and Windsor witnessed a line-up of trucks thirty-six kilometres long, a state of affairs that disrupted just-in-time production chains, closing down several US automobile plants. Cross-border shopping in the Tijuana-San Diego corridor plunged so precipitously as a result of stringent US border inspections that San Diego declared an economic emergency.[5] While powerful US business interests bewailed their millions in losses and called for the new border controls to be eased, it became clear that Washington would not modify its focus on security even to please the business lobbies which had historically dictated US commercial policy.

The 9/11 attacks shattered former American presumptions of domestic invulnerability, replacing them with a realization of their country's direct exposure to a hitherto underestimated form of attack. US politicians and the crisis-conscious media quickly blew their fear of sabotage into a threat of near apocalyptic proportions. The country suddenly had to mount an appropriate defence against an enemy who could 'strike at any place, at any time, and with virtually any weapon' against a society that 'presents an almost infinite array of potential targets.'[6] If just a handful of the wrong people slipped into the United States and attacked well-chosen targets, they could disrupt American society at a systemic level.[7] The Bush administration proclaimed its most 'important mission to be protecting the homeland from future terrorist attacks'[8] and subsequently launched military interventions abroad, while introducing draconian changes to policing, intelligence, and security practices at home. This urgent redefinition of homeland security impelled Washington to exert direct pressure on every country in the world to help it develop a completely global shield against Islamic terrorism.[9] None of the United States' allies were more affected than those in its periphery.

As we have just seen, Canada's and Mexico's importance for the United States' strategic defence had diminished after the Cold War when US military needs were decoupled from territorial considerations. The shock of 9/11 refocused Americans' security concerns on its North American neighbours, who were suddenly reborn as a major part of the US security problematic. Because of their geographic proximity, Canada and Mexico immediately came under suspicion as prime conduits for terrorists or their accomplices. Al-Qaeda's operatives might find cover within their communities before slipping into the United States. At the same time, while the United States' geographical periphery came to be understood as a critical security threat, the governments of Canada and Mexico became its indispensable partners in developing solutions for this new menace.

Leaving the question of narcotics security for the next chapter, we focus here on the differing roles that the periphery has played both as cause of and cure for the United States' vulnerability to terrorism in the new century. We argue that Canada's multicultural society and very high rate of immigrant reception made it easier in principle for terrorists to infiltrate; yet the Canadian government's sophisticated governance capability made it the United States' strongest security partner. By contrast, Mexico's much smaller intake of immigration from overseas made it less attractive as terrorist camouflage, but the government's institutional frailty required the Americans to bolster their southern neighbour's governing capacity to help it meet their continental security needs.

To understand the principal ways in which its periphery secures the United States' homeland against terrorist threats, we distinguish three interconnected dimensions along which it mediates US power. First, Canada and Mexico construct American power by improving the continent's security architecture *on their own initiative*. Canada and Mexico are often portrayed as reactive partners, simply conforming to American pressure to implement a US-directed homeland-security paradigm, but they can be important originators of security in their own right. This can happen when they increase their expenditures or act as first movers by adopting new security frameworks and sharing their domestic security best-practices or technological innovations with the United States. By the same token, inaction or foot dragging by the two neighbours can create insecurity for the United States.

Second, because borders are shared and all three North American governments have strong interests in combating terrorism together, *cooperation* can reduce the duplication of efforts and avoid creating a self-defeating incompatibility of divergent policies, technologies, and practices. Enhanced border cooperation and policy harmonization constitute forms of cost sharing which save the United States money.[10] Conversely, incompatible practices, data systems, or legal procedures can make cooperation more expensive, sometimes impossible.

Third, the periphery governments can become de facto extensions of the US security apparatus by harmonizing their policies and integrating their intelligence resources with those of the United States. In this way Canada and Mexico offer a *buffer zone* for its security, a territory where threats can be dealt with before they reach the American homeland. Such buffering extends the United States' security perimeter by expanding the amount of secured space beyond its own territory.

We can qualitatively assess the extent to which the periphery has initiated, cooperated with, and extended American counter-terrorist measures and we can quantitatively identify the resources – money, equipment, and personnel – devoted to providing the United States with greater security. But what ultimately counts as a measure of the perimeter's construction of US security is that, since 9/11, no terrorist attack has occurred at any scale. Although we argue that the periphery's contribution to this achievement is decisive, it nevertheless remains indeterminate because we cannot know how many terrorist plots were deterred by Canada's and Mexico's support.

Given the uncertain magnitude of the terrorist threat, we must keep two other conundrums in mind. Psychologically, whether Canadian and Mexican border policies genuinely bolster the United States' security or merely help Americans *feel* safer by mitigating their anxieties is one significant issue. Materially, while the governments of Canada and Mexico construct Americans' feeling of security insofar as they reduce the sense of threat that their geographical contiguity creates, the resulting border thickening impedes the exchange of the goods, investments, raw materials, and labour that help construct the *economic power* (analysed in Part One) on which US global power is premised.

This chapter will proceed to examine how Canada and Mexico construct US power by catering to their neighbour's anti-terrorism security needs. We will see that, although Canada offers a more likely space for infiltration by al-Qaeda, the government of Canada has had the resources and capacity to construct US security along all three dimensions. On the other hand, Mexican contributions to US security have been more ambiguous. Mexico let its policy rhetoric be largely determined by US security needs, but its inability to manage its own security agenda forced the United States at first to protect itself unilaterally from the security threats that it perceived to be originating in Mexico and then move to help its neighbour implement measures that would enhance both countries' interdependent security.

The Periphery as Initiator of Continental Security

Canada's Material Interests and the Construction of US Security

The North American continent's commercial asymmetry has produced a significant policy asymmetry. While the United States receives significant economic benefits from its massive trading relationship with Canada, it is Canada that stands to lose the most from a hardening of North American borders. We saw in chapter 1 that Canada bought about 17 per cent of US exports in 2008, while supplying 15 per cent of US imports. But these same trade figures represented over 75 per cent of Canadian exports and 63 per cent of Canadian imports.[11]

Having been frustrated that many of its carefully negotiated bilateral agreements from the 1990s – including the Shared Border Accord, the Border Vision Initiative, and the Canada-US Partnership[12] – remained unimplemented because of the Clinton administration's indifference to its border-security problems, the Canadian government signed a comprehensive bilateral Smart Border Declaration and Action Plan in December 2001, the bulk of whose thirty-two points had been initiated by Ottawa.[13] This far-reaching program for continental-security integration committed Canada and the United States to take carefully specified measures to guarantee that people and goods crossing the border would not threaten US security.

In the negotiation of this detailed plan, the overwhelming US government interest was to fortify its own border against terrorism. For its part,

Ottawa had its own pressing interest 'to ensure that issues surrounding the trade efficiency of the border ... not be relegated to the back burner, given the costs of border delays.'[14] Jointly administered programs to expedite safe traffic would use new technologies to separate flows of low-risk goods and people from higher-risk goods or people who required more scrutiny at border crossings. The NEXUS program created high-tech identity cards to streamline the transit of pre-cleared frequent business travellers, while the Free and Secure Trade (FAST) program was designed to sustain continental production networks by pre-clearing low-risk shipments from authorized companies.

Although these new border-screening technologies mitigated the economic impact of the US security measures, they did not restore the open trading environment that prevailed before 2001. Maximizing counter-terror security entails immense costs, and managing the tension between border trade and border security remained imperfect. Between the signing of the smart-border agreement and the end of 2004, the time required to process cross-border shipments actually tripled. While the creation of the mammoth Department of Homeland Security (DHS) was meant to have simplified border security, forty-four agencies still enjoyed some control over border policy. The annual cost of border delays was estimated at $12.5 billion, a burden that disadvantaged North American manufacturers competing with overseas firms which faced less onerous screening.[15]

The Canadian government backed its commitment to strengthened international security architecture with material contributions that reduced the costs of the United States' efforts and increased their efficiency. In the aftermath of 9/11, the Canadian minister of finance quickly allocated $7.7 billion for five years' worth of such measures to strengthen bilateral cooperation as enhancing emergency preparedness, air security, and border infrastructure.[16] This spending priority persisted well after the immediate urgency of 9/11 faded.

Having been vilified by Osama bin Laden in the same breath as Germany, Great Britain, and the United States as 'crusaders' fighting the Taliban in Afghanistan, Canada had its own reasons to worry about terrorists coming across the US border to attack Canadian targets. Ottawa built up its own border defences and emergency preparedness, investing over $10 billion to this end between 9/11 and 2009.[17] Canada also decided to provide customs officials with body armour and the authority to arrest and detain suspects coming from the United States.[18] In this way Canada contributed to the very border militarization of whose pernicious economic impact it has loudly complained since September 2001.

This increased deployment in personnel was supplemented along both sides of the land border with military technology that created a 'virtual wall' through the use of cameras, sensors, and even unmanned drones.[19] These border innovations ranged from gamma rays that could identify hidden explosives, contraband, and smuggled people to radiation detectors that could help intercept the passage of a small nuclear weapon.[20] It is impossible to quantify how much these large Canadian investments and expenditures on border personnel diminished the cost burden that the United States would otherwise have had to bear to raise its security to its desired level. But they gave psychic support to Americans by confirming that their northern neighbour had been made terrorist-proof – even against their own citizens heading north.

Canada's greatest contribution to the American defensive power against terrorism may be its heavy spending on counter-terror intelligence, which has functionally extended the US intelligence perimeter. In 2001 Canada budgeted an initial Cdn$646 million over five years for enhanced information-sharing technology to screen goods and travellers, the integration of Canadian officials with the US Foreign Terrorist Tracking Task Force, and the development of joint units to assess incoming air passengers before they reach Canadian air space so that the DHS's 'border management agencies could apply risk-based management tools.'[21]

In the immediate aftermath of 9/11, Canada, on its own initiative, also created Integrated National Security Enforcement Teams (INSETs) in Toronto, Montreal, Vancouver, and Ottawa, bringing together officers and resources from the Royal Canadian Mounted Police (RCMP), the Canada Border Services Agency (CBSA), Citizenship and Immigration Canada (CIC), and the Canadian Security Intelligence Service (CSIS) to collect, share, and analyse intelligence. In addition, Ottawa passed legislation that mirrored the Bush administration's security measures. The Immigration and Refugee Protection Act toughened Canada's visa policies and the Anti-Terrorism Act declared terrorism to be a distinct crime so serious that it justified infringing Canadians' civil liberties.[22] The latter measure included tougher sentencing for terrorism; criminalized any participation in, facilitation of, contribution to, or funding of a terrorist group; permitted electronic surveillance of suspected terrorist groups; and expanded police powers to arrest and deport suspected terrorists. In short, Canada adopted a number of US-style counter-terror measures. These acts constructed US security not just by enhancing the ability of Canadian law-enforcement officials to address the threat of terrorism but also by helping internationalize US security norms.

Canada's awareness of its dual vulnerability to terrorism itself and to the economic fallout from the US drive for maximum security led it to adopt a proactive approach. In implementing FAST and NEXUS and in passing new legislation, Ottawa demonstrated how it constructed US security on its own initiative.

Mexico: The Acquiescent Ally?

For two decades before 2001, the Mexico-US border had already become a contested policy space. Mexico's inability to impede the northward flow of drugs and migrants had entrenched American distrust, cynicism, and scepticism about cooperating with Mexican officials and police. The two countries' border-security agents often avoided each other for fear of being wrongfully arrested by officers of the other nation.[23] US border walls were unilaterally erected in Arizona (Operation Safeguard), California (Operation Gatekeeper), and Texas (Operation Hold the Line). The US Border Patrol employed over 9,000 agents, in striking contrast with its mere 334 agents deployed along the fenceless and far lengthier Canadian border.[24]

Having carefully worked out a 'smart border' with Canada in December 2001, Washington virtually imposed the relevant parts of this prototype on Mexico. The Mexico-US 22-Point Border Partnership Agreement of March 2002 mirrored the Canada-US Smart Border Declaration in its aim of tightening security through better technology and enhanced resources while facilitating the legitimate transit of people and trade. The agreement proposed initiatives for electronic-information exchange and tracking as well as for securing in-transit shipments, along with measures against fraud and contraband. Largely dictated by Washington without consultations having been carried out with the Mexican private sector as had been the case in Canada, this agenda did not generate much Mexican policy contribution. Mexican officials became not partners but administrators who felt little shared interest in designing mutual continental security.

While Mexico's financial and strategic contribution has not been on a par with Canada's, it has taken the initiative by trying to address another security concern that was seen as an emerging threat in the US intelligence community. Mexico's 1,146-kilometre-long, porous, mountainous, and tropical southern border with Guatemala and Belize constitutes the notional southern limit of the United States' North American security perimeter. It has eight official international crossing points with Guatemala and two with Belize, but there are at least 350 informal crossing points with Guatemala alone, through which some 400,000 undocumented persons are estimated to pass each year under conditions of high violence, widespread criminality, low human-rights protection, and rampant corruption.

Would-be immigrants to the United States from Central and South America flow mainly across the Mexico–Guatemala–Belize border, so potential terrorists exploiting this chaotic phenomenon became an additional element in Washington's cocktail of security worries. In response, the Mexican government has taken steps to reinforce its capacity to control the northward flow of people from Guatemala and Belize. To attack the root causes of the region's extremely low levels of social capital as measured by income, health, employment, housing, and education, the Fox administration presented in 2001 an ambitious economic infrastructure-construction project, the Puebla to Panama Plan, which garnered support from several international financial institutions because of its effort to address the structural problems which are limiting economic development and perpetuating social distress in the region. The Mexican government has also signed cooperation agreements with various Central American governments concerning the repatriation of undocumented immigrants and the protection of women and minors.[25]

Four years' experience with these security measures' stifling effects on cross-border economic flows generated such concern among senior officials in the three governments that a new Security and Prosperity Partnership of North America was announced at a 2005 trilateral meeting between President George W. Bush, President Vicente Fox, and Prime Minister Paul Martin. Despite its promises to reconcile border security with economic integration, it remains unclear how this circle was squared under the SPP's system of trinational working groups. It is certainly the case that the four summits involving North American leaders that followed – in Cancún (2006), Montebello (2007), New Orleans (2008), and Guadalajara (2009) – gave the Mexican president and Canadian prime minister regular opportunities to engage with their American counterpart about their concerns. But there is no evidence that they moderated DHS's monopoly over the US border-security dossier. When the SPP was quietly dropped by the Obama administration, it did not appear to have altered the basic dynamic of the periphery's uneven construction of US security.

The Periphery as a Cooperative Source of Security

Cooperation between US and Canadian officials at the border miti-gated the burden and increased the efficiency of security. Beyond the jointly administered FAST and NEXUS programs, the 1996 pilot project creating Integrated Border Enforcement Teams (IBETs) was expanded to become another key initiative in which agents from the RCMP, the CBSA, the US Coast Guard, the US Customs and Border Protection/ Border Patrol (CBP), and US Immigration and Customs Enforcement exchanged information and worked with local law-enforcement per-sonnel to administer the border. By 2004, there were twenty-four IBETs operating in fifteen border regions.[26]

To the south, the story has been less straightforward. Given its insist-ence on maintaining its sovereign autonomy, its consensus that ter-rorism was not a domestic priority, and the bitter arguments within Vicente Fox's cabinet about how to conduct the US relationship, the Mexican government's primary concession contributing to US security power was declaring its willingness to adopt Washington's counter-terror agenda.[27] However, shortfalls in institutional capacity and finan-cial resources severely curtailed the government's ability to implement those measures that had been agreed upon in a way that would mean-ingfully construct American anti-terror capacity. By not specifying such goals, programs, and modes of cooperation as the joint training of the integrated border teams that featured prominently in its Canada-US counterpart, the 2002 Mexico-US 22-Point Border Partnership Agree-ment anticipated Mexico's lesser capacity. Even the measures that were included required an immediate American contribution of US$25 million to jump-start their implementation. By 2008, the agreement's objectives remained far from realized in such critical areas as secur-ing the railways, combating fraud, interdicting contraband, exchanging electronic information, screening third-country nationals, and consult-ing on visa policy.[28] This discrepancy between stated goals and actual achievements explains the subsequent US effort under the Mérida Ini-tiative to build Mexico's capacity to support US narcotics security, a program that we consider more fully in chapter 6.

American concerns that Mexican border guards were neither well trained nor well paid (and thus susceptible to corruption) also reduced the prospects for effective continental cooperation,[29] a trend that was compounded by the Mexican Army's high desertion rate and bureaucratic corruption. Instead of relying on cooperation, the US government unilaterally deployed Border Enforcement Security Teams that were established solely by American agencies. Consequently, while the Mexican government has supported the US anti-terror agenda at the rhetorical level, its material contributions to continental security have been too slim to shift a significant portion of the United States' security burden off its shoulders.

The difference between Canada's massive and Mexico's minimal spending on security reflected the former's greater governance capacity and its sense of shared interests with the United States in emergency preparedness, air security, and border infrastructure. Canada committed itself to construct US security in the hope that a US government which felt safer would reduce its border barriers to commerce. In contrast, the Fox administration was divided over the merits of cooperation with the United States. Unlike Canada, whose interest in anti-terrorist security made it willing to construct US power through cooperation and burden sharing, Mexico lacked such a sense of shared interests and so was cool to American overtures.

The Periphery as a Security Perimeter and Buffer

Another thrust of Washington's continental efforts following 9/11 was to create a second US security perimeter along Canada's and Mexico's own outer boundaries. In policy matters, the United States pressed Mexico and Canada to bring their immigration and customs controls up to US-dictated standards.[30]

In physical terms, US pre-clearance facilities were moved into many of the periphery's ports and airports, enabling people and goods to be screened at their point of departure before being admitted to the United States. In the words of former Commissioner of US Customs and Border Protection Robert C. Bonner, pre-clearance would create 'a layered, defense-in-depth strategy that pushes our borders – our zone of security – out beyond our physical borders, so we know who and what is heading our way before they arrive.'[31]

The United States' concern with its security perimeter had two implications. If Canada's and Mexico's screening of people and goods coming from abroad were harmonized with US procedures, then the periphery's outer borders would be as secure as the United States'. Second, and by extension, this would turn the two neighbours into a buffer against al-Qaeda's suicide bombers, just as NORAD had made Canada a buffer against the Soviet Union's long-range bombers. As the *National Strategy for Homeland Security* explained, 'internationally, the United States will seek to screen and verify the security of goods and identities of people before they can harm the international transportation system and well before they reach our shores or land borders.'[32]

The 2001 Smart Border Declaration heralded secure procedures that allowed goods to be cleared away from the Canada-US border at rail and sea ports. In addition to tightening the Aeronautics Act and improving infrastructure, Canada armed its air marshals, trained airport passenger and baggage screeners, and purchased new explosive-detection systems that would not only secure flights from Canada to the United States but tighten screening for terrorists at the ports and airports abroad that acted as Canada's overseas border points. Under the Joint Targeting Initiative, specialists from the United States and Canada could identify and screen high-risk containers at their first point of arrival, operating jointly at the ports of Montreal, Halifax, Vancouver, Seattle, and Newark. The 2005 signing of the Container Security Initiative allowed Canadian and American security personnel to share intelligence and coordinate the inspection of suspect cargo in order to break potential terrorists' logistical chains, particularly the smuggling of weapons of mass destruction. More recently, with the 'Shiprider' pilot project, an initiative that emerged out of the Security and Prosperity Partnership, the United States and Canada conduct cross-border, jointly crewed maritime patrols in the St Lawrence Seaway and along British Columbia's coast.[33] Shiprider even played a role in providing integrated cross-border security for Vancouver's Olympic Games in 2010.[34]

Despite this high level of integration, not all attempts to push the US security perimeter into Canada have been compatible with perceived Canadian interests. The Canadian and US governments had been in talks since 2004 to establish a land pre-clearance pilot project at the Buffalo-Fort Erie crossing, an initiative that grew out of the Canada-US Smart Border Declaration.[35] As a result of this program, all US border operations would have been located on the Canadian side of the border, mirroring existing pre-clearance facilities in Canadian airports. Despite support from a wide range of stakeholders including the powerful North American Competitiveness Council and the SPP Leaders' Summit of 2007, the project was aborted by DHS Secretary Michael Chertoff because of Ottawa's concern that such US security practices on Canadian territory as mandatory fingerprinting would violate the Charter of Rights and Freedoms.[36]

In comparison, American efforts to extend the US security perimeter into Mexico were less intense. In the economic arena, the Customs and Trade Partners against Terror (C-TPAT) program registered truck drivers and sealed shipments at Mexican factories to enable pre-clearance and combat smuggling. Unlike the bilateral Canada-US FAST program, C-TPAT is a unilateral initiative of the US Department of Homeland Security whose burdens (including training, equipment, and paperwork) fall on private American importers and Mexican exporters. It still remains vulnerable to smuggling.[37] Similarly, the US SENTRI program facilitates the flow of people across the US-Mexico border but is unilateral – unlike the cooperative Canada-US NEXUS program.[38] Even the costs of screening the 4.5 million trucks that annually enter the United States from Mexico fall on US shoulders.[39]

The Mexican defence ministry undertook efforts to strengthen airport security and monitor the frontier, while the Centro de Investigación y Seguridad Nacional (CISEN) and the Instituto Nacional de Migración (National Immigration Institute) improved border vigilance and information sharing among intelligence agencies. But Mexico depended on both US technical and financial assistance in order to set up the necessary computer and data infrastructure in Mexican airports.[40] Similar efforts have been directed at Mexico's maritime borders. Under a 2007 agreement, the United States installed radiation-detection devices in the four busiest Mexican ports. Under the Sea Cargo Initiative, Mexico agreed to collect electronic data on Mexican-bound cargo at the shipment's point of origin.[41] Thus, while Mexico has provided its neighbour with the space to extend its security perimeter, it has often been up to the United States to develop that perimeter, making Mexico's contribution to US security at its northern border more permissive than proactive.

Mexican efforts to create a continental security perimeter have not caused the United States to reverse its projects to thicken its own borders. It conceives this extended perimeter not as a replacement for its existing borders but as a forward line of defence for the homeland's own strengthened fortifications. This double-fortification approach shoots down much of the periphery's hope that, if it meets US security standards, Washington will dismantle its land borders. Although the periphery's Americanization of its security policies was implemented to construct a continental security perimeter, it did not yield the hoped-for borderlessness inside North America.

While it has become more difficult for terrorists with destructive designs on the United States to enter via Canada and Mexico, it also became more difficult for Canadians, Mexicans, and even returning Americans to enter the United States. With the Western Hemisphere Travel Initiative, which came into effect in 2009, both Canadians and Mexicans were subjected to passport requirements for travel to the United States, or – in the Canadian case – an enhanced drivers' licence for land and sea crossings. The same requirement also made it more difficult for US citizens to return to the United States from Mexico or Canada.

As a policy corollary of developing a truly continental security perimeter, the periphery acts as a buffer, a zone where security threats can be dealt with before they reach the United States. One of the most dramatic examples of the periphery acting as buffer happened during the 9/11 attacks. While the United States shut down all its airports and airspace, many hundreds of US-inbound flights were diverted to Canadian airports. Of about 400 flights heading for the United States over the Atlantic Ocean, the Gander Area Control Centre in Labrador sent half back to Europe. Another 200 aircraft, many registered in the United States, landed in eastern Canadian airports. Inbound planes crossing the Pacific Ocean were redirected to western Canadian airports, while Canadian military aircraft escorted a San Francisco-bound Air China flight to Vancouver and a Korean Airlines New York-bound flight to Whitehorse. Gander accommodated 6,600 passengers from thirty-eight inbound flights, while Vancouver handled 8,500 passengers from thirty-five inbound flights.[42] In effect, Canadian airspace was the buffer space in which these possible threats to the United States were dealt with.

Following 9/11, the periphery's buffer-zone role has developed through integrated intelligence sharing. In addition to overseas visa screening, Canadian authorities also process passengers travelling into Canada from abroad and share this information with American intelligence officials.[43] US officials join Canadians to watch for threats approaching the United States and use Canadian airspace as the buffer zone.

In June 2006 authorities arrested the 'Toronto 18,' a group of fourteen adults and four youth who were plotting to detonate truck bombs in front of the Toronto Stock Exchange, the Toronto office of CSIS, and a Canadian military base. Although these were domestic terrorists aiming at Canadian rather than cross-border targets, the arrest showed

Washington that Canadian policing and intelligence efforts could block terrorist plots before they reached fruition – or the US border.

To the south, Vicente Fox's administration dismantled the notoriously corrupt Policía Judicial Federal, replacing it with the Agencía Federal de Investigación (AFI) as the main body dealing directly with terrorism and created an elite anti-terrorist group to cooperate with the Federal Bureau of Investigation (FBI). Staffed by former Mexican Interpol agents, AFI coordinates intelligence sharing with over 177 countries.[44] Immediately after 9/11, Mexico detained several hundred individuals with Middle Eastern backgrounds, provided the United States with information on terrorist suspects in Mexico, and toughened its entry conditions for several Middle Eastern and Central Asian countries.[45] Mexico also shares intelligence on visitors and potential immigrants to facilitate enhanced US background checks on applicants and to increase the tracking of foreign students headed for the United States. Yet the United States remains sceptical about Mexico's intelligence capacity, distrusting a service it perceives as weak, oriented towards domestic issues, starved for resources, and thus vulnerable to being corrupted by the cartels.[46] While Mexican intelligence and information-sharing capacities have improved, they are limited by the institutional rivalries between police, intelligence, and justice agencies for control over the terrorist agenda – a turf war that produces information hoarding and reduces the effectiveness of the government's anti-terrorism efforts.[47] While the Mexican government may have genuinely wanted to collaborate on the US anti-terror agenda, the degree to which Mexican officials can successfully create a buffer zone for the United States in Mexico remains in doubt.

Psychological versus Economic Security

These varied contributions to US security by Canada and Mexico must be measured both in objectively constructing the actual safety of US citizens and in subjectively reducing Americans' politically generated anxieties. Canada's 2001 Immigration and Refugee Protection Act, for example, limits access to appeal; widens the grounds for deportation; and allows the suspension or termination of refugee proceedings when there is reason to believe the claimant is a terrorist, war criminal, or senior official in a government engaged in terrorism. In essentially shifting its immigration and refugee policy from a humanitarian to a security configuration, the legislation addresses the persistent American misperception that weak Canadian immigration and asylum policies were the cause of 9/11 in the first place. In this way the symbolic purpose of the Canadian anti-terrorism effort was to assuage American fears even if its practical implications were indeterminate.

The admission of refugee claimants into Canada until their claims are processed sparked American fears that Canada could serve as a stepping stone for a terrorist incursion into the United States since these claimants can easily go underground. Canada immediately responded to these concerns after 9/11 by allocating an additional $9 million for detention, screening, and deportation and by spending $17.3 million to create a fraud-resistant permanent resident card.[48] However, a 2002 study found that Canada's greatest terrorist vulnerability is visitors – tourists, students, or business people – not applicants for immigration or asylum.[49]

Subscribing to the United States' anti-terrorism mandate may not always increase the security of Canada's own citizens. In September 2002 the RCMP provided intelligence to American authorities that led them to detain the Canadian citizen Mahar Arar as he was returning from Egypt to Canada via New York. Then, following the practice of 'rendition,' they sent him to Syria where, although completely innocent, he was tortured for nearly a year with the complicity of Canadian diplomats and police. Such faulty intelligence and human-rights violations suggest that Canadian support for Washington's excessive methods may strengthen Americans' feeling of security while actually creating insecurity for Canadian Muslims and even inducing some to join al-Qaeda's jihad in revenge.

Of course, Canada could be used as a staging ground for terrorist attacks against the United States. Most global terrorist organizations are thought to be present in Canada, suggesting that terrorists might subvert Canada's peaceful Islamic infrastructure to coordinate an attack against the United States.[50] In reality, however, this threat remains largely speculative and may even be completely unfounded, as was the case in the aftermath of 9/11, when a surprising number of Americans mistakenly blamed their neighbours rather than admit that their own intelligence failure was the immediate cause of al-Qaeda's attack.

Similar prejudices and misconceptions frame security threats at the US-Mexican border. After 9/11, migratory flows from Mexico, which we considered from an economic standpoint in chapter 3, began to be seen by the DHS as a growing security threat, potentially enabling a terrorist incursion. The testimony of Admiral James Loy at a hearing before the Senate Select Committee on Intelligence in February 2005 rang the alarm: 'Entrenched human smuggling networks and corruption in areas beyond our borders can be exploited by terrorist organizations. Recent information ... strongly suggests that al-Qaeda has considered using the southwest border to infiltrate the United States. Several al-Qaeda leaders believe operatives can pay their way into the country through Mexico and also believe illegal entry is more advantageous for operational security reasons.'[51]

Although Loy also noted the lack of evidence that operatives have successfully used this method, fieldwork revealed that, given the ease with which Mexican officials can be bribed, it might cost as little as US$1,000 to smuggle a Central Asian or Middle Eastern person into American border cities, while larger amounts would carry them farther into the US heartland.[52] Aggravating these fears was a report in the *Arizona Daily Star* that an American vigilante group called attention to the Mexican threat by smuggling a fake weapon of mass destruction across the border.[53] The DHS has suggested that the smuggling pipelines used by undocumented aliens and criminals seeking to enter the United States could also be used by terrorists.[54]

One exceptional example of bilateral cooperation is the Operation against Smuggling Initiative on Safety and Security, a program announced in 2005 to standardize US Border Control guidelines for the effective prosecution of migrant smugglers and human traffickers on both sides of the Mexican border through information sharing and coordinated enforcement.[55] More typical are US measures to merge its border-building measures against Mexican illegal immigrants with its anti-terrorism concerns. A 2003 Border Patrol assessment reported that 22,000 agents were needed to police the border adequately.[56] The US Border Patrol grew from a $200-million budget with 2,000 agents in 1986 to a $1,213-billion budget in 2006 with 12,200 agents, 9,000 of whom monitor the US-Mexico border.[57] Today's US-Mexico border involves trucks, jeeps, patrol agents, military personnel, expanding fences, night-vision technology, hundreds of cameras, high-tech communication technology, increasingly militarized training and operations, and the wall.[58]

Much political and environmental attention has focused on the Secure Fence Act of 2006, the bulk of whose 1,120-kilometre-long physical barrier has been built along the US-Mexican border. The barrier's efficacy has been questioned at all levels of government and US society, as the US government has increasingly endorsed technological fixes to the problem of controlling its southern border. The escalation in border-security measures has prompted the evolution of more adaptive smuggling – an illicit industry of professional 'coyotes' with the resources to bribe border guards in both nations; construct networks that, linked to the drug cartels, reach deep into the United States; and successfully traverse more remote regions while eluding points of enforcement.[59] These organizations have even manipulated the border fence in ingenious ways, from tunnels and holes to replacing portions of the barrier with camouflaged cardboard, creating access points that are not immediately identifiable to US authorities. If anything, the fence has transformed and diverted rather than reduced illegal border flows.[60] Unilateral American attempts to manage the perceived security threats at the southern border may have inadvertently produced an environment that fosters both terrorists and criminals.[61]

There are reasons to believe that Mexico's constraint on US security is not as grave as alarmists suggest. Mexico lacks Canada's large Muslim community and multicultural population that might conceal radical Islamic terrorist cells as they plan and execute a cross-border attack.[62] Non-Mexicans coming across the border potentially increase the chance that a terrorist could enter the United States; however, while the detention of 'other than Mexicans' (OTMs) at the US border rose by over 200 per cent between 2002 and 2005, the number of OTMs from countries with a relation to terrorism declined by 40 per cent.[63]

As we assess the extent to which the continental periphery constructs or constrains US anti-terrorist security, we need to remain mindful of an alternate reality. Were the Canadian and Mexican governments still preoccupied with the possibility of US military aggression against themselves – as they were 150 years ago – they would presumably have abetted the anti-US designs of their neighbour's fundamentalist enemies. In this counterfactual scenario of uncooperative and even hostile neighbours, the United States would have been forced to provide all of its security needs within the bounds of its own territory. Such unilateral security provision would have cost more, would have been less effective, and would have offset the economic openness that serves as the foundation for US global power.

In response to a single, if spectacular, terrorist act, the US government did what no foreign power could achieve – engineer a blockade that adversely affected its own economic well-being.[64] From the beginning, the US government's determination to 'rethink and renovate' its border security[65] led to confident assertions that security and trade policies could be mutually reinforcing.[66] Yet, despite claiming to reconcile the contradictory pressures between lowering economic barriers and raising security barriers, the new paradigm gave security policy priority over free commercial and human flows. In this respect, Canada's insistence on border-trade facilitation helped prevent Washington's exclusive focus on terrorism from undermining the economic component of its power.

Conclusion

Although the US Government Accountability Office announced as late as 2007 that it had discovered points along both borders where potential terrorists could slip across undetected,[67] Canada and Mexico may not be the source of terrorist insecurity that American conservatives have so vocally alleged. US homeland security envisions sustained cooperation with allies as a basic pillar of success, and Canada and Mexico have clearly played important roles in buttressing the United States' security architecture.

In some ways, Canada constrains US power more than Mexico, since its society could provide a better access point for inbound terrorists. Yet the Canadian government massively constructs the security of the United States, with whose policing apparatus it has closely integrated its own and with whose policies it has harmonized its own. This cooperation at the Canadian-US border at home and overseas has served to extend parts of the US security perimeter to include Canada's own sea and air borders and has turned Canada into a buffer where US security problems are dealt with before reaching the homeland. By working to develop its security policies, Canada has helped Washington manage its homeland-security needs without excessively jeopardizing the commerce that has been critical to the development of US power. Canada perceives a shared interest with the United States in both economics and security, and has constructed US power in a way that it believes fits with its own interests. Ultimately, even if much of the potential threat posed by Canada rests inside the heads of American policy makers, Canada has done much to calm their security fears, contributing both materially and psychically to US homeland security.

The Mexican government has been more passively responsive to US security demands, envisaging the same type of harmonized, integrated security architecture but, because of its relative institutional incapacity, hard-pressed to implement its commitments. This has led the US government to develop a less efficient and more expensive unilateral security defence along its southern border. US initiatives to enhance security while maintaining trade flows across that border cannot produce the efficiency gains that characterize the cooperative and harmonized US-Canada border-security system, yet Mexico's inadequacies are tempered by the fact that its potential as a major conduit for inbound terrorists seems limited.

The same modest degree of danger does not apply to drugs, a topic to which we now direct our attention. Here the Mexican state's institutional weaknesses have created real and significantly different security threats for the United States' homeland. Although 9/11 saw American policy makers conflate what are three very different issues – migration, drugs, and terrorism – each of which has its own distinctive logic, motivations, agents, and networks – and although the Department of Homeland Security institutionalized a combined approach to these distinct problems which nurtured an exaggerated association of migration with terrorism,[68] drug dealers carefully avoid any connection to terrorism in order to keep their particular networks off the US government's radar.[69] Since Canada and Mexico are – as with anti-terrorist security – both Uncle Sam's major constraint and major support in the area of drug control, the continental periphery has major negative and positive impacts on US societal power, a theme that we analyse in the next chapter.

6 Constraining and Reconstructing US Narcotics Security[1]

> The growing assault by the drug cartels and their thugs on the Mexican government reminds one that an unstable Mexico could represent a home-land security problem of immense proportions to the United States.
> – United States Joint Forces Command,
> *The Joint Operating Environment*, November 25, 2008[2]

The global drug trade has a wide-ranging and ever-increasing impact on American society. It affects the United States' health-care program and its justice system. It consumes immense resources and limits eco-nomic prosperity. By government estimates, the annual costs of health care associated with drug abuse rose from $11 to $16 billion in just ten years between 1992 and 2002; the direct costs of drug-related crime grew from $62 to $108 billion; indirect productivity losses doubled from $69 to $129 billion; the economic costs of premature death inched up from $23 to $25 billion; and losses related to narcotic-linked incarceration increased from $18 to $28 billion.[3] In September 2008 more than 52 per cent of all federal convicts were sentenced for drug-related crimes.[4] The total estimated cost of the drug problem – $190 billion as of 2002 – was equivalent in size to just under 2 per cent of US GDP.

Added to these costs are the billions of dollars spent on drug-control efforts that could otherwise be directed towards economic develop-ment or social welfare. Between 2002 and 2008, drug-control expen-ditures increased 31 per cent, including a 49 per cent increase in US spending abroad.[5] In 2009 the US federal budget allocated over $14 bil-lion for drug-related law enforcement, drug treatment and prevention, drug interdiction, and international counter-drug efforts.[6] Yet, despite the more than a quarter trillion dollars spent on anti-drug efforts over the past three decades, the illegal US drug industry flourishes.[7]

The US criminalization of narcotics production, sale, and consumption ensures that the continued supplying of American citizens' demand is inextricably accompanied by violence and criminality. These attendant effects threaten US power by undermining the state's ability to govern American society. Drug criminality defies the US government's ability to administer laws that determine the actual functioning of society while the intermingling of the markets for drugs and small arms undermines public safety to an extent that 'threatens the national security of the United States,' as President Ronald Reagan's National Security Decision Directive 221 already declared in 1986.[8]

Considered to be the world's second-largest industry after armaments, with estimates of annual revenues ranging widely between US$100 and $500 billion,[9] the international drug trade also affects the United States' global power by threatening and corrupting its allies, often by financing terrorist and insurgent movements. When friendly governments are unable to control large parts of their territories, sectors of their population, and even segments of their own military and judiciary, the consequences range from destabilizing the countries concerned to undermining US counter-narcotic programs themselves. In the words of the 1986 Security Directive: 'The national security threat posed by the drug trade is particularly serious outside US borders. Of primary concern are those nations with a flourishing narcotics industry, where a combination of international criminal trafficking organizations, rural insurgents, and urban terrorists can undermine the stability of the local government; corrupt efforts to curb drug crop production, processing and distribution; and distort public perceptions of the narcotics issue in such a way that it becomes part of an anti-US or anti-Western debate.'[10] The narcotics trade also threatens the United States' national security closer to home.

Enter Mexico and Canada.

Canada and Mexico as US Drug Threats

The North American drug trade's massive profits engender turf wars that weaken political and juridical institutions by corrupting officials, nourishing the global black economy to the detriment of legitimate commerce, aggravating existing social problems and cleavages, and – the subject matter of this chapter – spilling across borders.[11] As with military defence and security against terrorism, the US periphery harbours a paradox, presenting the United States with its largest foreign threat while simultaneously acting as its major ally. Its two neighbours are the primary gateways for the United States' five main drug threats (cocaine, methamphetamine, marijuana, heroin, and Ecstasy) and shelter the production of all of them except cocaine.[12] Segments of the periphery's criminal world are so deeply implicated in the United States' drug networks that the Canadian and Mexican governments have become Washington's most indispensable allies in its long-declared war on drugs. In this chapter, we will see how the geographical contiguity of Canada and Mexico and the differences between their jurisdictions ensure the continuing drug supply to the American market despite the US government's best interdiction efforts. At the same time, the governments of Canada and Mexico cooperate with Washington to disrupt production within their own borders and to interrupt trafficking operations across their borders. This alliance makes the United States directly dependent on its neighbouring administrations to resist their flow of drugs into its own market.

Together, Canada and Mexico act as the most important suppliers of, and the main conduits for, illegal narcotics entering the United States. Mexico is the largest supplier of marijuana and methamphetamines and has become an increasingly important source of heroin. For its part, Canada is the primary supplier of Ecstasy and a major supplier of high-grade marijuana to the American market. Of the major drugs, only cocaine is not produced in significant quantities in the North American periphery, although the vast majority of US-bound cocaine is smuggled through Mexico by its drug cartels. Mexico alone is estimated to be the source, whether as a conduit or production centre, of 70 per cent of all drugs consumed in the United States.[13]

Marijuana

Mexico is the United States' primary source of marijuana, which, with over twenty-five million users in 2007, is the most consumed drug there.[14] In 2007 approximately 15,500 metric tons of marijuana were grown in Mexico, with the vast majority of this production directed towards US markets.[15] To meet the immense scale of US demand for marijuana, Mexican suppliers have developed large outdoor farms boasting several thousand plants each.[16] While the Mexican government aggressively eradicates cannabis production in traditional growing areas, these efforts have only prompted producers to move from the southern states of Guerrero, Michoacán, and Nayarit northward to the more remote and mountainous parts of Durango, Sinaloa, and Sonora where they can more readily evade government pressure and more easily transport their product to the United States.[17] Many Mexican organizations have responded to increased government pressure by simply moving their outdoor cannabis-production sites to the United States itself, where cultivation is likely increasing.[18]

Canada also shelters significant marijuana operations. Smuggling thrives in the Great Lakes-St Lawrence Seaway area and in the border areas of the western US states.[19] Asian crime groups and gangs like the Hells Angels in Canada specialize in indoor 'grow-ops' and smuggle large quantities into the United States by land to established distribution networks.[20] It is known that these networks traffic huge quantities of high-potency marijuana per month for distribution in at least 100 American cities.[21]

Owing to the border-tightening measures discussed in the previous chapter, the US Customs and Border Patrol noted a decline in marijuana seizures from twelve tons in 2004 to six in 2006.[22] However, even with increased interdiction, the impact of Canadian marijuana production continues. Asian groups from Canada have shared their expertise in high-potency growing techniques with their US counterparts who have set up indoor cannabis cultivation throughout the country.[23] Although US growers are producing increasingly potent pot, the Canadian product is still prized for its high content of THC, the main psychoactive substance found in the cannabis plant, and has consequently held its high-end market share.[24]

The US National Drug Intelligence Center noted that, because of the Asian organizations' indoor grow-ops, 'marijuana potency has increased to the highest level ever recorded.'[25] The socio-economic impact of this development, according to the director of the White House Office of National Drug Control Policy (ONDCP), is that 'given the new levels of potency and the sheer prevalence of marijuana ... a case can be made that marijuana does the most social harm of any illegal drug. Marijuana is currently the leading cause of treatment need.'[26]

Ecstasy (MDMA)

Canada, where production has grown rapidly in response to burgeoning US demand, is the primary supplier of Ecstasy to the United States.

Seizures of MDMA – methylenedioxymethamphetamine – being smuggled into the United States increased five times between 2004 and 2006, from 1.1 million dosage units to 5.2 million in 2006, Canada having supplanted Belgium and the Netherlands as America's primary supplier in a mere two-year period.[27] It is estimated that Asian cartels based in Canada, smuggle many millions of dosage units of Ecstasy each month.[28] In October 2008 the RCMP declared Canada to be one of the world's largest producers of synthetic drugs.[29]

While MDMA production in the United States remains limited, Canadian labs are factory-sized production sites that often involve multiple buildings using industrial pill presses (which are not regulated in Canada).[30] All eighteen laboratories dismantled during 2007 were classified as 'super-labs.'[31] The finished product is transported across the border by private cars (75 per cent of seizures), commercial vehicles (15 per cent), and to a lesser extent through aircraft, boats, and the mail. The greatest sites of smuggling activity occur in Buffalo, New York; Detroit, Michigan; and Blaine, Washington – close to the chief production sites in Vancouver and the Greater Toronto Area.[32]

In economic terms, the Ecstasy trade shows how the periphery can also affect the US market. Clandestine MDMA production within Canada renders it more available to the American market, bringing down the street price and so augmenting the drug's socio-economic effects. Increased Canadian production contributed to price drops from Cdn$30–45 per tablet in 2004 to Cdn$10–15 per tablet in 2006.[33] The US National Drug Intelligence Center reported that 'the high, and possibly increasing, level of MDMA production in Canada is contributing to increased distribution of the drug in US drug markets. Moreover, distribution of MDMA tablets that have been adulterated with highly addictive drugs, particularly methamphetamine, is increasing.'[34] Given that the Drug Intelligence Center also predicts a consequent rise in treatment admissions for MDMA addiction, this trend exacerbates Canada's deleterious impact on US societal security.[35]

Heroin

An opoid drug synthesized from morphine, itself a derivative of the opium poppy, heroin is produced overseas and smuggled into Canada for domestic consumption rather than for smuggling to the south. By contrast, Mexican organizations are increasing their production and distribution of heroin in the United States.[36] Between 1999 and 2007,

Mexican heroin production doubled from nine to eighteen metric tons, with the majority shipped north.[37] Increased production coincides with the expansion of Mexican traffickers into markets formerly controlled by Colombian and Dominican networks. Mexican black-tar heroin is currently displacing white-powder heroin in eastern American markets, particularly New England, Ohio, and Pennsylvania.[38] The Central Intelligence Agency (CIA) reported in 2008 that Mexico was poised to become the main heroin producer for all of the United States.[39]

Methamphetamine

Mexico has also become the United States' chief source of methamphetamine.[40] There are no reliable estimates of overall 'meth' exports from Mexico, but seizures along the US border rose from 500 kilograms in 2000 to 2,700 kilograms in 2006, indicating the magnitude and growth of the problem.[41] To produce and distribute meth to American consumers more effectively, Mexican drug organizations are operating sophisticated laboratories north of the border, particularly in California. In just the first half of 2008, authorities in California seized nineteen super-labs, a drastic increase over the ten super-labs seized in all of 2007.[42]

For many drugs, geographical contiguity with the United States enables Canada and Mexico to enjoy a 'balloon effect': when enforcement efforts squeeze production or trafficking in one area, these activities simply bulge in another location, often owing to the cartels exploiting law-enforcement differences between jurisdictions. Canadian and Mexican drug organizations adapt to government efforts to control methamphetamine in order to maintain their continued supply to the American market. When, in 2004, the US government enacted comprehensive controls of the precursor chemicals, ephedrine and pseudoephedrine – the compounds that are required for synthetic drug production and become incorporated into the drug molecule – the number of domestic meth lab seizures decreased from a peak of 10,200 in 2003 to 2,600 in 2008.[43] Yet the amount of methamphetamine in the United States increased, because Mexico, and to a lesser extent Canada, offset the contraction in domestic production.[44] Accordingly, Canada implemented new precursor-chemical regulations in 2003 that substantially reduced their delivery to the United States and forced smuggling organizations to rely on overseas sources.[45] Similarly, in 2007, after Mexico banned the import of ephedrine and pseudoephedrine, the amount of seized methamphetamine decreased by 38 per cent.[46]

However, after a significant 2007 decline in Mexican production, many Mexican organizations relocated to California. The US National Drug Intelligence Center accordingly anticipated a resurgence of production and increased methamphetamine availability in the country.[47]

Cocaine

Obtained from the leaves of the coca plant, cocaine is considered the leading drug threat to the US societal security, because it is the narcotic most associated with violent crime, property crime, and arrests by the US Drug Enforcement Administration (DEA).[48] Colombia remains the world's primary producer of cocaine, but, without Mexico's essential role as its entry point for 90 per cent of the US cocaine supply,[49] the drug's scale and socio-economic impact would not be so severe. When American enforcement efforts closed the Caribbean trafficking routes from Colombia, Colombian producers and traffickers continued their business by forging relationships with Mexican cartels, thus managing to expand the flow of cocaine into the United States in another balloon effect. From 2000 to 2006, between 220 and 380 metric tons are estimated to have been smuggled into Mexico annually.[50]

The periphery is not only the major source of US-bound drugs, however. By rendering drugs cheaper and more readily available, it exacerbates their socio-economic impact and prevents enormous amount of counter-drug spending from accomplishing its aims. Geographical contiguity helps continentally scaled criminal drug networks evade national enforcement efforts in all three countries and provides further opportunities to forge hemispheric and global linkages. The result is more sophisticated and extensive criminality. For example, Canadian groups are able to specialize and divide labour: Vietnamese criminal groups focus on marijuana cultivation while Indo-Canadian crime groups do the actual cross-border smuggling.[51] Further, organizations in Canada and the United States can benefit from the comparative advantage of each other's national drug situation. Canadian traffickers barter bulk shipments of marijuana and/or MDMA to the United States in exchange for cocaine and firearms, alleviating the need to launder cash.[52]

Canada's outlaw society also provides American drug traffickers access to illicit global networks. One 2007 investigation of a trafficking network in British Columbia and Ontario traced its connections beyond the United States to Australia, New Zealand, China, and India.[53] Canadian organized-crime groups with deep links to China are increasingly involved in smuggling methamphetamine and MDMA precursor chemicals into Ontario and British Columbia, while Indo-Canadian organizations smuggle ephedrine from India to Canada for delivery to the United States.[54]

Criminal gangs have become a growing problem for border enforcement. Along the Atlantic provinces/New England border, large-scale drug smuggling is associated with both national and regional gangs, including the Asian Boyz, Hells Angels, and Outlaws. In the Pacific region, the Hells Angels are particularly notorious for their cross-border activities.[55] Vancouver has become Canada's gang capital, with over 130 operating, including the Red Scorpions, United Nations, MS-13, Bacon Brothers, and Hells Angels, along with other independent organizations. These groups' drug linkages include increasing ties to the Mexican cocaine market. In 2006 a Mexican crackdown on drug trafficking restricted Canadian supplies, with the result that violence erupted among these groups, including thirty shootings with escalating degrees of brutality, in just the first five months of 2009 as they struggled to get the supplies they needed for their desperate customers.[56] As the periphery's narcotics gangs deepen their linkages with continental drug networks, their criminality becomes more violent and much harder to control.

Given the Mexican government's failure to impose its authority in areas where the cartels have established their dominion, their emergence as a potent political, social, economic, and even military force has developed a new kind of US insecurity. It is estimated that Mexican drug cartels bring in between US$15 and $25 billion in cash from the United States each year.[57] Well resourced, the cartels corrupt law-enforcement officials in both countries, operating with few constraints in the border region.[58] By some accounts, almost all Mexican enforcement officials along the US border are either bought off or neutralized by threats to their own and their families' lives.[59]

Corruption may be spreading to the Mexican military, which has only limited civilian oversight and control. This hypothesis does not lack for evidence. In 1997 General Jesús Gutiérrez Rebollo, the former commissioner of the Instituto Nacional para el Combate a las Drogas (National Institute for Combating Drugs), was arrested on grounds of corruption. In 2008 four soldiers were arrested in Jalisco for complicity with the Beltrán-Leyva cartel. In 2009 twelve others linked to Los Zetas and allied with the Cartel del Golfo were imprisoned, and ten officers were discovered to be passing information to the Pacífico cartel.[60] Two other army generals have faced similar convictions since 1997.[61]

The problem of drug violence spilling over the border has occupied dozens of US government hearings.[62] In March 2009 Secretary of Homeland Security Janet Napolitano, confirming the importance to US security of Mexico's fight against the cartels, warned of the spillover of Mexican violence into the United States.[63] As a former director of the White House Office of National Drug Control Policy noted, 'the killing of rival traffickers is already spilling across the border. Witnesses are being killed. We do not think the border is a shield.'[64] Americans living in the United States now appear on cartel hit lists, with executions, kidnappings, and assassinations taking place on US soil.[65] In the past, drug traffickers would flee from US enforcement officials, but now they even confront and attack American officers on the US side of the border.[66] There have been hundreds of drug-related incursions by Mexican military personnel into American territory, sometimes in pursuit of drug traffickers – but sometimes in apparent support.[67] Los Zetas, the most violent paramilitary enforcement group that engages in protection services and other illegal activities including trafficking, was reported to be stockpiling weapons in American border towns in preparation for increased enforcement action within the United States.[68] Similarly, traffickers from the Sinaloa, Gulf, Juarez, and Tijuana cartels keep working relationships with numerous gangs inside the United States.[69] After the Calderón government dispatched the Mexican army to take on the cartels in a number of northern cities, violence there escalated. The implications for American citizens in Mexico have been serious. Between July 1, 2005 and June 30, 2008, 131 American citizens were killed, most along the US-Mexico border.[70] In Nuevo Laredo, more than sixty US citizens were kidnapped between 2003 and 2007, and almost two dozen more reported missing.[71] In March 2010 two US consular officials were assassinated after a birthday party at the American consulate in Ciudad Juarez, which was described as a 'war zone.'[72]

Pervasive corruption and violence, which increasingly features the assassination of high-level enforcement officials, erodes Mexico's historically weak state institutions in a downward spiral, edging it towards a governance crisis. Corruption impedes the development of a society governed by stable, law-bound, and accountable institutions rather than by the arbitrary dictates of violence and criminality. In this sense, the corruption engendered by the drug cartels undermines the United States' interest in having a stable democratic regime capable of maintaining a law-based social order within the large territory along its southern border.

In May 2007 the head of Mexico's drug-intelligence unit in the office of the attorney general was killed in Mexico City.[73] One year later, the city's chief of police was shot nine times.[74] That same month, three other police chiefs asked for US political asylum after their families were threatened by cartels.[75] This violence has continued, forcing the resignation of the police chief of Ciudad Juárez in Februrary 2009,[76] while in July 2010 the candidate for governor for the state of Tamaulipas, Rodolfo Torre Cantú, and seven campaign staff were shot just before election day.[77]

Though Mexican policy makers angrily dismiss the possibility, some US analysts believe there is a very real risk that drug-linked violence and instability could create a failed state on the United States' doorstep, a prospect that represents a new and ultimate level of threat to US power by the Mexican drug cartels.[78] A 2008 US Joint Forces Command report noted: 'In terms of worst-case scenarios for the Joint Force and indeed the world, two large and important states bear consideration for a rapid and sudden collapse: Pakistan and Mexico.'[79]

The debate on whether Mexico has become a failed state hangs on the distribution and intensity of the violence. Putting this situation in perspective, one expert wrote: 'Mexico suffers from localized violence in six of its thirty-two states with the national rate of 10 homicides per 100,000 inhabitants. Venezuela has 48; Colombia 37; Brazil 25; and Guatemala, Honduras, and El Salvador are over 50. At its peak in January 2010, Mexico's most violent state, Chihuahua, had a rate of 143 homicides per 100,000, with Sinaloa at 80, Durango at 49, Baja California at 44, and Michoacán at 25. In the early 1990s, Colombia's most violent city Medellín maintained a rate of 320.'[80] Whatever label is applied to the Mexican state, it seems clear that its ability to deliver security and social services is in jeopardy because of the cartels' unprecedented power.

The Canadian and Mexican Governments as US Drug Allies

Four decades ago, the Richard Nixon administration recognized that the transnational character of the narcotics trade required the cooperation of other governments for its war on drugs to succeed. Vigorously promoting its own criminal-justice norms around the world, the US government managed to universalize its narcotics-policy paradigm as the global standard to which other nations were expected to conform. This facet of US power relied on other states' endorsement of the assumption that the narcotics trade was a threat, not just to their own, but to international security.[81] National Security Decision Directive 221 explicitly stipulated that drug policy was to be 'guided by the principles of controlling crop production and targeting trafficking at the source and in transit.'[82] It further depended on foreign governments' adopting an approach based on total prohibition, a concentration on interdicting supply rather than mitigating demand, punitive enforcement (which particularly aimed at traffickers) rather than structural prevention (which focuses on the social, political, and economic context that nourishes the drug trade), and a heavy reliance on coercive force. The United States' global power was manifested in its ability to Americanize the domestic drug policies of other states and dictate the content of international drug-control treaties.[83]

For the most part, Canada and Mexico have endorsed the American war on drugs in their domestic policies and actions, in this way bolstering US power through their cooperation. However, Canada and Mexico also tailor their drug policies, which are often more liberal than those of the United States, to their own domestic contexts. Insofar as these key allies introduce such drug measures as decriminalizing marijuana and safe-injection sites that differ from the US model, they constrain US power, because these more liberal policies provide viable alternatives to the US approach, as we can see if we employ the same framework we used to analyse anti-terrorist border security in chapter 5.

A Cooperative Periphery as a Source of Security Resources

Direct cross-border cooperation limits the socio-economic and law-and-order effects of the drug trade on American societal security by increasing the US counter-narcotics war's efficacy. Successful actions by the Canadian and Mexican governments' law-enforcement agencies construct US power by impeding the operations of Canada's and Mexico's outlaw society.

To the north, a key cooperative institution is the Cross-Border Crime Forum (CBCF), which is co-chaired by Canada's ministers of public safety and justice and the US attorney general and brings law-enforcement and justice officials from both sides of the border together with provincial and state governments to coordinate a common response to drug smuggling, money laundering, firearms trafficking, and telemarketing fraud.[84] Project Northstar is another bilateral forum that coordinates law-enforcement agencies in both countries and builds transnational security relationships.[85] The Integrated Border Enforcement Teams mentioned in the last chapter augment this joint capacity with continued cooperation between Canadian and American officers. IBETs are organized in fifteen geographic regions and integrate land, air, and sea resources to fight cross-border criminality.[86] The DEA, the Customs Border Patrol, Immigration and Customs Enforcement (ICE), the Canada Border Services Agency, the RCMP, and local and provincial officers hold regular consultations at both the field and oversight levels, and Canadian agencies often receive specialized training from their American counterparts.[87]

The result of these joint initiatives, as the Crime Forum explains, is 'greater success in seizing illicit drugs crossing the US-Canada border and apprehending those that traffic them.'[88] Their impact on American drug security reveals itself in the many successful operations that break up drug-smuggling organizations and reduce drug supply in the region. In the 2002 Operation Mountain Express, the RCMP, Canada Customs, US DEA, US Customs Service, and the US Internal Revenue Service all worked together to disrupt Canadian pseudoephedrine exports, resulting in mass arrests as well as significant drug and currency seizures.[89]

To the south, American relations with Mexico on the issue of drugs have long been fraught with cynicism, distrust, and tension stemming from the many former Mexican administrations that tolerated, accommodated, and even cooperated with drug traffickers.[90] Under President Vicente Fox (2000–6) and especially under Felipe Calderón (2006–12), the bilateral relationship shifted dramatically towards cooperation.[91] Washington signalled its confidence in Fox's anti-narcotics actions by tripling its assistance to Mexican police and sharing critical drug intelligence with Mexican authorities.[92] Americans were even more impressed by Calderón's dramatically dispatching the Mexican army to battle the drug lords.

As we saw with border security in chapter 5, Mexico lacks the financial and institutional capacity to manage its drug problem alone. Recognizing their mutual interest, the United States agreed to contribute resources to help Mexico address its own insecurity. Financial support from the US Bureau of International Narcotics and Law Enforcement Affairs for Mexico's counter-narcotics initiatives amounted to $552 million between 1996 and 2008.[93] Within the United States, President

George W. Bush increased the budget for border security from $5 billion in 2001 to $12 billion in 2008.[94]

US-Mexican cooperation became more formalized under the Mérida Initiative. Jointly announced in October 2007, this program earmarked $1.4 billion over three years to combat drug trafficking, gangs, and organized crime in Mexico, Central America, Haiti, and the Dominican Republic.[95] After the US Congress appropriated US$700 million for Mexico, the Obama administration requested an additional $66 million[96] to enhance Mexico's anti-narcotics enforcement capacity by providing helicopters and surveillance aircraft; new inspection technology for interdicting drugs, arms, cash, and personnel; secure data and communications technologies; and technical advice and training to improve the professionalism, accountability, and efficiency of law-enforcement officials while promoting the reform of judicial institutions in the struggle against corruption.[97] At least $74 million was specifically devoted to strengthening the Mexican legal system.[98]

The Mérida Initiative marked a watershed in the two countries' cooperation in their war on drugs, with the United States publicly recognizing it must help Mexico, and Mexico recognizing it needed the United States' help if it was going to be able to defeat the cartels. Through this cooperation, the United States exerted its agency to construct its own security by expanding the Mexican government's capacity. Despite increased cooperation, corruption persists in some sectors. Nevertheless, US confidence in the Mexican government has been bolstered by the replacement of the Policía Judicial Federal with the Agencía Federal de Investigación (Federal Investigation Agency) and the Policía Ministerial (Ministerial Police), one of the Mexican government's most significant efforts to combat corruption. At the same time, military salaries have been raised significantly, reducing desertion rates from 21,000 in 2006 to 16,000 in 2007.[99]

Bilateral cooperation in real-time information sharing raises Mexican interdiction performance, and the US training of thousands of Mexican law-enforcement officers at the federal, state, and local levels improves their capabilities and professionalism.[100] In June 2008 the ICE and Mexico launched Operation Armas Cruzadas, a bilateral program to combat weapon smuggling through increased transborder intelligence and enforcement coordination.[101] During her April 2009 state visit to Mexico, Secretary of State Hillary Clinton unveiled plans with Mexican Foreign Minister Patricia Espinosa for a new bilateral implementation office where officials from both countries would work together to fight drug trade and violence.[102]

The Periphery as an Extension of the US Security Perimeter

Beyond joining with the United States in cooperative drug-enforcement efforts, both Canada and Mexico have taken steps to extend the US security perimeter by vigorously adopting the US war-on-drugs approach in their own territories. Policy convergence improves the American war on drugs' efficacy by reducing the differences between adjacent national jurisdictions and so narrowing the legal cracks within which drug traffickers can manoeuvre.

With some exceptions, Canada has come to adopt the US policy approach in every respect but for the word 'war.' When US President Ronald Reagan invigorated the American war on drugs in a 1986 speech, Canadian Prime Minister Brian Mulroney almost immediately echoed that 'drug abuse has become an epidemic that undermines our economic as well as our social fabric.'[103] The declaration did not arise from any sudden change in Canada's drug situation. It reflected a long-shared US-Canadian history of punitive and prohibitionist approaches that go back to the International Opium Commission of 1908. This convergence gave Canada one of the toughest Western drug regimes until, in 1982, the Charter of Rights and Freedoms reined in sweeping police powers and put legal limits on the aggressive pursuit of drug users and dealers.[104]

Canada's present approach is based in the 1997 Controlled Drugs and Substances Act, which parallels the US war on drugs by emphasizing prohibition, punishment, broad enforcement powers, and prosecution rather than prevention and harm reduction.[105] The 2001 Proceeds of Crime (Money Laundering) and Terrorist Financing Act strengthened Canada's capacity to interrupt money laundering and illicit financial transactions.[106] Canada has recently affirmed this aggressive support of the US approach by increasing the size of RCMP forces targeting drug trafficking and production and by improving the drug-detection and intelligence capabilities of the Canada Border Services Agency to boost its investigation, interdiction, and prosecution of drug offenders. Under the National Anti-Drug Strategy, Ottawa also passed legislation to increase existing mandatory prison sentences for major offences in order to deter growers and traffickers.[107] This policy convergence is built upon a diplomatic relationship with the United States that includes a Mutual Legal Assistance Treaty, an extradition treaty, and protocols delegating responsibility for cross-border drug enforcement coordination to the DEA and RCMP.[108]

Historically, Mexico's support for the US war on drugs has been much less enthusiastic, but its own spiralling drug problem has pushed it to take unprecedented action that supports US societal security by vigorously extending the American anti-drug campaign into Mexico. As soon as President Calderón took office in 2006, he decided to combat organized crime.[109] Declaring 'a war without quarter,'[110] he quickly pleased US drug warriors by drastically increasing extraditions of Mexican criminals to the United States.[111]

Drug Enforcement Administration agents have eleven offices in the country and undertake many joint missions with Mexican authorities.[112] The bilateral Operation All-Inclusive targeted the flow of drugs, money, and precursor chemicals from South America through Mexico, Central American, and the Caribbean into the United States, and, from January to September 2008, it made 1,278 arrests while seizing 100 metric tons of cocaine, 225 kilograms of heroin, 130 metric tons of marijuana, and $92 million in cash.[113] In March 2008 the DEA, in conjunction with an arrest warrant issued by the Southern District of California, helped the Mexican government's Special Investigations Unit arrest Gustavo Riviera-Martinez, then head of the Arellano-Felix cartel.[114] Similar examples of Mexican-DEA cooperation include Project Reckoning and Operation Xcellerator, which targeted the Gul cartel and the Sinaloa cartel respectively.[115] At the same time, a new maritime agreement streamlined US Coast Guard searches of Mexican-flagged vessels in international waters and facilitated the maritime seizure of over twenty metric tons of cocaine in 2008.[116]

The Periphery as a Security Buffer Zone

In addition to cooperative bilateral efforts, Canadian and Mexican authorities also construct US power by interdicting domestic drug traffic before it reaches the US border. By intercepting potential supplies to the US market, Canada and Mexico limit the impact of narcotics on US society.

In 2006 Canadian authorities broke up a Quebec- and New Brunswick-based-drug ring smuggling MDMA, methamphetamine, and marijuana into Maine for markets in Boston, New York, and Philadelphia, arrested eleven Canadians, and seized over 100,000 pills.[117] That year, Operation Frozen Timber, jointly coordinated by the ICE and RCMP, dismantled a major drug-smuggling operation that used public lands in British Columbia as an exchange point for marijuana heading south and cocaine shuttling back north via helicopter. The investigation seized 3,640 kilograms of marijuana, 365 kilograms of cocaine, three aircraft, and $1.5 million, leading to the arrest of over forty-five people in Canada and the United States.[118] Similarly, in June 2008, Canadian authorities busted a massive MDMA laboratory and seized materials capable of producing more than a million Ecstasy tablets.[119]

With the Mérida Initiative's resources and Calderón's increased resolve to destroy the domestic drug cartels, Mexico seemed to make strides in intercepting narcotics flows, arresting traffickers, including several cartel leaders,[120] and seizing caches of cocaine, marijuana, opium gum, heroin, methamphetamine, and illegal firearms. Also in 2008, authorities destroyed nineteen drug-processing laboratories, including five methamphetamine super-labs, and the Mexican military reduced the area under cannabis cultivation by eradicating some 15,756 hectares.[121]

The ultimate goal of all these initiatives is to limit the supply of drugs to the American market, and there are indications that Mexico's new-found vigour has supported US power in this way. Beginning in 2007, US authorities noted a significant decline in the availability of cocaine in certain key US markets. By August 2007, sustained cocaine shortages were reported in thirty-eight large and mid-size drug markets, causing the average price per gram for cocaine to increase 21 per cent in the first half of 2007. Multiple factors account for this fluctuation, including a series of abnormally large cocaine seizures in 2007, including one of 23.6 metric tons that was the largest recorded to that point.[122] Other factors included the Calderón government's increased pressure on Mexican drug-trafficking organizations, inter-cartel violence, coca eradication, and the anti-terrorist border-security measures already analysed in chapter 5.[123]

A much more pessimistic picture of these efforts can also be painted. The premise of the Mexican government's military strategy and the Mérida Initiative is that targeting the heads of drug cartels will cause their organizations to collapse and their operations to crumble. When the same strategy was applied during the 1990s against the Cali and Medellín cartels in Colombia, however, it failed to reduce drug criminality and flows of some drugs continued to increase. While the Cali and Medellín were disrupted by the policy, these large hierarchical structures dominating the drug trade were replaced by over three hundred smaller groups organized in a loose, cell-like network that could readily evade the more rigidly bureaucratic structures of state enforcement efforts.[124] The likelihood is that the narcotics industry will become decentralized, not eliminated, forcing Mexican and American officials to contend with dozens of more flexible organizations.[125]

This adaptive potential of drug-trafficking organizations is constantly demonstrated by the creative means they have used to elude increased interdiction efforts at the border. The cartels have channelled some of their immense profits into building remote-controlled submersible vehicles to transport multi-ton shipments of drugs to the United States through the Pacific Ocean.[126] Traffickers have also developed their use of cellphone and satellite-communications technology, re-routing traffic to evade enforcement attempts in real time.[127] Between 2000 and 2006, US border officials discovered forty-five tunnels – which became progressively longer and deeper – under the two borders, many used primarily for the drug trade.[128]

Optimists maintain that escalating violence represents the desperate death throes of a declining Mexican drug-export trade, fuelled by frustration at the increased difficulties associated with cross-border trafficking.[129] President Calderón's supporters argue that he has traced a brave path for the government and that his 'Let's Clean Up Mexico' (Limpiemos México) strategy is not mere rhetoric.[130] The opposite view interprets escalating violence as a symbol of the cartels' success in wresting control over substantial areas of Mexico from the government.

Similar debate surrounds Calderón's larger efforts to crack down on the drug trade within Mexico, with some already labelling the strategy a failure given continued corruption in the armed forces and police at all levels up to the leadership of the Procuraduría General de la República (Ministry of the Interior) and the Secretaría de Seguridad Publica (Ministry of Public Safety).[131] Moreover, the cartels' sophisticated technology and armaments – night-vision goggles, electronic interception, encrypted communications, anti-tank missiles, heavy machine guns, 50-calibre rifles, and the latest-model grenade launchers – often allow them to overwhelm the Mexican army and police when under attack.[132]

The use of extreme force by both the cartels and the army in Mexican cities produces victims among the local population, business people, and visitors alike.[133] Worse, as soon as the military decamp, the cartels take over again.[134] Vicente Fox's first foreign minister, the political scientist Jorge Castañeda, believes that the war has already been lost; as a result, the Mexican government has pivoted and pinned blame for its slow progress on US drug demand and the smuggling of weapons into Mexico from the United States.[135]

The Periphery as an Architect of Continental Drug Policy

While the Mexican government considers drug trafficking to be the principal threat to Mexican national security, it insists that it will not deviate from its tough approach,[136] but opinion leaders in Mexican society constantly advocate various degrees of decriminalization, given the failure of prohibition and a military approach to resolve the hemisphere's narcotics crisis. While Mexico plays a role in developing continental drug policy, Canada temporarily softened its support for the US war on drugs by developing some alternative approaches to managing drug issues.

Many American proponents of a softer approach to drugs looked to Canada's reputedly more humane approach and applauded change in Canadian drug policy as a first step towards their domestic goals.[137] At least on paper, Canada's drug strategy attempts to balance the punitive thrusts of the US approach with the 'harm reduction' principle of mitigating the damage that alcohol and other drugs cause to individuals, families, and communities even if it means relaxing strict prohibition.[138] Harm reduction is posited as a 'realistic, pragmatic, and humane approach ... as opposed to attempting solely to reduce the use of drugs.'[139] It promotes *safe* drug use as a goal that is more realistic than *zero* drug use. Insofar as Canada adopts this principle in its drug strategy, it challenges the US approach by framing drugs as an issue of public health rather than of war on crime.[140] Canada's harm-reduction approach also challenges the United States' supply-side focus by emphasizing the reduction of demand. Drug expert Charles Levinthal explains: 'Do we want total victory and complete annihilation of the enemy? Or do we want some kind of negotiated settlement, some type of compromise that gives us some semblance of peace and tranquility? If it is the former, then we require a total elimination, often expressed as "zero tolerance" of abusive drug-taking behavior, in America. If it is the latter, then we require a good deal less. We desire, in that case, only a reduction of the harmful consequences of abusive drug-taking behavior, knowing fully well that a total elimination is unrealistic.'[141]

Of the Cdn$210 million spent on the first phase of Canada's 1987–92

Drug Strategy, 77 per cent was allocated to demand-reduction measures including education, prevention, treatment, and rehabilitation to balance the previous supply-side approach that emphasized enforcement, interdiction, and control.[142] However, by 2001, Canada's approach had fallen back in line with the US war-on-drugs approach, with 85–95 per cent of its spending focusing on supply-side measures.[143]

The 'Insite' safe-injection site in Vancouver, British Columbia, provides the most striking example of how Canada's harm reduction acts as a US irritant. The project began in September 2003 as a drug-abuse management and treatment pilot project authorized by Health Canada and funded by British Columbia's Ministry of Health. It allows drug users to inject their own drugs using clean needles in a safe environment under the supervision of clinical staff and accompanied by registered nurses and addiction counsellors. US Drug Czar John Walters called the project 'state-sponsored suicide.'[144] A similar harm-reduction initiative, the North American Opiate Medication Initiative (NAOMI), is a Health Canada-approved research project studying the effects of treating heroin addicts with prescribed heroin.[145] White House ONDCP analyst David Murray called the study a mistake, saying 'there's a large moral-hazard question here about a government undertaking to become the official dispenser of addictive substances.'[146]

Canada has also sometimes demonstrated a significant tolerance of marijuana use that contrasts with the American war's exclusively prohibitionist approach. In 2001 Health Canada added the Marijuana Medical Access Regulations to the Controlled Drugs and Substances Act. This initiative permits medically approved applicants to access marijuana for medical purposes – particularly pain relief – allowing them to purchase their supply from a Heath Canada-contracted company, grow it themselves, or have someone grow it for them.[147] As of June 2009, 4,029 Canadians had legal access to medicinal marijuana, 2,841 were authorized to cultivate it, and the level of applications continued to increase.[148] In 2002 US Republican Congressman Mark Souder, chairman of the House Government Reform Subcommittee on Criminal Justice, Drug Policy, and Human Resources, warned that such a policy could result in border crackdowns and was a sign that the Canadian government was pursuing a dangerously lax drug policy.[149]

In a similar example of clashing 'pot cultures,' when the government of Prime Minister Jean Chrétien moved towards decriminalizing the possession of small amounts of marijuana for personal use, the move provoked considerable discontent among US officials. Walters again reacted, opining that liberalized marijuana laws would boost drug use and bring more of the drug into the United States.[150] Paul Cellucci, the US ambassador to Canada, warned that Canadian travellers might expect more delays at the Canadian-US border as a result of decriminalization.[151] Colonel Robert Maginnis, a drug-policy adviser to President George W. Bush, said that the policy would create some 'perception problems ... with regard to whether Canada is engaged in fighting drug use rather than contributing to drug use.'[152] Such negative reactions suggest that Canada's more liberal approach to marijuana was seen as a constraint in US governing circles. The legislation was subsequently thrown out in 2006 by the Conservative government, which has denounced the safe-injection program and toughened its approach to criminality.[153]

While the continental periphery is central to US counter-narcotics efforts, the relationship is not entirely straightforward. Though they are key suppliers to the US market, Canada and Mexico do not *cause* America's drug problem. If both Canada and Mexico sank into the sea, ceasing to be drug producers and suppliers, new networks would quickly spring up to supply the insatiable US demand.[154]

American policy makers expect Canada and Mexico to reduce the US drug problem by adopting their war on drugs, but forty years of the battle have only seen the drug trade escalate. Many experts consider the prohibitionist, supply-side, and enforcement-centred approach to have failed. The highly adaptive nature of the global drug industry ensures that the governments' tactical successes only lead to more imaginative responses which enable the narcotics trade to continue to prosper. This situation renders Canada and Mexico central to the efficacy of the American approach while simultaneously limiting their prospects for success. Paradoxically, greater enforcement vigour could prompt illegal society to adopt more sophisticated organizational forms and intensified violence, compounding narcotics' devastating impact on American societal security. Canada and Mexico may be endorsing a self-defeating US anti-narcotics strategy, the implication of which is that supporting US drug-control efforts may ultimately lead the periphery to constrain, not construct, US societal power.

Conclusion

The governments of both Mexico and Canada have taken concerted actions to support the United States' anti-drugs campaigns by cracking down on the production and flow of drugs from their territories into the United States. Their endorsement of the US war on drugs increases its efficiency through multiple types of direct bilateral cooperation that give continental depth to the US attack on an inherently transnational problem. These efforts to construct US societal power are, however, ultimately stopgap measures that are effectively eluded by drug traffickers operating in the criminal societies of both countries. Clandestine organizations in Mexico and Canada, enabled by their unique geographical location and by the associated impact of drug violence and organized criminality, undermine the American social order through their supply of drugs.

This three-decades-long pattern of the North American periphery's both constraining US societal security through the supply of narcotics and reconstructing it through the two governments' cooperation with US anti-drug forces has been significantly altered by the new war between the Mexican government and the cartels. Violence in the northern Mexican states has reached the point that it has been officially recognized as a new security threat for the United States. On a state visit to Mexico in April 2009, President Obama made a momentous admission when he acknowledged, 'I will not pretend that this is Mexico's responsibility alone. The demand for these drugs in the United States is what's helping keep these cartels in business.'[155] Beyond recognizing the United States' responsibility for generating its own narcotics problem, he went on to affirm his government's intention to support Mexico actively in its struggle: 'At a time when the Mexican government has so courageously taken on the drug cartels that have plagued both sides of the border, it is absolutely critical that the United States joins as a full partner in dealing with this issue.'[156] Secretary of State Hillary Clinton also publicly admitted that US sales of high-tech small arms to the cartels was a big contributing factor to drug violence in Mexico.[157] This still unfinished chapter in the history of US drug insecurity will centre on how well the United States succeeds in bolstering the Mexican government's capacity to support Washington in its weary war.

Weary or not, Mexico and Canada must also pursue their own foreign policies. Although their diplomacy with countries other than the United States might appear disconnected from their dealings with Uncle Sam, their goals overseas necessarily intersect with Washington's, constraining US power in some cases and, as we will see in the next chapter, constructing it in others.

PART THREE

Constructing and Constraining the
United States' Global Power

So far we have related the North American periphery's importance for US power to its geographical contiguity. Being physically located on the United States' northern and southern borders made Canada's and Mexico's economic and security contributions far greater than their GNP or military size would alone predict. If we shift our focus from the continental stage to the global arena, however, we find Mexico and Canada interacting with the United States less as unique neighbours than as two mid-sized members of the international community. Whether they affect the United States' structural power in world affairs or the achievement of its foreign-policy goals depends greatly on the issue and on each of the three states' shifting views of the challenges at stake and the interests it is pursuing. As a result, the periphery's role vis-à-vis US power within the multilateral arena has been contradictory, ranging along a spectrum from outright construction through negligible importance to overt constraint.

Successfully taking a global initiative can depend on putting together a bloc of like-minded states to create sufficient bargaining momentum. Canada and Mexico have often been necessary members of the United States' negotiating group, thus increasing the viability of its international initiatives. At other times, the two countries have been stubborn opponents, frustrating the United States' ability to achieve its objectives abroad and thus increasing its costs of pursuing its goals. In these processes, the periphery can provide institutional and moral support that can boost US foreign policy's effectiveness and legitimacy. However, this role should not be overstated. In the majority of international issues, the positions taken and roles played by these two middle powers are of marginal significance to Washington, whose attention generally focuses on mobilizing coalitions with larger powers.

Canada's and Mexico's multilateral contributions to the world order have had both intended and unintended effects on the United States' structural power to build global governance regimes. The continental periphery played the role of pivotal ally when collaborating to push the GATT's Uruguay Round towards its successful creation of the World Trade Organization. Later, when they negotiated their own trade and investment agreements with other states, the United States' two neighbours buttressed its global power only nominally by spreading and deepening investment and economic norms in which Washington had seemed to lose interest, as we will show in chapter 7.

While far from typical, there have been occasions when the two countries made concerted efforts to reduce the United States' room for unilateral manoeuvre by creating new multilateral instruments. A particularly striking example was their role in the creation and establishment of the International Criminal Court, which we examine in chapter 8. In this case, the periphery at-

tempted to blunt the power of its neighbouring colossus by forging governance norms that could constrain its military abroad. Canada was a major player in the ICC's negotiating phase. Mexico then played a significant role in resisting the Bush administration's efforts to defang the new institution when it negotiated immunity agreements with weaker countries that depended on US aid.

Our last case is Cuba, where Canada and Mexico directly thwarted US foreign policy, as we explain in chapter 9. While the PRI was in power, Mexico took the lead in resisting US intervention in Castro's Cuba, while Canada provided important economic support. As a result, in the crucial first years after the Soviet Union's collapse, the continental periphery was instrumental in frustrating the US embargo's objective of bringing down the hemisphere's only Marxist holdout.

While we do not wish to overstate the foreign-policy importance to the United States of its continental periphery, this concluding section of our study complements the book's previous two parts by illustrating that, from time to time, Washington has to pay serious attention to its neighbours' global positions.

7 Strengthening US International Economic Power[1]

In an imperfect world, we have something which will enable us to go forward together and to create a future that is worthy of our children and grandchildren, worthy of the legacy of America, and consistent with what we did at the end of World War II. We have to do that again. We have to create a new world economy. And if we don't do it, we cannot then point the finger at Europe and Japan or anybody else and say, why don't you pass the GATT agreement? Why don't you help to create a world economy? If we walk away from it, we have no right to say to other countries in the world, you're not fulfilling your world leadership, you're not being fair with us.

> – President Bill Clinton at the signing of the
> NAFTA side agreements, September 14, 1993[2]

American statesmen have always understood that their economy's strength is a function of its international reach. At first they endeavoured to increase the United States' economic size territorially, applying their diplomatic skills and military might to move the original Thirteen Colonies' boundaries southward to Florida and westward from the Atlantic. Having reached their political limits to both the north and the south by the end of the nineteenth century, Americans came too late to the Age of Empire to do more than seize arthritic Spain's few remaining possessions in the Caribbean and the Pacific.

The visible hand of trade and the less visible hand of investment then became the handmaidens of the United States' economic growth in the early twentieth century as it strove to expand its reach inside foreign economies by seeking – sometimes with the barrels of its Navy's cannons or its Marines' guns – an 'open door' for US enterprise. As we have already seen in chapter 1, the United States' material power was significantly constructed through the partial extension of its economic perimeter, opening large parts of the continental periphery's markets to its exporters and investors. This chapter explores the extent to which Canada and Mexico sometimes directly, sometimes indirectly, and often even inadvertently constructed US enterprise's overseas reach by supporting American efforts to mould the norms of global economic governance.

Emerging from the Second World War as the overwhelmingly dominant force in a capitalist world united by a common fear of the Soviet bloc, Washington had little trouble creating a US-friendly global economic regime. Based on the then prevailing Keynesian policy paradigm, which prescribed moderately interventionist management by governments, the United States led the process of designing an institutional architecture that would promote the capitalist economies' development while avoiding a reprise of the Great Depression. This mid-century version of global governance allowed it considerable leeway for protecting US agriculture and industry against more competitive imports while still nurturing the growth of trade and foreign investment – particularly that of its transnational corporations, which rapidly expanded their mining, manufacturing, and marketing operations abroad.

In the light of Europe's and Japan's wartime devastation, the newly industrialized Canada found itself with considerable military clout and political legitimacy. Exploiting these assets, it first inserted itself alongside the United States and Great Britain in the intense negotiations that produced the International Monetary Fund (1944), the World Bank (1944), and the General Agreement on Tariffs and Trade (1947) – the principal institutions that established a liberal economic order for the non-socialist world. Ottawa then proceeded to participate actively in the myriad new transnational organizations during what became known as the Golden Age of its short diplomatic history.

Throughout most of the Cold War, when Canada, responding to its public's pro-Western consensus, was an enthusiastic fellow traveller supporting the United States' liberal-internationalist leadership, Mexico, responding to internal pressures from the left, worked with other Latin American governments to obstruct US influence in the hemisphere.[3] At the same time as Canada was asserting its new-found international role after the Second World War by working alongside the United States and Britain, and only later partially recoiling from the United States' intimate economic embrace, Mexico played a mainly offsetting role by opposing these same powers' intrusion within Latin America.

Adopting the thesis of the charismatic Argentine economist Raúl Prebisch, who saw Latin America's underdevelopment as a trap perpetuated by its dependency on the industrialized economies' TNCs and raw-materials markets, Mexico led the resistance to the liberal economic values that it believed favoured US interests at the expense of such struggling Latin American economies as its own. Internally, its import-substitution industrialization strategy aimed to reduce Mexico's dependency on the industrialized West by constraining imports and foreign investment and by promoting its own production of the goods and services it would otherwise have imported. Instead of joining the GATT, it supported efforts to set up an alternative international economic order through the United Nations Conference on Trade and Development (UNCTAD), a body that championed the developing world's need to loosen the United States' control over global economic governance.[4] Recognizing that they would have difficulty putting pressure on the superpower through the traditional avenues of dialogue and advocacy, Mexican representatives helped found the Group of 77 (G-77) in 1964 to offset the industrialized nations' – in particular the United States' – capacity to define global economic and political norms. Mexico viewed the G-77, over which it presided in 1973–4 and again in 1983–4, as essential for achieving a more equitable international governance responsive to the developing countries' needs.[5] As late as 1983, it was insisting on reforming an international economic 'system which, in its unbalanced state, causes serious problems in developing countries.'[6]

Redesigning International Economic Governance under Neoconservatism

As the global balance of forces, industrial technologies, and resulting political-economic conflicts evolved in the 1970s, the post-war Keynesian consensus in the United States came under attack. With American pre-eminence in the world being challenged by Europe's and Japan's resurgence, Keynes's theories were questioned by new, conservatively inclined economists who trenchantly advocated the deregulation both of domestic government and of international governance.

As advances in technology were transforming existing industries and creating new ones, Washington's policy wonks came to believe that American knowledge-based industries could resuscitate and then sustain US power into the twenty-first century, with biotechnology, information processing, entertainment, and other service sectors playing the same, economy-boosting role that mass-production techniques had taken on in the twentieth. The catch was that, however huge it may have been, the United States' domestic market was not big enough to bring this dream to fruition. American TNCs could reap the full benefits of their high-tech superiority only if they could penetrate new markets overseas. Yet foreign economies with big public sectors and limited intellectual-property-rights regimes still generally discriminated against those burgeoning US industries.

Angered by well-publicized media reports of foreign sectors closed to US enterprise or overseas industries pirating US know-how, Congress instructed the administration to retaliate against governments suspected of unfairly subsidizing their exports, appropriating US technology, or failing to provide better access for US corporations to their protected sectors. By the early 1980s, US trade policy reflected a tension between lobbies championing the interests of competitive industries that demanded greater access to foreign markets and those expressing the protectionist need to defend uncompetitive American economic sectors.[7] This divide was refracted through struggles between a generally pro-trade administration and a largely protectionist US Congress, which won concessions protecting powerful domestic constituencies in return for approving the United States Trade Representative's further efforts to achieve global economic liberalization.[8]

As long as Cold War tensions remained acute, it would have been counterproductive for the United States to exert excessive market-opening pressure on governments whose military support it needed to sustain its containment strategy against the Soviet bloc. When the weakened USSR collapsed, Washington leveraged its new global dominance into a more muscular approach to its foreign economic policy. Its preferred route was to rewrite the rules of international trade during the GATT's Uruguay Round of negotiations which started in 1986. The USTR had both a strategy with an accompanying clear agenda and a game plan. The strategic goal was to achieve a market-oriented regulatory framework that would impose strict disciplines on other states' parochial regulations. The agenda was to require that trade partners wanting to benefit from access to the US market implement the rules that American TNCs wanted in order 'level the playing field' for their operations abroad: opening foreign markets to US service industries and introducing a new intellectual-property-rights regime for data-management, media, genetic-engineering, and pharmaceutical industries.[9]

The game plan involved playing simultaneously on the multilateral, bilateral, and unilateral levels. Achieving a multilateral consensus on rules that would apply to all capitalist countries proved difficult, given the resistance to US demands coming from Japan in East Asia, from India in South Asia, from Brazil in South America, from Mexico and the G-77's southern bloc, and, most seriously, from the European Union (EU) – powers that feared that their prospects of building up domestic economic sectors would be jeopardized by rules entrenching the first-entry advantages of American TNCs.[10] Since unilateral coercive tactics had proven counterproductive and since its multilateral efforts were blocked, Washington's fallback tactic was to negotiate with more compliant partners a series of separate bilateral agreements that would allow it two options for constructing a trade system to its liking.[11] A process of sequential liberalization could allow the United States to build its own trade bloc piece by piece in the face of continued resistance to its demands from the rest of the world, particularly the EU.[12] Alternatively, a network of bilateral agreements could establish precedents to be deployed as the basis for future multilateral negotiations should its interlocutors prove willing to come to the table.[13] With luck, the first scenario would create pressures that would trigger the second.

Enter Canada and Mexico once more.

Muscularly Reconstituting US Economic Power up to 1995

Canada and Mexico did much more to build US power than facilitate the extension of the United States' economic perimeter over the North American continent, as we showed in chapter 1. Because the international community took it for granted that Canada was already firmly attached to the US economy, Ottawa's willing negotiation of the 1989 Canada-United States Free Trade Agreement did not make much impression on the United States' other trading partners. Far more effective was Mexico's participation in expanding CUFTA to create the 1994 North American Free Trade Agreement, an event that triggered the consummation of Washington's global economic strategy, then stalled in the GATT's Uruguay Round.

Geopolitically, the Uruguay Round's major interlocutors were enjoying a post-Cold War peace dividend which allowed them to stand up against Washington's pressures without worrying about giving Moscow an opening. Besides, Washington's former Cold War allies understood perfectly well that its proposed new rules would reinforce its economic dominance through empowering American TNCs to make further incursions in their own markets. But, with NAFTA in hand, the US government signalled to its competitors that, if the GATT negotiations failed, it now had a credible fallback position that would present them with an even less attractive alternative – exclusion from a 'Fortress North America' where the United States would compete, now strengthened by its incorporation of the Mexican and Canadian economies within its economic perimeter, against a Fortress Europe or a Fortress Asia.[14] It was no coincidence that, just one year after NAFTA, the European Union came back to the bargaining table, bringing Japan with it, and the World Trade Organization came into effect: Washington's incremental trade bilateralism had proven a winning game in its strategic plan to reconstitutionalize the global economic system along the lines its TNCs had been seeking.[15]

Not only did NAFTA serve as a psychic stick with Europe; Mexico's adhesion to this comprehensive agreement provided a psychic carrot for the developing world. The very idea that a large but poor developing country could abandon its industrial-protection system and aspire to compete inside the world's most advanced capitalist economy helped assuage the qualms of such countries in the global South as Brazil and India which feared, among other things, that caving in to the US insistence on powerful rights for foreign corporations would jeopardize their chances of successfully projecting their own industries onto the international stage.[16]

Dangling before governments in the South, which had been resisting the neoconservative structural adjustments being imposed by the IMF and the World Bank, the Shangri-La of free access to the US market, NAFTA was a 'defining event in developing countries' attempts to engage in [the new phase of economic global governance] with a view to securing greater access to key markets and consolidating recent domestic reforms.'[17] But NAFTA did more than herald the end of host governments' abilities to squeeze greater economic and social benefits from foreign TNCs. As far as the contents of the new international economic constitution were concerned, NAFTA also helped blaze the trail to the WTO by introducing policy domains previously unheard of in trade agreements. Powerful investment rights for TNCs had barely been enshrined in investment treaties, let alone trade agreements. Services – whether offered by lawyers and architects, or banks and insurance companies, or tourism and education entrepreneurs – had nothing directly to do with goods being shipped across borders.

Ottawa's willingness to include provisions on services in CUFTA had already proved the critical catalyst for putting services on the agenda for the Uruguay Round.[18] CUFTA's services chapter, which was later refined in NAFTA, ended up in the WTO as its General Agreement on Trade in Services. NAFTA also directly helped the United States achieve its goal of getting powerful intellectual property rights (IPR) for pharmaceutical, bio-technology, and information-processing industries written into an international economic treaty. The USTR had taken the IPR clauses from the blocked Uruguay Round's Dunkel Draft (which expressed the US bargaining position) and required Canada and Mexico to accept them as NAFTA's Chapter 17. Washington turned this precedent to effect in the Uruguay Round's final deal: the text of the WTO's agreement on Trade-Related Aspects of Intellectual Property Rights (TRIPs) was almost word for word the same as NAFTA's, and Canada's soft-power–power legitimacy as a member of the so-called Quad helped muscle the deal through.[19] However, NAFTA's controversial Chapter 11, with its strong provisions enabling TNCs to sue states, failed to make its way into the WTO's agreement on Trade-Related Investment Measures (TRIMS).

The North American periphery was not passive during these long years of global constitution writing. Mexico contributed to writing the new global economic rule book by taking an active role in the GATT negotiations. For example, the Mexican secretary of the economy, Jaime Serra Puche, enthusiastically chaired the Uruguay Round's committee on services. For its part, Canada applied what it had learned from its disappointing experience with CUFTA's dispute-settlement process whose binational panels' judgments were inevitably denounced as biased by the losing side because the panels had been arbitrated by nationals from the two contending parties, that is, by American and Canadian experts whose neutrality could be questioned. Further, the United States government tended not to comply with dispute rulings that went against it in cases where powerful lobbies could mobilize political resistance by waving the flag of US sovereignty. Concerned with these bilateral experiences, Ottawa proposed a much more autonomous and muscular dispute-settlement body (DSB) – a proposal that ultimately won the EU's and the United States' support despite the fact that the WTO's proposed DSB would constrain their future trade behaviour.[20] An effective dispute-settlement institution that could even discipline the United States was an essential element in brokering the all-or-nothing 'single undertaking' which every national government had to sign to become a member of the new global-trade regime, a regime that, in universalizing most of Washington's desired norms, marked – at least in the short term – the culmination of the United States' effort to reconstruct the world's economic system in its image.

This long episode requires us to revise our causal chain. The Canadian and Mexican governments as agents did not simply construct US power as an object. Having had their own ideas reconstructed by a made-in-the-USA policy paradigm, they worked within this ideational hegemony to support their leader in achieving goals that they had adopted as their own. Thus, by overcoming considerable public opposition in each country, the North American periphery's political and economic elites had decisively boosted Washington's drive to rewrite the world's economic rule book.

Weakly Reconstituting US Economic Power after 1995

Although the World Trade Organization appeared to have constitutionalized the United States' trade-policy objectives, it was far from popular with the American public, whose opposition to multilateralism remained stubborn enough that Congress required, as a condition in its implementation legislation, that US membership in the WTO be revisited every five years. Indeed, the United States' initial experience with the new trade order was mixed. While Washington won some important trade disputes at the WTO, those it lost aroused strong negative feelings. American hostility to the organization grew as it came to be dominated by weaker states whose veto power in an institution operating on the principle of consensus became manifest in the ensuing paralysis of the next stage of negotiations, the Doha Round. The US economy's greater openness to imports flooding in from abroad, along with popular resentment about American jobs being lost as US firms outsourced their operations overseas, shattered the previous consensus in Washington about the merits of continual trade liberalization.[21] Although the Clinton administration launched negotiations for a Free Trade Area of the Americas (FTAA) in 1994, it did not invest much political capital in pursuing this goal. Nor did it put as much energy into incorporating other countries into NAFTA as Canada and Mexico had expected. Nevertheless, following the FTAA's collapse, President George W. Bush did secure Trade Promotion Authority to launch new bilateral negotiations of second-generation trade agreements with the intention of creating a network of separate agreements on a hub-and-spoke basis.[22] All told, from signing NAFTA till the end of 2010, the United States negotiated twelve such agreements.[23]

Frustrated that Washington was not promoting a coordinated approach to expanding NAFTA to include other countries, Ottawa and Mexico City pursued their own trade and investment agreements with third parties.[24] In this post-NAFTA period, Canada negotiated thirteen agreements and Mexico fourteen.[25] Canada innovated in content, while Mexico led the way in Latin America where it had more sway as a recent convert from protectionism to liberalism. We will proceed to assess to what extent these two countries' own negotiations supported US power during a period when, following its triumph with the WTO in 1995, the United States lost its sense of economic direction.

Mexico

By 1994, Mexico had effected a 180-degree turn in its position in the Western hemisphere. From having been the sworn enemy of the so-called Washington Consensus – shorthand for the new regime of free trade, deregulation, and fiscal and monetary restraint – it had entered a comprehensive trade and investment regime designed to accelerate its economic integration with the United States. Because Mexico had so overtly resisted US trade policy, its eventual embrace of neoconservative norms was carefully noted in some Latin American governments which were already having to experiment with the market-opening conditions imposed when receiving loans from the IMF or the World Bank. At the same time, they had to decide whether to join in the project to create an FTAA which would have had every country in Central America, South America, and the Caribbean – Cuba, of course, excepted – adopt powerful NAFTA-style rules.

Before NAFTA, Mexico's trade diplomacy had been conducted under the loose framework of the Asociación Latinoamericana de Integración (ALADI, Latin American Integration Association), which deals only with trade in goods within the continent, has very general criteria for rules of origin, and has no provisions on investment, services, intellectual-property rights, or dispute settlement. When President Salinas de Gortari started negotiating with Washington, he stopped negotiating other agreements in order to concentrate on his main game. Later, when the NAFTA deal was done, Mexico did not just present the spectacle of a new trade paradigm for other developing countries to ponder. It actively propagated this model by negotiating its own economic-liber-alization agreements with other trading partners, particularly those in Latin America.

In the decade and a half after 1995, when Mexico made concerted efforts to sign further trade and investment treaties, it insisted, on a take-it-or-leave-it basis, that NAFTA be the new negotiating template. A significant interlocutor in Latin America, Chile was enraged by Mex-ico's adoption of such an unyielding position. At first, Santiago wanted to bargain only about trade preferences, but when it saw how foreign investment was pouring into Mexico and when it found that Canada was also using NAFTA as the model for its own bilateral trade diplo-macy, it relented.

Despite Mexico being an insignificant foreign investor (coming thirti-eth as a source of direct investment for the Chilean economy) and only a minor export market, the Chilean government found a rationale for devoting bureaucratic resources to this new round of bilateral talks. By negotiating a new agreement with Mexico – and another with Canada (which, as we shall see, was eager to bargain) – Chilean officials reck-oned that they would learn what neoconservative legal clauses meant for a developing Latin economy and which of its own domestic regula-tions had to be amended to conform with them. Once they had mas-tered the subtleties of this latest-generation trade agenda, they felt they would be better prepared for launching their own negotiations with Washington, which they originally hoped would lead to Chile's entry into NAFTA.[26]

By 1999, Chile had signed a fully fledged, new-style FTA with Mexi-co, whose economic diplomacy thus served US power by helping bring another Latin American country into the new trade order and by pre-paring that country to work out the agreement with Washington that was ultimately sealed in 2000. This bilateral process had a multiplier effect, because Chile went on to negotiate and sign its own trade and investment agreements with other countries, including the European Union.

Mexico's post-NAFTA economic treaties in Latin America differed significantly from the ALADI framework. Rules-of-origin requirements were more demanding and regulations governing trade in goods more elaborate. Investment and services were now covered by strong rules and commitments.[27]

Between 1992 and 2004, Mexico signed six free-trade agreements with nine Latin American countries. It copied and pasted NAFTA clauses into the G-3 agreement with Colombia and Venezuela (1995), as well as into its agreements with Costa Rica (1995), Bolivia (1995), Nicaragua (1995), the Northern Triangle of El Salvador, Honduras, and Guatemala (2001), and Uruguay (2004).[28] It also worked on a new rules-of-origin norm in which origin could accumulate among Hispanic Pacific Rim countries exporting overseas.

Mexico's international economic diplomacy was not restricted to its own hemisphere. It negotiated an agreement with Japan that closely followed the NAFTA template.[29] With the European Union it engaged in a long process in which Brussels' negotiators, who were strongly committed both to political democratization and to trade liberalization, required Mexico to make commitments to improving human rights domestically while demanding the same treatment by Mexico for European goods and services as the United States had obtained in NAFTA. In this regard, Mexico's trade agreement with the EU caused Washington to lose ground since it had to share with EU companies its privileged access to the Mexican market.

The glitch from Mexico's point of view was investment over which the European Commission in Brussels did not have jurisdiction. As a result, Mexico had to negotiate separate investment agreements with the major European states. Since their leaders were still resisting neo-conservative investment liberalization and would not subscribe to the NAFTA model in which strong rights for foreign corporations trumped their own governments' powers, the resulting bilateral investment agreements were too weak to spread US investment norms across the Atlantic.[30]

Mexico did sign bilateral investment promotion and protection agreements with nineteen other governments outside the EU which accepted the investor-state dispute-settlement-mechanism model in NAFTA's Chapter 11. In these agreements Mexico contributed to broadening the scope of TNCs' powerful rights and their strengthened enforcement. With the addition of Romania and Bulgaria to the European Union, Mexico had signed twelve FTAs with forty-three countries by 2010 – thus confirming its considerable role in propagating the neo-conservative standard and encouraging its counterparts to deregulate their economic policies.[31]

These accomplishments did not necessarily serve Mexico's immediate interests in North America. Having little incentive to give up what it considered to be its privileged access to the US market, Mexico was only a token FTAA supporter since a comprehensive Western hemispheric trade agreement would have brought its preferential status in the United States' economy to an end.[32] The only option was for Mexico to defend its interests by being present at the negotiating table.

It would be far too much to claim that Mexico helped establish the preconditions for a US-style multilateral free-trade system in the Western hemisphere. The government of Brazil's defence of its own hegemonic position within the Mercosur group of South American countries and its antipathy to such NAFTA norms as national treatment that would prevent it using its powers to foster its own corporations' development presented a more serious obstacle to the hemispheric projection of US rules. President Lula da Silva's insistence that Washington put its subsidies for agriculture on the FTAA's negotiating table effectively sidelined the accord that Washington had considered its next objective after the WTO.[33]

In the face of Brazil's resistance, Washington abandoned its FTAA project and reverted once more to a bilateral strategy. The USTR launched a 'competitive negotiations strategy' in 2002 after obtaining Trade Promotion Authority[34] which granted the administration fast-track negotiating powers so that it could sign bilateral FTAs with individual Latin American countries and gradually make the region more receptive to US economic norms.

As for contributing to the strengthening of US economic power abroad by negotiating its own bilateral agreements with third parties, Mexico's positions were conflicted. It may well have contributed to the process in which other Latin American governments learned the ropes of the neoconservative trade and investment regime. But, as Washington began to negotiate its own bilateral FTAs with Latin American countries, Mexico found itself losing its own privileged status in the US market.[35]

By that point, political resistance to the neoconservative paradigm in the hemisphere was mounting. President Hugo Chávez abrogated Venezuela's agreement with Mexico in 2006, and Bolivia's President Evo Morales soon followed suit, downgrading its bilateral agreement to trade in goods under ALADI. Chávez's constant denunciations of US imperialism were given institutional form in his Alianza Bolivariana para los Pueblos de nuestra América (Bolivariana Alliance for the Peoples of our America), an alternative integration model that aimed to unite the region and help advance sustainable development by maximizing each country's potential to address its most urgent social needs.[36]

Paradoxically if unintentionally, Mexico also helped strengthen resistance to US trade initiatives in the hemisphere since its perceived experience with the neoconservative paradigm seemed to contradict its boosters' originally optimistic claims. At first in 1989, when the US Brady Plan rescheduled the country's debt in exchange for the government's market-opening moves, Mexico was considered to be Latin America's golden child.[37] Yet, although its structural-adjustment program of orthodox fiscal and monetary policy was meant to reduce its fiscal deficit and bring inflation under control,[38] its current account deficit actually jumped from $6 billion in 1989 to more than $20 billion by 1993.[39] Its concurrent overvaluation of the peso triggered a serious 1994–5 financial crisis whose feared 'tequila effect' threatened to spread around the world.

Many Latin American countries that were considering US-style reforms took note of Mexico's actual record with neoconservatism. Successes attributed to NAFTA were big increases in Mexico-US trade and an impressive inflow of foreign direct investment. At the same time, internal disparities grew between those regions that benefited from the deeper continental integration and those that suffered. Extreme poverty increased in agriculturally marginal areas whose subsistence economy was seriously affected by massive imports of US corn. The country's problems with corn production actually dated back to the 1970s, when difficulty meeting domestic demand, particularly for industrial needs, required growing imports, but NAFTA's rapid reduction of the tariff had provoked an increased flood of subsidized US corn which further devastated the campesinos' economy and aggravated their exodus from the pueblos. This spectacle discredited the Washington Consensus in countries with large rural populations and pre-industrial agriculture.[40]

When the United States did negotiate a number of its own agreements – the Central America Free Trade Agreement with Costa-Rica, El-Salvador, Guatemala, Honduras, and Nicaragua plus the Dominican Republic (CAFTA-DR, 2005), Peru (2006), and Panama (2006) – Mexico's controversial experience with NAFTA affected these documents' implementation.[41] Two months after the CAFTA-DR agreement was supposed to take effect on March 1, 2006, only one country had actually joined, while the other five still struggled to bring their laws in line with the new regime. Protests over CAFTA-DR in Guatemala cost two lives. In El Salvador, violent demonstrations against CAFTA in 2006 left five injured.[42] Costa Rica delayed its ratification entirely and made it conditional on a prior national public referendum in which the 'No' camp explicitly used Mexico's unhappy results under NAFTA as part of its case. Mexico's economic free fall following the 2008 global financial crisis – its 2009 GDP decline of 7.5 per cent was the greatest in the whole Western hemisphere[43] – further delegitimized the panacea of economic integration among opponents to liberalization in other countries.

Having lowered its protective barriers without having reformed its economy, Mexico suffered from a trade deficit with most of its partner countries. In the light of its continued difficulty in competing internationally, Mexican business came to oppose opening new commercial fronts until the internal market had strengthened.[44] Although Felipe Calderón's PAN government remained formally committed to trade liberalization and open markets, it gave way to its private sector's opposition and announced it would not negotiate any new agreements. As a result, Mexico's economic ministry switched from negotiating new deals (South Korea) to modifying existing ones.

With its NAFTA partners, Mexico sought to standardize norms for industry and agriculture and rework rules of origin which had become outdated.[45] With Colombia, it revised its agreement to include new products, expand existing quotas, and update the rules of origin because Venezuela's withdrawal from the G-3 agreement meant that its products could no longer be counted as originating in the region.[46] With Japan, the government made top-level efforts to obtain increased preferences for such agricultural products as pork, beef, and orange juice. With Brussels it proposed extending its treaty with the European Union to have it apply to more products. With Britain, Spain, and Germany it negotiated separately to raise the bar on foreign-investment protection from the somewhat vague standard of 'fair and equitable treatment' to the tougher 'minimum standard of treatment' used for NAFTA's investor-state dispute rulings which are not tempered by references to customary international law.[47] With Nicaragua, Costa Rica, Honduras, El Salvador, and Guatemala, it wanted a general Mexico-Central America agreement to enter into force by 2012.[48] The government also pursued unilateral liberalization: by 2013 it will have eliminated tariffs on 6,800 items.

All told, one can see that Mexico made concerted efforts to multilateralize the new economic-governance norms that it had adopted with NAFTA. Although these can be seen to have worked in the same direction that Washington was pursuing under Ronald Reagan, they were certainly not effective in helping the United States reach its goal, announced at the 1994 Miami Summit of the Americas, to extend NAFTA norms throughout the hemisphere.

Canada

While Mexico's economic diplomacy in the hemisphere was energetic but ultimately inconsequential for the United States, Canada's role in supporting Washington's foreign economic strategy after the WTO came into being was smaller, equally indirect, but possibly more helpful. This was not because Ottawa supported the negotiations of a Free Trade Area of the Americas any more enthusiastically than did Mexico: an FTAA would also have eroded the bilateral preferences it had gained in the US market. Like Mexico, Canada propagated such NAFTA norms as its investment rules. But unlike Mexico, Canada was the home of many companies that were major direct investors in mining operations throughout Latin America, as were US TNCs. As a result, Canadian successes in extracting greater privileges for its TNCs were likely soon to be extended to US companies and so helped construct US economic power.

Canada's economic diplomacy slowed down considerably after NAFTA. As had Mexico's efforts, Canada's had a somewhat contradictory significance for US power, primarily constructing and negligibly constraining it. In the first respect, by using NAFTA as its model in negotiating trade and investment agreements with other countries, Canada's Department of Foreign Affairs and International Trade (DFAIT) was not just promoting better conditions for its own transnational corporations' investments abroad. It was also strengthening the international economic regime which the United States had been instrumental in shaping to promote its own TNCs.

Chile considered Ottawa a more important interlocutor than Mexico City, because it was hoping to accede to NAFTA. Canada also offered an attractive export market and, after the United States and Spain, was the country's third-largest foreign source of investment capital, particularly for its mining industry. The 1997 Canada-Chile Free Trade Agreement (CCFTA) was Santiago's first new-generation trade and investment agreement. Because Canada also used NAFTA as its negotiating template, the CCFTA closely followed the North American model in its provisions concerning rules of origin, dispute settlement, services, and investment. While Canada was pursuing such interests of its own as achieving greater security for its mining companies operating in Chile, it was also pushing out the perimeter within which the norms that Washington had introduced in the international trade regime applied.

Although indirectly constructing US power by extending NAFTA's norms to Chile, DFAIT also attempted bilaterally to develop new norms that might ultimately constrain Washington's power. In its negotiations with Santiago, DFAIT tried to remedy its continuing failure to contain US unilateral behaviour by getting Washington to accept binding rules. It had long wanted to achieve genuine free trade with the United States in which Canadian exporters would be exempted from Washington's contingency trade-protection legislation. Anti-dumping (AD) rules had initially been designed to allow governments to protect their own enterprises against unfair foreign competition by imposing duties whenever foreign companies exported their goods at less than their 'fair value.' However, American firms routinely invoked anti-dumping actions against Canadian competitors as a strategic form of business harassment.[49] Notwithstanding its prior failures on this issue when negotiating CUFTA and NAFTA, Ottawa still dreamed of getting Washington to exempt Canadian exports from the application of its contingent trade-protectionist regime and, instead, to apply anti-trust policies to predatory corporate practices in North America, as happened in Europe. To make an end run around Washington's resistance on this issue, Ottawa tried creating a precedent with Chile in the hope that the United States might ultimately subscribe to it.[50]

Indeed, Chile did agree to phase out the use of anti-dumping and replace this instrument with competition policy.[51] Under the CCFTA, anti-dumping duties would no longer be placed on products whose tariff rate had already fallen to zero, an important innovation in global trade law and potentially significant as a precedent because Canada completed its agreement with Chile prior to the US-Chile FTA negotiations. But neither this breakthrough nor the fact that both the European Union's member states and Australia and New Zealand in their Closer Economic Relation Trade Agreement (1983) had abandoned the use of anti-dumping measures against each other made an impression in Washington.

Congress and the USTR kept insisting they must remain able to defend their less competitive industries with contingency protection measures. In a communication to the WTO in 1998, the US government even argued that anti-dumping measures were 'necessary for the maintenance of the multilateral trading system.'[52] In the face of such deep-seated resistance, any innovations made by middle powers concerning the use of anti-dumping norms would not easily be adopted by Washington even if it was in its longer-term interests to broaden and deepen the liberalized international trade order. Canada's capacity to constrain US trade unilateralism by negotiating new international norms had proven as feeble after 1995 as before.

After its agreement with Chile, DFAIT negotiated free-trade agreements with Israel (ratified 1997), El Salvador (ratified 1999), and Costa Rica (ratified 2002) in which NAFTA's Chapter 11 again served as the model that defined protections for Canadian direct investment abroad (CDIA). These NAFTA-type rules and disciplines included granting Canadian investors national treatment and forbidding signatories from imposing many performance requirements as conditions for Canadian investment.

Canada also entered into thirty-five Foreign Investment and Protection Agreements (FIPAs) aimed at protecting and promoting CDIA by obtaining legally binding rights for Canadian TNCs in these countries. In 2003 Canada updated its FIPA model, which had already adopted the main outlines of NAFTA Chapter 11's clauses after 1994, to respond to some objections from civil society. As a TNC-friendly document, this revised FIPA model continued 'to incorporate standards long promoted by the United States.'[53] Canada's new template imposed harsher restrictions on signatory governments by expanding the list of performance requirements that a host government was forbidden to impose as a condition for a Canadian company's proposed investment.[54]

Yet the new FIPA also incorporated some of Canadian civil-society's objections to the processes empowering foreign investors' NAFTA-style legal rights against host governments. The new model FIPA made the arbitration procedures used for Canadian companies suing host governments less offensive to normal legal standards of justice. In contrast with previous bilateral investment treaties, the FIPA model required the launching of investor-state cases to be publicly disclosed, the arbitration documents to be available for public scrutiny, and the proceedings to be open to public participation with provisions for amicus curiae interventions on behalf of civil-society groups. The definition of what constituted an indirect expropriation of a foreign investment was clarified to allow for governments to introduce legitimate public-interest regulations. The meaning of the loose notion, 'minimum standards of treatment,' which had been very broadly interpreted by earlier arbitrations to favour plaintiff TNCs, was made more precise and so less prone to abuse by tribunals biased in favour of transnational capital.

The significance of these improvements for US power has to be carefully weighed. On the one hand, restricting the scope of investor-state dispute settlement cannot be seen as constraining US interests if these are defined by what is prevailing US government policy. This is because, in response to American civil society's objections that NAFTA had given Canadian corporations greater powers to sue US govern- ments than domestic US corporations enjoyed, the USTR had made the provisions of US bilateral investment treaties negotiated after NAFTA more restrictive for investors challenging the regulatory power of the signatory state.[55] When granting the USTR its Trade Promotion Author- ity in 2002, Congress had required that the American model-investment treaty be modified so that foreign investors' rights could not exceed those available to US corporations under the American constitution.[56]

On the other hand, if US interests are defined in terms of freedom from foreign-government interference for American TNCs operating abroad, the new Canadian FIPA offered little new constraint on the arbi- tral outcomes of investor-state dispute resolution. This was because tri- bunals tended to ignore the fine legal distinctions between 'minimum standards of treatment,' 'fair and equitable treatment,' and 'customary international law'[57] and continued to award large damages to foreign corporations suing host governments for environmental, health, or cul- tural regulations promoting the public interest.[58] Seventeen of Canada's FIPAs were based on the new model. As a result, Canada has diffused NAFTA's US-favoured investment norms through many of its bilateral trade and investment agreements, albeit in slightly modified form.

With the electoral victory of Conservative Prime Minister Stephen Harper in 2006, Canadian foreign-policy makers appeared to rediscov- er Latin America.[59] With NAFTA still its model, Ottawa started a series of economic negotiations in order to improve its access to agricultural and financial-service markets and to strengthen protections for invest- ments by its mining TNCs, which had a growing presence throughout Latin America[60] and whose output was in great demand in Canada because of the declining availability of non-renewable resources there.[61] At the same time as it signed and ratified agreements with Jor- dan (2009) and the European Free Trade Association (2009), it signed and ratified FTAs with Peru (2009) and Colombia (2010), signed one with Panama in 2010,[62] and started negotiating with the Central Amer- ican Four – Guatemala, El Salvador, Honduras, and Nicaragua.[63]

Conclusion

Aruging that the WTO represented a triumph in Washington's efforts to recast the international economic order to favour its long-term interests, our analysis suggests that this achievement would have been almost impossible without Canada and Mexico having been eager to take the first steps in road testing the new model of expanded, intrusive, government-restricting economic-integration rules. With the logjam in the Uruguay Round's multilateral trade negotiations, the North American periphery's shift in the 1980s from resisting neoconservative policies to accepting them provided the United States with alternate avenues for promoting its trade agenda. By abandoning their countries' industrial-development strategies in favour of deepening their continental integration, the Mulroney and Salinas governments not only entrenched US norms on the North American continent but lent force to US demands in the global arena.

This is not to argue that the Canadian and Mexican governments were mere pawns in Washington's execution of its strategy. But their serendipitous desire to re-constitutionalize their countries with the norms contained in CUFTA and NAFTA allowed Washington credibly to threaten that it could establish a Fortress North America that would exclude Europe if the EU did not return to the negotiating table. Further, without CUFTA's dispute-settlement mechanism, which had been tested and found wanting by Canada, Ottawa would not have proposed the strengthened mechanism that was an essential component of the Uruguay Round's final compromise and helped forge the global consensus necessary for the WTO to be accepted. CUFTA also created the precedent that services could be included in global trade law, which led to the GATS agreements being included within the WTO. Since the United States completely shifted its priorities to homeland security after September 2001, it is difficult to imagine that it could have achieved its WTO triumph by that time without Canada's and Mexico's rarely recognized contributions.

Indispensable at the global level, the periphery was also helpful regionally. Having legitimized US norms at home, the periphery acted as their torchbearer in the Western hemisphere. By negotiating and signing NAFTA, Mexico became a much studied model in Latin America among both economic liberalization's proponents and its opponents. It had made its decisive policy reversal at a time when investors doubted Latin America's economic seriousness. Even in the severe currency crisis it experienced in the immediate wake of NAFTA's coming into effect, the Zedillo government kept its economy open, refusing to request an IMF exemption so that it could implement temporary high tariffs. It went on to prove that a developing country could fulfil its obligatons, however painful to its own citizens, as was the case when it undertook to reduce the tariff on corn to zero. By 2008, when it had implemented its last NAFTA pledge, Mexico had shown that it could keep its promises to the letter – from NAFTA's original signature to its final implementation.[64]

Both Canada and Mexico negotiated other neoconservative trade and investment treaties in their own interests that ipso facto propagated US-favoured investment norms and so indirectly promoted US economic interests in Latin America. Nevertheless, the increasing disfavour enjoyed by the neoconservative paradigm helped bring the FTAA negotiations to a halt after years of palavers.

Most Latin American states had been notorious throughout the Cold War for their closed-market policies and still resisted opening their economies to the United States.[65] Rating their readiness for signing free-trade agreements on a five-point scale which measured macroeconomic, micro-economic, trade, tax, and policy-sustainability indicators, Washington's Institute for International Economics (IIE) scored El Salvador, Guatemala, Honduras, Nicaragua, and Panama in 1994 at 2 or below.[66] By 2001, all five countries had met or surpassed the IIE's threshold for preparedness, scoring a cumulative average of 3.4.[67] These countries' negotiations with the North American periphery had made a significant contribution to this substantial evolution. Although it would be unjustifiable to claim an unmediated causal connection between Mexico's and Canada's economic diplomacy and the region's shift towards free-market policies, the agreements with these countries acted as training wheels for Latin governments wanting to learn how to ride around the neoconservative trade arena and subsequently made it easier for the United States to negotiate its own treaties with these countries.

From another point of view, it is debatable whether a multiplication of bilateral trade and investment agreements serves US interests. If its partners proliferate their own preferential arrangements, any future effort by Washington to consolidate its position in North America by upgrading NAFTA into a customs union or common market would come up against the problem of reconciling the different provisions of Mexico's and Canada's own bilateral agreements with other countries and regions such as the European Union.

The periphery's role in spreading and strengthening the network of neoconservative trade and investment norms can also be seen as possibly affecting US national security. To the extent that these rules promote economic growth and spread prosperity, they may help reduce the causes of instability within a partner state and its resulting international repercussions. But, if these agreements bolster the forces that are actually causing insecurity – for example, by aggravating extreme poverty and social inequalities in Mexico or violating human rights through the repression of labour unions in Colombia – they may exacerbate the conditions that underlie these countries' prolonged civil strife and consolidate their participation in the global narcotics industry.

Close to two decades after NAFTA's negotiation, Canada's and Mexico's importance for Washington as international liberalizers had patently diminished. Canadians' concerns that the WTO's rules were preventing urgently needed medications being made available to contain Africa's pandemics even led Ottawa to oppose Washington in the Doha Round on such an important issue as waiving intellectual-property rights to allow the production and export of generic versions of branded drugs. Mexico's PAN government listened more to its beleaguered business community than to its trade negotiators, and so adopted a much less aggressive approach to global market deregulation.

As for the United States after 2001, its single-minded quest for maximum security in its dual wars on terror and drugs continued to trump its previous goal of turning the world into its trade and investment oyster. To be sure, some American policy thinkers are aware of the value to the United States of its two neighbours both for their direct economic contribution to US prosperity and for their indirect support of US efforts to reconstitutionalize global governance.

Notwithstanding its occasional rhetorical assertions endorsing trade and investment liberalization, the Obama administration seems unsure about whether a liberal trading regime is more advantageous to the United States or to such rising competitors as China and Korea. Its Buy American Act required that all goods for public use that were financed by Washington's stimulus program be manufactured in the United States from American materials.[68] Having enthusiastically helped rewrite the global economic handbook in Uncle Sam's post-industrial image, the periphery's own neoconservative elite felt blindsided by this move. The Bush administration's commitment to achieving maximum border security against possible terrorist incursions had already stopped the continental trade momentum that the three countries had generated in the late 1990s and loosened the ties of economic integration that had been woven in NAFTA's aftermath by causing corporations to break their continental production chains. Obama's endorsement of an overt protectionism that directly negated NAFTA's spirit further reversed the process of economic continentalization. Canada's and Mexico's supportive role in consolidating US international economic power could no longer have much impact if Washington had itself lost interest in this goal. ·

By negotiating their own trade and investment agreements with third countries, the Mexican and Canadian governments were helping the United States while they tried to help themselves. But, as will now see, by negotiating and then launching the International Criminal Court, the two countries found themselves dealing with an angry Washington that considered this new manifestation of global governance to be a severe constraint on its military autonomy.

8 Thwarting the United States in International Criminal Law[1]

Our strategy is to keep the U.S. engaged ... Let's continue to work and massage and accommodate. But there has to be flexibility on the U.S. side. They have to adjust their sights now too and recognize that they are not going to get an exemption from this court. That's pretty clear. They've been told that.

– Lloyd Axworthy, quoted in 'U.S. Resists War-Crimes Court as Canada Conforms,' *New York Times*, July 22, 2000

Having designed with its victorious allies at the end of the Second World War a global governance regime that incorporated its liberal capitalist values, the United States subsequently deployed its enormous economic, military, and moral resources with impressive political success. Its first major post-war rival, the Soviet Union, manifested its resistance largely through political vetoes and military threats that prevented it acquiring significant support outside the areas under its direct control. Beyond this socialist bloc, many post-colonial states worked to create their own non-aligned order, often exploiting their numerical superiority in the United Nations to turn multilateral institutions to their own advantage. Although Washington insisted on its prerogative to proceed unilaterally when its national security was at stake (as it managed to disastrous effect in Vietnam), its own veto power in the Security Council, its financial clout, and its active participation in multilateral institutions helped ensure that, on major issues central to its national interests, it mainly got its way. Although it had its differences with the great powers in Europe and Asia, its dominance in the four-decades-long Cold War make it appropriate to describe the whole period as an American hegemony in which the leader led, and its followers followed, willingly contributing to the construction and development of a US-inspired and US-controlled international order. To be sure, the international community argued about the ways and means, but in the last resort it respected the United States' interests and acceded to its demands because it needed its leadership.

This context made what occurred on July 1, 2002 triply remarkable. On that day, the first permanent, truly international criminal tribunal created a global legal regime that would bring to justice the perpetrators of horrendous crimes against humanity. More unusual, having decided that this International Criminal Court jeopardized its national-security interests, the US government had waged a determined campaign to abort the new institution. For the purposes of this book, it was even more astonishing that the campaign's success in bringing the ICC to life and sustaining it in its infancy in the face of concerted US opposition was very largely due to the two countries which were the most economically and politically dependent on the superpower, Canada and Mexico.

This case of the diplomatic middle powers prevailing over the global giant is all the more extraordinary given that American opposition to the ICC was rooted in core security concerns, the object of the ICC's jurisdiction being the very men and women in uniform and their leaders who are the backbone of US military power. That Canada and its allies won an important multilateral policy battle against their immensely more powerful leader and that Mexico was able to defy US efforts to force it to subvert the ICC are two facts that challenge common assumptions depreciating the North American periphery's relationship with the United States and that suggest US diplomatic power is more dependent on its client states than is generally recognized.

In the debates before, during, and after the 1998 conference where the Rome Statute establishing the ICC was finalized, the North American community's three members asserted themselves in very different ways. The United States vehemently resisted the permanent international criminal regime both while it was being debated and when it was being established. Washington could not stomach an international criminal court exercising authority over US military personnel, particularly because it would lose the power it enjoyed as a permanent member of the Security Council to set up ad hoc international criminal tribunals.

Canada's default reluctance to defy its powerful neighbour was offset by its long-standing support for a broad, multilaterally developed human-security agenda. Having achieved a consensus around a strong and independent permanent court at the Rome Conference, Canada and its network of state and non-state allies spent the next four years bringing the ICC into being in the face of the United States' vigorous efforts to subvert the new institution. Canada's success can be attributed to:

- its reputation as a leader on human-security issues, which allowed it to work productively with a broad network of allies outside North America;
- its credentials as a solid supporter of multilateral governance, which it exploited to obtain and retain leadership roles in the formal UN negotiating process;
- its flexibility in bargaining on contentious issues, working always towards consensus; and
- its creative use of its financial resources as well as its legal and technical assistance to induce other countries to support the ICC.

Mexico's role in the negotiation process was far more modest, given that its position was hampered by domestic constitutional difficulties, but it emerged as a significant defender of the court in the early 2000s. A leading target of US pressure politics, it successfully resisted Washington's attempts to win immunity for US military personnel from the ICC's jurisdiction and so served as a model of autonomy for other Latin American states facing similar pressures. The United States was unwilling to go further in trying to coerce Mexico lest it jeopardize the two countries' strong economic and security ties. This suggested that the continent's deep integration tied the United States' hands when it was trying to combat its neighbours' attempts to constrain its power on the international stage.

We begin by depicting the historical context for the evolution of international humanitarian and criminal law up to the end of the Cold War. We then focus on the negotiations at the Rome Conference where Canada assumed a leadership role in outflanking a United States whose exceptionalist arguments had lost traction. Next, we follow the Rome Treaty's ratification, explaining Canada's large role in promoting the court's implementation and the part played by Mexico in resisting US pressure to subvert it. This diplomatic success appears ultimately to have overcome the Bush administration's continued opposition to the court.

The Bumpy Road to Rome

The ICC was the culmination of more than a century of activists' dreams, lawyers' debates, international efforts, and diplomats' attempts to regulate the conduct of warfare. The technologically advanced and brutally efficient forms of warfare that emerged in the second half of the nineteenth century shocked the conscience of many and prompted two peace conferences, at The Hague in 1899 and 1907, to define in law the limits of 'civilized' warfare. International humanitarian law has always been aimed at constraining states' conduct in their ultimate exercise of state power, but, as it developed over the course of the twentieth century, proponents soon realized that violations of these rules and other atrocities were committed not so much by states themselves as by individuals and in particular by those states' leaders.

The vision of an international criminal law and a corresponding global court to try individual perpetrators for breaches of these standards emerged in fits and starts. The victors of the First World War attempted but failed to try Kaiser Wilhelm and his collaborators for their 'supreme offence against international morality and the sanctity of treaties.'[2] Germany did bring a few of its own nationals to show trials, but most of those who were convicted promptly escaped.[3] Following the Second World War, the Allies tried some of the individuals accused of serious war crimes through the International Military Tribunal at Nuremberg and the International Military Tribunal for the Far East in Tokyo. The trials were largely successful, but they faced criticism because the international law enforced against the defendants was ad hoc. Worse, this retroactive justice was applied only to the losers: Allied atrocities were never investigated.[4] Efforts to establish a permanent international court with definite rules and universal application began in 1946, when the United Nations General Assembly set up the International Law Commission (ILC) and assigned it the task of developing the statute necessary to create such a court.

This was a period of great creativity in international law. The 1948 Genocide Convention carefully defined one of the gravest crimes that individuals can perpetrate (often on behalf of their state) and recognized that the charge of genocide might one day be tried by an international tribunal. The 1949 Geneva Conventions expanded the international regulation of the conduct of warfare. By 1953, a draft statute for a criminal court had been completed, but its serious consideration was delayed until the end of the Cold War, when the UN General Assembly invited the ILC to renew its efforts.

With civil war and ethnic conflict subsequently exploding in the Balkans after the break-up of Yugoslavia and in Rwanda, the Security Council created ad hoc criminal tribunals to bring the perpetrators of genocide to justice. The 1993 Yugoslavia and 1994 Rwanda tribunals demonstrated the viability of international criminal justice. They also proved the need for a permanent court,[5] because each time an ad hoc court was established suitable facilities had to be purchased or constructed, administrative costs were substantial, and achieving the necessary Security Council support required major investments of diplomatic capital.[6]

In 1994 the ILC reported to the General Assembly, which created an Ad Hoc Committee to develop the issue further and a Preparatory Committee (PrepCom) which was to present a draft statute of an international criminal court for final negotiation at a Diplomatic Conference of Plenipotentiaries to be held in Rome in 2002.

The Conflict at Rome over US Exceptionalism and Sovereignty

The draft statute that faced the conference delegates at Rome in 1998 was by no means final. The PrepCom's six meetings between 1996 and 1998 had produced a 173-page document riddled with some 1,400 unresolved proposals and counter-proposals[7] concerning such unsettled issues as the nature of the court's jurisdiction over individuals and its relationship to national courts, the relationship between the court and the Security Council, the role of the prosecutor, and even the definitions of the crimes that would come under the court's jurisdiction.

The ICC that emerged from the PrepCom was actually stronger than that proposed by the International Law Commission in 1994. This section traces Canada's leadership of a network of like-minded states that promoted the ICC from the early days of the negotiations. It also assesses the deep linkages between the United States' security concerns at Rome and its domestic constituencies. It then examines the issues and debates along with the manoeuvrings of Canada and its respective allies that led to a strengthened international court.

Canada in the Pre-Negotiation Phase

Alongside a coalition of non-governmental organizations, Canada was able to build this network, take leadership positions at Rome, and achieve its goal of a stronger, independent, and robust ICC – all the while resisting US obstructionism – by trading on its reputation as a robust multilateralist and advocate of human security.

The 1994 International Law Commission draft statute had presented a vision of a relatively weak court, with strong control by the Security Council and quite narrow jurisdiction,[8] more in line with the US position. Canada and its allies had wanted instead a stronger, more independent tribunal. Ultimately, Canada was able to outflank the United States at Rome in spite of the large power imbalance. As one observer at the Rome Conference remarked, 'Canada's fingerprints are over almost all of the final Rome Statute. To be honest, there is probably not a page of the statute that does not have directly-proposed language from Canada in it.'[9] The Canadian delegation helped build and maintain a robust coalition of like-minded states while at the same time securing key leadership roles for itself in the negotiation process and collaborating closely with the large network of NGOs involved in the Coalition for an International Criminal Court (CICC).

Canada engaged in the renewed debate about a permanent international criminal court almost immediately after the International Law Commission submitted its draft statute in 1994. An active participant at the Ad Hoc Committee meetings in 1995, Canada convened a group of states that supported the idea of a court.[10] This 'Like-Minded Group' (LMG) initially pushed for a diplomatic conference to finalize an ICC statute in the face of the Security Council's resistance.[11] Under initial Canadian chairmanship, the LMG grew to sixty states by the start of the Rome Conference and sixty-seven at its finish when it included all European Union members.[12] Other negotiating blocs were also active in the negotiations. The five permanent members (P-5) of the UN Security Council had been united in its opposition in the Ad Hoc Committee and PrepCom negotiations, but, prompted in part by a change in government, the United Kingdom joined the LMG shortly before Rome. France and Russia then rallied, leaving the United States and China as the only P-5 members in opposition by the end of the conference. The Non-Aligned Movement (NAM) was another large voting bloc but was torn. It had not decided what its basic principles were and had some of its own members inside the LMG who initially were all middle powers supporting a strong ICC.[13]

As the group's membership grew, agreement across all issues became less easy to achieve. Accordingly, Canada prodded the LMG 'to take on a substantive role' in the negotiations and to agree to a minimal set of 'cornerstone principles'[14] that committed its members to a court with a number of key features. The first was automatic jurisdiction over war crimes, genocide, crimes against humanity, and aggression. Sometimes referred to as 'inherent jurisdiction,' this concept meant that 'states parties' would not be free to submit to its jurisdiction only on a case-by-case basis or for a limited period of time, as is possible within the International Court of Justice. The second feature was a definition of war crimes that included internal armed conflict, a matter that was as yet unsettled in international humanitarian law.[15] Canada also wanted to ensure that the Security Council played no filtering role in the triggering process. On the contrary, the LMG fought for a prosecutor with enough autonomy to be able to initiate proceedings independent of a Security Council veto. Finally, the court should have the authority to decide on questions of its own jurisdiction and the admissibility of cases brought before it.[16]

These cornerstone principles provided a common-denominator basis for agreement among an increasingly diverse group of countries, but left each with flexibility to take divergent positions on other issues.[17] In fact, many LMG members aligned with the P-5 on some issues and with the LMG on others.[18] At the same time, these minimal principles ensured that, whatever shape the final court took, it would, in the words of the Canadian foreign minister, Lloyd Axworthy, not be just any court but 'one worth having.'[19]

The PrepCom meetings began just after Axworthy was sworn in as minister, and, sharing the view of many leading civil society voices, he made achieving the ICC a touchstone of Canada's new human-security diplomacy.[20] By the time the Rome Conference began, Canada already had significant reputational advantages as a leader on numerous human-rights issues, including its recent success in leading the campaign that achieved the Ottawa Treaty to ban anti-personnel landmines. That treaty had concluded successfully in part because of Canada's partnering with NGO groups around the world, and it was because of his leadership in that process that the Coalition for an International Criminal Court approached Axworthy, as the titular leader of the LMG, to collaborate on the ICC.[21]

As a result of this intervention, Axworthy decided to appoint the veteran diplomat Philippe Kirsch to energize the Canadian delegation in Rome. He also increased bilateral and multilateral contacts on the ICC issue and raised public awareness in Canada.[22] Consequently, Canadian officials and parliamentarians from the prime minister on down made the ICC negotiations a diplomatic priority with their foreign counterparts.[23] Canada also contributed to a fund established by the United Nations to help developing countries and NGO delegations – often members of the coalition with which Canada was informally allied – to participate.[24] The less-developed states were empowered by this NGO coalition whereas they would have normally been disadvantaged on an issue that impinged on the greater powers' core security concerns.[25]

Meanwhile, Canada urged the LMG, which by then spanned the traditional UN negotiating blocs and included members from every region except Asia, to move beyond its cornerstone principles and collaborate on 'substance and strategy, making it a more effective force in negotiations.'[26] It was the LMG's focus on principled negotiation (expressed most visibly in the cornerstones) that allowed it to attract new members even as the United States was courting them and to break up the United Nation's traditional regional negotiating blocs.[27] As one observer noted, 'the beauty of the like-minded caucus, indeed the key to its great success, was its ability to cut across the traditional regionalist lines.'[28] It would overstate the case to suggest that Canada caused this shake-up in UN diplomacy single-handed. Indeed, similar LMGs have formed at other UN conferences. But the LMG chaired by Canada until the Rome Conference began was recognized as the most organized and effective bloc in the negotiations[29] and as 'critical to the success of the Conference.'[30] Canadian leadership made the LMG negotiating bloc effective.

The United States Security Lobby

In the 1990s the United States supported efforts to strengthen international criminal justice. The Clinton administration and its ambassador to the United Nations, Madeleine Albright, were early promoters of the Yugoslavia and Rwanda tribunals.[31] President Clinton himself repeatedly spoke of the US commitment to bringing the perpetrators of heinous atrocities to justice,[32] and there was some support in Congress for creating a permanent international court.[33] Albright established an Office of War Crimes Issues in the State Department and appointed David Scheffer to head it as the first 'Ambassador-at-Large for War Crimes Issues,' thereby inspiring optimism abroad that the court would become a reality.[34]

But, as the Rome Conference approached, the US delegation was expressing serious reservations related to the effect of the proposed court's jurisdiction on American sovereignty.[35] Washington wanted to make the initiation of prosecutions subject to the UN Security Council's approval, a position supported at least initially by the other permanent members of the council,[36] all of whom saw eye-to-eye in the Ad Hoc Committee and PrepCom negotiations. Washington also had concerns about including aggression as a crime within the court's jurisdiction and how to define the other crimes with sufficient specificity to prevent future judges from taking undue interpretive license.[37] It argued, too, for provisions that would allow the prosecutions of individuals only with the consent of states on a case-by-case basis.[38] As a minimum, it wanted to ensure that the mere presence of an individual (such as an American soldier) on the territory of another state would not be a sufficient basis for the court to exercise jurisdiction over that person. It feared that physical presence alone might be a sufficient basis for the court to try US soldiers operating on the territory of a non-party state even if the United States was not a treaty signatory. It was also worried about the potential clash between its national-security concerns and the obligation to cooperate fully with the ICC, including in evidence gathering. More liberal US concerns had to do with the fair-trial rights of the accused and other substantive criminal law issues.[39]

The spectre of US troops being hauled into a court in The Hague was unpalatable domestically. George W. Bush neatly summarized this obdurate position almost a decade later when he said that 'every person who serves under the American flag will answer to his or her own superiors and to military law, and not to an external court beyond the control of the United States.'[40]

The United States' core sovereignty concerns were voiced by several domestic constituencies, particularly its military establishment and its congressional allies, who had long resisted any limits being put on how it conducted its wars. Because the United States had troops deployed around the world, there was a real possibility that American service members could be prosecuted by the ICC. The US secretary of defense himself tried to undermine support for the treaty at Rome.[41] The US military's fixation on the ICC's possible impact on US military operations, however remote that possibility might be, formed the basis of the US 'bottom line' position which gave no credence to the underlying purposes of an international criminal court.[42] The military lobby had allies in the Republican-controlled US Senate who were bent on derailing all the Clinton administration's multilateral diplomatic efforts but particularly the ICC in light of its potential for politically motivated prosecutions of US soldiers. Jesse Helms, the Republican chair of the Foreign Relations Committee, had no compunction about holding up appointments and budgets to blackmail the administration.[43]

Responding to this domestic pressure, the US delegation argued that the United States found itself in special circumstances owing to its unique responsibility for peace and security (shared with the rest of the P-5, by virtue of their membership on the Security Council) and its widespread military commitments.[44] This line was captured in a statement by the chief US negotiator shortly after the United States refused to sign the Rome Statute at the conference's conclusion: 'It is simply and logically untenable to expose the largest deployed military force in the world, stationed across the globe to help maintain international peace and security and to defend US allies and friends, to the jurisdiction of a criminal court the US Government has not yet joined and whose authority over US citizens the United States does not yet recognize.'[45]

Canada and the Final Negotiations

Until 1998, the PrepCom had been chaired by Adrian Boos, a senior Dutch diplomat who was also going to chair the Bureau of the Committee, the main negotiating organ within the structure of the Rome Conference. When Boos fell ill just weeks before negotiations began in Rome, he recommended that the delegates elect Philippe Kirsch, who was deputy head of the Canadian delegation and a veteran chair of many such multilateral negotiations.[46] Kirsch's election by acclamation was a testament to Canada's reputation in the negotiations to that date and its perceived potential for bridging some of the divides with its good neighbour, the United States.[47]

The LMG could not have been so effective without the subsequent Canadian leadership of the conference's chief negotiating body, the Committee of the Whole (CW), which was made up of all the negotiating members who would later have to adopt its outcomes in the senior body, the Plenary. Upon Kirsch also becoming chair of the CW, Canada gave up its seat as chair of the LMG.[48]

The Bureau of the Committee was charged with the CW's administration. It had several vice-presidents; one represented the United States but many were drawn from the LMG states. In reality, no serious negotiations occurred at the CW level, because Kirsch split it into working groups on individual issues, chaired by members of the bureau, who would then report back to the CW. Although the working groups were open to all states who were interested in a given issue, the Canadian delegation was often found acting as catalyst and consensus-builder to forge agreement.

Once Kirsch became the bureau's chair, the Canadian delegation refrained from advocating any particular set of outcomes in too partisan a fashion.[49] Instead, Canada focused its resources on reaching an agreement among all the conference's diverse set of interests. According to one delegate, 'the Canadian delegation played a brokering role in all areas of the new visions – the definition of crimes, jurisdiction, general principles, procedures, and the structure of the institution – by bridging gaps and finding creative ways to address legitimate concerns while maintaining a strong court.'[50] Kirsch's chairmanship of the bureau aided this new role, as Canada continued to work with other LMG members. Kirsch regularly hosted meetings where the bureau, the LMG, and the CICC would develop common strategies to move the negotiations forward. Significantly, the United States was not invited to any of these meetings, an absence that allowed Kirsch to implement key parts of his own strategy for bringing the conference to a successful conclusion.[51]

Recognizing that any permanent court's legitimacy and effectiveness would be greatly bolstered by the United States' significant financial, military, and diplomatic resources,[52] the Canadian delegation would have far preferred Washington to be a party to the statute and worked hard to keep it 'in' the final treaty. Along with its LMG allies, it often went out on a limb in an attempt to bridge the gap with the United States on issues related to the definition of crimes against humanity, the treatment of national law, the protection of national-security information, and the qualifications of judges.[53] Many of the concessions to the United States were made as a result of its neighbour's representations. But the deal to which the United States was prepared to agree did not meet the principled minimum standard that Canada and its LMG allies had set.[54]

By the conference's third week, the working groups had made significant progress, but Part 2 of the proposed treaty, which included the thorny issues of jurisdiction and what would trigger its exercise, remained unresolved.[55] Since the United States had not been prepared to compromise or even give an indication of where a middle ground might be found, Kirsch's bureau initiated the kind of diplomatic shuttle that generally remains unreported in the media and unanalysed in scholarship.

On July 5 Kirsch organized a meeting of twenty-eight select delegations at the Canadian embassy. Two observers noted that 'the United States, a participant, viewed the meeting as a Like-Minded Group setup and questioned Kirsch's impartiality as chair.'[56]

Two days later, the bureau distributed a discussion paper on Part 2 to the various delegations. For several days, delegates debated the proposals without moving forward.

On July 10, with time running out, Kirsch's bureau put out a formal proposal on Part 2 which contained draft language that adopted some of the most controversial positions, including ones related to the preconditions for the exercise of jurisdiction. This succeeded in narrowing discussion somewhat, but, with two days left in the conference, little progress had been made. Then, on July 17, with the conference coming to a close, the bureau pushed for a final agreement on a 'package deal,' a draft statute that picked and chose from the delegations' various positions to become what the bureau felt would be a compromise able to attract broad support. A race began to build support for the deal, which was not universally well liked. The US delegation was angry at having been 'confronted' and challenged Kirsch's impartiality.[57]

But insisting on its exceptionalism did not allow the United States much room to manoeuvre when facing the relatively coherent consensus of the other countries. Some have suggested that this was in part due to the US delegation having neither flexible nor detailed instructions either at the PrepCom or in Rome.[58] Others have judged that, particularly as the conference wore on, the administration was not well served by negotiators who neither sought solutions nor transmitted accurate reports back to Washington about the conference's dynamic.[59] As the conference progressed, US trade negotiator David Scheffer's arguments on behalf of the US military lost traction and were seen as pure unilateralism. As he subsequently affirmed, he 'spent many years seeking full immunity for [US] military forces and their civilian leadership in negotiations that quite frankly sometimes seemed the theatre of the absurd. I was given nothing to offer – certainly not signature or ratification – in return for an absolutist carve-out that other governments, particularly our closest allies, found arrogant and hypocritical.'[60] For its part, the Canadian delegation started a campaign to drum up support from states and NGOs that were not yet behind all aspects of the compromise package. By that point, Axworthy had appeared at the conference in person and led these efforts, which included a personal telephone call to Secretary of State Albright.[61] In the end, the Americans were not swayed. Although they were interested in every aspect of the ICC, they belonged to no negotiating group or bloc, so the compromise package effectively sidelined them.[62] As Scheffer wrote later that year, 'while most governments positioned themselves within some regional or functional grouping at the Rome Conference, the United States usually had to build support for its positions through time-consuming bilateral diplomacy.'[63]

The package that was ultimately adopted at the conference as the Rome Statute nevertheless contained a remarkable number of concessions to the US position.[64] The Security Council was accepted as one of the 'triggering mechanisms' that could refer violations to the prosecutor. While the final statute had (in US eyes) the untenable position of a prosecutor who could act on her or his own initiative, the Security Council could also *defer* the prosecutor's ensuing investigations for a year at a time. Solutions had also been found for some of the US national-security objections, and the Rome Statute even allayed many US due-process concerns. Despite winning these victories during the five-week conference, the United States would not deviate from its fundamental opposition.

Kirsch's gambit had worked because it caused other blocs, including the P-5 and the Non-Aligned Movement, to split apart, leaving individual governments to decide their own positions. Meanwhile, the Canadians' last-minute lobbying effort proved successful. Many delegations were happy to have an agreement that was generating consensus. The United States (and India) vainly attempted to reopen some of the issues at the final CW meeting, but procedural motions from Norway, supported by the vast majority of delegations, prevented those efforts from coming to a vote.[65] This allowed the Committee of the Whole to adopt the document and refer it to the Plenary where the package deal would be adopted as the Rome Statute on July 17, 1999 with only seven dissenting votes – China, Iraq, Israel, Libya, Qatar, and Yemen alongside the United States. These dissenters aside, the Rome Conference's agreement elicited jubilation from most of the delegates, many of whom were more committed to the ideal of an international court than were their own governments.[66]

Mexico had taken part in the PrepCom meetings and came to Rome prepared to negotiate a statute, but its success there was mixed. It was a relatively active participant in working groups and supported a view of an ICC that was very similar to that of the LMG.[67] It had not formally joined the LMG, preferring to work at different times with Latin American and non-aligned states. Although this autonomy allowed it to seek a number of provisions that were at odds with some LMG positions, it was not effective at the conference, having no solid network to draw on. Its objections to the final statute concerned the exclusion of nuclear weapons from the list of prohibited weapons, the role of the Security Council, and the 'no reservations' clause, which prohibited signatories from avoiding particular obligations by objecting to them at the time of ratification.[68] Mexico did vote for the Rome Statute in its final form, but, as we will see, its ratification efforts raised domestic constitutional issues.

The Promotion of the Court after 1998

Achieving the Rome Statute was not the end of the story. The negotiations were succeeded by another Preparatory Commission[69] which worked from 1999 to 2002 to specify many of the details of the court's functioning, including definitions of the crimes within the court's jurisdiction (the 'Elements of Crimes'), Rules of Procedure and Evidence, Rules for the Assembly of States Parties (ASP) – which would become the main body supervising the court's operation – and logistical and financial matters. Having shown how Canada played a hand in securing a consensus at Rome in the face of the United States' sustained objections, we now consider the efforts of the North American periphery to promote the ratification and effective implementation of the ICC while simultaneously resisting American US efforts to castrate it.

The PrepCom's deliberations began before the Rome Statute had even come into force and were attended by most of the same states that had attended Rome – including the United States, in spite of its 'no' vote.[70] The LMG remained intact at the opening of the Preparatory Commission sessions in 1999, as did the LMG's alliance with the CICC. As in Rome, Canada also held the chairmanship, with Philippe Kirsch heading the PrepCom's Secretariat, which was itself largely made up of LMG representatives. Not having supported the final Rome Statute, the United States could no longer play any leadership role.

The commission's individual working groups were also led by LMG states. A representative of the Netherlands chaired the meetings on the Elements of Crimes. The negotiations on the Rules of Procedure and Evidence were led by Argentina, assisted by others on specific issues, including representatives from Norway and Canada.

The United States tried to take an active role as part of the PrepCom process, because it recognized that, the court's final powers not yet being clear, it could still influence the outcome. The Rome Statute had granted the ICC jurisdiction over individuals if *either* they were a national of a state party *or* the crime was committed on the territory of a state party, which made the United States feel vulnerable to 'third party' jurisdiction over American personnel operating on the soil of such states.[71]

The United States' relationship with the LMG states was less antagonistic than formerly during the PrepCom meetings where it succeeded in achieving some of its objectives. Most important to Washington, it gained Rule 44(2), which effectively prevented a non-state party from referring only a portion of a 'situation.' This would have prevented, for example, Saddam Hussein from referring 'merely' US pilots for investigation by the prosecutor without also inviting scrutiny of his own forces.[72] But the LMG successfully resisted a Washington-proposed rule that would have required the permission both of the government of an accused and of the government upon whose territory a crime had been committed for the ICC to exercise its jurisdiction.

On December 31, 2000, part-way through the Preparatory Commission meetings, President Clinton signed the Rome Statute but made clear that he would not submit it for ratification in the Senate (where there was no chance for its acceptance in any event). This was meant as a gesture of goodwill from the United States to the existing signatories and also kept it 'engaged' with the PrepCom, despite its major reservations. In signing the Rome statute, Clinton declared, 'we are not abandoning our concerns about significant flaws in the treaty ... The United States should have the chance to observe and affect the functioning of the Court over time before choosing to [come] under its jurisdiction. I will not, and do not recommend that my successor, submit the treaty to the Senate for advice and consent until our fundamental concerns are satisfied.'[73]

The ICC's opponents in Washington immediately attacked Clinton's position as that of a lame-duck president hoping to hobble his successor,[74] but the Bush administration was set to be opposed to the International Criminal Court.[75] In a revelatory statement summarizing the new US government's unilateralist stance, John Bolton argued before the Senate Foreign Relations Committee: 'We should isolate and ignore the ICC. Specifically, I propose for United States policy – I got a title for it ... I call it the Three Noes: no financial support, directly or indirectly; no collaboration; and no further negotiations with other governments to improve the Statute ... this approach is likely to maximize the chances that the ICC will wither and collapse, which should be our objective.'[76]

Because the Rome Statute would not come into force until it had been ratified by sixty states, Canada under Axworthy's leadership kept up its diplomatic pressure.[77] Ottawa was among the first formally to sign the treaty and the first to draft legislation to bring the Canadian legal order into line with its new treaty obligations.[78] Its Crimes against Humanity and War Crimes Act (CAHWCA) introduced new offences corresponding to those in the Rome Statute and the procedural rules necessary to bring these into effect. Parallel legislation created a mechanism for extradition to the ICC and for the provision of Mutual Legal Assistance.[79] Canada then offered the CAHWCA as a model statute for other states implementing the Rome Statute, funded the NGO-led creation of an implementation manual, and provided technical expertise and legal staff to assist developing countries in this effort.[80] It sponsored seminars on ICC implementation in Africa, the South Pacific, Latin America, and the Caribbean; established ICC-related internships; held an international youth conference in 2001; and dedicated funding for NGOs which promoted the ICC by encouraging other governments to sign and ratify.[81]

The Mexican delegation to the 1998 conference, as we have seen, voted for the Rome Statute even though it had some reservations about the final document. It would have preferred to limit the court's jurisdiction to the most serious international crimes and to clarify its independence from the Security Council.[82] Mexico faced the additional hurdle of launching the constitutional-amendment process necessary for it to ratify the statute.[83] Mexico formally signalled its endorsement of the ICC by signing the Rome Statute on September 7, 2000,[84] but ratification would prove difficult.[85] A contentious political and legal debate erupted regarding the constitutional changes that would be required for Mexico to subject itself to the court's jurisdiction. In December 2001 the Vicente Fox government delivered to the Senate a draft reform of Article 21 of the Mexican constitution.[86] While specifying that the investigation of crimes and the imposition of penalties came under the exclusive jurisdiction of Mexico's judicial authorities, the amendment stated that 'the Federal Executive may recognize the jurisdiction of the International Criminal Court, subject to the Senate's approval in each case.'[87] The amendment process continued through Mexico's legislative bodies until, on October 28, 2005, Mexico's certified ratification of the treaty was deposited with the United Nations.

Once the 60th ratification of the Rome Statute had been deposited in 2002 and the court came into existence, the Bush administration's stance of muted ambivalence changed into open hostility. The United States had greatly expanded its military commitments abroad in Afghanistan and was considering other deployments in its 'war on terror,' including going to war against Iraq. The prospect that US service members would be charged by an ICC prosecutor and put on trial in The Hague became all the more credible, at least in the minds of American ICC opponents, as the court's territorial jurisdiction expanded with each ratification. In May 2002 Secretary of State Colin Powell officially announced that the United States was 'withdrawing' its signature on the Rome Statute[88] and that, accordingly, it considered itself bound neither by any of the treaty's obligations nor by its object and purpose.

Washington mounted an offensive against the court both bilaterally with signatories around the world and in the Security Council which authorized all UN peacekeeping missions. One of the largest commitments of US military personnel abroad was in Bosnia, and the council was due to renew the UN mission in Boznia-Herzegovina (UNMIBH) in June 2002. The United States threatened to veto this renewal (and all other UN peacekeeping missions) unless the council passed a resolution granting non-parties to the Rome Statute immunity from ICC jurisdiction for their troops who were members of UN peacekeeping operations.[89] The authority it claimed for such a resolution was Article 16 of the Rome Statute, which allowed the Security Council to defer prosecutions for a year. Despite this being a dubious interpretation,[90] the Security Council members were unwilling to jeopardize such an important peacekeeping mission, so the American threats won the day and the council passed Resolution 1422, which was effective from July 1, 2002. The United States successfully sought that resolution's renewal (as Resolution 1487) for a further one-year period in 2003.

In conjunction with its pressure on the Security Council, the United States began negotiating what it termed 'Bilateral Immunity Agreements' (BIAs) under the ostensible authority of the Rome Statute's Article 98.[91] Under these agreements, the United States and the other signatory agreed to extradite one another's nationals not to the ICC but to their home countries.[92]

The US Congress voted to cut off military and other aid to signatories who would neither 'unsign' the Rome Statute nor conclude such a BIA. The American Service-members' Protection Act (ASPA) was the most direct challenge to the ICC, because its main provisions effectively stopped most US military assistance to states parties and even authorized the military rescue of US servicemen being held by the ICC. The ASPA's financial-penalty provisions were bolstered by the Nethercutt Amendment, which cut non-military economic aid to ICC's signatories.

Those structural features of the UN negotiations that had helped Canada bring about agreement at Rome were relevant in the context of this new US offensive. Canada was in no position to resist US efforts in the Security Council because it did not hold a seat there, having just completed a temporary member's term in 2000. It did lobby the council and its members extensively, both publicly and in private, requesting and getting a public council meeting to debate the matter. These efforts were to no avail. Mexico did hold a temporary seat on the council but did not dissent from its unanimous vote supporting Resolution 1422.

Even though their countries were not affected directly, an informal coalition consisting of Canada, Australia, and New Zealand (CANZ) and headed by Canada's permanent representative at the UN worked to ensure a coordinated response by providing legal and technical support for states being subjected to US pressure.[93] The US campaign for BIAs proceeded via secret bilateral meetings closed to the LMG or its CICC allies, so there was no central negotiating forum for open multilateral diplomacy where the periphery might have had some influence.

The Canadian government refused to sign a BIA with the United States, but, since it was not the recipient of any assistance under the programs covered by the Nethercutt Amendment, it faced no meaningful sanction. Ottawa painted the BIA as 'unnecessary' in light of the existing Status of Force Agreement that covers the conduct of US military personnel on Canadian soil. Furthermore, the US legislation made an exception for important strategic partners, in particular other NATO members.

Mexico found itself in a very different situation. Although the effect of the US legislation was to cut off military and economic aid from the United States,[94] Mexico refused to sign a BIA and publicly denounced the US efforts. Its lower chamber announced that 'immunity is not allowed under the Rome Statute that established the ICC' and aligned itself with the EU's legal position that BIAs would not disqualify Americans from the ICC's jurisdiction.[95] In January 2003, in the context of Transparency International's tenth anniversary, the Mexican ambassador reaffirmed President Fox's position that 'Mexico is not inclined to sign any bilateral agreement with the United States that will limit the independence of the International Criminal Court.'[96] Citizens for Global Solutions claimed that Mexico lost some $11.5 million in economic and social aid in 2006 which had been earmarked for promoting 'democracy and improved economic competitiveness by strengthening the rule of law and supporting greater transparency and accountability in government,' but the figure may have been much smaller.[97] Mexico's signature and ratification of the Rome Statute in 2005 was widely seen as a rebuke to Washington for not having reformed its regulations concerning undocumented Mexican immigrants.

This rallying behind the ICC coincided with Mexicans' increasingly internationalist support for the human-rights movement and for broad multilateral regimes. The United States' attempts to coerce Latin American states were considered to be much more direct affronts to Mexico's cherished principle of non-intervention than were any perceived limits

to national sovereignty contained in the Rome Statute. Mexico's refusal to sign a BIA demonstrated that the diplomatic consequences of not
cooperating with the United States on this issue were not insurmount-
able. Across Central and South America, nations followed Mexico's
example. While ten Latin American nations are states parties to the
Rome Statute, only three of those have ratified a BIA.[98]

After several years, Washington's open hostility towards the ICC
mellowed. When in 2004 pictures of US abuses at Abu Ghraib prison in
Iraq appeared in the world's media, the opponents of US exceptionalism to the ICC regime pounced on this as an example of the conduct the
ICC should investigate. Those on the Security Council who had supported (or at least not opposed) resolutions granting immunity from
ICC jurisdiction to UN peacekeepers pushed back. Some permanent
members threatened to veto any resolution reauthorizing this immunity
for another year. The United States was forced to withdraw its proposal for an extension of resolutions 1422 and 1487 and had to rethink its
aggressive anti-ICC policy. Its BIA campaign had begun to appear ineffective, a waste of diplomatic capital, and counter-productive because it
negated other American programs designed to stabilize governments,
promote human security, and support a range of other high-priority US
objectives. When the Nethercutt Amendment was first introduced, the
chair of the Subcommittee on Foreign Operations predicted these very
problems: 'At a time when we are fighting the War on Terrorism, reducing this tool of diplomatic influence is not a good idea ... the United
States will be hamstringing itself, placing a straitjacket on its diplomatic
tools, when we have a lot of US national security objectives.'[99]

Military voices were concerned about the impact that the hard-line
anti-ICC policy was having on US hemispheric security interests. The
Pentagon's Quadrennial Defence Review in 2005 suggested that US
foreign-policy objectives were being constrained by its own actions.
General Jon Craddock, commander of US Southern Command, told the
House Armed Service Committee in 2006 that the void in military training and economic aid in South America was increasingly being filled by
China.[100] Mexico's ratification of the Rome Statute and defiance of the
United States' BIA demands was particularly alarming for one official,
who noted that 'in the case of Mexico, which is one of our most important relationships, there's no question this is a setback. Suddenly we
find we are in this glass box where we can't reach out to them.'[101]

It is unclear whether and to what extent the CICC or LMG network
had a hand in successfully resisting the BIA campaign. Canada's and

Mexico's impact are even more difficult to pin down precisely. What is evident is the US administration's growing recognition that open antagonism was only further undermining its already diminished international legitimacy. Demanding immunity from international criminal law made the United States look even more overbearing. The Bush administration eventually reversed itself. No BIA agreements were signed after 2006. Of the over 100 BIAs that were signed, only one-third were ratified.[102] President Bush granted ASPA waivers to twenty-four states in 2006 and 2007, including Mexico, most of which were renewed in 2008.[103] For its part, Congress removed the restrictions on most military financing in an amendment to the ASPA in 2007 and allowed the Nethercutt Amendment to expire in 2009.[104] The Obama administration did not signal its intent to ratify the Rome Statute but adopted a positive attitude towards the court.[105]

Further evidence of the decline in US antipathy towards the court was the Security Council's action in referring the situation in Darfur to the ICC. Voices had been demanding action on the atrocities committed in the Darfur region of Sudan for some years, and the UN Security Council had begun to monitor the situation.[106] Among these voices was Secretary of State Colin Powell, whose department completed a study of Sudanese refugees and, for the first time in any official US governmental statement, used the word 'genocide.'[107] Powell urged the council to establish a commission of inquiry, headed by leading international lawyer Antonio Cassese, whose report detailed numerous international crimes.[108] Washington now found itself in a dilemma when council members and others pushed for Darfur situation's referral to the ICC. It did not want to legitimize the ICC, but its arguments for an African Union-backed ad hoc court fell on deaf ears. The calls for action on Darfur were so great that the US government could not ignore them without alienating the international community.[109] Apparently at the urging of incoming Secretary of State Condolezza Rice, the United States abstained from the vote, allowing Resolution 1593 to pass.[110]

The United States had consistently presented its anti-ICC case in starkly realist terms – its own capacity to engage in military operations would be undermined – but this argument had little purchase. The statute was aimed at the Milosevics and the Husseins, not at a Clinton or a Bush. In any event, should any allegations of US abuse arise, the ICC's rules would allow the US government and its fully capable legal system to handle the case itself, obviating the need for ICC involvement.[111] Washington gained the upper hand in the ICC diplomatic battle only when it made arguments that were also relevant to other states' core security interests.

Its threat to withdraw military support and funding was, for many states, a serious menace. But the United States was unable to pressure Canada or Mexico on the ICC issue because it was unwilling to jeopardize the North American security relationship. Canada's deep military cooperation with the Washington was never in question, and the $2.5 million in military spending that Mexico lost in 2006 was a very small figure in the overall US-Mexico security relationship.[112] Paradoxically, the periphery's close security relationship with the United States contributed to its ability to resist US efforts to force its hand on the ICC issue.

Conclusion

The ICC is a unique institution in modern international affairs. There has not been a similarly global and powerful institution that has come into being in the face of open hostility on the part of the United States, certainly not an institution that strikes (figuratively if not necessarily literally) so directly at the heart of states' sovereignty. In many respects, the Rome Statute's rapid negotiation, its relatively quick national ratification and implementation, and its early development are the result of a unique confluence of factors in which the North American periphery played a decisive role owing to Mexico's stubborn resistance to gringo pressure and to Canada's legitimacy in transnational networks and its skills in diplomatic manoeuvring.

Canada and Mexico clearly constrained US interests as defined by conservatives for whom the United States' military power is the pre-eminent value. But, if a functioning international system governed by institutions in which members states play their parts responsibly better promotes US values in an orderly world, then Canada and Mexico were supporting United States' best interests even if they were constraining the US administration of the day. An international court to bring perpetrators of atrocities to justice had been an explicit US foreign-policy goal since the end of the Cold War. And yet the Pentagon had a compelling interest in preventing American service members from being brought before such a court, particularly if any trial would invite scrutiny of US actions and create a forum for embarrassment or criticism. The tension between these two priorities goes some way to explaining US policy schizophrenia on a permanent international criminal court over the two decades of its negotiation and implementation. At the intersection of these two competing policy principles, Canada primarily and Mexico secondarily were able to take advantage of their reputation and networks to constrain Washington in the short term and so support it in the longer term.

In showing how Canada played such a decisive role, we saw that it was perceived to have considerable legitimacy on issues of multilateral governance. It had enough credibility to assemble allies and to adopt a position of leadership. Also, Canada was able to create organizational parameters for international negotiations that prevented the United States and its supporters from setting the agenda, dominating the debate, or having an undue influence in the drafting stages. Canada further created new structural elements in the negotiating process by involving a broad range of NGOs in international lobbying efforts – thus enhancing the periphery's diplomatic capacity. In addition to lobbying governments and interest groups, the global reach of both Canadian and international NGOs extended technical and material support more broadly than the Canadian government would have been able to alone. Coincidentally, the movements favouring collective enforcement had grown considerably in the 1990s. International sentiment is not easily manipulated by middle powers, and this narrative suggests that timing as well as structural power were especially important factors determining the periphery's success.

The story of the Rome Statute shows that the North American periphery can not only constrain the United States but may help reorient its positions. That President George W. Bush ended his term supporting the enforcement of ICC warrants relating to violence in the Sudan indicates that Canada and Mexico had had some success in moving the United States from a false to a truer understanding of its best interests. If Canada and Mexico had not existed, the International Criminal Court might not have come into being at all or would now be considerably weaker than it is.

In chapter 7 we saw how Canada and Mexico negotiated economic agreements alongside the United States or alone. With the ICC, the two countries were resisting the United States in a United Nations forum. In our final chapter, we look at how their engagement with a single foreign power, Cuba, constrained the effectiveness of Washington's embargo on Fidel Castro's regime.

9 Offsetting the US Embargo of Revolutionary Cuba[1]

If you gentlemen allow me I will tell you something ... Our people have greeted [Mexican] President Echeverria ... as a fighter for relations with Cuba, as a statesman who condemned the economic blockade against Cuba throughout Latin America and who urged governments everywhere to maintain relations with Cuba, as the president of a country with which we have close and profound relations ... We paid Mexico and its president the honor, the love and the enthusiasm that they deserve from our people.
– Fidel Castro speaking at a joint press conference with Mexican President Luis Echeverria Alvarez in Havana, August 22, 1975[2]

Viva Cuba ... Viva el primer ministro Fidel Castro!
– Prime Minister Pierre Trudeau addressing a crowd of 25,000 during an official visit to Cuba, February 3, 1976

Cuba's revolutionary government survived for over fifty years despite the declared hostility of the world's most powerful state looming just 140 kilometres over the horizon. Citizens and scholars alike have long asked how Cuba was able to resist not so much a botched CIA invasion but decades of the United States' economic embargo. While most answers focus on the three decades of military protection and economic aid that the Soviet Union offered Fidel Castro's Cuba, analysts generally disregard the roles played by smaller nations in offsetting the United States' political might within the inter-American system. Mexico and Canada never approached Great Power stature, yet they proved to be important players in the Cuban dossier by mostly resisting – although on occasion supporting – their shared superpower neighbour's anti-Castro strategy.

Despite themselves being vulnerable to US pressure, Mexico and Canada are the only two countries in the hemisphere to have maintained political and economic ties with the island throughout the Cold War and its aftermath. In this chapter we examine whether and in what way their respective foreign policies, from Fidel Castro's ousting of Fulgencio Batista in 1959 until the end of Mexico's PRI regime in 2000, frustrated US policy towards Cuba. We will show that the principles proclaimed in the Mexican Revolution shaped how the PRI government defended Cuban sovereignty by resisting the United States in multilateral forums and providing Havana financial support. The text will then review Canada's less complex but more profitable relationship with Cuba.

Neither Canada nor Mexico had the capability to alter US policy. In some cases they even cooperated with Washington, the crisis over Soviet missiles being an important example. But, by establishing binding regional norms, challenging the legitimacy of key US actions, and pursuing their own relationships with Cuba, Mexico primarily and Canada secondarily stymied Washington's Cuba strategy, playing a particularly crucial role in undermining the American embargo's effectiveness following the Soviet Union's collapse.

The Origins of Mexican Foreign Policy

After Mexico gained its independence from Spain, its experience of invasions by Spanish, French, and American forces made national self-determination the central preoccupation of its twentieth-century diplomacy. The United States' military occupation and subsequent annexation of almost half of their territory in 1848 created in Mexicans a deep distrust for their powerful neighbour which was reactivated by such other incursions as Woodrow Wilson's sending in the Marines to defend US interests in 1914. It was primarily in response to these interventions that Mexico developed a nearly unshakeable commitment to the principle of non-intervention during the Reagan administration's involvement in Central America's civil wars.[3] In 2002 Mexico's secretary of external relations, Bernardo Sepúlveda Amor, was so concerned about US interventionism that he persuaded President Miguel de la Madrid to insert a foundational definition of Mexican foreign policy in the constitution. Paragraph 10 of Article 89 now states that in 'conducting [foreign] policy the head of the Executive Power will observe the following standard principles: self-determination of peoples, non-intervention, peaceful resolution of disputes, the proscription of threat and the use of force in international relations, juridical equality of states, international cooperation for development, and the struggle for international peace and security.'[4]

Basing its foreign policy on the central principles of international law provided the Mexican state some legitimacy abroad in the face of its obvious economic and military weakness. At the same time, its loud advocacy of these same principles gave the authoritarian Partido Revolucionario Institucional some domestic legitimacy in the face of its lack of democratic credentials.[5] PRI leaders were accordingly happy to play to domestic anti-American sentiment in publicly articulating, if not always privately honouring, their proclaimed foreign-policy principles. The external appeal of non-interventionism and the internal appeal of anti-gringo rhetoric would ultimately prompt it to challenge the United States after 1980 in Central America, as we saw in chapter 4, and after 1960 in Cuba, the subject of this final chapter.

Sister Revolution: Cuba Revolucionaria

The Cuban Revolution inspired a natural sympathy among Mexicans since it proclaimed the same social values as had their own. Because the PRI justified its foreign policy to the Mexican public from within its own emancipatory discourse, it found itself obliged to support Castro's project. This shared rhetoric made sovereignty, self-determination, international justice, and pluralism in the hemisphere among the most prominent themes of the bilateral relationship.[6]

This solidarity had diplomatic consequences. Mexico resisted US policy beginning with the 1960 meeting of the Organization of American States (OAS) in Costa Rica which had been convened to sanction the Castro government. The resulting Declaration of San José was interpreted as a victory for Mexico and non-interventionism given that the document made no mention of Cuba at all. Mexico went even further by including a reservation to its vote which specified that the declaration in no way constituted a condemnation of Cuba, although that was precisely how the United States had hoped to portray it.[7]

The two states clashed more dramatically later the same year following a comment made by Senator Manuel Moreno Sánchez, who suggested that 'Mexico might assist Cuba in her hour of need by supplying oil to keep her refineries operating.' This provoked an immediate reaction by the State Department, which demanded reassurances that the comment did not represent Mexico's official position. The notion that Mexico could break Washington's oil embargo was interpreted as a 'stunning blow' to US economic aggression by Cuba's news media,[8] which was no doubt one reason why the US response was so strong. Mexico gained substantial kudos throughout Latin America for what was seen as its surprisingly courageous defiance of Washington.

Castro's success bolstered the Mexican left, especially after the charismatic former president, Lázaro Cárdenas, declared himself a keen supporter of Fidel. Cárdenas's popularity with the Mexican campesinos and labourers gave his pro-Castro position considerable political weight but provoked a strong reaction from the Mexican right. When the disastrous failure of the CIA-orchestrated assault in the Bay of Pigs gave Mexican Castroism a filip, President Adolpho López Mateos (1958–64) attempted a balancing act designed to cater to both pro- and anti-Cuba sentiment without jeopardizing either Mexico's relationship with the United States or its own internal stability.[9] This balancing act led Mateos to adopt a position of political support for Cuba which did not endanger Mexico's larger interests.[10]

Numerous official statements confirmed the Mexican people's solidarity with the goals of the Cuban Revolution and some pointedly contrasted the Mexican position to that of the United States.[11] As the Cuban government showed more explicit communist tendencies, President Mateos was careful to emphasize both that he in no way endorsed Marxism-Leninism or the export of revolution to other Latin American nations and that these reservations did not diminish his defence of Cuba's right to self-determination or the island's prerogatives as a sovereign state. Although the Mexican government at first declined to condemn United States' aggressiveness, it became much more critical after the Bay of Pigs disaster.

Beyond its bilateral relationship, Mexico used its role in transnational governance to check US influence in the hemisphere. It was during the UN General Assembly's debate about the Bay of Pigs attack that Mexico spoke most clearly against US intervention in Cuba. When Ambassador Luis Padilla Nervo addressed the Assembly, he reiterated Mexico's sympathy for the Cuban Revolution and impugned the US government's initial denials of responsibility for the invasion. He reminded the Assembly of the numerous treaties undertaken by states in the Americas to prevent direct intervention or the use of one territory to launch acts against the 'political independence and the territorial integrity of another State.'[12] He declared that no nation had the right to try by any means to bring about the overthrow of a government not to its liking.[13] Further, Secretary of External Relations Manuel Tello Barraud called on all UN members urging them to deny their territories' use as bases for fomenting civil war in Cuba. Both of these high-ranking Mexican officials' statements implicitly condemned US aggression against Cuba as violations of international law.

Washington nevertheless wanted the OAS to support a series of punitive measures against Cuba. In October 1961 Peru's representative to the regional body invoked the Rio Treaty's Article 6 – which deals with cases of aggression or other threats to members' political independence – to convene a meeting of foreign ministers to discuss the Cuban case and investigate the country's civil rights. A majority of the Latin American states joined Mexico in rejecting the proposal on the grounds that it would constitute interference in Cuban domestic affairs. The Peruvian motion was duly defeated, only to be reintroduced a month later by Colombia's representative. Mexico again opposed holding the meeting on the grounds that, since Colombia was not itself a victim of aggression, it had no authority under Article 6 to call for a foreign ministers' meeting.[14] Given Fidel Castro's recent proclamation that he was a life-long Marxist-Leninist, Mexico was the only nation other than Cuba to oppose holding the meeting, although there were five abstentions.

This obstruction represented another setback for Washington. Mexico's importance to the United States on the Cuba issue was underlined at a press conference called by US Senator George Smathers in December 1961 following his meeting with Secretary of External Relations Tello. Smathers expressed his country's disappointment with Mexico's stance, which he dismissed as based on 'juridical obscurities.' He went on to stress that Tello had explained that the Mexican vote was not an expression of support for the Castro regime. The US embassy in Mexico then distributed copies of the text of the press conference in Spanish, taking pains to ensure that the Mexican position was not seen as a direct challenge to the United States.[15]

In the aftermath of the embarrassing failure in the Bay of Pigs, the United States wanted to affirm a hemispheric front against socialism, to impose economic and diplomatic sanctions that would isolate Cuba from the rest of the Americas, and to strengthen the OAS in advance of what Washington feared would become a stronger communist presence in Cuba by expelling it from the organization.[16] When an OAS Meeting of Consultation was scheduled for Punta del Este, Uruguay, in

1962 ostensibly to discuss regional security, it did not escape the Mexicans' attention that its agenda was politically motivated. The US-leaning nations, which sought to isolate Cuba, needed a regional meeting to endorse collective measures. Mexico viewed the proposed measures as clearly violating Cuba's right to self-determination and refused to support them. It acted with Brazil as leaders of the 'soft-liner' nations – those who opposed collective measures against Cuba – while the United States directed the 'hard-liners.'[17]

Because Mexican-led opposition denied Washington the unified regional front it desired, the US delegation had to lower its sights.[18] After the initial Mexican vote against the expulsion of Cuba at Punta del Este, the US media portrayed Mexico as supporting Cuban communism and opposing American democracy. Indicating how seriously Mexico's position was taken by the United States, the US Congress declared that financial aid through the Alliance for Progress and even President John F. Kennedy's planned trip to Mexico should be 'reviewed.'[19]

In astonishing denial of what the events of the Bay of Pigs had clearly demonstrated, Secretary of State Dean Rusk subsequently disclaimed any US quarrel with the Cuban Revolution or with its establishment of socialist economic and political institutions. Instead, the US government chose to adopt the Argentine characterization of the Cuban communism as 'incompatible' with the OAS, an organization whose member states endorsed the ideal of representative democracy. Having so changed its stance, the United States was able to gain Mexico's agreement that the inter-American system could not be indifferent to political philosophies, but Mexico still opposed the expulsion of Cuba from the organization on the grounds that the OAS Charter did not provide for the expulsion of any member. It failed to prevail on this most important point, however: Cuba was expelled from the OAS.

By July 1964, at the OAS's ninth Meeting of Consultation, Mexico, Brazil, Chile, and Bolivia were the only countries still maintaining relations with the Cuban government. Even before the meeting took place, the Mexican government announced that it would oppose any sanctions against Cuba, particularly the anticipated resolution requiring the compliance of only a small number of OAS member states.[20] For example, the general prohibition of air communications with Cuba singled out Mexico, since it was the only OAS member that had air links with the island. By articulating this position beforehand, Mexico indicated that its stance was non-negotiable. Not only did Mexico vote against the resolution that outlined these sanctions, it also refused to honour the resolution when it was passed, making it the only Western-hemisphere nation to maintain diplomatic and commercial relations with the island (besides Canada, which was not yet an OAS member).[21]

Mexico's support for the United Nations' decision to send observers to monitor disturbances in the Dominican Republic in 1965 – the first example of the UN's involvement in a Western hemisphere conflict – illustrated its desire to offset the OAS's tolerance for US interventionism. In the face of US disapproval, Mexico maintained that it was critical for the United Nations to retain its jurisdiction even where such a regional organization as the OAS existed.[22] Even though it endorsed a regional role for this global institution, Mexico tried to keep the Cold War out of Latin America. At OAS Council meetings, Mexico consistently opposed Cuba's characterization as a regional-security threat warranting collective measures under the Rio Treaty. In these ways Mexico became the key country constraining the United States' power within the OAS to legitimize its Cuba policy.[23]

President Luis Echeverría (1970–6) went on later to establish much closer contacts with Castro than had his predecessors.[24] He intensified diplomatic efforts to readmit the ostracized regime to the OAS, so that, in the words of the joint communiqué issued on the occasion of his state visit to Peru, 'the Republic of Cuba be definitively incorporated in the Inter-American dialogue.'[25] Mexico's lobbying led to the approval of a resolution at the OAS's San José meeting in July 1975 that let members re-establish relations with Cuba, effectively nullifying its 1962 ostracization.

But in his domestic politics, President Echeverría was playing a double game. Although he presented himself publicly as a spokesman for the Mexican left at international meetings, he was secretly directing the Mexican police in its own dirty war against Mexican dissidents whose links with Cuba were treated as treasonous subversion. Perhaps for this reason, President Richard Nixon would later indicate in conversation with Echeverría that the United States viewed Mexico as an important ally in promoting US economic and political interests in Latin America.[26]

An explanation for the United States' toleration of Mexico's pro-Castro posturing came to light in 2003 when Kate Doyle of the *National Security Archive* released a report indicating that during Lyndon Johnson's presidency the two countries had actually reached a tacit agreement in which Mexico passed along information on the island's political, economic, and social developments to US intelligence. Indeed, the CIA covertly photographed everyone leaving Mexico for Havana by plane.[27] For this reason, some members of the Johnson administration saw the 'practical desirability of having one Latin American embassy there if possible.'[28] Private tapes of conversations between Nixon and Echeverría demonstrate that the two presidents saw the mutual benefits of Mexico being perceived as the independent, left-leaning country in Latin America to ensure that Cuba did not become the region's leader in this sense. In Nixon's words, 'Let the voice of Echeverría rather than the voice of Castro be the voice of Latin America.'[29]

Nixon's perception of Mexico as a valuable ally could be seen in his encouraging it to promote internal stability in other Latin American countries in order to make foreign (that is, US) investments more secure, something that the United States could not do without being seen to be interfering in these states' internal affairs. Whether Mexico negotiated its position directly in Washington or at the OAS meetings, the result was the same: Mexico acted as Cuba's spokesmen at the OAS but did not in fact obstruct the United States in this period. This interpretation is consistent with Echeverría supporting the establishment of a regional economic-cooperation organization in 1974, the Latin American Economic System.

Although this behind-the-scenes cooperation likely improved Mexican-American relations, the actual benefit to US power was small. Mexico did not displace Cuba as a regional spokesperson for the left in Latin America where the Cuban Revolution did have a fundamental impact, as could be seen in the spread of insurrectionary movements in Nicaragua, Peru, Colombia, El Salvador, and even Mexico itself.

After the Soviet Union's collapse caused American hostility to lose some intensity, Cuba's relationship with Mexico took on more economic value. According to both Cuban and IMF data, Mexico was Cuba's second-largest foreign investor and trade partner after Canada by 1997. The U.S.-Cuba Trade and Economic Council reported that, in the period from 1990 through the first quarter of 1999,[30] Mexico had delivered US$450 million in foreign direct investment to Cuba. Although enhanced integration with the US economy during the PRI's last decade in power intensified Mexico's relations with Washington, its trade with Cuba also increased after 1994.[31]

Given its commercial interests in the island, Mexico worked closely with Canada to oppose US legislation penalizing Cuba's trade partners, particularly the Cuban Liberty and Democratic Solidarity Act (Helms-Burton Act), which it denounced as violating the trade-liberalization principles that the three North American countries had affirmed by signing NAFTA.[32] The Mexican government passed counter-legislation – the Law to Protect Commerce and Investment from Foreign Norms That Contravene International Law – in 1996[33] in consultation with Ottawa, which had longer experience combating US extraterritorial legislation that used American transnational corporations to further Washington's foreign-policy goals.

Compared to the considerable benefits that Cuba received from these economic relations, covert Mexican collaboration with US intelligence appears relatively insignificant. More meaningful was the role that Mexico periodically played trying to improve relations between the two enemies.[34] Mexico had originally begun its mediation efforts in 1960 under the leadership of President Mateos, who coordinated Mexican, Canadian, and Brazilian efforts to defuse the rising tensions between Havana and Washington. Although these efforts were initially rebuffed by President Eisenhower, the Mexican presidency attempted to promote dialogue between the two antagonists for the next four decades.

Some officials in Washington viewed Mexico's mediating role as a nuisance, hesitant to allow the Cuba file too much stature.[35] Yet, on some occasions, the Mexican president also helped facilitate the dialogue that both Castro and the US administration were seeking. When secret Cuban-American talks took place in 1978, for instance, Mexico provided the meeting place where they could occur. Since the White House believed that it would be politically too risky to hold talks in Cuba, hiding them in Cuernavaca was a mutually acceptable alternative that allowed the Americans to meet the Cubans on neutral ground.[36] When the talks were unsuccessful but both parties wanted to keep the dialogue open, Mexico was a key player because it had gained the confidence of both sides, having established itself in the credible position of being both the Cuban Revolution's main defender and Washington's key interlocutor in the hemisphere.

At no time did Mexico encourage palavers between the two opponents with more conviction than in the 1980s, when civil wars were raging in Nicaragua and El Salvador. President Lopez Portillo believed that these dangerous conflagrations could not be resolved without reducing the tensions between the United States and Cuba which he considered the core of the Central American conflict.[37] Because Washington alleged that Cuba was inciting revolution by arming the left-wing Sandinistas in Nicaragua and aiding the Frente Farabundo Martí de Liberación Nacional (FMLN) in El Salvador, it attempted to counter

Cuban influence by funding and training the Contra forces and other paramilitary groups in the region.

Both as an independent actor and as a member of the Contadora Group, Mexico was a major player in conflict-resolution efforts, and, with Cuba's cooperation, it played a central role in bringing the left-leaning groups to the table for the negotiations that led to the final peace accords.[38] Compared to its involvement with Cuba, Mexico's role in pacifying Central America did far more to limit US hegemony, since its efforts helped institutionalize and legalize the radical, anti-American movements which then came to power – an outcome diametrically opposed to the United States' goals. Far from disappearing as Washington wanted, these armed movements morphed into political parties which participated in elections. In 1984 the Sandinistas won country-wide elections, and the following year the former guerrilla leader, Daniel Ortega, was elected president of Nicaragua.[39] On December 14, 1992, the day before armed conflict formally came to an end, El Salvador's supreme electoral court accepted the FMLN's legal registration as a political party which went on to participate in the 1994, 1999, and 2004 elections and to win the presidency in 2009.

Communication with the Cubans again became a matter of great political importance in August 1994 when Washington confronted the problem of the *balseros* – the thousands of Cubans who set sail for Florida following Castro's galvanizing declaration that anyone who wanted to leave the island could do so. In order to find a resolution to the ensuing immigration crisis, the US administration wanted to know Castro's real position and to negotiate a solution.

Despite the PRI government having been seen as supporting George H.W. Bush's candidacy in the 1992 presidential election campaign, President Bill Clinton called President Carlos Salinas de Gortari to ask for his help in contacting the Cubans and communicating his message. Salinas, who was the last to play a double game with both US and Cuban intelligence in order to keep tabs on Cuban-trained guerillas in Mexico,[40] facilitated dialogue between the two hostile nations by discreetly passing messages back and forth with the help of Colombian Nobel laureate Gabriel Garcia Márquez. By early September 1994, Castro and Clinton were able to reach an agreement on how to resolve the problem, including establishing an annual limit to the number of Cuban immigrants the United States would accept and obtaining Castro's assurance he would take measures to control the outflow.[41]

Mexico's role as mediator served both Cuban and US interests by maintaining a dialogue that helped to defuse tensions at moments when they could easily have escalated. This was a tangible benefit to Washington, which wanted to have a dialogue with Cuba but needed a way to maintain its official hard line with Castro's government. Having achieved this diplomatic balance, Mexico was uniquely placed to defend the Cuban regime from US intervention while also facilitating a working relationship between the two.

Constructive Engagement: Canada's Relationship with Cuba

Significant parallels can be drawn between Mexico's and Canada's relations with Cuba despite the two countries' considerable differences. Since Canada was not a member of the OAS until 1990, it was not bound by the organization's 1962 resolution that attempted to isolate Cuba. Because of its support for ideological pluralism abroad and its long and fruitful history of commercial relations with the island, Ottawa resisted the United States' considerable pressure to break diplomatic relations with the Castro regime. Canadian nationalism and the need to demonstrate some policy autonomy ensured that even those governments that were more ideologically aligned with the current US administration maintained a relationship with the island which they could describe as one of 'constructive engagement.'[42]

Given its regular practice of 'recognizing the government of the day, regardless of its ideology, provided that it enjoyed popular support – which was clearly the case in Cuba,'[43] Canada recognized the Castro government when it came to power, as did Mexico. Though Prime Minister John Diefenbaker was strongly anti-communist, his fierce sense of nationalism led him to maintain good relations with Cuba throughout his term in office (1959–63), a policy that was sustained by all succeeding Canadian leaders, notwithstanding changes in party and a later warming of Canadian-US relations.[44] As with Mexico, the Cuba question became a domestic symbol of foreign-policy independence from the United States, but it was complicated by an early diplomatic incident.

The discovery of a memorandum by the Kennedy administration official Walt Rostow provided documentary proof to Prime Minister Diefenbaker that the United States was intent on 'pushing' Canada around. 'What We Want from Ottawa Trip,' the confidential memo prepared for President Kennedy in advance of his May 1961 visit to Ottawa, documented the US government's goals as follows:

1. To push the Canadians towards an increased commitment to the Alliance for Progress ...
2. To push them towards a decision to join the OAS.
3. To push them towards a larger contribution for the India consortium foreign aid generally ...
4. We want their active support at Geneva and beyond for a more effective monitoring of the borders of Laos and Vietnam.[45]

The Rostow memo's emphasis on getting Canada to join the OAS illustrated not only the United States' recognition of Canada's value as a generally supportive ally but its desire to get its material and moral contribution to the Alliance for Progress, which was an integral component of the United States' broader strategy to curb Cuban influence in Latin America. Washington clearly believed that Canada could be an important regional ally which could build support for US initiatives in the hemisphere because it did not have the imperialist baggage that Uncle Sam carried.

Exacerbated by the Rostow memo incident, Diefenbaker's personal antipathy for Kennedy helped bring Canada-US tensions to a crisis point in October 1962, when the United States detected Soviet missiles being installed in Cuba. Kennedy instructed his ambassador to Canada to insist on assurances that, in accordance with its NORAD obligations, Ottawa would put its own military machine on the same level of alert as were US armed forces. Diefenbaker, who considered it yet another affront that he had not been consulted earlier by the Americans, not only declined to order Canadian forces on the same level of alert but also called into question the US interpretation of events in Cuba by recommending that the United Nations undertake a formal investigation before Ottawa decided on a course of action.[46] Prime ministerial posturing was one thing; action was another. The Canadian Navy and Air Force effectively ignored the prime minister's instructions and cooperated closely with their American counterparts.

Canada's political position on Cuba was rooted in the two economies' productive trade relationship, which Ottawa was not prepared to compromise just for ideological reasons. The Canadian private sector had a history of profitable banking, trade, and investment with the island, and Canadians continued to reap the significant commercial benefits that came from accessing a market that the United States had gratuitously abandoned. For this reason, Ottawa also enjoyed Canadian business's support for an independent Cuba policy. Indeed, Canada was in a strategically advantageous position to supply the North American technology (spare parts and machinery) that Cubans needed once the United States cut off ties with the island, although it did honour a commitment it made not to 'bootleg' US-made goods through Canada.[47]

While Diefenbaker's much more US-friendly Liberal successor, Lester Pearson, maintained a cordial and correct relationship with Cuba, he made no special effort to improve it. In fact, while the Pearson government would not support the Castro government's overthrow, its shock that Castro's complicity with Moscow had brought the world to the edge of nuclear holocaust in 1962 led it to agree to have its diplomats provide Washington with intelligence on Soviet military installations and Soviet ships' comings and goings.[48]

In contrast, commercial relations between Canada and Cuba progressed greatly during the early Trudeau years. Canadian exports to Cuba rose tenfold, from $45 million in 1968 to $450 million by 1981. Over the same period, Cuban exports to Canada rose exponentially from $5 million to $197 million, an increase that turned Canada into Cuba's major capitalist trading partner, displacing both Japan and France.[49] Canada also played a significant role in facilitating Cuba's trade with the Soviet Union in a triangular trade relationship that allowed Moscow to use its Canadian credit lines to buy food which it sent directly to Havana.[50] Indeed, between 1979 and 1987, Canada provided over some Cdn$300 million in cereal (primarily wheat) exports to Cuba per year.[51]

This trade increase should be understood in the context of Trudeau's overall move to revise Canada's defence, economic, and aid policies in the light of Canadians' sensitivity to the United States' overpowering presence in their economy and its resulting threat to their national identity.[52] The 'Third Option' policy of diversifying Canada's trading partners included expanding trade with Havana and even Moscow.

After Castro came to power and US businesses either withdrew or were nationalized, the island had been dependent on Washington's Cold War enemies for economic support. When the Cold War ended, Cuba lost some $6 billion it had been receiving in the form of sugar subsidies because the USSR had paid up to five times the world price for Cuban sugar and had agreed to a sugar-for-oil exchange. What followed in the early 1990s was known euphemistically in Cuba as the 'special period' of economic hardship, which hit its worst point in 1993. In light of this disaster, trade relations with Canada and Mexico, as well as Spain and other partners, became critical lifelines that allowed Cuba slowly to regain its footing and stave off what would have been a much

Table 9.1
Cuba's major sources of imports (millions of Cuban pesos)

	1988	1995	2000
USSR/Russia	5364.4	56.8	111.3
Western Hemisphere, of which	360.4	1441.3	2163.4
Canada	28.6	220.3	311.1
China	175.9	170.8	443.7
Spain	n.a.	353.0	743.2
World	**7580.0**	**2882.5**	**4793.2**

Cuba's major export markets (millions of Cuban pesos)

	1988	1995	2000
USSR/Russia	3683.1	194.5	324.6
Western Hemisphere, of which	98.1	351.1	466.7
Canada	38.5	230.8	277.9
China	226.2	188.9	80.5
Spain	n.a.	93.3	150.2
World	**5518.3**	**1491.6**	**1675.3**

Source: Archibald R.M. Ritter, 'Canadian-Cuban Economic Relations: Past, Present, and Prospective,' in Robert Wright and Lana Wylie, eds., *Our Place in the Sun: Canada and Cuba in the Castro Era* (Toronto: University of Toronto Press 2009), 251.

more serious internal crisis, as suggested by Table 9.1. Subsequently, Cuba recorded a growth in its GDP of 2 per cent in 1994, 2.5 per cent in 1995, and 5 per cent in 1996[53] – a remarkable recovery in the context of its prior 35 per cent contraction.

During the decade of the 1990s, annual two-way trade between Canada and Cuba rose from some US$260 to $500 million.[54] Their historic friendship led Cubans to attach greater value to contracts with Canadians even as Americans began to penetrate the Cuban market. The Atlantic Council of the United States reported that Canada was Cuba's largest source of FDI in the 1990s.[55] In the period, some estimates put Canadian direct investments in Cuba at US$600 million, with proposed investments of US$1.8 billion.[56] By the turn of the century, Canada was Cuba's biggest export market in the Western hemisphere.[57]

When Russia could no longer sustain its purchases, tourism steadily gained importance for Cuba, displacing sugar as its most lucrative economic sector. Between 1990 and 2009, Canada was consistently the single largest source of tourists for Cuba, often by a significant margin.[58] Through its tourists' dollars and its other trade relationships, Canada supplied the island with desperately needed hard currency.

From first seizing power, Castro was well aware of the benefits flowing from a strong relationship with Canada, a US ally and industrialized middle power. Accordingly, Canadian companies were treated in a manner that was totally different from the reception given their American counterparts.[59] For example, when all foreign banks were nationalized in 1960, the only exceptions were the Royal Bank of Canada and the Bank of Nova Scotia, two of the first banks ever established in Cuba in the early 1900s. In a TV interview, Castro indicated that the banks were exempted because they were providing important services to the Revolution. In fact, the Royal Bank also provided an important service to the United States in 1961 by facilitating a transfer of funds to the Banco Nacional de Cuba as a payment for the release of the 1,200 American prisoners taken during the Bay of Pigs invasion. Kennedy felt an obligation to the prisoners and their families, and the Royal Bank aided the delivery of food and medicine to the detainees.[60] After breaking relations with Washington, the Cuban government came to rely on the Canadian banks as its connection to the external financial world. Indeed, Castro emphasized that 'notwithstanding the blockade imposed by Washington, [Cuba] was surviving and developing without too much hardship, due in part to a good working relationship with Canada. The Canadian banks were helping Havana in external financial matters, manufactured goods from Canada were filling the vacuum left in the wake of the US withdrawal, and Cuba was extremely appreciative of [Canada's] independent nationalistic stance despite ongoing US pressure.'[61]

Cuba used Canadian dollars in its international transactions. The relationship also benefited from Trudeau's warm friendship with Castro, which allowed relations to flourish even when the two leaders disagreed. Indeed, Trudeau became the first NATO head of government to make an official visit to Cuba.[62] It was also valuable for Castro's international legitimacy to be able to showcase a good working relationship with a member of the G-7 Economic Summit which represented the world's biggest industrialized countries.

Prime Minister Brian Mulroney's decision to have Canada finally occupy its empty seat in the OAS in 1989 helped strengthen and legitimate its voice on Latin American issues.[63] After the collapse of the Soviet Union, he actually became a more outspoken ally promoting the island's reintegration into the OAS and hemispheric community at large by arguing that Cuba could no longer reasonably be considered a security threat. Secretary of State for External Affairs Joe Clark indicated that Latin American issues could be best managed if Cuba were to be 'brought back into the family of hemispheric nations,' a view – reiterated by his successor, Barbara McDougall – that came to characterize the Canadian position of constructive engagement. While Canada's and the United States' long-term goals for Cuba (democratization and the development of a capitalist economy) were similar, their proposed means for achieving that goal were diametrically opposed.

The clash of perspectives came into higher relief during the prime ministership of Jean Chrétien owing to a series of high-level Canadian political trips to Havana. First came the speaker of the House of Commons in 1995. Then Minister of Foreign Affairs Lloyd Axworthy's visit in 1997 caught the attention of the Washington press, which normally consigns things Canadian to its back pages.[64] Prime Minister Chrétien made his own official visit in 1998, the same year that Pope John Paul II condemned the US embargo, causing many Americans to question whether this was still the correct approach to Cuba.[65]

The Canadian government continued to maintain that the best way to bring about positive change within Cuba was to engage diplomatically and economically with the country. Canada repeatedly voted against the US embargo at the United Nations and spoke out strongly against US legislative actions in the 1990s that sought to tighten the embargo and curb investment in Cuba.[66] Some of Canada's most significant challenges to the United States' Cuban policy were its responses to these extraterritorial pieces of legislation.

The 1990 Mack Amendment extended the US embargo by making it illegal for American subsidiaries in other countries to do business with Cuba and by halting aid or imposing sanctions on those countries that bought Cuban products. This legislation directly targeted Canada, and Ottawa reacted strongly. Beyond its diplomatic protest, the Mulroney government invoked its 1985 Foreign Extraterritorial Measures Act (FEMA), which required any implicated Canadian companies (including US subsidiaries) to ignore the Mack Amendment and report any attempts by American TNC head offices to implement it in Canada.[67] In a letter to US Secretary of State James Baker, Ottawa's own secretary of state for external affairs called on Washington to 'weigh fully the impact the Mack Amendment will have on US-owned enterprises in Canada as well as on our bilateral relationship.'[68] The combination of Canadian and international pressure eventually led President George H.W. Bush to veto the amendment.

Nevertheless, the Mack Amendment was followed in 1992 by the Cuban Democracy Act (CDA), which tightened the embargo on Cuba by stipulating that any ship that had visited Cuba in the previous six months could not dock in American ports. This raised shipping costs dramatically for Cubans at a time when they had limited access to hard currency and so made Canadian and Mexican imports more important, given that shipping distances from these two countries were much shorter than from Europe or Asia. The CDA also made direct Canadian investments and joint business ventures more critical for Cuba as a source of hard currency. Ottawa again responded to the CDA's extraterritoriality by revising FEMA, its own counter-legislation, to make compliance with the US law illegal in Canada.

The largest foreign investor in Cuba, the Saskatchewan company Sherritt International, runs highly successful operations in Cuban mining (including bauxite and nickel), oil and natural gas, tourism, and agricultural projects. It was the source of some aggravation in the American business community because it had partnered with a Cuban state company to run what was formerly Moa Bay Mining. The CDA placed Sherritt on a list of entities banned from doing business in the United States and even with US subsidiaries, so the company had to forego the US market in favour of doing business in Canada, Asia, Europe, and Cuba.[69]

Wal-Mart Canada, however, had a more difficult time navigating the political and legal minefield the CDA had created. When it decided to remove Cuban-made pyjamas from its inventory in order to avoid penalties from its headquarters, Ottawa used FEMA to order Wal-Mart to have the pyjamas put back on the shelves. A US Treasury official warned the Canadians that it was not going to let the matter drop.[70] To demonstrate as much, Republican senators Jesse Helms and Dan Burton proposed the Cuban Liberty and Democratic Solidarity Act soon after.

The Helms-Burton Act, as the measure was commonly known, was signed into law by President Clinton in March 1996. Though Clinton had not initially supported the legislation, he faced increased pressure to pass it following the shooting down in February of two planes of a dissident group, the Brothers-to-the-Rescue, which were attempting to drop anti-Castro leaflets over the island. Support also came from the business community: Otto Reich, a lobbyist for Bacardi Rum, drafted sections of the law. Since Helms-Burton gave non-US citizens standing to make expropriation claims, Bacardi's owners were hoping to get compensation for the Cuban government's expropriation of their facilities in 1960.[71]

Helms-Burton also extended US jurisdiction extraterritorially by allowing a US citizen to bring a suit against, for example, a Canadian citizen or company for 'trafficking' in stolen property. Title IV allowed Washington to ban implicated companies' officials as well as their families from entering the United States. This restriction was placed on Sherritt officials and their children in July 1996, effective unless the company terminated its activity in Cuba within forty-five days. Sherritt was one of only three companies specifically targeted under Title IV – the others being the Mexican Grupo Domos and the Italian Stet International.[72]

Canada reacted forcefully. Within months, Canada's secretary of state for external affairs, Lloyd Axworthy, had established coalitions with allies in a number of international organizations in order to fight the act, including the World Trade Organization, the Organization for Economic Cooperation and Development, the European Union, and the G-7.[73] Axworthy reminded the US administration, which had consistently opposed secondary boycotts against Israel, that 'one cannot have it both ways ... One cannot unilaterally pick and choose which international rules to accept and which to ignore.'[74] The Canadians also worked closely with the Mexicans to draft a resolution challenging the legal validity of Helms-Burton and calling for an official review by the Inter-American Juridical Committee. The resolution passed by a vote of 33 to 1 at the June 1996 OAS meeting in Panama, much to the United States' displeasure.[75] The international criticism of the US legislation's extraterritoriality left Washington looking like a bully for imposing its own outdated Cuba policy on its neighbours and allies in contravention of both international law and the pro-business norms articulated in NAFTA.

Canada's 'unrelenting position, coupled with international support provided by Mexico, the 15-member European Union, and others, forced Bill Clinton to. relent.'[76] The president exercised his authority under Title III of Helms-Burton to suspend the effective date of its implementation for six months, a suspension he continued to renew until he left office in 2001. President George W. Bush maintained the policy of suspending Title III, which as a result never came into operation. The US administration's retreat on Title III 'amounted to an admission that other options needed to be explored to avoid a disruption of good relations with its major trading allies.'[77] Mirroring Mexico's success in mobilizing important allies to change the US approach to Cuba in the OAS, Canada had successfully rallied the support of the United States' trade partners to alter its extraterritorial proclivities.

Given this strong reaction to its unilateralism, the United States attempted to harness a tool that had worked well for Mexico and Canada. As part of a new strategy, President Clinton made Ambassador Stuart Eizenstat a special envoy on Cuba to promote a multilateral effort to establish democracy on the island. He was charged with persuading Canada, Mexico, the countries of Europe, and others to adopt core US principles for regime change. Eizenstat visited Canada in August 1996, only five months after Helms-Burton had been initially signed into law. During this trip, he attempted to make additional demands on Canadian businesses but was firmly rebuffed even by the Business Council on National Issues (BCNI), which represented some 150 of the largest American and Canadian corporations in the Canadian economy.[78] The official Canadian position also had the support of the Canadian Labour Congress (CLC). The change in United States strategy and the speed with which it reacted to Canadian-led opposition indicates that Washington had hoped to create a united front against Cuba rather than pursue its policy alone. The Mexican government pushed equally hard against Helms-Burton, telling its ambassadors abroad to lobby against it.[79]

There is debate as to whether these three pieces of US legislation were in fact designed to create a united international front against Cuba, to send a message to Canada, Mexico, and other Cuban trade partners, or simply to appease the Miami lobby. Perhaps they were designed to do all three. Whatever the motivations, the United States knowingly provoked a confrontation with some of its major allies, including its two NAFTA partners. The legal and political dispute highlighted the emotive nature of the US stance when, in the aftermath of the Cold War, Cuba could no longer be perceived as a security threat and when the effect was only to penalize the Cuban people whom the United States claimed to support. Moreover, the United States' aggressiveness kept the memory of the Bay of Pigs and its other interventionist tactics alive, rallying many Cubans against the ever-present Yankee threat and justifying Castro's crackdown on suspected subversives. It further made Washington appear arrogant in its unilateral attempt to enforce an embargo that had been consistently censured at the UN General Assembly. As a result, the United States was left more isolated than Castro himself.

To Constrain the Constrainer

Arguably, Mexican and Canadian efforts would have had little effect on US power if the United States had been bent on pursuing its interests through coercive measures, but there are clear indicators that the United States recognized the importance of Mexican and Canadian support. One is the US response to Mexico's policy. As we saw, the US reaction to Mexico's voting record in the OAS indicated that Washington hoped either to gain Mexico's support or prevent it from exercising its own influence. Other key regional events highlight the US view that Mexico's was a 'bridge between the United States and the rest of Latin America.'[80]

For example, the settlement in 1963 of the hundred year-old Chamizal border dispute has been interpreted as an effort by the United States to improve its image in the region and with Mexico specifically. A flood in 1864 had caused a slight but symbolic change in the path of the Rio Grande, in effect turning 240 hectares into American property. In 1911 Mexico and the United States agreed to submit the issue to arbitration at the International Boundary Commission, but the proposed settlement was not accepted by the United States until 1963. By improving bilateral relations with Mexico in the 1960s, the United States likely also hoped to gain critical Mexican support for its policy initiatives against Cuba.

There is even some evidence that the United States hoped to end Mexican opposition to its policies through increasing the two countries' economic ties. Ex-president Salinas de Gortari recalls of the NAFTA negotiations: 'Practically the same day as the [US Congress'] approval for fast-track [negotiation authority], the magazine *Proceso* published a memorandum attributed to the US ambassador in Mexico. In that document ... the ambassador informed his country that with NAFTA "the institutionalization of the acceptance of a US orientation in Mexico's foreign policy" would be achieved.'[81]

Canada faced similar pressure from the United States at all official levels for the position it took on Cuba. The Rostow memo demonstrated Washington's interest in securing Canada as an international ally. When this failed to materialize with Cuba, some Americans accused Canada of simply wanting to make a fast buck and exploit the absence of the United States even if it meant 'trading with the enemy.' The former US ambassador to Cuba, the US ambassador to Mexico, members of US Congress, and President Kennedy's adviser Arthur Schlesinger all expressed their disappointment and concern to their Canadian counterparts with varying degrees of menace. Two analysts of the Canada-Cuba relationship note that 'this ongoing criticism reflected the

Kennedy administration's concern that a trusted ally would dare to pursue an independent policy that tended – in a minor way at least – to contradict that taken by the North American superpower.'[82] At times during the early 1960s, anger at Canada over its Cuban policy was strong south of the 49th parallel among American officials, private citizens, and the American media. This sentiment was expressed publicly by protesters who drove from New York to demonstrate outside the Canadian embassy in Washington.[83]

Canada was seen to be undermining US authority and control. Yet Canadian policy was not blindly supportive of Castro and his Revolution. Canada did maintain primary loyalty to the NATO and NORAD alliances and expressed the desire that Cuba would break ties with the Soviet Union. Its position was in fact much more in line with the US government's than Washington seemed willing to realize, but, in the atmosphere of the Cold War's ideological polarization, the overriding American criterion for assessing its neighbours' foreign policies was whether they were 'for us or against us.'

Conclusion

Taken together, Mexico and Canada clearly acted as the Western hemisphere's – indeed, the Western world's – two most important political supports for the Castro regime's consolidation and maturity. That these countries did not carry the Soviet Union's ideological stigma made their support especially valuable in providing greater legitimacy for the Cuban regime. The two US neighbours were instrumental in breaking the US air blockade: Mexico allowed Cubana de Aviación to fly to Mexico City, and Canada gave transit rights to Soviet civilian aircraft so that they could refuel in Gander, Newfoundland. The two countries contributed significantly to Cuba's economic survival after the communist superpower's collapse by helping it earn crucial hard currency through trade, investment, and tourism. The failure of Washington's embargo is understood in the United States as Moscow's work, but in the early 1990s, when Cuba felt the worst effects of the Soviet Union's demise and when the United States was still passing legislation designed to tighten the noose, Mexico and Canada became crucial for the Castro regime's arrival. While their support became relatively less important than Spain's and Venezuela's after the mid-1990s, both remained major economic partners during the whole decade and beyond.

The two governments used different means to achieve the same results, domestic political factors and the hemisphere's dynamics explaining how each chose to act. Each country's relationship with Cuba was made with one eye on Washington, though not in the sense that US pressure forced policy convergence. Ottawa and Mexico City did give priority to their relationship with Washington. At the same time, the United States proved unwilling to let its Cuba policy negatively affect its relationship with its two allies and so accommodated Canadian and Mexican protests against the Mack Amendment and Helms-Burton by vetoing the former and waiving Title III of the latter.

Despite the fact that neither Canada nor Mexico was willing to jeopardize its relationship with the United States for Cuba's sake, both felt the political imperative to satisfy domestic sentiment by adopting an independent stance which held high those foreign-policy tenets differentiating them from the United States. This was especially true once the perceived US economic domination of Canada became a politically sensitive question. The commercial relations that drove the Canada-Cuba relationship buoyed the tradition of recognizing, and trading with, foreign governments in spite of ideological differences.

Mexico's approach was equally pragmatic. Its official relationship with Castro's Cuba was shaped largely by the principle of non-intervention, aimed at both resisting US interventionism and maintaining the ruling PRI's rhetorical consistency, but the principle was tempered in practice by Mexico's need to survive next to the United States. Both Mexico City's and Ottawa's defence of non-intervention, ideological plurality, and Cuba's sovereignty made it difficult for Washington to contemplate overt military action against the Castro regime.

Neither country offered blind support for Castro. Both governments cooperated with Washington to some degree by sharing information and both repeatedly criticized Cuba on its human-rights record. When Cuba intervened in the Angolan war, Canada stopped its foreign aid (which it subsequently reinstated).

One way to assess the net impact of Mexican and Canadian foreign policy on US power in the case of Cuba is to evaluate what impact these policies had on the ability of the US to achieve its goals. In 1963 the US assistant secretary of state for interamerican affairs, Edwin Martin, defined American strategy as twofold – 'to isolate Cuba from the hemisphere and discredit the image of the Cuban revolution in the hemisphere.'[84] Mexico and Canada prevented the United States from isolating Cuba from the hemisphere by maintaining full diplomatic and commercial relations. Following Mexico's example, all Latin American nations re-established relations with the island over the following years, starting with Chile in 1970. To this extent, Mexico can claim victory for its early policy towards Cuba.[85]

Neither was the Cuban Revolution fully discredited during the Cold War since Mexico defended Cuba's right to self-determination and both Canada and Mexico provided significant financial support. Both nations maintained healthy trade flows despite various US attempts at curbing foreign commercial relationships with Cuba. Following his 1998 visit to Havana, Prime Minister Jean Chrétien was able to announce significant progress on a bilateral investment-protection treaty under which Cuba agreed to compensate Canadian life-insurance companies which had been nationalized after 1959. A Canadian government official publicly contrasted this progress with the United States' approach, observing that the Canadian experience should provide 'a lesson to the Americans about what they ought to be doing instead of passing the Helms-Burton law and placing an embargo on Cuba.'[86]

As late as October 2003, a US assistant secretary of state indicated that the US position on Cuba, whether for domestic political reasons or others, would not change. He reported to the Senate Foreign Relations Committee that 'the president is determined to see the end of the Castro regime and the dismantling of the apparatus that has kept him in office for so long.'[87] This ideological hard line became an embarrassment to Washington and an obstacle to its relationships with important allies, leaving it looking like a bully in an age when multilateralism was seen to be more legitimate. Annual UN General Assembly votes regularly expressed international condemnation of the embargo, with only three dissenting votes – from the United States itself, Israel (the number one recipient of US foreign aid), and the Marshall Islands or Uzbekistan in alternating years.[88]

As a gesture of reconciliation by the other hemispheric nations, Cuba was elected to a temporary seat on the UN Security Council in 1989[89] and it assumed leadership of the Non-Aligned Movement in 2006.[90] When Castro retired in 2008, he did so on his own terms, having seen the Revolution through almost fifty years of an embargo, the devastating 'special period,' no fewer than ten US presidents, and some 600 plots on his life, one as late as 2000.[91] Castro's triumph was in large part the result of international economic and diplomatic partnerships. As neighbours with economies and societies that were highly integrated with the United States, no two countries were more vulnerable to US arm twisting than Canada and Mexico, a dependency that made their contributions to Cuba's Revolution all the more remarkable.

Thinking counterfactually, if the two governments had taken Washington's side in the debate on Cuba as members of the United Nations or the inter-American system, all Western hemisphere nations would have broken relations with Cuba. With Castro entirely ostracized in the hemisphere, the United States would probably have obtained the region's consent to intervene militarily under the Rio Treaty. Failing its forced regime change, the Castro regime would have experienced an even more severe economic shock in the early 1990s. The resulting social distress might have been enough to inspire such discontent domestically that the Cuban people themselves would have overthrown the government and handed Washington the success it had long craved.

Conclusion to the Book: How the United States Needs Canada and Mexico

At the outset of our quest, we laid out a problematic that we can now review:

- To what extent do Canada and Mexico as *agents* construct US power?
- Do these contributions create a dependency that makes the United States as *object* vulnerable to its neighbours' withdrawal of their support?
- Taking the policy initiative as *agent*, has Washington been able to neutralize the autonomy-reducing consequence of such dependence?

Addressing our first question, our nine chapters argued that the United States derives a noteworthy portion of its material assets, its domestic security, and its international influence from its North American neighbours. When these external supports are thoroughly analysed, it becomes clear that they are constantly varying over time and by issue. As far as our second question was concerned, we unearthed little evidence that Canada's and Mexico's contributions to US economic, military, and international power translated into any palpable US *dependency* on its continental neighbours. This puzzle – that the periphery can simultaneously be so important and so unimportant – set up the answer to our third question: the United State has been able to shape the policy space within which Canada and Mexico relate to it by encouraging their support and weakening any leverage that might otherwise have accrued to them. Washington's agency has both *fostered* Canada's and Mexico's contributions to its power and *forestalled* their constraints on it.

This Conclusion reviews our core research results. In the Epilogue that follows it, we will relate these findings to the larger question of the three states' interrelationships and what they signify for North America as a region. There, we will see what light our conclusions shed on the political economy of the continent's three states, an issue that *Uncle Sam and Us* addressed for Canada alone in 2002. Next, we will reflect on what the analysis developed in *Dependent America?* suggests about the nature of the North American region, to bring up to date the analysis laid out in *Does North America Exist?* in 2008. Finally, the Epilogue will speculate about the possible futures and looming choices that face the region's three members.

But first we will review the six principal findings of this study.

Finding One: The Periphery Constructs the United States' Economic Strength

In a nutshell, Part One argued that, because of the trade and investment opportunities offered by their markets, their abundant non-renewable natural resources, and their ever-renewing supplies of skilled and unskilled labour, Canada and Mexico are the United States' largest external sources of its material power.

Mexican and Canadian contributions to US prosperity have deep roots. In basic but decisive ways, the precondition for the United States' ultimate geopolitical supremacy was its early successes in forcing its northern and southern neighbours to cede it vast territories. More out of war weariness than necessity, Great Britain handed over the lands to the west of its thirteen ex-colonies and to the east of the Mississippi River in the 1783 Treaty of Paris, territories that would form the heart of the US midwest. Then, in the Treaty of Guadalupe Hidalgo signed in 1848 at the end of its triumphant war with its Mexican neighbours, the United States appropriated almost half their territory. This gigantic secession comprised present-day California, Nevada, Utah, Oklahoma, Kansas, Colorado, and Wyoming, and parts of Arizona and New Mexico. In a further treaty signed in 1853, Washington bought the rest of Arizona and New Mexico and managed to move Texas's frontier south to the Rio Grande.

These eighteenth-century acquisitions from the Canadian colonies' distracted guardian and nineteenth-century annexations from a vanquished Mexico ultimately helped transform the United States of America into the twentieth century's global strongman, a country powerful enough to contribute decisively to the destruction of the German and Japanese empires in the Second World War and engineer a global containment of the communist bloc during the Cold War. Of course, its overwhelming superiority in material and military power also had destructive consequences, prompting Washington to overreach itself in Southeast Asia in the 1960s and the Middle East four decades later.

Although the GDP of present-day Mexico and Canada taken together would constitute only the fifth-largest economy in the world, their intense, proximity-driven economic ties with the United States make them by far the largest foreign consumers of its exports and the biggest suppliers of its imports. While Canada has lost its earlier position as the primary site for US foreign direct investment, it remains in the top tier of investment targets for US transnational corporations abroad. The US market's perimeter has been extended to embrace large parts – and in some economic sectors such as mass retailing, almost all – of the continental periphery. Taken together, Canadian and Mexican economic and political spaces increase US competitiveness, and this continental trade and investment raises US GDP and the average American's wealth by some 2 to 3 per cent.

While the availability of their supplies and the demand for their resources have fluctuated with the passage of time and the evolution of technology, Canada principally and Mexico secondarily are the US economy's largest foreign vendors of oil, and Canada its principal external source of natural gas. Despite oil's inherent fungibility, the decline of Mexican oil production, and the recent shale-gas discoveries in the continental United States, both Canada and Mexico remain central contributors to US energy security, a fact that is acknowledged by American economic and political decision makers, if not always by their fellow citizens.

On the human-power front, the North American periphery has for decades been the largest purveyor of skilled and unskilled men and women to the US labour force. This low-cost, flexible, and highly productive labour, primarily from Mexico, has inserted itself into American production and service chains, greasing key cogs in the US economy while having little impact on domestic workers' wages. Rather than compromising their country's interests as American xenophobes maintain, these immigrants help spread US norms and values back in the periphery where they bolster the United States' legitimacy. Across both time and space we can see that the North American periphery has in the past and continues in the present to construct US material wealth – and so global power – to an impressive, even surprising, degree.

Finding Two: The Periphery as Security Ally

Geographical contiguity turns Canada's and Mexico's land and populations into a potential menace to the United States, but this proximity also makes the Canadian and Mexican governments its closest allies in securing the US homeland.

The United States' acknowledgement of its security vulnerability has risen and fallen over time but came into urgent relief in the aftermath of the 9/11 terrorist attacks on New York and Washington. In Part Two, we addressed the paradox of North American security in which Canada's and Mexico's territories and their criminal underworlds present the main foreign threats facing the United States at the same time as their governments become its most important partners in countering these dangers. While the two countries have played mixed roles in the past, sometimes supporting and sometimes resisting the United States' military power, the recent harmonization of Canadian and Mexican security practices with US standards has turned both countries into Washington's prime associates in its wars on terror and drugs.

Large differences between their military institutions, defence capabilities, and strategic doctrines highlight the historic disparity between Canada's hand-in-glove and Mexico's hand-on-sword defence relations with the United States. At its extreme in the Cold War, Canada was so integrated in the American military system that the US defence perimeter's anti-Soviet early-warning systems extended right up to the Canadian Arctic.

While the geographical facts of Mexico's and Canada's existence pose a challenge for United States to secure its land borders, the persistence with which it has pressed its neighbours into action indicates its recognition of their significance for its security. Without Canada's and Mexico's agreeing to harmonize their immigration policies and integrate their intelligence capacities, thus pushing the US anti-terrorist defence perimeter outwards towards the periphery's far-flung frontiers, the United States' exposure to unconventional threats would increase markedly.

The United States' abrupt shift in 2001 to an anti-terrorism paradigm precipitated multiple types of cooperation among the three countries' police and intelligence forces. When it came to security against non-state actors, Ottawa focused on financing joint border-toughening measures, harmonizing its visa policies, supplying the Department of Homeland Security with police records on suspects and data about its citizens' air-travel movements, and integrating its counter-intelligence capacities with Washington's. Mexico's more restrictive immigration stance made it less attractive as a route for al-Qaeda's recruits, but it nevertheless upgraded and integrated many of its data systems with those of the United States and started to militarize its southern border with Guatemala to extend the US security perimeter southward.

In the United States' struggle with narcotics, Canada's and Mexico's relative importance is reversed. The criminal underworld in Canada ships a lesser volume and a less societally damaging array of illegal narcotics to the United States, while Canadian police forces cooperate seamlessly with their cross-border counterparts. With the largest American intake of the most socially dangerous and addictive narcotics coming from a Mexico that was reluctant to cooperate, the United States grew used to acting unilaterally, whether by waging its war on drugs in Mexico though US agents or by building a border wall without Mexican agreement. Once Mexico recognized that its own public's safety was jeopardized by the narcotics scourge to such an extent that it had shared interests with the United States in controlling the cartels, it took the initiative. Soon after his election in 2006, President Felipe Calderón's sent the Mexican army into action against the most violent gangs, a measure seen by Washington as an important gesture in support of its escalating, if unsuccessful, war on drugs.

Finding Three: The Periphery as Constraint

Implicit in the notion of construction is its opposite – the possibility of constraint. While Parts One and Two documented the substantial ways in which the North American periphery constructs US power, they also showed that Canada and Mexico have constrained the United States, although rarely have these constraints significantly undermined US power.

Within the energy realm, both countries have made determined attempts to reduce their US exports. The outright nationalization of Mexico's oil sector just before the Second World War represented the extreme case. Canada's most ambitious effort to extract greater national benefit from its domestic resources was the comprehensive 1980 National Energy Program, which was designed to restructure the country's (meaning in practice Alberta's) oil and gas sectors by redirecting them from the US market to servicing the populations and industries of central and eastern Canada. Washington's consternation made it clear that the NEP was regarded as harmful to both the United States' prosperity and its national security. More generally, Canadian and Mexican industrial-development policies that promoted domestic industries and restricted American TNCs also fell into this category. Placing such key sectors as financial institutions out of bounds for foreign corporations or instituting various regulatory instruments to support the competitiveness of their domestic enterprises was resisted by Washington, even when it practised such strategies itself.

To the extent that the United States' wealth derives from its transnational corporations' operations abroad, any foreign law or regulation that explicitly restricts their room for expansion by favouring domestic enterprises can also be considered a constraint on US power. Nominally, the two neighbours may also be deemed to constrain the United States' economic power by not giving its corporations license to make more gains in their economies. For example, not further liberalizing intellectual-property-rights laws to expand the monopoly controls of US pharmaceutical corporations can be construed according to this hypothetical logic as constraining US power.

Constraints from the periphery on US military security have largely come from Mexico's opposing the Pentagon's strategic vision. The impact of the Mexican military – either by not cooperating with or by actively seeking to block US designs – has been uneven in light of Mexico's marginal military importance in US eyes. By contrast, Canada's military constraints are more annoying than effective. On occasion, Ottawa has queried aspects of the Pentagon's strategic planning, has refused to participate in some weapons projects, has demurred over allowing it to test its missiles over Canadian territory, or has not spent enough dollars on its own armed forces to keep Washington happy. Many of these defence-policy constraints have been more due to public opinion than to the government rejecting US policies, as happened in 2003 when, because of the Chrétien government's sensitivity, Ottawa deferred to popular resistance and decided to rebuff the Bush administration's demands that Canada line up behind its war against Iraq.

Mexican and Canadian constraints on US anti-terrorism security since 2001 are largely hypothetical. If reckoned by actual incidents, no attacks on the United States have originated from its periphery. If measured in governmental capabilities to monitor potential terrorists and screen incoming passengers, Mexico's institutional weakness could be considered a constraint. Its tenuous governance capacity and its less enthusiastic commitment to anti-terrorism raise concerns in the Department of Homeland Security.

If societal cohesion is integral to a country's global power, Canadian gangs and Mexican cartels constrain the United States' power when they funnel illegal drugs into the hands of American addicts. As a result of their huge profit margins, the drug cartels have become so rich, so lethally armed, so ruthless – in a word, so powerful – that they can corrupt or fend off any government effort to inhibit them. Horrendous levels of violence along the Mexican frontier certainly aggravate insecurity for Americans in the border regions. The Canadian and Mexican governments contribute to this constraint on US societal security if and when their policing capacity fails to control this traffic.

Finding Four: The Periphery as Multilateral Help and Hindrance

While Parts One and Two addressed the material and security areas, where the periphery's geographical contiguity makes its capacity to construct US power unique in the world, Part Three discussed Canada and Mexico as middle powers on the international stage where their actions rarely affect Washington's capacity to achieve its international goals. Our three chapters provided examples of how, in pursuing what they deemed their own national interests, Canada's and Mexico's economic and political diplomacy have supported and opposed US global objectives.

We made the case that, without first Canada's and then Mexico's cooperation in developing the path-breaking North American Free Trade Agreement, the United States would not have managed to pull off its remarkable post-Cold War achievement of transforming the limited and weak General Agreement on Tariffs and Trade into the intrusive and muscular World Trade Organization. With its own commercial diplomacy, Mexico subsequently supported US efforts to spread neoconservative economic norms throughout Latin America. Canada also negotiated trade-liberalization and investment-protection agreements that further strengthened the rights of TNCs in weaker countries. But the periphery could hardly contribute to US global economic power when Washington lost its focus on its own economic liberalization agenda by fixating instead on anti-terrorism.

The impact on US interests of Canada and Mexico pursuing their own policies in the multilateral realm depends on how these interests are conceived. The Clinton administration believed that a strong International Criminal Court with universal jurisdiction would serve the United States' soft-power interests by bringing to justice political leaders whose crimes against humanity within their failed states threatened regional security. The election of George W. Bush overturned the executive branch's position. This reversal in domestic US politics inverted the way in which the periphery's actions impinged on the United States' perceived interests, so that the new administration viewed Canada's and Mexico's creation of and support for the ICC as a clear impediment to its armed forces' acting freely around the world. Our discussion of the ICC showed that, when the continental periphery had little sense of shared interests with the United States, it could use its diplomatic assets to considerable effect, whether by Canada's negotiating the court's creation as part of a like-minded coalition or by Mexico's resisting US efforts to hamstring the new institution's functioning.

Revolutionary Cuba presents a country-specific example of Washington's foreign policy being blocked by its two neighbours. While the story was laced with back-channel ambiguities, Washington's embargo of Fidel Castro's regime was undermined by Mexico and Canada providing moderate but regime-saving levels of both political and economic support which stymied initial US attempts to get hemispheric backing for military intervention and later kept the country from collapse when it was on the ropes after the Soviet Union's demise.

When Canada's and Mexico's declared interests do not coincide with those of their giant neighbour, they may indeed constrain the United States' economic strength, impair its sense of security, or block it from achieving its international objectives, but overall the periphery constrains far fewer aspects of US power than it constructs.

Finding Five: The United States Is Not Politically Dependent

Despite its material dependence on its neighbours for a good part of its wealth and security and a smaller part of its foreign-policy effectiveness, we found that the United States has largely neutralized any resulting potential dependency on Canada or Mexico.

Our book's title plays on the ambiguity inherent in the notion of dependency both to suggest the logical novelty of our approach and to make an analytical point. Novel was our endeavour to treat the United States as *object* and to research its two neighbours' roles as causal *agents* in the construction of its wealth, security, and global influence. Analytically we wanted to establish how much the United States is in fact beneficially dependent on Canada and Mexico for its economic growth and prosperity, for its security, and even for some of its global sway.

Given the considerable economic and military significance of both Canada and Mexico in the construction of the United States' power, it is noteworthy how few of our probes uncovered any empirical evidence of actual policy dependence. Absent trade with and investment in Canada, the US economy would lose some eight million jobs, but it would hardly go into shock the way we might expect the manufacturing industry in Ontario to implode if the United States blockaded its northern border.

Despite the United States' chronic concerns about its energy dependence, it is hard to make a convincing case that it is so vulnerable to the interruption of Canadian or Mexican imports that it would be crippled if they were cut off. Deprived of Canadian oil, the US economy would find more suppliers offshore, though, admittedly, they are politically far less stable and reliable. And, while the United States is dependent on Canada for virtually all its natural-gas imports, domestic shale-gas discoveries may satiate US demand. The American oil sector's anger at the nationalization of its Mexican assets and Washington's fuming against Trudeau's National Energy Program both signalled their recognition that the periphery's energy reserves were very important. But these strong reactions did not so much demonstrate a US dependency on its periphery as they revealed the proprietary belief that the periphery's resources were what Americans call 'North American' when they feel Mexican or Canadian assets should be freely available for their commercial exploitation.

In the case of labour, the marked dependence of key US industries and a range of core service sectors on Mexican immigrants for maintaining their competitiveness has unclear implications. If the need for below-minimum-wage workers persisted in the face of Mexicans' disappearance from the labour market, the United States could open its doors to motivated immigrants from many other lands, although these new arrivals would not be likely to leave the country and return home during periods of high unemployment as illegal Mexican immigrants have tended to do. The loss of a sustained inflow of highly skilled young Canadians would be far less perceptible but would accentuate the United States' serious inadequacies in producing enough well-trained graduates to sustain its primacy as an innovation-based economy.

A clear example of the United States' freedom from policy dependence on its periphery is Mexico's inability to leverage its emigrants' centrality to the US economy into political influence. With the exception of its bargaining success during the Second World War, when it resolved US claims over Mexico's oil-company nationalization by making security commitments and later laid down preconditions for the establishment of a guest-worker program, Mexico has been unable to translate the key role played by its migrant labour into even such minimal concessions as preventing their harassment by some US political constituencies.

To the north, while Canada was able to shape the Smart Border negotiations in the aftermath of September 11, 2001 so that the ultimate agreement focused on maintaining commercial flows across the border, this process did not so much illustrate a one-way dependency of the United States on Canada for its security as it demonstrated both sides' recognition of their mutual interdependence in dealing with a shared security challenge. The parameters of this challenge were defined by Washington, but the goal of neutralizing the Islamic terrorist threat was adopted by Canada as its own. While the Mexican government's failures to eliminate its domestic narcotics cartels and to maintain public safety in its own border cities expose Americans in the border region to greater violence, this social vulnerability does not give Mexico clout over US policy. Instead, it obliges the United States to invest in trying to construct a stronger and less corrupt Mexican governance capacity by funding a good deal of the technology and training required for putting its desired reforms there into effect.

Finding Six: Washington's Efforts Have Pre-empted Its Dependence

If the United States is not 'dependent' on its two neighbours in the sense that it is subject to their influence over its policy, this is in good part because, over time, Washington has successfully managed to blunt their capacities to take actions that would prejudice its interests.

As we have shown throughout this book, agency flows in both directions in the continuing dialectic between the United States and its periphery, a condition referred to academically as 'complex interdependence' when there are multiple channels of contact between the regimes over a very broad range of issues, reducing the importance of military force.[1] Although we have focused on how Canada and Mexico (seen as agents) have constructed US power (as the object of this agency), it is clear that the US government has seldom been passive in these matters. From the first days of its gunboat diplomacy, when warships from the US Navy opened up foreign markets, Washington has been assiduous in pushing its international partners to discontinue policies that restrict the wealth-making potential of US enterprise abroad, to help build its security, and to support its foreign policies.

Where it has found resistance to these goals, it has made every feasible effort to eliminate such constraints on its economic, military, or diplomatic power. Over the past half-century, the bread and butter of US embassies' work has been making representations to their host governments on behalf of American economic interests. From threatening retaliation against foreign government's national film-promotion policies to lobbying for changes in the fine print of specific banking regulations, American diplomacy has laboured diligently to have measures it considers prejudicial to its overseas business' interests dismantled.

That Canada and Mexico have so little leverage on Washington does not suggest their objective unimportance. Rather, their impotence speaks to the United States' success in shaping the political, economic, and military structures within which continental policy processes play out – including disempowering any governance institutions that could give the perimeter a voice in determining the content of US policies.

In this regard, the United States has followed a dual strategy. Positively, it has worked to make the Canadian and Mexican economies complementary to its interests by obtaining for its corporations full access to the periphery's raw materials and extending their operations into the periphery's manufacturing and consumer markets. Negatively, Washington has sought to prevent the periphery from emerging as a competitor. Before CUFTA and NAFTA, this prevention strategy was implemented at the border by three principal devices. Instituting high tariffs on manufactured imports encouraged raw-material exports while discouraging industrial exports. Anti-dumping duties let US businesses harass their Canadian competitors' exports. Countervailing duties could negate the neighbours' public programs for making their exports to the United States more competitive. Notwithstanding the rhetoric about North America as a free-trade area, Washington's less competitive industries retained their powers to invoke these contingency measures to block the imports of such cheaper Canadian and Mexican products as lumber, fruit, and vegetables.

US agency has not been restricted to reactive damage control. When it came to promoting the inflow of needed raw materials from abroad, the US government's tax incentives stimulated US corporations' exploration, development, and production of many resources in Canada and Mexico beyond oil and natural gas. US foreign economic policies sensitively distinguished between its competitive and its complementary interests. Whereas its contingent protectionism was designed to retaliate against foreign-government subsidies on the grounds that they gave their companies' exports to the United States unfair advantages, Washington explicitly endorsed government subsidies for the exploration and development of Canadian energy resources by having authorization for Canadian energy subsidies written into the Canada-US Free Trade Agreement.

Institutionalizing its two bilateral relationships with CUFTA and NAFTA was a masterstroke of US agency. Although the negotiations were formally initiated at the request of Canada, then Mexico, the US government resolved long lists of irritants by transforming its ad hoc protests into general rules that constitutionally bound Canada's and Mexico's behaviour. Thereafter, American business could effectively discipline any breaching of these rules since investor-state dispute-settlement arbitration would be uninhibited by the kind of diplomatic considerations that might restrain the US government from prosecuting one of its corporation's complaints.

Washington did not always act alone in countermanding unacceptable actions by its neighbours. It often worked with business allies in Canada or Mexico or with their provinces and states. When the US State Department was deeply alarmed by the prospect of Trudeau's National Energy Program diverting what it had believed to be a secure and stable supply of western Canadian petroleum, it cooperated closely with the Albertan government and petroleum sector which were just as outraged by what they saw as Ottawa's power grab. A shared concern about a possible resurgence of energy nationalism led Alberta to support Washington's insistence that CUFTA contain guarantees that would prevent Ottawa from interfering with the southward flow or pricing of Canadian energy.

In matters of national defence, overcoming Canada's minor constraints has generally had a low priority for the Pentagon, which prudently leaves differences with Ottawa to be resolved through the passage of time and the processes of domestic Canadian politics. Given Mexicans' hyper-sensitivity to any intervention by gringos in their affairs, US efforts to reverse Mexico's deep-rooted antipathy and cajole it into military and naval cooperation have had to be modestly designed and patiently implemented.

As threats to the United States changed, so did Washington's efforts to persuade the periphery to construct its security. Al-Qaeda's shocking attacks prompted Washington's insistence on intense security collaboration from its two neighbours. Since it believed that Canada's multicultural social space gave attractive cover for jihadists planning to mount further assaults, it pressed Ottawa to harmonize Canadian policies with its many anti-terrorism initiatives.

Even when the United States was vulnerable to security threats coming from Canada and Mexico and depended on the periphery's cooperation to keep its territory safe, it exploited its neighbours' more extreme dependence on US markets by linking its security demands to their economic needs. If Canadian business wanted to regain some of its ease of access to the US economy, it was for Ottawa to integrate its security practices with US systems and to prove to the Department of Homeland Security that its anti-terrorism laws were sufficiently strict. Otherwise, it was understood that the DHS would further thicken the US-Canadian border, impeding Canadian commerce.

The United States' agency in constraining the Canadian and Mexican underworlds' threat is largely directed through intergovernmental channels, and its pressure to toughen, preferably to harmonize, Canadian policies with American approaches was welcomed in Ottawa. For several decades, Washington pushed Mexico to support its war against the narcotics underworld. As with its security against terrorism, the United States' dependence on its Hispanic ally for its anti-narcotics security has obliged it to offer greater funding for reforming its neighbour's institutional, legal, and policing capacities.

The US government has not always succeeded in constraining its constrainers. We showed in Part Three that, in the domain of diplomacy, its efforts could prove counter-productive, particularly when its actions veered towards bullying. In those foreign-policy issues where Canada and Mexico opposed it, Washington's efforts to reverse their international actions were sometimes ill-conceived and poorly executed. Its influence over the negotiating process leading up to the Rome Statue was marginal. US manoeuvres to undermine what it felt were the International Criminal Court's constraints on its power by coercing weaker states to sign bilateral immunity agreements backfired in the Western hemisphere when Mexico refused to toe Washington's line. Similarly, US diplomacy proved ineffectual in disabling the periphery's resistance to its Cuba strategy. Indeed, such provocative actions as the Helms-Burton Act made its neighbours even more determined to maintain their business-as-usual stance vis-à-vis Fidel Castro's regime. US agency is less effective in constraining the periphery when Canada and Mexico act against US interests in the multilateral domain than when they do so bilaterally in a situation where a consciousness of their extreme dependence creates a feeling of great vulnerability to US retaliation and where a sense of shared purpose breeds their willingness to cooperate.

While we have been discussing US agency as a separate factor, the United States' interactions with its periphery are only rarely unilateral. Normally they involve negotiations in which Canada and Mexico press their own causes even if the bargaining outcomes may generally favour the more powerful party.

In short, despite the extent to which US power is determined by its relationships with Canada and Mexico, Washington's behaviour towards these two neighbours demonstrates neither deference towards its benefactors nor concern about their continuing to supply the assets it needs. Armed with a self-confident political culture developed since their Revolutionary War, American citizens and politicians have seen themselves unquestioningly as agents in the world, not as objects – as masters, not servants. While President Barack Obama changed the United States' official discourse vis-à-vis the rest of the world by emphasizing his country's need to cooperate with its international partners, consciousness of its interdependence has not caused Washington to rethink how it relates to its continental periphery.

On the other side of the same coin, its two neighbours constantly demonstrate dependent-country comportment towards the United States. Mexican and Canadian politicians may complain about US behaviour and become angry at American politicians, but they never try to flex their economic or security muscle to impose their will on Uncle Sam. If Washington complies with a Canadian demand, it is either because it accepts Ottawa's rationale or because domestic US pressures have pushed it in the desired direction.

This lack of psychological and behavioural dependency on the United States' part is explained by its having – through its *own* agency – turned Mexico and Canada's greater economic, security, and multilateral dependence on it into rules, policies, or practices that minimize any vulnerability it might have experienced in their regard. 'Dependent America' acts independently because it has systematically laid down markers that prevent Canada and Mexico from leveraging US material dependency on them into their policy influence over it.

Even when Ottawa has an irritant to be resolved, the two countries' differing negotiating cultures generally result in arrangements that further American interests over Canadian ones. In exchange for Canadian corporations' access to a remnant of the Obama administration's stimulus program, the 2010 Canada–United States Government Procurement Agreement opened access for US companies to almost all provincial governments' public-sector procurement, a major concession they had refused to make in the 1990s. At the subfederal level, where provinces and states interact across the international boundary, the cross-border balance of forces tends to be more equal. In border regions characterized by more symmetrical, cooperative, and sustained power relations, the resolution by provincial and state governments of such mutual problems as water management consequently yields more balanced outcomes.

The timidity of Canadian officials and their readiness to accept small gains while making large concessions contrasts with the tough-minded assertiveness of US negotiators and illustrates a different point. The deeply rooted bilateral relationship between Canada and the United States has developed a negotiating culture in which US agency generally prevails, so that the ultimate intergovernmental arrangement serves the US interest more than it meets Canada's needs. In the 2011 bargaining over an enhanced continental security perimeter, for example, Washington inserted a completely extraneous demand for greater intellectual property rights for its pharmaceutical industry as part of a deal that was meant to thin down the previously thickened barriers to cross-border trade.

This negotiating aggressiveness underlines a contradiction that pervades American trade discourse. Notwithstanding its positive-sum, we-all-win market-liberation rhetoric, Washington typically bargains in a zero-sum mercantilist mode, pressing for its companies' greater access to the periphery's market while resisting concessions that would expand opportunities for the periphery's TNCs in its own market.

Our purpose was to elucidate the North American periphery's relationship to US power, and, with our nine studies, we rest our dual case. On the one hand, the United States derives a considerable part of its economic wealth, security, and global efficacy from its relationship with Canada and Mexico. On the other, it has successfully disabled these two neighbours' political capacity to turn its material dependency against it. By considering the United States as the object of other forces, we can better understand that its power is not entirely self-determined. Yet the spaces for Canada's and Mexico's agency are generally bounded by policy frameworks put in place through US efforts. In recognizing how much agency Washington exerts in boosting Canada's and Mexico's constructive role and containing their potential to constrain it, we can understand why its neighbours so consistently punch below their weight in their own region.

What North America has become is our last concern. In the following Epilogue we consider what further light this book's analysis has to shed on the internal autonomy and external capacity of the continent's three states and the character of their region on the world stage.

Epilogue to the Trilogy:
The Disunited States of North America

This study of how Canada and Mexico support US power brings to an end a three-tier research project on the impact of globalization on North America's political economy that goes back to the mid-1990s. The norms, rules, and rights laid out in NAFTA for Mexico, Canada, and the United States and in the WTO for most of the world's states were so comprehensive in their scope and so intrusive in their reach that they gave analysts cause to investigate their implications for individual nation-states. For the signatory states, which were being dubbed 'post-national' because they seemed to be losing some of the core sovereignty that had been their defining feature, the question was whether this reduced autonomy in regulating their own economies was being offset by greater external capacity for their corporations in others.

In contrast with scholars' historic interest in the nation-state, analysing the regional governance arrangements that were springing up on all continents was a comparatively new enterprise. Regional institutions had long existed in the security sphere, most notably NATO and the Warsaw Pact. Similarly, specialized cross-border agreements that coordinated the management of such shared resources as joint watersheds were not uncommon. Yet only in Western Europe had multi-state governance evolved to a significant degree. When Brazil, Argentina, Uruguay, and Paraguay came together in 1991 to set up Mercosur (Market of the South), broadly modelled after the European Community, and when, three years later, developing Mexico entered an economic-integration agreement with the two rich and highly developed states to its north, scholars had reason to ask whether North America was joining an apparently global trend by taking on the character of a governance region.

The next section will review how the analysis that we have just completed for *Dependent America?* requires us to update our understanding of the Canadian, Mexican, and American states' relationship to each other that was developed in *Uncle Sam and Us* (2002) and *Does North America Exist?* (2008). This Epilogue will then look at how the six findings summarized in our Conclusion require us to adjust our understanding of North America as a regional entity – first its political economy and then its future prospects as a transnational governance region.

Globalization, Neoconservatism, and the Canadian State

In the context of NAFTA's and the WTO's economic-governance innovations, *Uncle Sam and Us* (2002) identified how three sets of influences had shaped the Canadian state's internal autonomy (its ability to meet its citizens' needs) and its external capacity (its ability to promote their interests abroad): first, the external pressures from new transnational regimes; second, the shift to a neoconservative paradigm in domestic policy; and third, such path-dependent forces as the continuing impact of the Canadian constitution's Charter of Rights and Freedoms.

Uncle Sam's conceptual originality was to argue that NAFTA and the WTO had 're-constitutionalized' Canada's legal order by adding to it a demanding new set of norms, rules, and rights that limited the federal, municipal, and provincial governments' powers. These changes also gave foreign corporations a powerful new capacity to challenge domestic regulations. The investor-state dispute-settlement mechanism was NAFTA's only significant governance instrument but it inhibited governments at all levels from passing environmental, economic, social, or cultural measures that might give a NAFTA company reason to launch often extravagant claims against them.

International economic agreements are negotiated as an exchange of concessions in which each signatory agrees to reduce certain protectionist measures (and so sacrifice some internal autonomy) in return for equivalently valued increases in their firms' capacity to sell to or operate in the other signatories' economies. These arrangements generally institutionalize some greater influence for the signatory states over their counterparts through their participation in transnational institutions designed to manage the newly increased collective interests of participating states.

As *Uncle Sam and Us* showed, Canada did not gain the increased external capacity vis-à-vis the United States it had expected because

Washington would not comply with important trade-dispute rulings. *Does North America Exist?* explained how Washington then imposed a new, security-justified border thickening that had the same effect as protectionist barriers, slowing the growth of trade and investment relations with its periphery. Thus, while NAFTA was originally touted for having persuaded the United States to accept a dispute-settlement mechanism that made American protectionist trade measures harassing Canadian exports subject to reversal by binational panels, this gold-medal governance achievement turned to dross.

In practice, Canada's external capacity vis-à-vis the United States has actually diminished. It is now so locked into the US market that its options are very restricted, while its hopes for continental economic integration are constrained by the United States' security and economic nationalism. If there is a silver lining in this story, it is the United States' general reluctance to link demands in one issue domain with another. Early in the Cold War, a diplomatic culture developed that tried to have even the most politically fraught bilateral disputes settled privately by the two countries' officials. While this mutual restraint subsequently eroded, 'coercive issue linkage' still remains rare in the US-Canadian relationship. Thanks to its own self-restraint, the complexities of American domestic politics, and a US preference to retaliate passively by closing off Canadian officials' access to the Beltway, Canada may enjoy more autonomy than its extreme economic integration might otherwise lead one to expect.[1]

The basic question for *Uncle Sam and Us* was not whether Canada would survive US-led globalization but what kind of post-national state it would become. Nine years later, the answer has become clearer. The fairly generous and relatively egalitarian socio-economic system that it had developed during the Keynesian era was gradually eroded in the ensuing decades, a transformation that was due less to the forces of globalization impinging directly on Canada than to the internal changes that moved the Liberal and Progressive Conservative parties to embrace neoconservatism and later brought Stephen Harper's far more radical Conservative Party to power. Harper's ideas and stances may appear imported from the Republican Party's right wing but they were homegrown at the University of Calgary whose political thinkers have had a transformative impact on the whole country.

If the Harper government cuts back its own environmental department, rejects a national childcare program, builds more prisons during a period of falling crime rates, and eviscerates the decennial census, this is not because the forces of globalization have twisted its arm. It is because most of the Canadian business community actively supports and much of the Canadian public passively condones policies that promote growing social inequality, deny environmental degradation, and advance simplistic law-and-order solutions to complex problems of public safety. Canada's diminished internal autonomy is best illustrated by the Harper government's straightforward declaration that it would not decide on its climate-change policy until the US Congress had determined its approach.

In a similar fashion, Canada's capacity abroad has been affected not so much by changes in the international rule book as by its own decisions. Downplaying its diplomatic focus on human security in favour of military interventions while flouting its Kyoto-Protocol obligations showed clearly that the Canadian government still has enough external capacity to make the shifts in its international positions that it wishes – even if these actions diminish its own international legitimacy to the point of its 2010 bid for a temporary seat on the United Nations' Security Council being decisively rejected.

Globalization, Neoconservatism, and the Mexican State

Like Canada, Mexico has experienced globalization's reduction of its internal autonomy primarily through its relationship with the United States and the international institutions it dominates. Preaching the Washington Consensus, the IMF imposed tough conditions for Mexico's bailout following its 1982 financial crisis, and the GATT insisted, when Mexico joined in 1986, that Mexico bring its foreign-investment and trade restrictions into line with liberal economic norms. It was at US graduate schools in the 1980s that the Mexican elite's next generation learned the new thinking on market reform. Meanwhile, it became clear that, if it were to convince the US Congress that it was a worthy candidate for negotiating its own trade and investment agreement, Mexico had first to make significant reforms in its economic policies and democratic practices.

On top of these pre-emptive structural shifts, NAFTA clauses required far more substantial changes in Mexico's legislative order than they had done for Canada. Most strikingly, the government agreed to install within its legal system a regime that let American and Canadian companies operate in Mexico within the same administrative framework concerning anti-dumping and countervailing duties as they enjoyed in each other's jurisdictions.

Unlike Canada's external constitution, which was inserted into an

already effective, highly sophisticated, liberal-democratic state structure and had pushed the country in a direction that its business and
political elites were already advocating, Mexico's was superimposed
on an impoverished, haltingly functioning state that was required to
administer numerous and virtually simultaneous policy shocks on
itself. This made the country's transition to neoconservatism far more
abrupt than Canada's. Having operated within the closed borders of an
autarchic state, it suddenly faced an open border with the world's most
powerful economy while having to transform such policy systems as
its intellectual-property-rights regime. The measures were more radical,
with hundreds of state-owned corporations being sold off, and the consequences were more traumatic, with US chains (Wal-Mart, Starbucks,
and the like) and manufacturers spreading around the country and helping to drive legions of small and medium enterprises into bankruptcy.

A state's autonomy is only partly derived from its constitutional
powers and so is only partly reduced by the international agreements
that it signs. Its ability to adopt the policies it wants for its citizens also
depends on its institutions' inherent effectiveness. Mexico became a
laboratory for neoconservative reform designed by sophisticated technocrats whose drawing boards were in some respects far removed from
the Mexican reality. Policy makers could issue edicts and prescribe the
necessary legislation but could not determine how individual and business behaviour would respond, in particular the deeply entrenched
corporatist systems which were ingrained in the Mexican political culture. Just because the various economic sectors' chambers of commerce
accepted the merits of Mexico's opening up to a fiercely competitive
global economy did not mean that these business interests could rein-
carnate their family-controlled members' firms as budding Microsofts
or junior Cargills. Underlying and impeding Mexico's transformation
program was a universal but resource-starved education and health
infrastructure and a justice system blighted by poorly trained judges
and worse-paid police officers. These public services' archaic relationships with the government presented a stultifying obstacle to Mexico's
anticipated economic revolution.

Beyond the existing institutional inefficacy that impeded the changes
which the Mexican government wished to bring about, its new external
constitution came into effect at the same time as other factors shook up
the country's political machinery. Because NAFTA and the WTO were
implemented under the PRI's muzzling autocracy, the political fallout
they engendered was not expressed publicly until after 2000, when

Vicente Fox wrested the presidency away from the ruling party. The polarization that then gave voice to Mexico's impoverished and unemployed, many the casualties of free trade, largely paralysed Fox's six years in office.

Even if his successor was more adept at finding allies in Congress to push through some partial energy and finance reforms, Felipe Calderón could not resolve the Mexican polity's double dilemma. First, it had introduced a new legal superstructure before it had transformed its socio-political infrastructure, a modernization that would have given its neoconservative restructuring a better chance to succeed.

A more daunting impediment to Mexico's autonomy came from its second dilemma. The narcotics industry, which had quietly entangled its operations throughout the Mexican underworld in tandem with the PRI regime, rapidly morphed into such a lethally armed set of ruthlessly warring cartels that the Mexican state lost its ability to assure its citizens their rights to a minimal degree of security in many parts of the country. At the same time, it could not eradicate the judicial and police corruption that sustained this insecurity. To understand the impact of globalization and neoconservatism on the Mexican state, it is now futile to debate whether its narcotics insecurity is exogenously created (demand coming from the United States and supply flowing in from Colombia) or endogenously generated (by the locally operating cartels). The point is that pervasive and horrific violence has added a crushing handicap to Mexico's prospects for having its neoconservative wager succeed, because it has undermined the state's ability to function.

Nor did help come from the outside. The United States' and Canada's unwillingness to address these realities and launch a serious effort dedicated to pulling their large, southern partner up to northern standards speaks both to the narrow thinking of NAFTA's founders and to the institutional inadequacy of what they created. Having dismissed the pertinence of the European Union's complex institutions, NAFTA's negotiators apparently believed their own rhetoric: once liberated from government regulations and reinstitutionalized with weak dispute-settlement mechanisms, the market's invisible hand would do the heavy lifting. Since they insisted that theirs was simply a trade and investment deal, they maintained that there was no need to create mechanisms to handle the societal or environmental side effects of neoconservatism's prescriptions. Above all, there were to be no solidarity programs transferring major funding from rich Canada and the United States to help Mexico overcome its heavy handicaps and effect the necessary transformations of its ailing educational, medical, social, judicial, policing, and military systems.

If visitors to Mexico are selective, they can find evidence that belies any talk of the country's failure within NAFTA. A stroll through the leafy Polanco or hyper-modern Santa Fe districts of Mexico City reveals gorgeous restaurants and luxury stores, dazzling hotels and apartment blocks, and office buildings that house consultants and legal firms who serve a high-tech economy fuelled by Mexico's new economic model. But the country's overall data do not suggest that these germs of super-prosperity have been contagious. On the contrary, its recent record has been discouraging, particularly in comparison with the other large developing countries that are emerging as rising powers.

These deficits in Mexico's internal autonomy have not been offset by any increase in its external capacity. Mexican labourers play a big role in helping the US economy confront its challenges, and Mexicans in the underworld manage a cross-border trade in narcotics so violent that it inflicts horrendous costs on American society. But Mexico as a government plays virtually no part in determining the contours of the continent to which it contributes 24 per cent of the population and 6 per cent of the Gross National Income. It can protest the American ambassador's undiplomatic assessment when his words are leaked in the media and have him recalled, but it cannot prevail on Washington to interdict the flow of high-powered US weapons to its cartels. Still less can it persuade the United States to address the root cause of the narcotics industry's socially catastrophic impact in both countries, the criminalization of drug consumption. That so much attention was paid to President Obama's March 2011 agreement to restore a pilot project allowing a few Mexican truckers to deliver their goods within the United States on a trial basis after years of US non-compliance with its clear NAFTA commitment is testimony to Mexico's muted political voice in Washington.

Globalization, Neoconservatism, and the American State

Because of its economy's huge size and diversity, its complex political structure, and the worldwide scope of its commercial, military, and cultural interests, the United States is affected, in terms of both internal autonomy and external capacity, by a diverse set of factors other than those related to its immediate continental periphery. However, if we are to understand what constructs and constrains US power overall, we need to appreciate the surprising contrast between the growth of the United States' capacity to shape its own continental neighbourhood and the decline in its power vis-à-vis the rest of the world – two tetonic shifts in the international political economy which help us comprehend the varied impact of globalization and neoconservatism on the United States' standing in the twenty-first century.

As with Canada and Mexico, changes in its global interactions have caused the United States to lose external capacity over the past two decades. The 2007–9 financial crisis punctured American policy makers' sense of economic control and international leadership, as they struggled to rescue the US automobile industry and were forced to bail out scores of banks and insurers. The mortgage crisis may well have been made in the USA, but its repercussions could not be contained there because so much of the US debt was held elsewhere, particularly in Asia. The resonance of anti-China and anti-NAFTA rhetoric indicates how many Americans feel besieged and powerless. Stretched by its exhausting wars in the Middle East, the US military is even criticized for overreach by conservative US voices, most notably in its 2011 aerial bombardment of Colonel Muammar Gaddafi's Libya.

This global weakening has sparked vigorous academic stocktaking. For some, the United States' days as the world's pre-eminent superpower are numbered. Immobilized by domestic political fractures and contained by the rise of competitor powers both in the developing world and through regionalized blocs, the United States will increasingly need to reconcile itself to its gradual decline.[2] Yet, at the same time as America has faltered globally, the American state has become more assertive within its own region where it has been able to offload onto its continental neighbours some of globalization's negative externalities. Whereas the periphery's internal autonomy was constricted without its gaining any offsetting external capacity in Washington, the United States' external capacity vis-à-vis its neighbours was significantly extended without it losing domestic autonomy.

Since NAFTA's and the WTO's norms and rules were largely projections of American norms and rules onto other states' external constitutions, signing onto these agreements had little impact on the United States' sovereignty. Even where it had made concessions sacrificing some internal autonomy, the United States' huge power differential with Canada and Mexico afforded it impunity when it chose not to respect even its minimal NAFTA obligations. When Washington refused to comply with its trade obligations in the still-festering trucking issue analysed in *Does North America Exist?* Mexico was helpless. And when it lost most of the NAFTA and WTO dispute-settlement rulings in its long-running softwood-lumber dispute with Canada, it was Ottawa that capitulated in the face of Washington's non-compliance. In other words, the United States' internal autonomy has been largely uncompromised in its continental relationships, even as it has been diminished by its global challengers' increasing influence over it. Thanks to both NAFTA and the WTO, the United States has extended its dominion over both of its continental relationships. Even as the Obama administration publicly reset the clock on US multilateralism by emphasizing the United States' interdependence with its counterparts and by engaging with the expanded G-20 Economic Summit, it has attempted no such reinvigoration of its continental relations. North America's trilateral institutions – from the SPP to the North American leaders' summit – have been left to wither, and Washington has reasserted its security problematic with continued border militarization to its north and south alike.

Moreover, the overlapping regimes of the WTO and NAFTA have enhanced American continental economic capacity. NAFTA's national-treatment norm required Canadian governments to treat American firms in the same way as they would domestic companies. This barely noticed concession spliced into the Canadian legal order an overarching, constitution-like imperative that invalidated any measures designed to help domestic corporations compete with their giant American rivals. Through its handling of the *Sports Illustrated* case at the WTO and under NAFTA – discussed in *Uncle Sam and Us* – the United States leveraged its new economic agreements to reach back in time and undo Canada's carefully constructed protections for its magazine industry, allowing US magazines to publish split-run editions in Canada.[3]

With NAFTA further locking in such other US objectives as the guaranteed export of Canadian oil, the United States Trade Representative's office has little to do besides the congressionally required annual monitoring of other issues of concern, for instance, Canadian legislation on intellectual property rights for pharmaceuticals. In its relationship with Canada, the United States has a friendly, stable, democratic state that participates enthusiastically in its cultural life, believes in the virtues of market principles, accepts a re-engineering of the bilateral relationship devoted to entrenching the Canadian contribution to US prosperity, and willingly conforms to Washington's demands that both countries 'securitize' its their territory against terrorism and narcotics.

The parallel with Washington's Mexico relationship is clear, but the differences are stark. Before the free-trade era, the United States could see in its southern neighbour another vast, coast-to coast, European-settled federation with a basically capitalist economy and a formally democratic constitution. But its culture was Hispanic, its indigenous population impoverished, its social disparities large, its governance systems weak, its ruling PRI dictatorial, and its heavily regulated economy stultifyingly bureaucratized. There were so many factors that constituted significant obstacles to its becoming a viable economic partner that the United States' efforts to have the Mexican economy serve its interests were at first cautiously undertaken. US congressional reports took issue with human-rights violations. American environmental activists encouraged their Mexican counterparts to get on their feet.

As it had with CUFTA for Canada, the US government achieved a breakthrough in having Mexico accept NAFTA's rigorous disciplines. Its capacity to persuade Mexico to adapt its economic system to suit American interests was not restricted to changing Mexico's external constitution under NAFTA and the WTO's aegis. Initially, NAFTA's Chapter 17 on intellectual property rights was applied to Mexico's pharmaceuticals sector. Then, lobbied by Big Pharma, Congress instructed the USTR to maintain pressure on Mexico to extend its intellectual property rights still further.[4] Having failed to extract from Mexico the same concessions on energy exports and pricing that it had won in CUFTA from Canada, Washington did not give up. American TNCs contracted their services to Pemex and, under the George W. Bush administration, Mexican officials were seconded into the North America Energy Working Group to start them thinking about energy security in continental terms.

The proof that NAFTA was initially strengthening the US economy by spreading its footprint in Mexico was what the 1992 US presidential candidate Ross Perot had memorably called a 'giant sucking sound' – the early flood of investment by American TNCs building maquiladora assembly plants, relocating parts of their production chains, and expanding US retail franchises. And, had other things been equal, the modernization dreams of NAFTA's Mexican negotiators at the end of the twentieth century might have been realized. But, at the beginning of the twentieth-first century, Mexico's domestic and external security threats changed catastrophically.

Although it is often opined that, with NAFTA, the United States had lost its capacity to impose its will on its neighbours by threatening retaliation, the security paradigm it introduced after 9/11 used the possibility of restricting market access to force Canada and Mexico to tighten their border-security, policing, and counter-intelligence capabilities. There is little doubt that the United States has increased its security capacity by extending its anti-terrorist perimeter throughout Canada. But, because the Mexican government has been unable to control the havoc generated by the heavily armed cartels, the United States' capacity to ensure narcotics stability beyond its southern border has decreased even as the two countries' socio-economic integration has intensified.

The United States' relationship with Canada and Mexico thus presents a paradox. *Does North America Exist?* showed that globalization was reducing the salience of North America as an economic entity, whether in the steel sector's global restructuring or in the international consolidation of banking regulations. However, even as North American regionalism falters, the United States' immediate periphery is becoming a more important partner in sustaining its material power. Constrained by its global partners' superior growth rates, the United States can still count on the unusually beneficial economic relationship it quietly maintains with its continental periphery. Although it normally ignores its neighbours' interests when dealing with other countries, its gradual decline no longer affords Washington this luxury without having to pay a price.

That price is its two neighbours expanding their strategic gaze from the continent to the world. Canada and Mexico are endeavouring to strengthen their economic links with other countries. Indian capital is already investing in iron-ore extraction in Quebec, while Chinese firms are staking out Alberta's tar sands. Even with disputes over Newfoundland's seal industry and its visa restrictions on Czech visitors, Canada has busily negotiated a comprehensive economic trade agreement with the European Union. Hosting the G-20 Economic Summit in 2012, Mexico is positioning itself as the champion of emerging economies and the developing world. This economic internationalization could mitigate Canada's and Mexico's lopsided dependencies on a US market to which their access has been curtailed since 9/11. Should they succeed in diversifying their economic links by attracting more FDI from overseas and should their extra-regional imports and exports abroad begin to expand more than their intra-regional trade, the United States' economic perimeter in North America will contract, and their construction of US material strength will ipso facto diminish. The North American periphery has been Uncle Sam's gold-laying goose for as long as most can remember. It would make an ironic epitaph for the United States' hegemonic decline if alienating its most valuable and easily cultivated foreign asset accelerated its self-induced fall.

Globalization, Neoconservatism, and the State of North America

Having reviewed how our new research updates our understanding of North America's three states and their interrelationships, we can now reflect on what it has to tell us about the nature of North America itself as a global region. This will in turn enable us to see how North America's evolution – either as a governance region or as a giant's region – will determine its three members' interlocked destinies in the years ahead.

North America as a Governance Region

Compared to such parts of the world as South Asia and the Middle East or Latin America and Africa, North America was one of the most promising candidates for academic standing as a 'world region' in the Cold War's aftermath. Defined geographically by oceans to the east, west, and north and by Guatemala to the south, its contours were clearly demarcated. With its European-settler populations, its indigenous communities, and its huge multi-ethnic diasporas, the continent enjoyed in its diversity a comparatively high level of cultural coherence. As for stability, it had not experienced inter-state war since 1848 or intra-state civil war since Mexico's Revolution came to a bloody end in 1917.

Economically speaking, the three-economy entity was roughly equal to the whole European Union in gross national product and in population. By the Cold War's end, much of the Mexican economy was uncompetitive, but it was complementary to that of the United States. Foreign direct investment was expected to pour in because of its low labour costs and its proximity to the US market, sparking an economic transformation. In short, North America was believed to have a strong potential for intensifying the already advanced state of commercial integration that had developed between the United States and its two neighbours.

Canada and the United States had effectively functioning governments, and Mexico's was stable, albeit autocratic. The neoconservative consensus of the three member states' political and economic elites and the consequent convergence of the periphery's political values and public attitudes with those of the United States heralded compatible approaches to new economic challenges. If there was a cloud on the new North America's horizon, it was the towering dominance over the continent of the world's most powerful state, but the official rhetoric in the three countries and the seriousness with which NAFTA was taken in capitals overseas suggested that North America might become not just an entity that was treated as a new global actor by its three signatories but one whose 'regionness' was recognized by the world community.

Fifteen years after NAFTA was signed by the Clinton, Salinas, and Mulroney governments, such hopes were dashed. Although the region was becoming economically and socially more integrated, it was not showing signs of growing transnational governance. NAFTA welcomed Mexico into the US and Canadian markets under a detailed rule book for trade and investment, but the region was not evolving through the standard textbook stages from its partial free trade towards a common market let alone a monetary union. North America's failure to meet some of its proponents' optimistic expectations lies in its flawed conceptualization as Europe-lite. Most analysts' thinking about North America under NAFTA was largely conditioned by Brussels' extraordinary asymmetry-reducing, institutionally muscular, societally inspired approach to achieving a multi-state continent. But North America's differences with the EU overwhelm the similarities. It has no collective vision similar to Europe's aspirations for peace. It has no identity roots reaching back millennia to ancient Greece and beyond. It has no overarching sense of the community solidarity that would prompt its stronger members to help pull the weaker ones up to their level of well-being or its student populations to mingle.

In this vein, *Does North America Exist?* confirmed in 2008 that the continent was not an embryonic European Union steadily developing transnational governance forms. On the contrary, in its first decade it had displayed quite distinct characteristics. Institutionally speaking, it was much less than the word 'NAFTA' conjured up. It had virtually no legislative, executive, or administrative presence, and five of its six dispute-settlement processes had been shown to have no effective judicial capacity. Proof of the institutional vacuum created by NAFTA was the addition in 2005 of a trilateral, executive-driven Security and Prosperity Partnership that spawned an annual Leaders' Summit and a big-business North American Competitiveness Council. The SPP and NACC enjoyed scant democratic legitimacy but gave the periphery's political and business elites much coveted 'face time' with their US counterparts, including the president himself.

The next three years saw this phenomenon reversed. That the newly elected President Obama could mothball the SPP's effort to reinstitutionalize North America showed that Washington needs no institutions at all to get what it wants from its periphery – including unilaterally abolishing one that the three countries had spent two years negotiating before its launch in 2005. At the same time, the annual trilateral Leaders' Summit has been discontinued. While these new North American institutions have flamed out, old ones have slowly fizzled. In 2010 one of NAFTA's vaunted innovations – the North American Commission on Labour Cooperation – quietly closed its doors, although its sister commission on environmental cooperation bravely continued despite being largely ignored by its three sponsoring governments.

In parallel with the SPP's development, Canada's and Mexico's discovery of each other had motivated them to generate what appeared to be the continent's gradually strengthening 'third bilateral.' Yet, in the past three years, Canada has played its own part in breaking down whatever trilateral solidarity NAFTA originally represented. Because it feared that its influence in Washington was contaminated by being associated with Mexico, Ottawa has taken pains to turn its back on Mexico. Openly, it instituted offensive visa requirements on Mexican travellers to Canada. Privately, it expressed reticence for a continental trilateralism that would link itself with Mexico in Washington's eyes. Although the political, economic, and military conditions that had sustained Canada's cordial transnational political culture with the United States have long since eroded,[5] the Harper government is bent on resurrecting the two countries' special relationship.

NAFTA's potential for economic integration was initially signalled by significant increases in trade, investment, and corporate mergers. Such parts of the North American economy as agriculture and energy, where geographical propinquity reinforced continental integration, were integrating on a continental basis. Where some sectors such as the automobile and textile industries had first appeared to be continentalizing thanks to NAFTA's rules of origin, global corporate restructuring and China's eruption as an export colossus caused the three countries' putative merging to falter. The disintegration of the continent's trinational coherence through a process of global restructuring accelerated in the late 2000s, with China, India, and Brazil increasing their stakes in the periphery's resource, manufacturing, and information-technology sectors and so diminishing the dominance of US foreign direct investment in the Canadian and Mexican economies. Other sectors' regulatory harmonization was due to global, not continental, governance, as in the case of banking, whose continental consolidation has only been moderate.

While globalizing market forces had *centrifugal* effects on North America's regional coherence, security issues were *centripetal* in their impact. In the wake of 9/11, North America appeared just what it had originally seemed: an intergovernmentally managed zone in which Canada and Mexico – on pain of facing thickened borders obstructing their exports – were obliged to conform to Washington's anti-terrorist, immigration, intelligence, and information-monitoring standards.

In the short term, this governance-lite institutional model served particular corporate interests in the United States very well. Whereas US businesses had benefited from their expanded North American rights under NAFTA's investment arbitration tribunals, so too did they prefer the absence of continental decision-making institutions that might have offset their new-found capacity by imposing greater responsibilities for environmental or social responsibility. Without the region having its own governance institutions, US-Canadian and US-Mexican conflicts are naturally resolved in the continent's de facto capital, Washington. Leaving its irritants to be addressed on an ad hoc basis generally suits the most powerful US party in any dispute, because the American political system's processes are highly responsive to pressure from business lobbies or social coalitions from which Canadians or Mexicans as non-citizens are excluded.

In the medium term, this kind of responsiveness to its special interests acted against the United States' broader national interests. For instance, the American firearms lobby resisted government attempts to control the southward flow of US weaponry and so enabled the Mexican cartels to cause mayhem along both sides of the United States' border. But the connection between economic liberalization's externalities and Mexico's losing battles with the cartels are not recognized, since neoconservative thinking can compartmentalize this US security threat as a separate issue to be addressed under the rubric of the war on drugs.

The two periphery governments had clearly believed that the NAFTA bargain would be advantageous, because they assumed their increased economic integration in the North American market would attract more job-creating foreign direct investment. Even before September 2001, this confidence had been undermined, for NAFTA had turned out in practice to be somewhat different from the way it had been presented in theory. Continuing harassment by US anti-dumping and countervailing measures had negated the benefits that such highly competitive sectors as Canadian steel had expected from the new 'free-trade' era. This continuing US protectionism, which would have been incompatible with a genuine free-trade area, impelled Canada's leading steel concerns to put all their new investments in the United States. In the three years since *Does North America Exist?* was published, the US economy's gravitational tendency to attract investment at Canada's and Mexico's expense has been reinforced by Buy American pressure on TNCs to break up their continental production chains and relocate all their operations within the United States' territory.

Nor have the continent's three countries shown signs of a growing regional cohesion. On the contrary, in the frantic international efforts at the end of the 2000s to rethink the global regulation of financial institutions, North America had no collective voice. Its members even took actions against each other. The Obama administration's stimulus program endorsed Buy America provisions that caused US-based transnationals to source all their inputs in the United States. As for security, although Washington pushed to extend its anti-terrorist perimeter to include its continental neighbours, it nevertheless militarized its own land boundaries against them, extending the US-Mexican border wall and toughening its treatment of undocumented Mexican immigrants. Throughout the United States and Mexico, public venom focused on NAFTA has limited the capacity of any government to promote the institutional innovations that could yet shape continental economic trajectories.[6] When Canada failed to organize the North American Leaders' Summit, for which it was responsible as the designated host for 2010, the only thing more remarkable than how few cared was how few appeared even to notice.

In sum, North America meets none of the criteria that scholars have laid down as the test for world 'regionness.'[7] It shows few signs of rule making that is institutionally generated and governs its three members. It is not recognized as a significant entity by actors within the continent: the three governments barely show any consideration of each others' interests in their international behaviour. Nor is it treated as an entity by actors overseas: the Argentine foreign office's North American affairs bureau, for instance, does not include Mexico in its remit. Functionally driven needs for regulatory changes do not generate collective decision making. Transnational regulatory changes happen on an ad hoc basis when Washington's intergovernmental lobbying induces Mexico and Canada to alter existing rules or introduce new legislation.

This collapse of trilateralism has pushed both Mexico and Canada back to dealing separately with Washington and belatedly attempting diversification. In response to its worsened prospects for a northward-directed integration, the Mexican government made a show in 2010 of establishing a new hemispheric entity which included all the Latin American and Caribbean states but *excluded* the United States and Canada. It also made efforts to strengthen the trade and investment agreements it had already signed with other countries. But gestures of solidarity towards its Latin American counterparts and aspirations for internationalization do little to disentangle Mexico's conflicted embrace of the United States. Managing its one overpowering bilateral relationship remains its central preoccupation. Although the issues remained too inflamed in 2011 – whether from public outcries over American border agents killing an unarmed migrant or US drones violating Mexico's airspace sovereignty – for the border's administration to be depoliticized, regulatory harmonization efforts continued apace, and a High-Level Regulatory Cooperation Council created in May 2010 delivered an action plan with specific bureaucratic goals the following March.

Canada upped this ante by agreeing with the White House in February 2011 to establish two frankly bilateral joint executive-level institutions. A Regulatory Cooperation Council (RCC) was mandated to adopt compatible approaches to public regulations in the interests of deepening economic integration. Like its Mexican counterpart, the RCC promised to push ahead with the business-inspired agenda already worked out by the SPP's Competitiveness Council. While this policy harmonization was to proceed, a joint Beyond the Border Working Group was set up to pick up the traces of the 2001 US-Canada smart-border agreement and its 2002 follow-up action plan. A decade after these agreements were signed, the United States was still pushing Canada to deliver more Charter of Rights-protected information on Canadian citizens and travellers. For its part, Canada was still dreaming that the Department of Homeland Security could be induced to trust Canadian security policies enough that it would lighten its restrictions on goods and people crossing the common border.[8] The Harper government's requiring Canadians crossing the border – along with all other travellers – to have a passport so that their entry into Canada could be shared with US immigration authorities would mark a major concession, meeting DHS's desire to verify whether all who had entered the United States had eventually exited.[9] Whether such a concession would lead to significant US border thinning or border-infrastructure enhancement requiring congressional approval or financing, however, remained extremely doubtful.[10]

While Canada's break with trilateralism might suggest that North America has returned to its pre-free-trade, hub-and-spoke profile, its two-speed bilateralism is nevertheless different from the cross-border governance of three decades ago. Bilateral relations are becoming lightly institutionalized by regulatory harmonization bodies staffed by government officials. Such executive-level consultations as the Clean Energy Dialogue established when President Obama visited Ottawa in February 2009 leads to Canada 'paralleling' the policies that emerge from the US political process.[11] And this invisibly harmonizing North America still contains a Mexico whose relationship with Canada has developed significantly under NAFTA and after 9/11.

North America as a Giant's Region

If North America is looking less and less like a transnational governance region, how should we understand it? In the 1990s the international system was morphing into a 'world of regions embedded in the American imperium.'[12] From this perspective, in which the US superpower was the world's hub, Canada and Mexico played primarily supportive roles, and North America had little existence in its own right. But by 2008, the continent appeared sui generis, with its new forms of business autonomy and corporate judicial capacity, its resulting deepened asymmetries, and its negligible institutional constraints on its leader, which also served as global hegemon. Having put as many eggs as they could in their NAFTA basket, the Canadian and Mexican governments appeared to have no options but to hope for a border-thinning reduction of the United States' anti-terrorist fixation.

Three years later, the United States was no longer the master at the centre of a unipolar universe. Following the implosion of its economic system and the uneven success of its military efforts in Iraq and Afghanistan, it was declining from unchallengeable supremacy to being the first among a group of global giants. In Latin American, African, and Asian markets, it was losing its primacy to a resilient Europe, a burgeoning China, and even an emerging India. This rebalancing of the United States' relationship with the rest of the world contrasts with its continuing dominance within its own continent.

What we can infer from the United States' capacity to gain economically and militarily from its neighbours without having to interact with them institutionally is that North America has developed a no-formal-governance model quite distinct from the European Union's asymmetry-reducing transnational approach. Instead, the North American region is characterized by such a high disparity in size that its Goliath has the capacity to extract economic gains, security guarantees, and diplomatic support from its immediate neighbours without letting them play Davids who participate in any meaningful, member-driven collective decision making. This immunity to their influence affords the dominant state the luxury of being able to keep control within its neighbourhood while devoting most of its externally oriented energies to dealing with the rest of the world.

These characteristics do not make North America a lonely exception to the general rule of global regionalization. On the contrary, North America is actually more like some other major regions in the world than is the European Union. Consider Russia in the domain formerly known as the Union of Soviet Socialist Republics, or India in South Asia, and even China in territorial East Asia. These areas are not so much *world* regions as *giants'* regions in the sense that their hegemon wields enough de facto control over its geographical periphery that it can take its immediate neighbours for granted, treating its dealings with them as secondary in importance to its relations with the rest of the world. The giant focusing its attention outside its immediate continent creates further centripetal pressures, since, in their frustration with their cavalier treatment, its neighbours join in the competition to negotiate special arrangements with partners overseas.

Seeing the United States in this way helps us understand why North America does not 'exist' as a region in the same way as does Europe with its complex, powerful, and productive governance processes. This insight should now assist us in envisaging the alternative futures facing it and each of its three states.

North America's Alternative Futures

To envisage North America's prospects, it will help if we take a step back historically and see how fundamentally the US approach to world regions has changed.

In the Second World War's immediate aftermath, the ambitious model that the United States applied to fostering regionalism had three characteristics. It took a long-term view. It acknowledged the causal complexity of the various processes that it wanted to see reformed. And it accepted its responsibility to engage actively in the region with a creative generosity. The exemplar of this policy-making trinity was the Marshall Plan, a far-sighted, all-embracing, well-financed program which helped war-devastated Europe get back on its feet and become the United States' most significant partner for growing its economy and winning its Cold War against the Soviet Union.

This expansive and sophisticated approach to global policy at the beginning of the Keynesian period contrasts strikingly with the narrower ways that the United States has approached its own region during the last thirty years. It focused on the short term. It compartmentalized issues. It committed minimal resources, maintaining that the inevitably rising tide would ultimately raise all boats. As a result, NAFTA was a narrowly conceived deal designed to resolve Washington's ongoing economic irritants with its neighbours without worrying about the social, environmental, or security consequences that its sometimes harsh measures might engender. That breaking down Mexico's barriers to a flood of Washington-subsidized US corn might hasten the northward streaming of dispossessed campesinos was barely a consideration. And, even when this possibility was envisaged, the negotiators' blinkered vision kept them from understanding that, as conditions changed, some forums would be required to deliberate about the alternatives, consider the best courses of action, and effect their implementation.

Because neoconservatives assumed their market-based prescriptions were inevitably going to generate greater prosperity, they felt there was neither a practical need nor a moral justification for rich Canada and the still richer United States to commit massive funding to help raise Mexico's poor out of their deep poverty, to lift its judiciary out of its clientelism, to purify its policing culture, to modernize its armed forces, and to transform its education system, let alone to eradicate its deeply rooted narcotics underworld. When Vicente Fox made a plea for EU-like solidarity from its NAFTA partners to help Mexico overcome its multiple and interrelated social, political, and economic challenges, Canada and the United States dismissed the proposal out of hand. These two countries might practise some income redistribution and even interregional redistribution within their own borders, but their vision was too tunnelled to foresee how their long-term interests in a just and secure North America urgently required Mexico to be rebuilt as a prosperous, fair, and effectively functioning political economy.

The mistake was not just the United States' and Canada's unwillingness to provide enough financial support to pull an institutionally weak Mexico out of its political and economic straits. More damaging has been the three national elites' incapacity to think outside the narrow confines of their ideological paradigm, a lack of imagination that has left them stubbornly inert in the face of their persisting dilemmas.

In this state of suspension, North America faces two starkly opposed options. It can continue along the path of regional disintegration it has followed since 2001. This would see the United States go beyond its present mild economic nationalism and reinforce its historical proclivities for isolationism. It could become a Lone Ranger vigilante focusing on sealing its borders rather than promoting connections with its periphery. Its new El Dorado of shale gas could diminish its concern that Europe, China, and India might gain greater access to Canada's resources. Such a blinkered vision would ignore the loss for the average American's standard of living of the United States' already declining share of Canada's and Mexico's foreign investment.[13] To the south it could try fortifying its border still further against would-be Mexican workers and narcotics merchants, without paying heed to the economic distress, political chaos, and security bedlam pushing people across the Rio Grande.

Faced with their heightened exclusion, the United States' backyard neighbours would have to build on their own global strategies' present reorientation. Negotiating more bilateral economic agreements that invite other countries to trade with their markets and reap the benefits of investing in their resources, they would be forced to free themselves from their dependency on Uncle Sam and operate in a multipolar world of dizzying economic complexity. Such ventures would sit uneasily in the minds of neoconservative Mexican elites who have invested intellectually and emotionally in the project of shifting Mexico from its previous Latin American to a North American orientation. Canadian leaders would encounter similar difficulties in giving up their fantasy of operating across a completely erased US boundary and in reorienting their efforts to compete in a broader and tougher global market.

The alternative scenario to a future centrifugal North America is a centripetal world region in which the periphery plays a special role through its extensive social, economic, cultural, and security linkages in rebuilding the continent's 'regionness' and so constructing US power itself. Repairing the region would require Americans to shrink their obsession with terrorism to realistic dimensions in the aftermath of their having killed Osama bin Laden. The United States would also need to accept its own responsibility for narcotics violence as the source of demand for illegal narcotics and the source of armaments for the Mexican and Canadian underworlds. Recognizing the positive rather than the negative value of the huge Mexican presence both inside and outside their borders, Americans might consider the possibility of extending to Mexicans the open-border approach that integrated Canadians so intimately in their society.

Taking North America's interdependencies seriously would also require sacrifices on the part of Canadians who would have to rediscover their moral compass and accept their own responsibility – and long-term self-interest – in helping Mexico break out of its vicious circles of corruption, criminality, and social disintegration. A Marshall Plan for a sustainable Mexico would be an expensive but strategic investment for Canada – perhaps costing as much as did its war in Afghanistan –

and would provide no quick or easy fix. But launching such a visionary scheme could give Canada a pragmatic program for international engagement that suits its diminished global importance while engaging its citizens' and NGOs' liberal idealism in an effort tailored to their constructive culture and considerable talents.

Mexico's challenge is not one of knowing what to do. Its problem is to achieve the kind of effective democratic governance, economic well-being, and social stability to which all young Mexicans outside its underworld aspire. Reintegrating the politically excluded and reanimating the hopes of civil society would require reformulating a social project that replaces neoconservatism's narrowly compartmentalized thinking with a comprehensive alternative and weaves together the various reforms needed by the Mexican state's different sectors into a coherent program aimed less at narrowly defined economic growth than at broadly conceived social emancipation.

For the United States, North America has played a passively positive role, moderating the impacts of globalization on US citizens and corporations. But it does not come close to constituting a constructive governance space which can assist the United States in facing its looming policy challenges, from climate change to deindustrialization. To meet this more demanding standard, a trinational effort would require institutions that give Canada and Mexico a meaningful degree of participation in making continental decisions that also work to their advantage. The continent needs a far-sighted vision involving real power sharing in which North America's two historical dyads function on a more symmetrical and so more effective footing. The chances of such an outcome appear dim, given Mexico's partisan polarization, Canada's demagogic conservatism, and the United States' tempestuous fragmentation. Responding piecemeal to ad hoc crises is unlikely to bring North America to a point from which all three states would benefit. North America needs what Europe got sixty years ago: not just the intelligent articulation of the United States' long-term interests in a changed balance of global forces but smart and generous leadership able to realize its goals. Otherwise, Canada and Mexico's construction of US economic strength and security will decline while they continue to have little say in determining the continent's future direction.

The question for North America is no longer whether it exists but whether it can become more than the sum of its increasingly disunited parts.

Notes

Introduction

1 Paul Kennedy, 'Back to Normalcy: Is America Really in Decline?' *The New Republic*, December 21, 2010.
2 All figures from World Bank Development Indicators Database, http://www.data.worldbank.org/indicator (accessed March 16, 2011). Population figures are for 2009. GDP figures are for 2009 and given in current US dollars.
3 Stephen Clarkson, *Uncle Sam and Us: Globalization, Neoconservatism and the Canadian State* (Toronto: University of Toronto Press 2008), chapter 4.

1. Making the US Economy Stronger and More Competitive

1 Parts of this chapter were originally researched by Derek Carnegie. The chapter has benefited greatly from critical reading in Canada by Marjorie Cohen (Simon Fraser University); John Helliwell (University of British Columbia); Ed Safarian, Gerald Helleiner, and Mel Watkins (University of Toronto); in Mexico by Alejandro Álvarez, Federico Manchón Cohen, Gabriel Mendoza Pichardo, and Bruce Wallace (Universidad Nacional Autónoma de México); and in the United States by Gary Hufbauer (Peterson Institute for International Economics).
2 David Sanger, 'Huge Deficits May Alter U.S. Politics and Global Power,' *New York Times*, February 2, 2010, A15.
3 World Bank, 'Gross Domestic Product 2008 Quick Reference Table,' http://www.web.worldbank.org/WBSITE/ EXTERNAL/DATASTATISTICS/0,,contentMDK:20399244~menuPK:1504474~pagePK:64133150~piPK:64133175~theSitePK:239419,00.html (accessed February 10, 2010).

4 Mira Wilkins, *The Emergence of Multinational Enterprise: American Business Abroad from the Colonial Era to 1914* (Cambridge, Mass.: Harvard University Press 1970).

5 Gordon Stewart, 'A Special Contiguous Country Economic Regime: America's Canadian Policy,' *Diplomatic History*, fall 1982, 339–57.

6 Kari Levitt, *Silent Surrender: The Multinational Corporation in Canada*, new ed. (Montreal and Kingston: McGill-Queen's University Press 2002).

7 Government of Canada, 'Foreign Direct Investment in Canada [Gray Report]' (Ottawa: Queen's Printer 1972).

8 Josefina Z. Vazquez and Lorenzo Meyer, *México frente a Estados Unidos: Un ensayo histórico 1776–1980* (Mexico City: El Colegio de México 1982), 2: 178–9.

9 Ibid., 2: 169, 171–2.

10 W. Dirk Raat, *Mexico and the United States: Ambivalent Vistas* (Athens, Ga.: University of Georgia Press 1992), 153–4.

11 Dale Story, 'Trade Politics in the Third World: A Case Study of the Mexican GATT Decision,' *International Organization*, 36 (1982): 770.

12 Nora Lustig, *The Remaking of an Economy* (Washington, D.C.: Brookings Institution 1992), 133.

13 President Carlos Salinas, Remarks at the NAFTA at 10 Conference, Woodrow Wilson International Center for Scholars, in *NAFTA at 10: Progress, Potential, and Precedents*, vol. 2 (2005), 34.

14 Data used throughout this section derives from United States, Department of Commerce, Bureau of Economic Analysis (BEA), 'International Transaction Accounts Data,' http://www.bea.gov/international/ bp_web/list. cfm?anon=71 (accessed July 15, 2008; updated July 30, 2011).

15 Figures 1.1 through 1.4 and Table 1.1 are all derived from data presented in ibid.

16 Whether Canada or China have a larger export-trading relationship with the United States depends on the criterion used to create the trade figures. In the 2008 figures released by the US Department of Commerce, Canada exports some $16 billion more to the United States in narrowly defined goods and services; however, when international income payments are also factored into the statistics, Chinese exports to the United States are valued at around $4 billion more than Canadian exports. In the text, following the general convention, the more narrow goods-and-services figure is used, although income payments and other new types of international economic relationships are projected to become increasingly important over the coming years. During the 2008–9 financial crisis, US-Canada

trade haemorrhaged significantly more than trade between China and the United States. As a result, China became the largest US importer by over $50 billion.

17 Scott C. Bradford, Paul L.E. Grieco, and Gary Hufbauer, 'The Payoff to America from Global Integration,' in C. Fred Bergsten, ed., *The United States and the World Economy: Foreign Economic Policy for the Next Decade* (Washington, D.C.: Institute for International Economics 2005), 68.

18 By contrast, there has been a small literature on the impacts of CUFTA and NAFTA on the US economy, with most studies suggesting that the trade agreement would have – or has had – a marginal to modest impact. This literature is less useful for our analysis because it focuses on the benefits to the US economy of additional trade generated by NAFTA, not on the overall impacts of Canada and Mexico on US strength. For both Canada and Mexico, sustained trading relationships would have developed even in NAFTA's absence, and, in particular for Canada, much trade liberalization preceded both NAFTA and CUFTA. For a sampling of these estimates, see: President of the United States, 'Statement of Administrative Action, in Communication from the President of the United States Transmitting the Final Legal Text of the U.S.-Canada Free-Trade Agreement, the Proposed U.S.-Canada Free-Trade Agreement Implementation Act of 1988, and a Statement of Administrative Action, pursuant to 19 U.S.C. 2112(e)(2), 2212(a), 100th Cong., 2d Sess., H. Doc. 100–216,' July 26, 1988 (Washington, D.C.: GPO 1993), 3–7; results of private contract work by DRI/McGraw described in a Clinton administration report of 1997; Arlene Wilson, 'NAFTA: Economic Effects on the United States after Five Years,' in C.V. Anderson, ed., *NAFTA Revisited* (Hauppague, N.Y.: Nova Publishers 2003); Council of Economic Advisors, *Economic Report to the President 2002*, 279–80; United States, International Trade Commission, *The Impact of Trade Agreements: Effects of the Tokyo Round, the US-Israel FTA, the US-Canada FTA, NAFTA, and the Uruguay Round on the US Economy*, International Trade Commission Publication 3621 (Washington, D.C., 2003).

19 OECD, 'The Sources of Economic Growth in OECD Countries,' ISBN 92-64-19945-4 (Paris: Organization for Economic Co-operation and Development 2003), in Bradford, Grieco, and Hufbauer, 'The Payoff to America from Global Integration,' 73.

20 Bradford, Grieco, and hufbauer, 'The Payoff to America from Global Integration,' 66.

21 Our calculations follow from the analysis set out in ibid.; the methodology behind that work is described in detail on 72–4. Briefly, the authors use

an OECD estimate of the elasticity between US trade exposure (total US imports and exports divided by US GDP) and per-capita growth to provide a crude value for the pay-off to the United States of its international trading relationships. Using parallel data on the trade exposure of Canada and Mexico to the United States over the same time period, we extrapolate the fraction of the total change in US trade exposure that is attributable to Canada and to Mexico, and assume that an equivalent fraction of the benefits of trade for the United States can be attributed to Canada and Mexico respectively. These estimates are from the years 1970–2003 for Canada and from 1990–2003 for Mexico. Data sets used in this exercise, like those of Bradford, Grieco, and Hufbauer, are all derived from the BEA, 2004, National Income and Product Account Tables (NIPA), and are available at http://www.bea.gov/bea/dn/nipaweb/index.asp (accessed July 14, 2008). Note that, as described in the text, these estimates do not account for trade diversion and thus may overstate the value of Canadian and Mexican trade; on the other hand, these estimates are based on changes in trade exposure and thus cannot account for changes in trade levels previous to 1990 for Mexico, and 1970 for Canada. In this sense, the estimates may understate the value of Canadian and Mexican trade to the United States.

22 Mary Jane Bolle, 'NAFTA: Estimated US Job "Gains" and "Losses" by State over 5½ Years,' in Anderson, ed., *Nafta Revisited*, 15.

23 Laura Baughman and Joseph Francois, 'U.S.-Canada Trade and U.S. State-Level Production and Employment: 2008,' Government of Canada, 2008, http://www.canadainternational.gc.ca/washington/offices-bureaux/media_room-salle_de_presse/media-medias-20100511.aspx?lang=eng, p.8 (accessed March 16, 2011).

24 Ibid., 11.

25 Representative publications that lay out this economic position and its implied scepticism are: John F. Helliwell and Alan Chung, 'Are Bigger Countries Better Off?' in R. Boadway, T. Courchene, and D. Purvis, eds., *Economic Dimensions of Constitutional Change* (Kingston, Ont.: John Deutsch Institute 1991), 345–67; Christopher M. Meissner and Alan M. Taylor, 'Losing Our Marbles in the New Century?: The Great Rebalancing in Historical Perspective,' Conference Series, [Proceedings], Federal Reserve Bank of Boston, 2006. Available as NBER Working Paper no. 12580.

26 Glen Williams, *Not for Export*, 3rd ed. (Toronto: McClelland and Stewart 1994).

27 Walid Hejazi and A.E. Safarian, 'The Complementarity between US Foreign Direct Investment Stock and Trade,' *Atlantic Economic Journal*, December 2001, 1.

28 United States, Office of the US Trade Representative (USTR), 'U.S.-Canada Trade Facts,' http://www.ustr.gov/ countries-regions/americas/canada (accessed April 18, 2010).

29 United States, Department of Commerce, BEA, 'US Direct Investment Abroad, US Direct Investment Position Abroad on a Historical Cost Basis/ Operations of Multinational Companies,' http://www.bea.gov/international/index.htm (accessed June 12, 2011). All figures here are in current dollars on a historical-cost basis. These data reflect only investment flows through multinational corporations operating on a continental scale.

30 Ibid.

31 United States, Department of Commerce, BEA, 'U.S. Direct Investment Abroad, Direct Investment Income without Current-Cost Adjustment,' http://www.bea.gov/ international/index.htm (accessed March 9, 2010; accessed June 12, 2011).

32 USTR, 'U.S.-Canada Trade Facts,' http://www.ustr.gov/ countries-regions/americas/canada (accessed April 18, 2010).

33 United States, Department of Commerce, BEA, 'Foreign Direct Investment Position in the United States on a Historical-Cost Basis,' http://www.bea.gov/international/index.htm (accessed June 12, 2011).

34 BEA, 'US Direct Investment Abroad,' US Direct Investment Position Abroad on a Historical Cost Basis/Operations of Multinational Companies.'

35 USTR, 'U.S.-Mexico Trade Facts.'

36 BEA, 'U.S. Direct Investment Abroad, Direct Investment Income without Current-Cost Adjustment.'

37 USTR, 'U.S.-Mexico Trade Facts.'

38 BEA, 'Foreign Direct Investment Position in the United States on a Historical-Cost Basis.'

39 Alvin Paul Drischler, 'NAFTA and Foreign Direct Investment in the US,' in Charles Doran and Alvin Paul Drischler, eds., *A New North America: Cooperation and Enhanced Interdependence* (Westport, Conn.: Praeger 1996), 60.

40 Lorraine Eden and Dan Li, 'The New Regionalism and Foreign Direct Investment in the Americas,' in S. Weintraub, ed., *NAFTA's Impact on North America: The First Decade* (Washington, D.C.: Centre for Strategic and International Studies Press 2004), 50.

41 Gary Gereffi et al., 'The Governance of Global Value Chains,' *Review of International Political Economy*, 12 (2005): 9.

42 Ibid., 57.

43 United States, Central Intelligence Agency, 'The World Factbook,' http://www.cia.gov/library/publications/the-world-factbook/rankorder/2119rank.html (accessed July 15, 2010). Population estimates are

accurate as of July 2010. Also, World Bank, 'World Development Indicators,' http://www.data.worldbank.org/data-catalog/world-development-indicators (accessed July 15, 2010). Per-capita income estimates are from the World Bank, gross national income per capita 2009 using Purchasing Power Parity (PPP). All figures are in current international dollars, which has the same purchasing power that a US dollar has in the United States.

44 World Bank, 'World Development Indicators.' GNP figures are for 2008 using Atlas Method (current US$).

45 Walid Hejazi and A. Edward Safarian, *Canada and Foreign Direct Investment: A Study of Determinants* (Toronto: University of Toronto, Centre for Public Management, 2001), 22.

46 Walid Hejazi and A. Edward Safarian, 'Trade, Foreign Direct Investment, and R & D Spillovers,' *Journal of International Business Studies*, 30 (1999): 496.

47 Mary E. Burfisher et al., 'The Impact of NAFTA on the United States,' *Journal of Economic Perspectives*, 15 (2001): 137.

48 United States, Boston Federal Reserve Bank, Michael W. Klein et al., 'Job Creation, Job Destruction, and International Competition: Job Flows and Trade – the Case of NAFTA' (Working Paper 02–8), http://www.bos.frb.org/economic/wp/wp2002/wp028.pdf (accessed January 15, 2011), 18.

49 Duke University, 'The Automobile Industry: Global Value Chain,' http://www.duke.edu/web/soc142/ team1/valuechain.html (accessed August 25, 2009).

50 John Humphrey and Olga Memedovic, *The Global Automotive Industry Value Chain: What Prospects for Upgrading by Developing Countries* (Vienna: UNIDO Sectoral Studies Series Working Paper, 2003), 11.

51 Klein et al., 'Job Creation, Job Destruction, and International Competition,' 19.

52 Canadian Steel Producers Association, 'The Integrated North American Market: The Details,' available in web-archived format at http://www.web.archive.org/web/20061010023245/www.canadiansteel.ca/industry/factsheets/intnamarketdetails.htm (accessed January 17, 2011).

53 Peter Warrian and Celine Mulhern, 'Learning in Steel: Agents and Deficits' (presented at the Annual Meeting of the Innovation System Research Network, Quebec City, May 9–10, 2002), 12.

54 Canadian Steel Producers Association, 'Integrated North American Market: The Details.'

55 Nancy E. Kelly, 'Employment Stats Tell the Real Story, Steel Union Says,' *American Metal Market*, 110, no. 23 (2002): 2.

56 Timothy J. Considine, *The Transformation of the North American Steel Industry: Drivers, Prospects, and Vulnerabilities* (University Park: Penn State University Press, April 21, 2005), http://www.steel.org/AM/Template Redirect.cfm?Template=/CM/ContentDisplay.cfm&ContentID=11021 (accessed May 1, 2008), 27.

57 Canadian Press, 'US Steel Challenges Investment Act,' *Toronto Star*, November 26, 2009, http://www.thestar.com/business/article/730899--us-steel-challenges-investment-act (accessed January 15, 2011).

58 Harry W. Arthurs, *The Hollowing out of Corporate Canada?* (Toronto: York University Working Paper Series on Globalizing Societies), http://www.yorku.ca/robarts/archives/pub_domain/pdf/apd_arthurs.pdf (accessed June 29, 2010).

59 Insituto Nacional de Estadistica y Geografia (INEGI), Banco de Información Económica (BIE), http://www.inegi.gob.mx (accessed March 22, 2010).

60 Secretaría de Economía, 'IED de maquiladoras por país de origen,' Dirección General de Inversión Extranjera Directa. Secretaría de Economía, personal communication, March 23, 2010.

61 Per Stromberg. 'La Industria Maquiladora Mexicana y el medio ambiente: una revisión de los problemas,' in Jorge Carrillo and Claudia Schatan, ed., *El Medio Ambiente y la maquila en México: un problema ineludible* (Mexico City: Comisión Económica para América Latina y el Caribe [CEPAL] 2005), 36.

62 Roberto A. Sánchez, 'Contaminación industrial en la frontera norte: algunas consideraciones para la década de los noventa,' Colegio de México, *Estudios Sociológicos*, 8, no. 23 (1990): 308.

63 Alicia Puyana, 'Introducción,' in *La maquila en México: Los desafíos de la globalización* (Mexico City: FLACSO 2008), 16.

64 Roberto Sánchez, 'Contaminación de la industria fronteriza: Riesgos para la salud y el medio ambiente,' in Rocío Barajas et al., *Las Maquiladoras: ajuste estructural y desarrollo regional* (Mexico City: El Colegio de la Frontera Norte, Fundación Friedrich Ebert, 1989), 168.

65 Bradford, Grieco, and Hufbauer, 'The Payoff to America from Global Integration,' 66–7.

66 Oliver Cadot et al., *Assessing the Effects of NAFTA's Rules of Origin* (Washington, D.C.: World Bank 2002), 11.

67 Aziz Elbehri, *MFA Quota Removal and Global Textile and Cotton Trade: Estimating Quota Trade Restrictiveness and Quantifying Post-MFA Trade Patterns* (Washington, D.C.: USDA Economic Research Service 2004), 5. In the Americas, the United States established the Caribbean Basin and Andean

initiatives partially in hopes of replacing imports from MFA producers with those from nearby countries which would be required to use American textiles to gain preferential access to the US market.

68 Hyunjoo Oh and Moon W. Suh, 'What Is Happening to the US Textile Industry? Reflections on NAFTA and US Corporate Strategies,' *Journal of Fashion Marketing and Management*, 7, no. 2 (2003): 120, 128.

69 Staci Bonner, 'Convergence: One-Stop Shopping in the Apparel Supply Chain,' *Apparel Industry Magazine*, 58, no. 9 (1997): 82.

70 Oh and Suh, 'What Is Happening to the US Textile Industry?' 120.

71 Jennifer Bair et al., *Free Trade and Uneven Development: The North American Apparel Industry after NAFTA* (Philidelphia, Penn.: Temple University Press 2002), 70.

72 Judi A. Kessler, 'The North American Free Trade Agreement, Emerging Apparel Production Networks and Industrial Upgrading: The Southern California/Mexico Connection,' *Review of International Political Economy*, 6, no. 4 (1999): 584.

73 Jennifer Bair and Gary Gereffi, 'Upgrading, Uneven Development, and Jobs in the North American Apparel Industry,' *Global Networks*, 3, no. 2 (2003): 162.

74 William A. Amponsah and Victor Ofori Boadu, 'Crisis in the U.S. Textile and Apparel Industry: Is It Caused by Trade Agreements and Asian Currency Meltdowns?' American Textile Manufacturers Institute, http://www.cnas.tamu.edu/publications/powerpoint/papers/Amponsaht.pdf (accessed May 2, 2008), 6.

2. Supporting US Energy Security

1 This chapter was originally researched by Sarah Yun in Toronto and by Haidy Durán Gil in Mexico. Its successive drafts benefited enormously from critical reviews by Rosío Vargas, Angel de la Vega Navarro, and Nora Lina Montes (Universidad Nacional Autónoma de México); and Guillermo Velasco (Capital Sustenable) in Mexico City; Annette Hester (CIGI/CSIS) in Calgary, Alberta; Leah Stokes (MIT) in Cambridge, Massachusetts; and Robert Johnston (Eurasia Group) in Washington, D.C. Joseph Dukert (Centre for Strategic and International Studies) in Washington, D.C., gave us a particularly exhaustive and thoughtful critique.

2 United States, Energy Information Administration (EIA), 'U.S. Primary Energy Flow by Source and Sector, 2009,' http://www.eia.doe.gov/aer/pecss_diagram.html (accessed March 18, 2011). See also EIA, 'US Energy

History,' http://www.eia.doe.gov/aer/eh/eh.html (accessed March 18, 2011).

3 EIA, 'US Imports by Country of Origin,' http://www.tonto.eia.doe.gov/dnav/pet/pet_move_impcus_a2_ nus_ep00_im0_mbblpd_a.htm (accessed June 12, 2011).

4 EIA, 'How Dependent Are We on Foreign Oil?' *Energy in Brief,* June 24, 2011, www.eia.gov/energy_in_brief/foreign_oil_dependence.cfm (accessed July 22, 2011).

5 Formally, this is the 'net import' figure, which corrects for the export of petroleum products from the United States and considers the theoretical US ability to quench its own oil thirst. Ibid.

6 Ibid.

7 United States, Central Intelligence Agency, 'Oil Production,' *The World Factbook,* http://www.cia.gov/library/publications/the-world-factbook/rankorder/2173rank.html (accessed January 15, 2011).

8 EIA, 'US Imports by Country of Origin.' The statistics on 'net imports' in the paragraph below are drawn from: EIA, 'How Dependent Are We on Foreign Oil?'

9 EIA, 'Chapter 3: World Oil Markets,' *International Energy Outlook 2006,* June 2006, http://www. eia.doe.gov/oiaf/archive/ieo06/pdf/oil.pdf (accessed December 15, 2007), 29, 37. Ecuador is bundled with non-OPEC states because of its comparatively small reserves.

10 Annette Hester and Sidney Weintraub, 'Canada,' in Annette Hester et al., eds., *Energy Cooperation in the Western Hemisphere: Benefits and Impediments* (Washington, D.C.: Center for Strategic and International Studies 2007), 74.

11 Personal communication from Joseph Duckert, November 2010.

12 Christina Babylon, 'The Biggest Oil Discovery in US History,' *Mining Top News,* April 17, 2008, http://www.miningtopnews.com/the-biggest-oil-discovery-in-us-history.html (accessed July 28, 2008).

13 EIA, 'Country Analysis Briefs: Mexico,' *Country Analysis Briefs,* December 2007, http://www.eia.doe. gov/cabs/Mexico/Background.html (accessed December 20, 2007).

14 Sidney Weintraub, 'Introduction,' in Hester et al., eds., *Energy Cooperation in the Western Hemisphere,* 17.

15 Frank Verrastro, 'The United States,' in ibid., 47.

16 Pietro S. Nivola, 'Energy Independence or Interdependence? Integrating the North American Energy Market,' *Brookings Review,* 20, no. 2 (2002), http://www.brookings.edu/articles/2002/spring_ energy_nivola.aspx (accessed August 12, 2008).

17 EIA, 'World Dry Natural Gas Consumption, Most Recent Annual Estimates, 1980–2006,' *International Energy Annual 2006*, August 28, 2008, http://www.eia.gov/emeu/international/gasconsumption. html (accessed January 15, 2011), Table 1.3.

18 EIA, 'What Role Does Liquified Natural Gas (LNG) Play as an Energy Source for the United States?' *Energy in Brief*, December 11, 2009, http://www.tonto.eia.doe.gov/energy_in_brief/liquefied_natural_gas_lng.cfm (accessed January 15, 2011).

19 Energy interdependence is so pervasive that even official natural-gas statistics are complicated to interpret. For example, much of the Canadian natural gas that is exported to Michigan is then exported back to Canada for use in Ontario. Inconsistent tracking creates some inflation of natural-gas trade data, at least at the subfederal level. See Christopher Kukucha, 'Sub-Federal Trade and the Politics of North American Economic Integration: Evaluating the Cross-Border Exports of American States,' in Monica Gattinger and Geofffey Hale, eds., *Borders and Bridges: Canada's Policy Relations in North America* (Toronto: Oxford University Press 2010), 283.

20 Petróleos Mexicanos (Pemex), *Principales Desafíos de PEMEX: Los 25 principales desafíos de Petróleos Mexicanos*, Conclusión de los Foros, July 2008, http://www.pemex.com.mx (accessed July 26, 2010).

21 Joseph M. Dukert, 'North America,' in Hester et al., eds., *Energy Cooperation in the Western Hemisphere*, 140.

22 EIA, 'US Natural Gas Imports by Country,' http://www.tonto.eia.doe.gov/dnav/ng/ng_move_impc_ s1_a.htm (accessed June 2, 2011).

23 Nivola, 'Energy Independence or Interdependence?'

24 Petroleos Mexicanos, 'Gas y Petroquímica Básica. Gas Natural. Estadísticas,' http://www.gas.pemex.com (accessed January 15, 2011).

25 See note 22.

26 EIA, 'What Is Shale Gas and Why Is It Important?' *Energy in Brief*, http://www.eia.doe.gov/energy_in_brief/about_shale_gas.cfm (accessed January 17, 2011).

27 EIA, 'Foreign Direct Investment in US Energy in 2000,' *Energy Finance*, http://www.tonto.eia.doe.gov /ftproot/financial/2000_fdi.pdf, 14 (accessed February 17, 2008).

28 EIA, 'Annual Energy Outlook 2010 with Projections to 2035,' http://www.eia.doe.gov/oiaf/archive/aeo10/gas.html (accessed January 17, 2011), Figure 77.

29 EIA, 'Foreign Direct Investment in US Energy in 2000,' *Energy Finance*, http://www.tonto.eia.doe.gov /ftproot/financial/2000_fdi.pdf, 15 (accessed February 17, 2008).

30 For the mainstream political view that the United States needs to worry

about oil imports, see Henry Lee, 'Oil Security and the Transportation Sector,' in Kelly Gallagher, ed., *Acting in Time on Energy Policy* (Washington, D.C.: Brookings Institution 2009), 56–88; and Pietro Nivola and Erin Carter, 'Making Sense of "Energy Independence,"' in Carlos Pascual et al., eds., *Energy Security: Economics, Politics, Strategies and Implication* (Washington, D.C.: Brookings Institution 2009), 105–18.

31 PEMEX Anuario Estadístico 1977, Coordinación y Estudios Técnicos, Sistemas de Información, Instituto Mexicano del Petroleo, 30, http://www.ri.pemex.com/index.cfm?action=content&sectionID=134&catID=12202&contentID=18442 (accessed June 11, 2011).

32 Mario Ojeda, *Alcances y límites de la política exterior de México* (Mexico City: El Colegio de México 2006), 39–41.

33 United States, Department of the Interior, *Resources for Freedom: The President's Materials Policy Commission (Paley Commission)*, vol. 1 (Washington, D.C.: GPO 1952).

34 Ibid., 1: 3.

35 Ibid., vol. 1.

36 Ibid., 1: 91.

37 Ibid., 1: 92.

38 Ibid., 1: 2.

39 Ibid., 1: 16.

40 Ibid.

41 Ibid., 1: 20.

42 Wallace Clement and Glen Williams, 'Resources and Manufacturing in Canada's Political Economy,' in Wallace Clement, ed., *Understanding Canada: Building on the New Canadian Political Economy* (Montreal and Kingston: McGill-Queen's University Press 1997), 49.

43 Glyn R. Berry, 'The Oil Lobby and the Energy Crisis,' in Richard Schultz et al., *The Canadian Political Process*, 3rd ed. (Toronto: Holt, Rinehart, and Winston 1979), 255.

44 Annette Hester, 'Canada as the Emerging Energy Superpower: Testing the Case,' *Canadian Defence & Foreign Affairs Institute*, October 2007, http://www.cdfai.org/PDF/CDFAIConference2007.pdf, p.9 (accessed November 27, 2007).

45 United States, Cabinet Task Force on Oil Import Control, *The Oil Import Question: A Report on the Relationship of Oil Imports to National Security ('Shultz Report')* (Washington, D.C.: GPO 1970); A.W. Cockerill, 'Whose Continental Resources Did You Say?' *Guardian Weekly*, December 1971, http:// www.achart.ca/publications/essays_resources.html#bottom (accessed December 29, 2007).

46 *Shultz Report*, para. 218.

47 Ibid., para. 235a.
48 Ibid., para. 252b.
49 Ibid., para. 335c.
50 Hester, 'Canada as the Emerging Energy Superpower,' 9.
51 Gary Clyde Hufbauer and Jeffrey J. Schott, *NAFTA Revisited: Achievements and Challenges* (Washington, D.C.: Institute for International Economics 2005), 397.
52 Ibid., 395.
53 Ibid., 397.
54 *Schultz Report*, para. 336h.
55 Hufbauer and Schott, *NAFTA Revisited*, 418–19.
56 Stephen Clarkson et al., 'De-Institutionalizing North America: NAFTA's Committees and Working Groups' (Paper presented at the Third EnviReform Conference, Toronto, November 8, 2002), 20.
57 United States, National Energy Policy Development Group, *National Energy Policy: Report of the National Energy Policy Development Group* [*Cheney Report*] (Washington, D.C.: GPO 2001), 8–4.
58 Ibid., 8–7.
59 Ibid., 8–9.
60 Ibid., 8–8.
61 Ibid., 8–9.
62 Ibid., 8–18.
63 Stephen Clarkson et al., 'A North American "Community of Law" with Minimal Institutions: NAFTA's Committees and Working Groups,' in John Kirton and Peter Haynal, eds., *Sustainability, Civil Society, and International Governance: Local, North American and Global Perspectives* (New York: Ashgate 2006), 105–22.
64 John W. Foster, 'Beyond NAFTA: The Security and Prosperity Partnership,' Council of Canadians, http://www.canadians.org/DI/documents/NAFTA_SPP_Foster.pdf, p.3 (accessed April 27, 2008).
65 Joseph M. Dukert, 'North America,' in Hester et al., eds., *Energy Cooperation in the Western Hemisphere*, 138; Hufbauer and Schott, *NAFTA Revisited*, 425.
66 Joseph M. Dukert, 'The Quiet Reality of North American Energy Interdependence,' in *Mapping the New North American Reality* (Montreal: Institute for Research on Public Policy, Working Paper Series, 2004), 2.
67 North American Energy Working Group (NAEWG), *North America: The Energy Picture*, June 2002, http://www.eia.doe.gov/emeu/northamerica/engindex.htm (accessed December 20, 2007).
68 Joseph M. Dukert, 'U.S., Canada and Mexico: Depending on Interdepen-

dence,' *SAISPHERE 2005* (Washington, D.C.: Paul H. Nitze School of Advanced International Studies 2005), http://www.sais-jhu.edu/pressroom/ publications/saisphere/2005/dukert.htm (accessed August 23, 2008).

69 NAEWG, *North America: The Energy Picture II*, January 2006, http://www. pi.energy.gov/documents/North AmericaEnergyPictureII.pdf (accessed December 27, 2007).

70 United States, Department of Energy, 'The Office of Policy and International Affairs,' 2007, http://www.pi.energy.gov/naewg.htm (accessed February 6, 2008).

71 The nine expert groups are the Electricity Experts Group, Energy Efficiency Experts Group, Energy Picture Experts Group, Hydrocarbons Experts Group, Natural Gas Trade and Interconnections Experts Group, Nuclear Collaboration Experts Group, Oil Sands Experts Group, Regulatory Experts Group, and Science and Technology Experts Group.

72 US, Department of Energy, 'The Office of Policy and International Affairs,' 2007.

73 Security and Prosperity Partnership of North America (SPP), *2006 Report to Leaders*, August 2006, http:// www.spp.gov/2006_report_to_leaders/index. asp?dName=2006_report_to_leaders (accessed August 23, 2008); Greg Anderson and Christopher Sands, *Negotiating North America: The Security and Prosperity Partnership* (Washington, D.C.: Hudson Institute, summer 2007), 22.

74 United States Chamber of Commerce, 'US Chamber of Commerce – North American Competitiveness Council (NACC),' 2008, http://www.uschamber.com/issues/index/international/nacc.htm (accessed August 23, 2008).

75 Israel Rodriquez, 'Plantea Pemex incluir a petroleras internacionales para compartir riesgos,' *La Jornada*, April 10, 2007, http://www.jornada. unam.mx/2007/04/10/index.php?section=economia&article=021n1eco (accessed February 4, 2008).

76 PEMEX, 'Proyectos Estratégicos,' http://www.pemex.com (accessed July 26, 2010).

77 Sidney Weintraub and Rafael Fernández de Castro, 'Mexico,' in Hester et al., eds., *Energy Cooperation in the Western Hemisphere*, 107; Sidney Weintraub, 'Mexico's Oil, Gas, and Energy Policy Options,' *Issues in International Political Economy* (August 2005), http://www.csis.org/media/csis/pubs/ issues200508. pdf (accessed August 24, 2008).

78 PEMEX and Secretaría de Energía, 'Documento Diagnóstico: Situación de PEMEX Resumen Ejecutivo,' March 2008, http://www.pemex.com.

79 US Chamber of Commerce and NACC, *Enhancing Competitiveness in Canada, Mexico, and the United States: Private-Sector Priorities for the Security*

and Prosperity Partnership in North America (Washington, D.C.: GPO, February 23, 2007).

80 *Cheney Report.*

81 Dukert, 'U.S., Canada and Mexico: Depending on Interdependence.'

82 These data come from a reply on April 6, 2010 to access-to-information request no. 1857200037010 made through the Federal Institute for Access to Governmental Information (Instituto Federal de Acceso a la Información Gubernamental). Data prior to 2003 was not provided.

83 Centro de investigacion y Docencia Economicas, 'Mexico and the World Economy,' *Mexico and the World in 2006: Public Opinion and Foreign Policy in Mexico* (Mexico City: Consejo Mexicano de Asuntos Internacionales 2006), 45.

84 Ibid., 51–2.

85 Hufbauer and Schott, *NAFTA Revisited*, 404.

86 Geoffrey E. Hale. '"In the Pipeline" or "Over a Barrel"? Assessing Canadian Efforts to Manage US-Canadian Energy Interdependence,' *Canadian-American Public Policy*, 76 (February 2011): 25.

87 For the argument that Canada and Mexico have more soft power with Washington than is generally thought, see Joseph M. Dukert, 'The Search for Best Practices and Models,' in Andrés Rozental and Alex Bugailiskis, eds., *Building Bridges: Canada among Nations 2011* (forthcoming).

88 Jennifer Welch, *At Home in the World: Canada's Global Vision for the 21st Century* (Toronto: Harper Canada 2005), 101–4.

3. Supplying Workers for the US Labour Market

1 This chapter profited greatly from the critical comments received on earlier drafts from Tamara Woroby (School of Advanced International Studies) in Washington; Isabel Studer (Instituto Tecnológico de Monterrey) in Mexico City; and Morley Gunderson (University of Toronto) in Canada. A small portion of this text appeared previously in Stephen Clarkson's *Does North America Exist?* (Toronto: University of Toronto Press 2008), 29–37.

2 Sidney Weintraub, 'US Foreign Policy and Mexican Immigration,' in Frank Bean et al., eds., *At the Crossroads: Mexico and US Immigration Policy* (Lanham, Md.: Rowman and Littlefield 1997), 283. The translation is Weintraub's own.

3 United States, Central Intelligence Agency, *The World Factbook*, http://www.cia.gov/cia/publications/factbook/rankorder/2095rank. html (accessed July 4, 2010).

4 Michael Rosenfeld and Marta Tienda, 'Labor Market Implications of Mexi-

can Migration: Economies of Scale, Innovation and Entrepreneurship,' in Bean et al., eds., *At the Crossroads*, 183.

5 Patrick Smith, *The New Americans: Economic, Demographic, and Fiscal Effects of Immigration* (Washington, D.C.: National Academy Press 1997), 5.

6 US-Mexico Binational Council, Center for Strategic and International Studies, and Instituto Tecnológico Autónomo de México, *Managing Mexican Migration to the United States: Recommendations for Policymakers* (2004), xiv.

7 Lynn Karoly and Constantin Panis, 'The 21st Century at Work: Forces Shaping the Future Workforce and Workplace in the United States,' Rand Corporation Report (Santa Monica, Calif.: Rand Corporation 2004), xv–xvi, 20.

8 Ibid., xxxv.

9 Walter Nugent, 'Crossing Borders, Countering Exceptionalism,' in M. Rodriguez, ed., *Repositioning North American Migration History: New Directions in Modern Continental Migration, Citizenship, and Community* (Rochester, N.Y.: University of Rochester Press 2004), 7.

10 Bruno Ramirez, 'Borderland Studies and Migration: The Canada/United States Case,' in Rodriguez, ed., *Repositioning North American Migration History*, 23.

11 United States, Department of Homeland Security (DHS), *Persons Obtaining Legal Permanent Resident Status by Region and Selected Country of Last Residence: Fiscal Years 1820–2009*, http://www.dhs.gov/files/statistics/publications/ LPR08.shtm (accessed June 28, 2010). Data table available online through Yearbook of Immigration Statistics, 2008.

12 Ramirez, 'Borderland Studies and Migration,' 21.

13 DHS, *Persons Obtaining Legal Permanent Resident Status by Region*.

14 Jeffrey Passel et al., 'Estimates of the Legal and Unauthorized Foreign-Born Population for the United States and Selected States, Based on Census 2000,' Draft paper, 2004, http://www.google.com/url?sa=t&source=web&cd=1&sqi=2&ved=0CBIQFjAA&url=http%3A%2F%2Fwww.copafs.org%2FUserFiles%2Ffile%2Fseminars%2Fmethodology_and_data_quality%2FEstimates%2520of%2520the%2520Legal%2520and%2520Unauthorized%2520Foreign-Born%2520Population%2520for%2520the%2520United%2520States%2520and%2520Selected%2520States%2C%2520Based%2520on%2520Census%25202000.pdf&rct=j&q=122%2C000%20unauthorized%20Canadians%20passel&ei=etmoTJ6R MZS-sQPKnviPDQ&usg=AFQjCNGpdVNUxuKgLxTdZxKhRtCmb0akHg&sig2=VTfsLWicfHomIzd7T-GBn9Q (accessed October 2, 2010).

15 Sister Mary Colette Standard, 'The Sonoran Migration to California 1848–1856: A study in Prejudice,' in David Gutierrez, ed., *Between Two*

Worlds: Mexican Immigrants in the United States (Wilmington, Del.: Jaguar Publications 1996), 3–22.

16 DHS, *Persons Obtaining Legal Permanent Resident Status by Region.*
17 M. Ngai, 'Braceros, Wetbacks, and the National Boundaries of Class,' in Rodriguez, ed., *Repositioning North American Migration History*, 206–64.
18 Ibid., 234–5.
19 Ibid.
20 Ibid.
21 Emma Lazarus, *The New Collosus*, http://www.en.wikipedia.org/wiki/The_New_Colossus (accessed June 7, 2011).
22 Gary Freeman and Frank Bean, 'Mexico and US Immigration Policy,' in Bean et al., eds., *At the Crossroads*, 27.
23 Alene Gelbard and Marion Carter, 'Mexican Immigration and US Population,' in ibid., 120.
24 Freeman and Bean, 'Mexico and US Immigration Policy,' 34.
25 Gelbard and Carter, 'Mexican Immigration and US Population,' 120.
26 Rogelio Sanchez, Maria Morales, and Janie Filotea, 'The Demography of Mexicans in the United States,' in Roberto de Anda, ed., *Chicanas and Chicanos in Contemporary Society* (Lanham Md.: Rowman and Littlefield 2004), 3–20.
27 Freeman and Bean, 'Mexico and US Immigration Policy,' 28.
28 Ibid., 33.
29 Jeffrey Passel, *Unauthorized Migrants: Numbers and Characteristics.* Background briefing prepared for the Taskforce on Immigration and America's Future, 2005, http://www.pewhispanic.org/files/reports/46.pdf, p.6 (accessed June 7, 2011).
30 The data in this table are adapted from United States, Congressional Budget Office (CBO), 'The Role of Immigrants in the US Labor Market: An Update,' Table 2, 'Composition and Educational Attainment of the U.S. Labor Force, by Birthplace, 2009,' July 2010, 3–4.
31 Jeffrey S. Passel and D'Vera Cohn, *Mexican Immigrants: How Many Come? How Many Leave?* (Washington, D.C.: Pew Hispanic Center, July 2009).
32 Pia Orrenius, 'The Effect of US Border Enforcement on the Crossing Behaviour of Mexican Migrants,' in Jorge Durand and Douglas Massey, eds., *Crossing the Border: Research from the Mexican Migration Project* (New York: Russell Sage Foundation 2004), 281–99.
33 Ibid., 2.
34 George Borjas, 'The New Economics of Immigration,' *Atlantic Monthly*, 278 (November 1996): 75; George Borjas and Lawrence Katz, 'The Evolution of the Mexican-Born Workforce in the United States,' National Bureau for Economic Research (NBER), Working Paper 11281 (Cambridge, Mass.:

National Bureau of Economic Research 2005).

35 Doris Meissner et al., *Immigration and America's Future: A New Chapter*, Report of the Independent Taskforce on Immigration and America's Future, Co-Chairs Spencer Abraham and Lee Hamilton, 2006, 10; Smith, *The New Americans* 1997, 6.

36 Giovanni Peri and Chad Sparber, 'Rethinking the Effect of Immigration on Wages,' *Journal of the European Economic Association*, forthcoming; Smith, *The New Americans*, 7. Also see Michael Fix and Jeffrey Passel, *Immigration and Immigrants: Setting the Record Straight* (Washington, D.C.: Urban Institute 1994), http://www.urban.org/publications/305184.html 1994 (accessed June 7, 2011).

37 Giovanni Peri, 'Rethinking the Area Approach: Immigrants and the Labor Market in California, 1960–2005,' NBER, Working Paper 16217.

38 Susan Baker, Robert Cushing, and Charles Haynes, 'Fiscal Impacts of Mexican Migration to the United States,' in Bean et al., eds., *Mexico and US Immigration Policy*, 172.

39 Borjas, 'The New Economics of Immigration,' 75.

40 Tony Payan, *The Three U.S.-Mexico Border Wars* (Westport, Conn., and London: Praeger Security International 2006), 77, referring to a *New York Times* article: Eduardo Porter, 'Illegal Immigrants Are Bolstering Social Security with Billions,' *New York Times*, April 5, 2005. See also testimony of Jorge Casteñeda at United States Senate Committee on Foreign Relations, 'North American Cooperation on the Border,' Committee Hearing S. HRG. 109–423 (July 12, 2005), 22.

41 Fernando Romero, *Hyper-Border: The Contemporary U.S.-Mexico Border and Its Future* (New York: Princeton Architectural Press 2008), 100.

42 William Kandel, 'A Profile of Mexican Workers in Agriculture,' in Durand and Massey, eds., *Crossing the Border*, 261.

43 Baker et al., 'Fiscal Impacts of Mexican Migration to the United States,' 147.

44 Smith, *The New Americans*, 7.

45 Ibid.

46 D. DeVoretz, 'The Brain Drain is Real and It Costs Us,' *Policy Options*, 20, no. 7 (1999): 21.

47 David Stewart-Patterson, 'The Brain Drain Will Be a Torrent if We Don't Staunch It Now,' *Policy Options*, 20, no. 7 (1999): 30–3.

48 William Gibson, 'Canadian Students in the United States,' in Richard Harris, Stephen Easton, and Nicholas Schmitt, eds., *Brains on the Move: Essays on Human Capital Mobility in a Globalizing World and Implications for the Canadian Economy* (Toronto: C.D. Howe Institute 2005), 49.

49 Matthew Bloch et al., 'Immigration and Jobs: Where U.S. Workers Come From,' Special to the New York Times Online, April 7, 2009, http://www.

nytimes.com/interactive/2009/04/07/us/20090407-immigration-occupa-
tion.html?emc=eta3 (accessed January 17, 2011).

50 Jorge Durand and Douglas Massey, 'What We Learned from the Mexican
    Migration Project,' in Durand and Massey, eds., *Crossing the Border*, 6.

51 Rosenfeld and Tienda, 'Labor Market Implications of Mexican Migration,'
    195.

52 United States Census Bureau, 'Growth of Hispanic-Owned Businesses
    Triples the National Average,' Press release, 2006, CB06–41, http://www.
    census.gov/newsroom/releases/archives/business_ownership/cb06–41.
    html (accessed June 7, 2011)

53 Meissner et al., *Immigration and America's Future*, xiv.

54 Ngai, 'Braceros, Wetbacks, and the National Boundaries of Class,' 209.

55 David Gutierrez, 'Introduction,' xiii, in Gutierrez, ed., *Between Two Worlds*.

56 Mark Reisler, 'Always the Laborer, Never the Citizen: Anglo Perceptions of
    the Mexican Immigrant during the 1920s,' in ibid., 35.

57 Arthur Irwin and Walter Fogel, 'Shadow Labor Force: Mexican Workers
    in the American Economy,' in Arthur Corwin, ed., *Immigrants and Immi-
    grants: Perspectives on Mexican Labor Migration to the United States* (Westport,
    Conn.: Greenwood Press 1978), 262.

58 Ibid.

59 Jeffrey Passel, *The Size and Characteristics of the Unauthorized Migrant
    Population in the United States: Estimates Based on the March 2005 Population
    Survey* (Pew Hispanic Center Research Report, 2006), 16.

60 Wayne Cornelius, Leo Chávez, and Jorge Castro, 'Mexican Immigrants and
    Southern California: A Summary of Current Knowledge,' Center for US-
    Mexican Studies, University of California at San Diego, Research Report
    Series 36 (1982), 8.

61 US-Mexico Binational Council, *Managing Mexican Migration to the United
    States: Recommendations for Policymakers*. Report of the US-Mexico Bina-
    tional Council, (Washington DC and Mexico City: Center for Strategic and
    International Studies and Instituto Tecnológico Autónomo de México,
    2004), 6.

62 Estimaciones de CONAPO con base en Bureau of Census, Current
    Population Survey (CPS), 1994–2007, http://www.conapo.mx/index.
    php?option=com_content&view=article&id=323&Itemid=251 (accessed
    July 27, 2010).

63 CBO, 'The Role of Immigrants in the US Labor Market,' 13.

64 Wayne Cornelius, 'Mexican Migration to the United States: An Introduc-
    tion,' in Wayne Cornelius and Jorge Bustamente, eds., *Mexican Migration
    to the United States: Origins, Consequences, and Policy Options* (San Diego:

Center for US-Mexican Studies, University of California at San Diego, 1989), 3.

65 Wayne Cornelius, 'The Structural Embeddedness of Demand for Mexican Immigrant Labor: New Evidence from California,' in Manueal Suarez-Orozco, ed., *Crossings: Mexican Immigration in Interdisciplinary Perspectives* (Cambridge, Mass.: Harvard University Press 1998), 134.

66 Giovanni Peri, 'The Effect of Immigration on Productivity: Evidence from US States,' *Review of Economics and Statistics*, forthcoming.

67 Borjas and Katz, 'The Evolution of the Mexican-Born Workforce in the United States.'

68 CBO, 'The Role of Immigrants in the US Labor Market,' 8, 13.

69 Isabel Studer, 'Editor's Note,' in 'North American Crossroads, *Quarterly Report of the North American Center for Transborder Studies*, 4, *Labor Markets Interdependence in North America* (Tempe: Arizona State University Press 2007).

70 Cornelius, 'Mexican Migration to the United States: An Introduction,' 3.

71 Wayne Cornelius, 'The US Demand for Labor,' in Cornelius and Bustamenta, eds., *Mexican Migration to the United States*, 41.

72 Cornelius, 'Mexican Migration to the United States: An Introduction,' 7.

73 Smith, *The New Americans*, 147.

74 Manuel Garcia y Griego, 'The Importance of Mexican Contract Laborers to the United States, 1942–1964,' in Gutierrez, ed., *Between Two Worlds*, 44.

75 Freeman and Bean, 'Mexico and US Immigration Policy,' 40.

76 Cornelius, 'The Structural Embeddedness of Demand for Mexican Immigrant Labor,' 135.

77 United States, Senate Committee on Foreign Relations, 'North American Cooperation on the Border,' Committee Hearing S. HRG. 109–423 (July 12, 2005), 9.

78 We are grateful to Eric Helleiner (University of Waterloo) for this point.

79 Cornelius, Chávez, and Castro, 'Mexican Immigrants and Southern California,' 47.

80 Weintraub, 'US Foreign Policy and Mexican Immigration.'

81 Griego, 'The Importance of Mexican Contract Laborers to the United States, 1942–1964,' 71.

82 Weintraub, 'US Foreign Policy and Mexican Immigration,' 285.

83 Saskia Sassen, 'US Immigration Policy towards Mexico in a Global Economy,' in Gutierrez, ed., *Between Two Worlds*,' 225.

84 Cornelius, 'The Structural Embeddedness of Demand for Mexican Immigrant Labor,' 139.

85 Ana María Aragonés, 'Explosivo retorno de migrantes?' *La Jornada*, October 25, 2008, http://www.lajornada.com.mx (accessed July 24, 2010).

86 Cornelius, 'Mexican Migration to the United States: An Introduction,' 4.
87 Ibid.
88 Rebecca Morales, 'Transition Labor: Undocumented Workers in the Los Angeles Automobile Industry,' *Journal of International Migration*, 17, no. 4 (1983): 576.
89 Philip Martin, Richard Chen, and Mark Madamba, *United States Policies for Admission of Professional and Technical Workers: Objectives and Outcomes*, International Migration Paper 35 (Geneva: International Labour Office 2000), 3.
90 Maia Jochimowicz and Deborah Myers, 'Temporary High-Skilled Migration' (Washington, D.C.: Migration Policy Institute), November 2002, http://www.migrationinformation.org/feature/display.cfm? ID=69 (accessed November 10, 2006).
91 Meissner et al., *Immigration and America's Future*, 97.
92 Migration Policy Institute, http://www.migrationinformation.org/feature/ display.cfm ?ID=69.
93 Some important ones are the L visa (up to seven years and for intra-company executive transfers) and the E visa (one year, for a trader or investor who needs to manage a large personal investment in the US). See D. DeVoretz and D. Coulumbe, 'Labour Mobility between Canada and the United States: Quo Vadis 2003?' second draft, March 2003, 6. Prepared for Session 5 at Social and Labour Market Aspects of North American Linkages Workshop, an Industry Canada-Human Resources Development Workshop, Ottawa, November 21, 2002, 5.
94 Though, as will be considered, there was a cap of 5000 TN-Visas from Mexico in place until 2004.
95 Martin, Chen, and Madamba, *United States Policies*, 19.
96 Mahmood Iqbal, 'Are We Losing Our Minds?' *Policy Options*, 20, no. 7 (1999): 34–8.
97 Mahmood Iqbal, 'Brain Drain: Empirical Evidence of Emigration of Canadian Professionals to the United States,' *Canadian Tax Journal*, 48, no. 3 (2000): 674–88. 681.
98 DeVoretz and Coulombe, 'Labour Mobility,' 6.
99 DHS Office of Immigration Statistics, *2009 Yearbook of Immigration Statistics*, August 2010 (Washington, D.C.: US Department of Homeland Security), 65.
100 John Zhao, Doug Drew, and Scott Murray, 'Brain Drain and Brain Gain: The Migration of Knowledge Workers to and from Canada,' *Education Quarterly Review*, 6, no. 3 (2000): 15, 18.
101 John McHale, 'Canadian Immigration Policy in Comparative Perspective.'

Paper presented at John Deutsch Conference, Canadian Immigration Policy for the 21st Century, Queen's University, Kingston, Ont., October 2002.

102 Stephen Easton, 'Where Canadian Scientists Work,' in Harris, Easton, and Schmitt, eds., *Brains on the Move*, 25–7.

103 Ibid., 37.

104 K. Richardson, 'Sieve or Shield: Cascadia and High Tech Labor Mobility under Nafta,' in D. Wolfish and R. Roberge, eds., *3* (Ottawa: Policy Research Initiatives 2002).

105 DeVoretz and Coulombe, 'Labour Mobility,' 4.

106 DHS, *Non-Immigrant Admissions to the US: 2009*, April 2010.

107 Some analysts also feel that the increased use of TN visas is simply a function of substitution of these visas for H1-B visas and other working arrangements. Richard Harris and Nicholas Schmitt, 'Labour Mobility and a North American Common Market: Implications for Canada,' in Harris, Easton, and Schmitt, eds., *Brains on the Move*, 138. See also John Helliwell, 'Checking the Brain Drain: Evidence and Implications,' *Policy Options*, 20, no. 7 (1999): 12.

108 DeVoretz and Coulombe, 'Labour Mobility,' 2.

109 J. Vazquez-Azpiri, 'Through the Eye of a Needle: Canadian Information Technology Professionals and the TN Category of the NAFTA,' *Interpreter Releases*, 77, no. 24 (2000), as discussed in DeVoretz and Coulombe, 'Labour Mobility.'

110 Tamara Woroby, 'North American Immigration and the Search for Positive-Sum Returns,' in *Requiem or Revival? The Promise of North American Integration* (Washington, D.C.: Brookings Institution 2007), 14.

111 Heriberta Castonos-Lomnitz, *La migración de talentos en México* (Mexico City: Instituto de Investigaciones Económicas, Universidad Nacional Autónoma de México, 2005).

112 Woroby, 'North American Immigration,' 14.

113 Alicia Alonso, 'Regional Migration under NAFTA's Chapter 16: Then and Now.' Paper presented at the *North America at the Cross-Roads* Seminar, Universidad Iberoamericana, Mexico City, April 9, 2008.

114 Richard, 'Costing the Brain Drain,' in Harris, Easton, and Schmitt, eds., *Brains on the Move*, 62.

115 Ibid., 71.

116 Ibid., 69.

117 Michael Teitelbaum, 'U.S. Science and Engineering Workforce: An Unconventional Portrait,' in MaryAnne Foxx, ed., *Pan-Organizational Summit on the US Science and Engineering Workforce, Meeting Summary* (Washington, D.C.: National Academies Press 2002), 3.

118 Report quoted in Martin, Chen, and Madamba, *United States Policies*, 4.
119 Meissner et al., *Immigration and America's Future* 2006, xiv.
120 Teitelbaum, 'U.S. Science and Engineering Workforce,' 3.
121 Bryant LeEarl, 'Trying Times for U.S. Engineers,' in Fox, ed., *Pan-Organizational Summit*, 109.
122 Michael Crosby and Jean Pomeroy, 'What Will It Take for the United States to Maintain Global Leadership in Discovery and Innovation?' in William Butz et al., eds., *The US Science and Engineering Workforce*. Prepared for RAND Science and Technology, Office of Science and Technology Policy, Santa Monica, Calif., 2004, 21–6.
123 Jacob Kirkegaard, *The Accelerating Decline in America's High-Skilled Workforce: Implications for Immigration Policy* (Washington, D.C.: Peterson Institute for International Economics 2007), 60.
124 Sergio Diaz-Briquets and Charles Cheney, *Biomedical Globalization: The International Migration of Scientists* (New Brunswick, N.J.: Transaction Publishers 2002), 8.
125 Griego, 'The Importance of Mexican Contract Laborers to the United States, 1942–1964,' 52, 61.
126 Ibid., 60.
127 Weintraub, 'US Foreign policy and Mexican Immigration,' 290.
128 Ibid., 197.
129 Yossi Shain, 'The Mexican-American Diaspora's Impact on Mexico,' *Political Science Quarterly*, 114, no. 4 (2000): 669.
130 Ibid.
131 Ibid., 670.
132 Rodolfo de la Garza, 'Interests not Passions: Mexican-American Attitudes toward Mexico, Immigration from Mexico, and Other Issues Shaping U.S.-Mexico Relations,' *International Migration Review*, 32, no. 2 (1998): 401.
133 Gaspar Rivera-Saldana, 'Mexican Migrants and the Mexican Political System,' in Xochitl Bada, Jonathan Fox, and Andrew Selee, eds., *Invisible No More: Mexican Migrant Civic Participation in the United States* (Washington, D.C.: Woodrow Wilson Center 2006), 32.
134 Shain, 'The Mexican-American Diaspora's Impact on Mexico,' 681.
135 Ibid., 683.
136 de la Garza, 'Interests not Passions,' 404.
137 Ibid.
138 Rivera-Saldana, 'Mexican Migrants and the Mexican Political System,' 31.
139 Ibid.
140 The consular identification card may also be useful to US authorities, since it can help keep track of unauthorized residents.

141 Rivera-Saldana, 'Mexican Migrants and the Mexican Political System,' 33.
142 Myron Weiner and Michael Teitelbaum, *Political Demography, Demographic Engineering* (New York: Bergahn Books 2001), 79.
143 de la Garza, 'Interests not Passions,' 403.
144 Rodolpho de la Garza, Angelo Falcon, and Chris Garcia, 'Will the Real Americans Please Stand Up? Anglo and Mexican-American Support for Core American Values,' *American Journal of Political Science*, 40, no. 2 (1996): 348.
145 Jonathan Fox, Andrew Selee, and Xochtil Bada, 'Conclusion,' in Bada, Fox, and Selee, eds., *Invisible No More*, 35–40.
146 de la Garza, 'Interests not Passions,' 401.
147 David Ayón, 'Mexican Policy & Émigré Communities in the U.S.' Background paper presented at the seminar 'Mexican Migrant Social and Civic Participation in the United States,' Woodrow Wilson International Center for Scholars, Washington, D.C., November 4–5, 2005.
148 Fox, Selee, and Mada, 'Conclusion,' 38.
149 de la Garza, 'Interests not Passions,' 416–17.
150 Ibid., 417.
151 Meissner et al., *Immigration and America's Future*, 15.
152 Shain, 'The Mexican-American Diaspora's Impact on Mexico,' 690.
153 Jorge Chabat, 'The Vicious Circle of Nationalism: How the Mexican Elites Created the Myth of Mexican Anti-US Feeling.' Paper presented at the Annual Meeting of the International Studies Association, March 22–25, 2006, San Diego, Calif., http://www.allacademic.com (accessed July 28, 2010).
154 Meissner et al., *Immigration and America's Future*, 16.
155 Mark P. Sullivan and June S. Beittel, 'Mexico-U.S. Relations: Issues for Congress,' (United States Congressional Research Service, May 1, 2009), 29; Romero, *Hyper-Border*, 101, 104.

4. Extending the United States' Military Perimeter

1 This is chapter was researched by Erin Fitzgerald and Ariana Lopes Morey. We are indebted to General de Brigado Juan Alfredo Oropeza Garnica (Colegio de Defensa Nacional, México); Joel Sokolsky (Royal Military College of Canada); and Joseph Jockel (State University of New York, Plattsburgh) for their very helpful comments on earlier drafts of this chapter. An earlier version of this chapter was published as: Stephen Clarkson and Erin Fitzgerald, 'A Special Military Relationship? Canada's Role in Constructing US Military Power,' *Journal of Military and Strategic Studies*, 12, no. 1 (2009).
2 White House, *National Security Strategy*, May 2010, 42.

3 John Bailey and Sergio Aguayo Quezada, *Strategy and Security in U.S.-Mexican Relations beyond the Cold War* (San Diego, Calif.: Center for U.S.-Mexican Studies at the University of California 1996), 65–6.
4 Communication to the authors from Joseph Jockel, November 2010.
5 Rupert Smith, *The Utility of Force: The Art of War in the Modern World* (London: Penguin 2005), 182.
6 David Haglund, 'North American Cooperation in an Era of Homeland Security,' *Orbis*, 47 (autumn 2003): 684.
7 David G. Haglund and Joel J. Sokolsky, *The U.S.-Canada Security Relationship: The Politics, Strategy, and Technology of Defense* (Boulder, Colo.: Westview Press 1989), 2.
8 J.L. Granatstein, 'Staring into the Abyss,' in Granatsein, ed., *Towards a New World: Readings in the History of Canadian Foreign Policy* (Toronto: Copp Clark 1992), 52.
9 Jack Granatstein, *How Britain's Weakness Forced Canada into the Arms of the United States* (Toronto: University of Toronto Press 1989), 28.
10 Christopher Conliffe, 'The Permanent Joint Board on Defense, 1940–1988,' in Haglund and Sokolsky, eds., *The U.S.-Canada Security Relationship*, 150–1.
11 Robert Bothwell et al., *Canada, 1900–1945* (Toronto: University of Toronto Press 1990), 366.
12 Norman Hillmer and J.L. Granatstein, *Empire to Umpire: Canada and the World into the Twenty-First Century* (Toronto: Thompson Nelson 2008), 143.
13 Ibid., 153.
14 Raúl Benítez Manaut, 'Sovereignty, Foreign Policy, and National Security in Mexico, 1821–1989,' in H.P. Klepak, ed., *Natural Allies? Canadian and Mexican Perspectives on International Security* (Ottawa: Carleton University Press 1996), 67–8.
15 Ibid., 67.
16 Ibid. Emphasis added.
17 Ibid., 67–8.
18 Ibid.
19 Christopher Minster, 'The Unsung Ally: Mexican Involvement in World War Two,' *About.com Guide*, under 'About.com: Latin American History,' http://www.latinamericanhistory.about.com/od/thehistoryofmexico/a/09mexicoww2.htm (accessed February 11, 2010), 2.
20 Joseph T. Jockel, *Canada in NORAD, 1957–2007: A History* (Montreal and Kingston, Ont.: McGill-Queen's University Press 2007), 10.
21 Melvin Conant, *The Long Polar Watch: Canada and the Defense of North America* (New York: Council on Foreign Relations, Harper and Brothers, 1962), 39.
22 Quoted in Jockel, *Canada in NORAD*, 10.

23 Ibid., 54.
24 Quoted in ibid., 77.
25 Quoted in ibid., 127.
26 Elinor C. Sloan, *Security and Defence in the Terrorist Era: Canada and North America* (Montreal and Kingston, Ont.: McGill-Queen's University Press 2005), 102.
27 Jockel, *Canada in NORAD*, 136.
28 John A. Cope, 'In Search of Convergence: U.S.-Mexican Military Relations into the Twenty-First Century,' in Bailey and Quezada, eds., *Strategy and Security*, 186.
29 Luis Herrera-Lasso, 'Mexico in the Sphere of Hemispheric Security,' in Bailey and Quezada, eds., *Strategy and Security*, 42.
30 Manaut, 'Sovereignty, Foreign Policy, and National Security,' 68.
31 Quoted in ibid., 68–9.
32 Michael J. Dziedzic, 'Mexico and U.S. Grand Strategy: The Geo-Strategic Linchpin to Security and Prosperity,' in Bailey and Quezada, eds., *Strategy and Security*, 66.
33 Manaut, 'Sovereignty, Foreign Policy, and National Security,' 76.
34 Ibid., 75.
35 Ibid., 76.
36 Athanasios Hristoulas, 'Trading Places: Canada, Mexico, and North American Security,' in Peter Andreas and Thomas J. Biersteker, eds., *The Rebordering of North America: Integration and Exclusion in a New Security Context* (New York: Routledge 2003), 28.
37 Manaut, 'Sovereignty, Foreign Policy, and National Security,' 76.
38 Ibid., 77.
39 Herrera-Lasso, 'Mexico in the Sphere of Hemispheric Security,' 43.
40 Alfonso Garcia Robles (1967), 'El Tratado de Tlatelolco,' in *Génesis, Alcance y Propósitos de la proscripción de las armas nucleares en la América Latina* (Mexico City: Colegio de México 1967) 40.
41 Sloan, *Security and Defence in the Terrorist Era*, 31.
42 T.X. Hammes. *The Sling and the Stone: On War in the 21st Century* (New York: Zenith Imprint 2006), 2.
43 United States National Security Council, *The National Security Strategy of the United States of America* (Washington, D.C.: GPO 2002), 6, http://www.globalsecurity.org/military/library/policy/national/nss-020920.pdf (accessed January 15, 2011).
44 José Manuel Villalpando, *Las Fuerzas Armadas y la Ley: una introducción al derecho militar mexicano*, 2nd ed. (Mexico City: Escuela Libre de Derecho 2002), 210–12.
45 Ahmed Rashid, *Descent into Chaos: The United States and the Failure of Nation*

Building in Pakistan, Afghanistan and Central Asia (New York: Viking 2008), 371.

46 Julian Beltrame, 'Canada to Stay out of Iraq War,' *Maclean's*, March 31 2003.

47 Janice Gross Stein and Eugene Lang, *The Unexpected War: Canada in Kandahar* (Toronto: Viking Canada 2007).

48 Jockel, *Canada in NORAD*, 179.

49 Canada, Department of National Defence (DND), 'Enhance Canada-US Security Cooperation: Backgrounder,' December 9, 2002 (Ottawa: Queen's Printer for Canada 2002), http://www.forces.gc.ca/site/mobil/news-nouv-elles-eng.asp?cat=00&id=509 (accessed January 17, 2011).

50 Sloan, *Security and Defense in the Terrorist Era*, 74.

51 Communication from Joseph Jockel, November 2010.

52 William Knight, 'Homeland Security: Roles and Mission for United States Northern Command,' *Congressional Research Service*, June 3, 2008, CRS-7, http://www.fas.org/sgp/crs/homesec/RL34342.pdf (accessed January 15, 2011).

53 Interview with General Victor Renuart, commander, US Northern Command and North American Aerospace Command, Center for Strategic and International Studies, Washington, D.C., June 16, 2009.

54 Sloan, *Security and Defense in the Terrorist Era*, 109–11.

55 US National Security Council, *National Security Strategy*, 3.

56 Ibid., 42.

57 Ibid.

58 Ibid., 43.

59 Haglund and Sokolsky, *The U.S.-Canada Security Relationship*, 11.

60 DND, 'Canada First Defence Strategy: Three Roles,' March 3, 2010, http://www.forces.gc.ca/site/pri/first-premier/roles-eng.aspin (accessed December 2010).

5. Building US Homeland Security against Terrorism

1 This chapter was researched by Gilleen Witkowski, Jim Mylonas, and Mike Lawrence. It benefited enormously from detailed comments on earlier drafts by Raúl Benítez Manaud (Universidad Nacional Autónoma de México) and Athanasios Hristoulas (Instituto Tecnológico Autónomo de México); and Wesley Wark (University of Toronto).

2 United States, Department of Homeland Security (DHS), *National Strategy for Homeland Security*, July 2002 (Washington, D.C.: GPO), 21.

3 United States, Department of Commerce, Bureau of Economic Analysis

(BEA), *US International Transactions Accounts Data*, http://www.bea.gov/international/bp_web/list.cfm?anon=71 (accessed July 10, 2009).

4   Ibid.

5   Peter Andreas, 'A Tale of Two Borders,' in Peter Andreas and Thomas J. Biersteker, eds., *The Rebordering of North America* (New York and London: Routledge 2005), 10; Stephen Flynn, 'The False Conundrum: Continental Integration versus Homeland Security,' in ibid., 115.

6   DHS, *National Strategy for Homeland Security*, 1 and vii, respectively. See also 7–10 and 67 on the uncertainty surrounding the threat.

7   DHS, *National Strategy for Combating Terrorism*, September 2006 (Washington, D.C.: GPO), 13.

8   President George W. Bush, 'Preface,' DHS, *National Strategy for Homeland Security*.

9   Ibid.

10 Athanasios Hristoulas, 'Trading Places: Canada, Mexico, and North American Security,' in Andreas and Biersteker, eds., *The Rebordering of North America,* 33; Flynn, 'The False Conundrum,' 111.

11 Statistics Canada, 'Imports, Exports and Trade Balance of Goods on a Balance-of-Payments Basis, by Country or Country Grouping,' http://www.40.statcan.gc.ca/l01/cst01/gblec02a-eng.htm (accessed March 30, 2011).

12 Canada, Department of Foreign Affairs and International Trade (DFAIT), *Building a Border for the 21st Century: CUSP Forum Report* (Ottawa: DFAIT 2000), 15–17; Christopher Sands, 'Fading Power or Rising Power: 11 Sept. and Lessons from the Section 110 Experience,' in Norman Hillmer and M. Appel Molot, eds., *Canada among Nations: A Fading Power* (Toronto: Oxford University Press 2002), 51–64.

13 DFAIT, 'Action Plan for Creating a Secure and Smart Border,' December 2001, http://www.international.gc.ca/anti-terrorism/declaration-en.asp (accessed January 15, 2011).

14 Canada, House of Commons Sub-Committee on International Trade, Trade Disputes and Investment (Bill Graham, chair), *Towards a Secure and Trade-Efficient Border* (November 2001), 1. Also: Public Policy Forum, *Canada's Policy Choices: Managing Our Border with the United States* (Ottawa: Public Policy Forum 2001), 23.

15 Senate Committee on Foreign Relations, *North American Cooperation on the Border: Prepared Statement of Hon. Perrin Beatty, President and CEO of the Canadian Manufacturers and Exporters and Former Canadian Foreign Minister*, 109th Cong., 1st sess., 12 July 2005, S. HRG. 109–423, p. 21.

16 DFAIT, 'Backgrounder: Canada's Actions against Terrorism since Septem-

ber 11,' February 7, 2003, http://www.international.gc.ca/anti-terrorism/canadaactions-en.asp (accessed January 15, 2011).

17 Government of Canada, *Border Cooperation*, January 22, 2009 (Washington, D.C.: Government of Canada 2009), http://www.canadainternational.gc.ca/washington/bilat_can/border_frontiere.aspx? lang=eng&menu_id=34& menu=L (accessed January 15, 2011).

18 Elinor C. Sloan, *Security and Defence in the Terrorist Era: Canada and North America* (Montreal and Kingston, Ont.: McGill-Queen's University Press 2005), 59.

19 Victor Konrad and Heather N. Nicol, *Beyond Walls: Re-inventing the Canada-United States Borderlands* (Aldershot, U.K., and Burlington, Vt.: Ashgate 2008), 1, 16.

20 Sloan, *Security and Defence in the Terrorist Era*, 62–3.

21 DFAIT, Backgrounder – Canada's Actions against Terrorism since September 11'; Canada, Department of Finance, 'Budget 2001 – Budget Plan: Chapter 5 – Enhancing Security for Canadians,' http://www.fin.gc.ca/budget01/bp/bpch5-eng.asp (accessed March 14, 2011); DHS, *National Strategy for Homeland Security*, 22.

22 Audrey Macklin, 'Borderline Security,' in Ronald J. Daniels et al., *The Security of Freedom: Essays on Canada's Anti-Terrorism Bill* (Toronto: University of Toronto Press 2001), 393–8; Canadian Centre for Policy Alternatives, 'CCPA Analysis of Bill C-36: An Act to Combat Terrorism,' November 1, 2001 (Ottawa: Canadian Centre for Policy Alternatives 2001), 1, http://www.policyalternatives.ca/ publications/reports/ccpa-analysis-bill-c-36 (accessed December 4, 2010).

23 Athanasios Hristoulas, 'North American Security Policy: Rhetoric and Reality.' Paper prepared for presentation at the Annual International Studies Association Meeting, San Francisco, March 26–29, 2008, 14–16.

24 Peter Andreas, 'The Mexicanization of the US-Canada Border: Asymmetric Interdependence in a Changing Security Context,' *International Journal*, 60, no. 2 (2005): 452.

25 Information in these two paragraphs comes from a Mexican government memorandum transmitted to the author confidentially in January 2011.

26 Royal Canadian Mounted Police, 'IBETs across Canada,' http://www.rcmp-grc.gc.ca/ibet-eipf/map-carte-eng.htm (accessed January 17, 2011).

27 Mario Arroyo Juárez and Gerardo Rodríguez. 'Terrorismo en México,' in Raúl Benítez Manaut, Abelardo Rodríguez Sumano, and Armando Rodríguez Luna, eds., *Atlas de la Seguridad y la Defensa de México 2009* (Mexico City: Colectivo de Análisis de la Seguridad con Democracía AC 2009), 114.

28 Hristoulas, 'North American Security Policy,' 11.

29 Hristoulas, 'Trading Places,' 37.

30 United States, Senate Committee on the Judiciary, *The War against Terror-ism: Working Together to Protect America*, testimony of US Attorney General John Ashcroft, March 4, 2003, 108th Cong., 1st sess., S. HRG. 108–37, http://www.globalsecurity.org/security/library/ congress/2003_h/03-04-03_ashcroft.htm (accessed January 15, 2011).

31 United States, Customs and Border Protection, 'Remarks by Robert C. Bonner, Kansas City Chamber of Commerce, Kansas City, Missouri,' May 16, 2005, http://www.customs.gov/xp/cgov/newsroom/speeches_state-ments/archives/2005/05162005_kansas.xml (accessed March 6, 2011).

32 DHS, *National Strategy for Homeland Security*, 22; George Haynal, 'Inter-dependence, Globalization and North American Borders,' *Policy Options*, September 2002, 25–6.

33 *Vancouver Sun*, 'U.S., Canada Share Police Powers in Mutual Waters,' Sep-tember 14, 2007.

34 Canada, British Columbia, RCMP, 'Border Integrity – Canada and the Unit-ed States Announce Shared Coastal Law Enforcement Operations during the 2010 Winter Games,' February 3, 2010 (Vancouver, B.C.: RCMP 2010), http://www.bc.rcmp.ca/ViewPage.action?siteNodeId=50&languageId=1&contentId=13191 (accessed February 17, 2010).

35 DHS, 'Joint U.S.-Canada Agreement for Land Pre-Clearance Pilots,' Press Release, December 17, 2004 (Washington, D.C.: GPO 2004), http://www.dhs.gov/xnews/releases/press_release_0571.shtm (accessed February 17, 2010).

36 United States, Government Accountability Office (GAO), 'Various Issues Led to the Termination of the United States-Canada Shared Border Man-agement Pilot Project,' September 4, 2008, GAO-08-1038R (Washington, D.C.: GPO 2008).

37 Tony Payan, *The Three U.S.-Mexico Border Wars* (Westport, Conn., and Lon-don: Praeger Security International 2006), 34–6, 104–5.

38 Lisa M. Seghetti et al., *Border Security and the Southwest Border: Background, Legislation, and Issues* (Washington, D.C.: United States Congressional Research Service 2005), CRS10–11.

39 Payan, *The Three U.S.-Mexico Border Wars*, 105.

40 US-Mexico Binational Council, *US-Mexico Border Security and the Evolving Security Relationship: Recommendations for Policymakers* (Washington, D.C.: Center for Strategic and International Studies 2004), 10–11.

41 Mark P. Sullivan and June S. Beittel, *Mexico-U.S. Relations: Issues for Con-gress* (Washington, D.C.: United States Congressional Research Service 2009), 28.

42 NAV Canada, 'NAV Canada and the 9/11 crisis,' Backgrounder, http://www.navcanada.ca/NavCanada.asp? Language=en&Content=ContentDefinitionFiles\Newsroom\Backgrounders\911crisis.xml (accessed February 17, 2010).

43 DFAIT, 'Smart Border Action Plan Status Report,' December 17, 2004, http://www.migration.ucdavis.edu/rs/more.php?id=170_0_2_0 (accessed January 17, 2011); Stephen Brill, *After: How America Confronted the September 12 Era* (New York: Simon and Schuster 2003), 219.

44 Fernando Romero, *Hyper-Border: The Contemporary U.S.-Mexico Border and Its Future* (New York: Princeton Architectural Press 2008), 121.

45 Andreas, 'A Tale of Two Borders', 12.

46 Interview with Raúl Benítez, CISAN, Universidad Nacional Autónoma de México, Mexico City, February 21, 2006.

47 Hristoulas, 'North American Security Policy,' 132–43.

48 Macklin, 'Borderline Security,' 391.

49 John J. Noble, 'A Secure Border? The Canadian View,' in Alexander Moens and Martin Collacott, eds., *Immigration Policy and the Terrorist Threat in Canada and the United States* (Vancouver: Fraser Institute 2008), 171–2.

50 CSIS report quoted by Martin Collacott. 'Canada's Inadequate Response to Terrorism: The Need for Policy Reform,' Fraser Institute Digital Publication, February 2006, 4–5.

51 Quoted in Payan, *The Three U.S.-Mexico Border Wars*, 96–7.

52 Ibid., 69.

53 Ibid., 93–4.

54 Seghetti et al., *Border Security and the Southwest Border*, CRS45.

55 See United States Customs and Border Patrol, 'U.S./Mexico Initiative Targets Alien Smugglers & Human Traffickers,' August 17, 2005, http://www.cbp.gov/xp/cgov/newsroom/news_releases/archives/2005_press_releases/082005/ 08172005.xml (accessed January 15, 2011).

56 Seghetti et al., 'Border Security and the Southwest Border,' CRS54.

57 Payan, *The Three U.S.-Mexico Border Wars*, 56–7.

58 Ibid., 78.

59 Flynn, 'The False Conundrum,' 111–14; Payan, *The Three U.S.-Mexico Border Wars*, 58.

60 Stephanie Simon, 'Border-Fence Project Hits a Snag.' *Wall Street Journal*, February 4, 2009.

61 Flynn, 'The False Conundrum,' 111.

62 Hristoulas, 'Trading Places,' 32.

63 Blas Nuñez-Neto et al., *Border Security: Apprehensions of 'Other Than Mexican' Aliens*, September 22, 2005 (Washington D.C.: United States Congressional Research Service 2005), CRS20–1.

64 Flynn, 'The False Conundrum,' 111, 117.
65 DHS, *National Strategy for Homeland Security*, viii.
66 Ibid., 22.
67 United States, GAO, 'Border Security: Security Vulnerabilities at Unmanned and Unmonitored U.S. Border Locations,' Statement of Gregory D. Kutz, testimony before the Committee on Finance, U.S. Senate, GAO-07-884T, September 27, 2007 (Washington D.C.: GPO 2007).
68 Payan, *The Three U.S.-Mexico Border Wars*, 16–17, 87–9. Payan comments: 'Conflating these issues can only prevent the U.S. government from dealing more effectively with each of them. Creating what looks like a single strategy with a unilateral, short-term focus seems counterproductive as well, given that the problems of the border are better solved in partnership with one's neighbor, with a long-term focus to tackle the very origins of each concern' (17).
69 Ibid., 16.

6. Constraining and Reconstructing US Narcotics Security

1 This chapter was researched by Mike Lawrence and Harry Skinner. It benefited enormously from detailed comments on earlier drafts by Raúl Benítez Manaud (Universidad Nacional Autónoma de México), Athanasios Hristoulas (Instituto Tecnológico Autónomo de México), and Wesley Wark (University of Toronto).
2 United States, Joint Forces Command, 'The Joint Operating Environment 2008: Challenges and Implications for the Future Joint Force,' November 25, 2008, 34, http://www.jfcom.mil/ newslink/storyarchive/2008/JOE2008.pdf (accessed March 12, 2011).
3 White House Office of National Drug Control Policy (ONDCP), 'The Economic Costs of Drug Abuse in the United States, 1992–2002, December 2004, http://www.ncjrs.gov/ondcppubs/publications/pdf/economic_costs.pdf (accessed June 12, 2011).
4 United States, Department of Justice, National Drug Intelligence Center, *National Drug Threat Assessment 2009* (December 2008), iii.
5 ONDCP, Executive Office of the President, 'National Drug Control Strategy: FY2009 Budget Summary,' February 2008, 13, http://www.whitehouse-drugpolicy.gov/publications/policy/ndcs08/2008ndcs.pdf (accessed March 8, 2011).
6 US, Department of Justice, *National Drug Threat Assessment 2009*, iii.
7 Stephen E. Flynn, 'The Global Drug Trade versus the Nation-State,' in Maryann Cusimano Love, ed., *Beyond Sovereignty: Issues for a Global Agenda*, 2nd ed. (Toronto: Thompson-Wadsworth 2003), 168.

8 United States, Office of the White House, National Security Decision Directive 221, 'Narcotics and National Security,' April 8, 1986, 1, http://www.fas.org/irp/offdocs/nsdd/nsdd-221.htm (accessed June 12, 2011)

9 Flynn, 'The Global Drug Trade,' 168.

10 Office of the White House, Security Decision Directive 221, 2.

11 Flynn, 'The Global Drug Trade,' 170.

12 US, Department of Justice, *National Drug Threat Assessment 2009.*

13 Ibid., 2; United States, Department of State, Bureau for International Narcotics and Law Enforcement Affairs, *2009 International Narcotics Control Strategy Report: Vol. 1, Drug and Chemical Control, Mexico Country Report*, February 27, 2009, http://www.state.gov/p/inl/rls/nrcrpt/2009/vol1/116522.htm (accessed June 12, 2011); Tony Payan, *The Three U.S.-Mexico Border Wars: Drugs, Immigration, and Homeland Security* (Westport, Conn.: Praeger Security International 2006), 27.

14 US, Department of Justice, *National Drug Threat Assessment 2009*, 17, referring to National Survey on Drug Use and Health (NSDUH) data.

15 Ibid., 22.

16 Ibid., 17.

17 Ibid., 22.

18 Ibid., iv.

19 Royal Canadian Mounted Police, Criminal Intelligence, *Drug Situation in Canada – 2007* (2007), 4, http://www.rcmp-grc.gc.ca/drugs-drogues/pdf/drug-drogue-situation-2007-eng.pdf (accessed June 12, 2011)

20 United States/Canada Cross-Border Crime Forum (CBCF), *United States-Canada Border Drug Threat Assessment 2007* (2007), 11–12, 35, http://www.publicsafety.gc.ca/prg/le/oc/_fl/us-canadian-report-drugs-eng.pdf (accessed June 12, 2011).

21 US, Department of Justice, *National Drug Threat Assessment 2009*, v; 46.

22 CBCF, *United States-Canada Border Drug Threat Assessment 2007*, vii.

23 Ibid., vii, 12, 35.

24 Ibid., 9.

25 US, Department of Justice, *National Drug Threat Assessment 2009*, iv.

26 John Walters, 'No Surrender: The Drug War Saves Lives,' in Laura E. Huggins, ed., *Drug War Deadlock: The Policy Battle Continues* (Stanford, Calif.: Hoover Institution Press and Stanford University 2005), 238. Walters also notes that 'marijuana's role in emergency-room cases has tripled in the past decade' (239).

27 CBCF, *United States-Canada Border Drug Threat Assessment 2007*, vii, 1.

28 US, Department of Justice, *National Drug Threat Assessment 2009*, v, 46.

29 CTV.ca News Staff, 'Canada Now a Major Producer of Ecstasy,' CTV

News, December 17, 2007, http://www.ctv.ca/servlet/ArticleNews/story/
CTVNews/20071217/rcmp_drugs_071217/20071217?hub=CTVNews
At11; US, Department of State, Bureau for International Narcotics and Law
Enforcement Affairs, *2009 International Narcotics Control Strategy Report:
Vol. 1, Drug and Chemical Control, Canada Country Report*, February 27, 2009,
http://www.state.gov/p/inl/rls/nrcrpt/2009/vol1/116520.htm (accessed
June 12, 2011); RCMP, *Drug Situation in Canada – 2007*, 14.

30 CBCF, *United States-Canada Border Drug Threat Assessment 2007*, 2; RCMP,
Drug Situation in Canada – 2007, 14, 18–19.

31 US, Department of Justice, *National Drug Threat Assessment 2009*, 37.

32 RCMP, *Drug Situation in Canada – 2007*, 15.

33 Ibid., 14.

34 US, Department of Justice, *National Drug Threat Assessment 2009*, v.

35 Ibid., vi.

36 Ibid., 25.

37 Ibid., 27–8, 32.

38 Ibid., 25–7.

39 Central Intelligence Agency, *World Factbook*, 'Field Listings – Illicit Drugs
– Mexico,' November 10, 2008, http://www.cia.gov/library/publications/
the-world-factbook/fields/2086.html (accessed February 2010).

40 CBCF, *United States-Canada Border Drug Threat Assessment 2007*, 13.

41 United States, Government Accountability Office (GAO), 'Drug Control:
U.S. Assistance Has Helped Mexican Counternarcotics Efforts, but the
Flow of Drugs into the United States Remains High,' testimony of Jess T.
Ford before the Subcommittee on the Western Hemisphere, Committee on
Foreign Affairs, House of Representatives, October 25, 2007, 3.

42 US, Department of Justice, *National Drug Threat Assessment 2009*, 12. A
'superlab' is a lab with a production scale that can produce ten or more
pounds of meth per production cycle.

43 Ibid., Figure 11, p. 15.

44 Ibid., 15–16.

45 CBCF, *United States-Canada Border Drug Threat Assessment 2007*, 16–18.

46 US, Department of Justice, *National Drug Threat Assessment 2009*, 9–11; US,
Department of State, Bureau for International Narcotics and Law Enforce-
ment Affairs, *2009 International Narcotics Control Strategy Report: Vol. 1,
Drug and Chemical Control, Mexico Country Report*.

47 US, Department of Justice, *National Drug Threat Assessment 2009*, iv–v, 9,
12.

48 Ibid., 1.

49 Ibid., 2; US, Department of State, *2009 International Narcotics Control Strat-*

egy Report: Vol. 1, Drug and Chemical Control, Mexico Country Report; Payan, *The Three U.S.-Mexico Border Wars*, 27.

50 GAO, testimony of Jess T. Ford, 7.

51 RCMP, *Drug Situation in Canada – 2007*, 4; CBCF, *United States-Canada Border Drug Threat Assessment 2007*, 7.

52 RCMP, *Drug Situation in Canada – 2007*, 9; CBCF, *United States-Canada Border Drug Threat Assessment 2007*, 6–7.

53 RCMP, *Drug Situation in Canada – 2007*, 10.

54 Ibid., 31. One of the key precursor chemicals for MDMA is MDP2P, which is typically smuggled into Canada from China in quantities of one ton or greater. US, Department of Justice, *National Drug Threat Assessment 2009*, 38.

55 Ibid., 44.

56 Linda Diebel, 'How Mexico's Drug War Washed up on Canada's West Coast,' *Toronto Star*, May 30, 2009, http://www.thestar.com/article/642966 (accessed January 15, 2011).

57 Mexico Institute, Woodrow Wilson International Center for Scholars, *The United States and Mexico: Towards a Strategic Partnership*, January 2009.

58 Ignacio Alvarado y Evangelina Hernández, 'Narcos Corrompen Autoridades de EU,' *El Universal*, October 19, 2009, http://www.eluniversal.com.mx (accessed July 13, 2010).

59 Payan, *The Three U.S.-Mexico Border Wars*, 39–40.

60 Grupo Reforma, 'Caen 10 militares ligados al "chapo,"' *Reforma*, June 14, 2009, http://www.grupoSreforma.com (accessed July 14, 2010).

61 Maureen Meyer, 'At a Crossroads: Drug Trafficking, Violence and the Mexican State,' (Washington Office on Latin America and the Beckley Foundation Drug Policy Program, November 2007), 9.

62 For a list of fourteen House and Senate hearings on this threat in just part of the 111th United States Congress, see June S. Beittel, 'Mexico's Drug-Related Violence' (Congressional Research Service: May 27, 2009), 20–4.

63 Ibid., 14.

64 Quoted in Danna Harman, 'Mexican Drug Cartels' Wars Move Closer to U.S. Border,' *USA Today*, August 17, 2005.

65 Ted Galen Carpenter, 'Troubled Neighbor: Mexico's Drug Violence Poses a Threat to the United States,' *Policy Analysis* (CATO), 631 (February 2, 2009): 4; US, Department of State, *2009 International Narcotics Control Strategy Report: Vol. 1, Drug and Chemical Control, Mexico Country Report*, 414.

66 Carpenter, 'Troubled Neighbor,' 4.

67 Ibid.

68 Ibid., 4–5.

69 US, Department of Justice, *National Drug Threat Assessment 2009*, 43–4.
70 Carpenter, 'Troubled Neighbor,' 3. Only some of these victims are believed to have been involved in drug trafficking.
71 Colleen W. Cook, 'Mexico's Drug Cartels' (Congressional Research Service: October 16, 2007), 11.
72 Raúl Benítez Manaut, 'Ciudad Juárez: War Zone,' 81, http://www.socialde-mocracia.org (accessed July 13, 2010).
73 GAO, testimony of Jess T. Ford, 11.
74 Catherine R. Dooley and Adriade Medler, 'A Farewell to Arms: Managing Cross-Border Weapons Trafficking,' *Hemisphere Focus*, 16, no. 2 (2008), http://www.csis.org/media/csis/pubs/hf_v16_02.pdf. (accessed June 12, 2011)
75 Carpenter, 'Troubled Neighbor,' 2.
76 Mark P. Sullivan and June S. Beittel, 'Mexico-U.S. Relations: Issues for Congress' (Congressional Research Service: May 1, 2009), 16–17.
77 Salvador Camarena, 'Asesinado a Balazos el candidato del PRI a la gobernación del Estado de Tamaulipas,' *El País*, June 26, 2010, http://www.elpais.com (accessed July 14, 2010).
78 For a thoughtful reading of this debate, see George Grayson, *Mexico: Narco-Violence and a Failed State?* (New Brunswick, N.J.: Transaction Publishers 2010).
79 US, Joint Forces Command, 'The Joint Operating Environment 2008.' The assessment continues: 'The Mexican possibility may seem less likely, but the government, its politicians, police, and judicial infrastructure are all under sustained assault and pressure by criminal gangs and drug cartels. How that internal conflict turns out over the next several years will have a major impact on the stability of the Mexican state. Any descent by Mexico into chaos would demand an American response based on the serious implications for homeland security alone.'
80 Joaquín Villalobos, 'Doce mitos de la guerra contra el Narco,' *Revista Nexos*, January 1, 2010, http://www.nexos.com.mx (accessed July 14, 2010).
81 Office of the White House, National Security Decision Directive 221, 3–4.
82 Ibid., 3. Indeed, since 2001 there has been a 20.9 per cent decrease in US spending on domestic prevention programs, owing to budgetary constraints forced by increased involvement overseas. ONDCP, 'National Drug Control Strategy.'
83 Ethan E. Nadelmann, *Cops across Borders: The Internationalization of U.S. Criminal Law Enforcement* (University Park: Pennsylvania State University Press 1993).
84 CBCF, *United States-Canada Border Drug Threat Assessment 2007*, 28.

85 Ibid., 28–9.

86 Ibid., 28.

87 US, Department of State, *2009 International Narcotics Control Strategy Report: Vol. 1, Drug and Chemical Control, Canada Country Report*, 186.

88 CBCF, *United States-Canada Border Drug Threat Assessment 2007*, vii.

89 Government of Canada, *United States-Canada Border Drug Threat Assessment 2004*, http://www.publicsafety.gc.ca/prg/le/bs/uscabdta-eng. aspx#a14 (accessed March 8, 2011).

90 Beittel, 'Mexico's Drug-Related Violence,' 2.

91 Ted Galen Carpenter, *Bad Neighbor Policy: Washington's Futile War on Drugs in Latin America* (New York: Palgrave 2003), 186.

92 Ibid.

93 Raúl Benitez Manaut et al., eds., *Atlas de la Seguridad y la Defensa de México 2009* (Mexico City: Colectivo de Análisis de la Seguridad con Democracía [CASEDE] 2009), 383–5.

94 David Francis, 'As Violence Grows along Border, Congress Debates Funding for Fighting Mexican Drug Cartels,' *World Politics Review*, March 7, 2008, http://www.worldpoliticsreview.com/article. aspx?id=1735 (accessed January 15, 2011).

95 Raúl Benítez Manaut, 'La Iniciativa Mérida: nuevo paradigma en la relación de seguridad México-Estados Unidos-Centroamérica,' *Revista mexicana de política exterior*, 87 (October 2009): 193–267; Clare Ribando Seelke, 'Mérida Initiative for Mexico and Central America: Funding and Policy Issues' (Congressional Research Service: August 21, 2009); US Department of State and Government of Mexico, 'Joint Statement on the Mérida Initiative, October 22, 2007, http://www.cfr.org/mexico/joint-statement-merida-initiative/p14603 (accessed June 12, 2011).

96 Sullivan and Beittel, 'Mexico-U.S. Relations,' summary.

97 Seelke, 'Mérida Initiative,' 4–5; Sullivan and Beittel, 'Mexico-U.S. Relations,' 21.

98 Sullivan and Beittel, 'Mexico-U.S. Relations,' 20.

99 Sergio Aguayo Quezada, '¿Quién gana la guerra contra el narcotráfico?' in Manaut et al., eds., *Atlas de la Seguridad*, 33.

100 GAO, testimony of Jess T. Ford, 17–18; US, Department of State, *2009 International Narcotics Control Strategy Report: Vol. 1, Drug and Chemical Control, Mexico Country Report*, 417–18.

101 Sullivan and Beittel, 'Mexico-U.S. Relations,' 26–7.

102 Ibid., 13.

103 Patricia G. Erickson and David L. Haans, 'Drug War, Canadian Style,' in Jurg Gerber and Eric L. Jensen, eds., *Drug War, American Style: The*

Internationalization of Failed Policy and its Alternatives (New York: Garland Publishing 2001), 123.

104 Ibid. 122–3.

105 Ibid., 123–6.

106 CBCF, *United States-Canada Border Drug Threat Assessment 2007*, 25.

107 Ibid., 33.

108 US, Department of State, *2009 International Narcotics Control Strategy Report: Vol. 1, Drug and Chemical Control, Canada Country Report*, 184.

109 Gerardo Rodríguez Sanchéz Lara, 'Seguridad Nacional en México: Evaluación a dos años de gobierno del Presidente Calderón,' http://www. seguridadcondemocracio.org (accessed July 14, 2010).

110 Felipe Calderón Hinojosa, 'La Guerra contra el crimen organizado,' in Manaut et al., eds., *Atlas de la Seguridad*, 17.

111 General Barry R. McCaffrey, 'El Desafío mexicano: corrupción, crímenes y drogas,' in ibid., 132.

112 Sullivan and Beittel, 'Mexico-U.S. Relations,' 24.

113 US, Department of State, *2009 International Narcotics Control Strategy Report: Vol. 1, Drug and Chemical Control, Mexico Country Report*, 52.

114 Ibid., 51.

115 Sullivan and Beittel, 'Mexico-U.S. Relations,' 23–4.

116 US, Department of State, *2009 International Narcotics Control Strategy Report: Vol. 1, Drug and Chemical Control, Mexico Country Report*, 417.

117 CBCF, *United States-Canada Border Drug Threat Assessment 2007*, 14.

118 Ibid., 11.

119 US, Department of Justice, *National Drug Threat Assessment 2009*, 37.

120 US, Department of State, *2009 International Narcotics Control Strategy Report: Vol. 1, Drug and Chemical Control, Mexico Country Report*, 415.

121 Ibid., 416.

122 US, Department of Justice, *National Drug Threat Assessment 2009*, 3–4.

123 Ibid., 1.

124 Carpenter, 'Troubled Neighbor,' 7–8, and *Bad Neighbor Policy*, 187–8; Payan, *The Three U.S.-Mexico Border Wars*, 30–1.

125 Carpenter, 'Troubled Neighbor,' 192–3.

126 US, Department of Justice, *National Drug Threat Assessment 2009*, 3; US, Department of State, *2009 International Narcotics Control Strategy Report: Vol. 1, Drug and Chemical Control, Mexico Country Report*, 415.

127 GAO, testimony of Jess T. Ford, 11.

128 Ibid.

129 David Aguilar, 'Confronting the Issue of Border Incursions,' statement of David Aguilar, chief, Office of Border Patrol, United States Customs and

Border Protection, Department of Homeland Security, before the U.S House of Representatives Committee on Homeland Security, Subcommittee on Investigations, January 28, 2008, http://www.cbp.gov/xp/cgov/newsroom/congressional_test/border_problem.xml (accessed June 12, 2011).
130 McCaffrey, 'El Desafío mexicano,' 132–3.
131 Quezada, '¿Quién gana la guerra contra el narcotráfico?' 35.
132 McCaffrey, 'El Desafío mexicano,' 131.
133 Jorge Luis Sierra, 'La Guerra en la frontera México-Estados Unidos,' in Manaut et al., eds., Atlas de la Seguridad, 167.
134 Jospe María Moreno, 'La seguridad en la frontera con Estados Unidos: de la ineficacia a políticas estratégicas,' in ibid., 160.
135 Jorge Castañeda, 'Mexico's Failed Drug War,' CATO Institute, Economic Development Bulletin, Center for Global Liberty and Prosperity, 13 (May 16, 2010): 2–3.
136 Marcos Pablo Moloeznik, 'Sistema de defensa, fuerzas armadas y profesión militar,' in Manaut et al., eds., Atlas de la Seguridad, 55.
137 Erickson and Haans, 'Drug War, Canadian Style,' 135–6.
138 Government of Canada, Canada's Drug Strategy (Ottawa: Health Canada 1998), 4.
139 Ibid.
140 Patty Torsney, chair, Policy for the New Millennium: Working Together to Redefine Canada's Drug Strategy (Ottawa: Special Committee on Non-Medical Use of Drugs 2002), 26, 43.
141 Charles Levinthal, 'Should Harm Reduction Be Our Overall Goal in Fighting Drug Abuse?' in Huggins, ed., Drug War Deadlock, 203.
142 Torsney, Policy for the New Millennium, 23–4.
143 Ibid., 31–3.
144 Canadian Press, 'Support Grows for Vancouver's Safe-Injection Site,' CTV.ca, July 18, 2006, http://www.ctv.ca/servlet/ArticleNews/story/CTVNews/20060718/vancouver_safe_injection_060718/20060718?hub=Health (accessed January 15, 2011).
145 North American Opiate Medication Initiative, 'Status Report, March 2008,' http://www.naomistudy.ca/documents.html (accessed January 15, 2011).
146 Steven Frank, 'Fighting Heroin with … Heroin,' Time, February 7, 2005, http://www.time.com/time /magazine/article/0,9171,1025170,00.html (accessed January 15, 2011).
147 Health Canada, 'Marihuana for Medical Purposes – Statistics, June 5, 2009, http://www.hc-sc.gc.ca/dhp-mps/marihuana/stat/_2009/june-juin-eng.php (accessed June 12, 2011)

148 Ibid.
149 Erin Anderssen, 'Would Softer Pot Laws Stir Wrath of US?' *Globe and Mail*, July 13, 2002.
150 'U.S. Frets Canada May Ease Marijuana Law,' *New York Times*, December 12, 2002.
151 Robert MacCoun, 'American Laws, Foreign Lands: O Cannabis! Pot Decriminalization in Canada Highlights U.S. Isolation,' *San Francisco Chronicle*, June 11, 2003, http://www.sfgate.com/cgi-bin/article.cgi?file=/chronicle/archive/2003/06/11/ED254167.DTL (accessed January 15, 2011).
152 Ibid.
153 *CBC News*, 'PM Says Pot Soon to Be Decriminalized,' April 30, 2003, http://www.cbc.ca/news/story /2003/04/29/marijuana_chretien030429.html (accessed January 15, 2011); CTV.ca News Staff, 'Harper's Crime Agenda Getting Mixed Reviews,' *CTV.ca*, April 3, 2006, http://www.ctv.ca/servlet/ArticleNews/story/CTVNews/20060403/ marijuana_crime_harper_060403/20060403?hub=Canada (accessed January 15, 2011).
154 In Mexico's case, see George W. Grayson, *Mexico's Struggle with 'Drugs and Thugs'* (New York: Foreign Policy Association 2009), 56.
155 Stephen Dinan, 'Obama Blames U.S. Guns in Mexico,' *Washington Post*, April 17, 2009, http://www.washingtontimes.com/news/2009/apr/17/obama-blames-us-guns-in-mexico/ (accessed June 12, 2011).
156 BBC News, 'Obama Backs Mexico War on Drugs,' April 19, 2009, http://www.news.bbc.co.uk/2/hi/americOtras/8001733.stm (accessed July 14, 2010).
157 Mark Landler, 'Clinton Says U.S. Feeds Mexico Drug Trade,' *New York Times*, March 25, 2009.

7. Strengthening US International Economic Power

1 This chapter was partly researched by Denitza Koev and benefited greatly from research by Haidy Durán Gil in Mexico and from invaluable interviews there with Juan Carlos Baker Pineda, Luz María de la Mora, Hugo Perezcano, Eloy Cantú Segovia, and Roberto Zapata Barradas; and from discussions at the Canadian embassy with Heather Brason, John Gartke, and Sean Sunderland. Earlier drafts benefited from comments by Juan Carlos Baker Pineda, Luz María de la Mora, and Roberto Zapata Barradas and professors Greg Anderson (University of Alberta) and David Schneiderman (University of Toronto).

2 White House, Office of the Press Secretary, 'Remarks by President Clinton, President Bush, President Carter, President Ford, and Vice President Gore in Signing of NAFTA Side Agreements,' September 14, 2009, http://www.historycentral.com/Documents/Clinton/SigningNaFTA.html (accessed June 12, 2011).

3 Teresa Guttierrez-Haces, 'The Rise and Fall of an "Organized Fantasy": The Negotiation of Status as Periphery and Semi-Periphery by Mexico and Latin America,' in Stephen Clarkson and Marjorie Cohen, eds., *Governing under Stress: Middle Powers and the Challenge of Globalization* (New York: Zed Books 2004), 71–3.

4 David R. Mares, 'Strategic Interests in the U.S.-Mexican Relationship,' in John Bailey and Sergio Aguayo Quezada, eds., *Strategy and Security in U.S.-Mexican Relations beyond the Cold War* (San Diego: Centre for U.S.-Mexican Studies, University of California, 1996), 24.

5 Contadora information bulletin, Contadora Island, January 9, 1983. Reprinted in Bruce Michael Bagley, Roberto Alvarez, and Katherine J. Hagedorn, eds., *Contadora and the Central American Peace Process: Selected Documents* (Boulder, Colo., and London: Westview Press 1985), 165.

6 Ibid., 165–6.

7 Frank Cain, *Economic Statecraft during the Cold War: European Responses to the US Trade Embargo* (New York: Routledge 2006).

8 Pietro Nivola, 'Commercializing Foreign Policy? American Trade Policy, Then and Now,' *Brookings Review*, 15, no. 2 (1997).

9 Isidro Morales, *Post-NAFTA North America: Reshaping the Economic and Political Governance of a Changing Region* (New York: Palgrave Macmillan 2008), 2 and 9.

10 Gustavo del Castillo V, 'NAFTA and the Struggle for Neoliberalism,' in Gerardo Otero, ed., *Neoliberalism Revisited: Economic Restructuring and Mexico's Political Future* (Boulder, Colo.: Westview Press 1996), 33.

11 Charles Pearson, *United States Trade Policy: A Work in Progress* (Hoboken, N.J.: Wiley and Sons 2004), 108–9.

12 Sylvia Ostry, 'Regional Dominoes and the WTO: Building Blocks or Boomerang?' in Mordechai Kreinin, ed., *Building a Partnership: The Canada-United States Free Trade Agreement* (East Lansing: Michian State University Press 2000), 156.

13 Nicola Phillips, 'The New Politics of Trade in the Americas,' in Dominic Kelly and Wyn Grant, eds., *The Politics of International Trade in the Twenty-First Century: Actors, Issues, and Regional Dynamics* (Hampshire, U.K.: Palgrave Macmillan 2005), 192.

14 Bardly J. Condon, *NAFTA, WTO and Global Business Strategy* (Westport, Conn.: Quorum Books 2002), 14.

15 Richard E. Feinberg, 'The Political Economy of the United States' Free Trade Arrangements,' *World Economy*, 26. no. 7 (2003): 1027.

16 Stephen Clarkson interview with Luis de la Calle, Washington, D.C., March 15, 1987.

17 Marilyne Pereira Goncalves and Stephanou Constantinos, 'Financial Services and Trade Agreements in Latin America and the Caribbean: An Overview,' World Bank Policy Research Working Paper 4181, April 2007, n.p., cited in Emma Lavoie-Evans, 'Canada's Free Trade Agreements with Latin America' (Ottawa: Latin American Trade Network, North-South Institute, May 2010), 4.

18 Geza Feketekuty, 'Trade in Services,' in Kreinin, ed., *Building a Partnership*, 146–8; Ostry, 'Regional Dominoes,' 158.

19 See Peter Drakos and John Braithwaite, *Information Feudalism* (New York: New Press 2003), chapters 7–9.

20 Sylvia Ostry, *The Post-Cold War Trading System: Who's On First* (Chicago: University of Chicago Press 1997).

21 Greg Anderson to Stephen Clarkson, December 2, 2010.

22 Morales, *Post-NAFTA North America*, 5.

23 Robert A. Pastor, *The North American Idea: A Vision of a Continental Future* (New York: Oxford University Press 2011), 26.

24 Castillo, 'Nafta and the Struggle for Neoliberalism,' 33.

25 Pastor, *The North American Idea*, 26.

26 Stephen Clarkson's confidential interviews in Secretaría de Relaciones Exteriores Santiago, Chile, March 1999.

27 Sebastián Sáez, 'Implementing Trade Policy in Latin America: The Cases of Chile and Mexico,' *Comercio Internacional*, 54 (October 2005): 13.

28 Organization of American States, Foreign Trade Information System, 'Mexico: Trade Agreements,' http://www.sice.oas.org/ctyindex/MEX/MEXagreements_e.asp (accessed April 29, 2009).

29 Secretaria de Economía, Comercio Exterior, 'Ficha de Publicaciones,' http://www.economia.gob.mx (accessed June 24, 2010).

30 Stephen Clarkson interview with Hugo Perezcano, Secretaria de Economia, Mexico City, February 11, 2009.

31 Hugo Perezcano, 'International Investment Agreements: Competing for Foreign Investment in Latin America,' 5. Paper presented at Canning House, London, October 11, 2005.

32 Jeffrey J. Schott, 'Trade Negotiations among NAFTA Partners: The Future

of North American Economic Integration,' in Isabel Studer and Carol Wise, eds., *Requiem or Revival? The Promise of North American Integration* (Washington, D.C.: Brookings Institution 2007), 81.

33 Ibid., 79.

34 Jaime Zabludovsky and Sergio Gomez Lora, 'Beyond the FTAA: Perspectives for Hemispheric Integration,' in ibid., 93.

35 Carol Wise, 'Introduction,' in ibid., 9.

36 Alianza Bolivariana para los Pueblos de nuestra América/Tratado de Comercio de los Pueblos, http://www.alianzabolivariana.org (acessed September 16, 2010).

37 Interview with Professor Alejandro Alvaréz at the Department of Economics, Universidad Nacional Autónoma de México, Mexico City, March 6, 2008.

38 Rogelio Ramirez de la O, 'Prospects for North American Monetary Cooperation in the Next Decade,' in Sidney Weintraub, ed., *NAFTA's Impact on North America – The First Decade* (Washington, D.C.: Center for Strategic and International Studies 2004), 71.

39 Joseph A. Whitt, Jr, 'The Mexican Peso Crisis,' Federal Reserve Bank of Atlanta, http://www.frbatlanta.org/publica/eco-rev/REV_ABS/96ER/J_whi811.pdf, n.d., p. 2 (accessed April 7, 2008).

40 Dixia Vania Valdivia y Pablo Ramírez, 'Situación y Perspectivas del Maíz en México,' Universidad de Chapingo, March 2004, http://www.senado. gob.mx/comisiones/LX/grupo_tlcan/content/banco de datos/maiz/maiz1.pdf (accessed June 28, 2010).

41 United States Trade Representative (USTR), 'USTR Announces Agreement on Extension of Time for Costa Rica to Join the CAFTA-DR,' http://www. ustr.gov/assets/Document_Library/Press_Releases/2008/February/ asset_upload_file527_14507.pdf (accessed October 31, 2009).

42 Elisabeth Malkin, 'Central American Trade Deal Is Being Delayed by Partners,' *New York Times*, March 2, 2006, http://www.nytimes. com/2006/03/02/business/02cafta.html?ex=1298955600&en=bb00ddc3e8 7779b3&ei=5090&partner=rssuserland&emc=rss (accessed April 9, 2008).

43 Sidney Weintraub, 'Latin America Is in Good Shape,' *CSIS Issues in International Political Economy*, no. 130 (October 2010) (Washington, D.C.: Center for Strategic and International Studies).

44 Lilia González Velázquez, 'Antes de firmar más Tratados, demanda IP aprovechar actuales,' *El Economista*, February 25, 2010, http://www. eleconomista.com.mx (accessed June 22, 2010).

45 Lilia González Velázquez, 'Profundizan TLC México-EU,' *El Economista*, June 20, 2010, http://www.eleconomista.com.mx (accessed June 29, 2010).

46 'México y Colombia aumentarán comercio tras acuerdo bilateral,' *El Economista, Notimex*, January 6, 2010, http://www.eleconomista.com.mx (accessed June 29, 2010).

47 David Schneiderman to Stephen Clarkson, December 10, 2010.

48 Ulises Díaz, 'Arranca éste año revisión de tratados,' *Reforma*, June 1, 2010, http://www.reforma.com (accessed June 29, 2010).

49 Ian Wooton and Maurizio Zanardi, 'Trade and Competition Policy: Anti-Dumping versus Anti-Trust,' Department of Economics, University of Glasgow (October 2002), 11.

50 Schott, 'Trade Negotiations among NAFTA Partners,' 81.

51 Antonio Ortiz Mena L.N., 'Mexico in the Multilateral Trading System: A Long and Winding Road,' in Studer and Wise, eds., *Requiem or Revival?* 202.

52 Wooton and Zanardi, 'Trade and Competition Policy,' 6.

53 David Schneiderman, *Constitutionalizing Economic Globalization: Investment Rules and Democracy's Promise* (Cambridge: Cambridge University Press 2008), 136.

54 Luke Eric Peterson, 'Evaluating Canada's 2004 Model Foreign Investment Protection Agreement in Light of Civil Society Concerns,' *Canadian Council for International Co-operation Briefing Note* (Ottawa: June 2006), 1–10.

55 Greg Anderson to Stephen Clarkson, December 2, 2010.

56 Schneiderman, *Constitutionalizing Economic Globalization*, 73–4.

57 David Schneiderman to Stephen Clarkson, December 10, 2010.

58 Gus Van Harten, 'Private Authority and Transnational Governance: The Contours of the International System of Investor Protection,' *Review of International Political Economy*, 12, no. 4 (2005): 600–23.

59 Laura Macdonald and Ame Rucket, 'A New Role for Canada in the Hemisphere? Canada's Americas Strategy,' *LATN Nexos*, 4, no. 10 (2009): 5.

60 Pablo Heidrich, 'Contexto de la Relación comercial y de inversión entre Canadá y América Latina,' *LATN Nexos*, 4, no. 10 (2009): 3.

61 Department of Foreign Affairs and International Trade Canada (DFAIT), 'Canada – Central America Four (CA4) – Free Trade Agreement Negotiations,' http://www.international.gc.ca/trade-agreements-accords-commerciaux/agr-acc/ca4.aspx?lang=eng (accessed August 27, 2010).

62 DFAIT, 'Negotiations and Agreements,' http://www.international.gc.ca /trade-agreements-accords-commerciaux/agr-acc/index.aspx?lang=en#free (accessed June 24, 2010).

63 DFAIT, 'Canada – Central America Four (CA4) – Free Trade Agreement Negotiations.'

64 Stephen Clarkson interview with Juan Carlos Baker, Secretaría de la Economía, March 11, 2010.
65 Phillips, 'The New Politics of Trade in the Americas,' 191.
66 El Salvador – 2; Guatemala – 1; Honduras – 2; Nicaragua – 1.5; Panama – 2. See Table 2.9 in Jeffrey J. Schott's *Prospects for Free Trade in the Americas* (Washington, D.C.: Institute for International Economics 2001), 63–77.
67 El Salvador – 4.5; Guatemala – 3; Honduras – 3; Nicaragua – 2.5; Panama – 4.
68 United States, House of Representatives, US Code, 01/05/2009 Sec. 10a, American Materials Required for Public Use, http://www.uscode.house. gov/lawrevisioncounsel.shtml (accessed July 7, 2010).

8. Thwarting the United States in International Criminal Law

1 This chapter was researched and drafted by Brian Kolenda, with assistance from Artiom Komarov, Paul Jarvey, and Haidy Durán Gil. It benefited enormously from two critical reviews by Darryl Robinson (Queens University).
2 Treaty of Peace between the Allied and Associated Powers and Germany, Article 227, June 28, 1919, 225 Consol. T.S. 188, 285.
3 Leila Nadya Sadat, 'The Evolution of the ICC: From Hague to Rome and Back Again,' in Sarah B. Sewall and Carl Kaysen, eds., *The United States and the International Criminal Court: National Security and International Law* (New York: Roman and Littlefield 2000), 34; M. Cherif Bassiouni, 'Establishing an International Criminal Court: Historical Survey,' *Military Law Review*, 149 (1995): 53.
4 See Sadat, 'The Evolution of the ICC,' 35.
5 John Washburn, 'The Negotiation of the Rome Statute for the International Criminal Court and International Lawmaking in the 21st Century,' *Pace International Law Review*, 11 (1999): 361, 364.
6 See Elizabeth Riddel-Dixon, 'Canada's Human Security Agenda: Walking the Talk,' *International Journal*, 60 (2005): 1071; M. Cherif Bassiouni, 'From Versailles to Rwanda in Seventy-Five Years: The Need to Establish a Permanent International Criminal Court,' *Harvard Human Rights Journal*, 10 (1997): 11, 12–13, 59.
7 Philippe Kirsch and John T. Holmes, 'The Rome Conference on an International Criminal Court: The Negotiating Process,' *American Journal of International Law*, 93 (1999): 3.
8 Philippe Kirsch and Darryl Robinson, 'Reaching Agreement at the Rome Conference,' in Antonio Cassese, Paola Gaeta, and John R.W.D. Jones, eds., *The Rome Statute of the International Criminal Court: A Commentary* (Oxford: Oxford University Press 2002), 88.

9 Interview with Valerie Oosterveld, cited in Chris Tenove, 'Canada and the ICC. Part One: The Backstory,' Liu Institute – Reports from the Field, http://www.blogs.ubc.ca/ligi/2010/05/31/canada-and-the-icc-part-one-the-backstory/ (accessed July 29, 2010).

10 Bruce Broomhall, *International Justice and the International Criminal Court: Between Sovereignty and the Rule of Law* (Oxford: Oxford University Press, 2003), 74.

11 Darryl Robinson, 'Case Study: The International Criminal Court,' in Robert Grant McRae and Don Hubert, eds., *Human Security and the New Diplomacy: Protecting People, Promoting Peace* (Montreal and Kingston, Ont.: McGill-Queen's University Press 2001), 170, 172; William R. Pace and Jennifer Schense, 'The Role of Non-Governmental Organizations,' in Cassese, Gaeta, and Jones, eds., *The Rome Statute*, 113.

12 William Schabas, *The International Criminal Court: An Introduction*, 3rd ed. (New York: Oxford University Press 2010), 18; Dominic McGoldrick, 'Political and Legal Responses to the ICC,' in Dominic McGoldrick, Peter Rowe, and Eric Donnelly, eds., *The Permanent International Criminal Court: Legal and Policy Issues* (Oxford: Hart Publishing 2004), 389, 391

13 Kirsch and Robinson, 'Reaching Agreement,' 70–1.

14 Lloyd Axworthy, *Navigating a New World* (Toronto: Alfred A. Knopf 2003), 202.

15 See M. Cherif Bassiouni, 'Normative Framework of International Humanitarian Law: Overlaps, Gaps, and Ambiguities,' *Transnational Law and Contemporary Problems*, 8 (1998): 221–33.

16 See Kirsch and Robinson, 'Reaching Agreement,' 67, 70–1.

17 Philippe Kirsch and John T. Holmes, 'The Birth of the International Criminal Court: The 1998 Rome Conference,' *Canadian Yearbook of International Law*, 36 (1998): 3, 36.

18 Nicole Deitelhoff, 'The Discursive Process of Legalization: Charting Island of Persuasion in the ICC Case,' *International Organization*, 63 (2009): 33, 50.

19 Lloyd Axworthy, 'Address to the Diplomatic Conference of Plenipotentiaries on the Establishment of an International Criminal Court,' Rome, June 15, 1998, United Nations, http://www.un.org/icc/speeches/615can.htm (accessed August 1, 2010).

20 Ibid.; Darryl Robinson, 'The Canadian Perspective on the International Criminal Court,' *Michigan State University-DCL Journal of International Law*, 9 (1999), and 'Case Study,' 172.

21 Pace and Schense, 'The Role of Non-Governmental Organizations,' 120; Robinson, 'Case Study,' 172; Axworthy, *Navigating a New World*, 202.

22 Robinson, 'Case Study,' 172.

23 Ibid.; Axworthy, *Navigating a New World*, 202.
24 Robinson, 'Case Study,' 172.
25 Deitelhoff, 'The Discursive Process,' 57.
26 Robinson, 'Case Study,' 172.
27 Deitelhoff, 'The Discursive Process,' 58.
28 Schabas, *The International Criminal Court*, 16.
29 Kirsch and Holmes, 'The Negotiating Process,' 4; Kirsch and Holmes, 'The Birth of the International Criminal Court,' 8; Robinson, 'Case Study,' 174.
30 Kirsch and Holmes, 'Birth of the International Criminal Court,' 3–37.
31 Henry T. King and Theodore C. Theofrastous, 'From Nuremberg to Rome: A Step Backward for U.S. Foreign Policy,' *Case Western Reserve Journal of International Law*, 31 (1999): 47.
32 Ibid., 73–6; Axworthy, *Navigating a New World*, 203.
33 King and Theofrastous, 'From Nuremberg to Rome,' 73.
34 Ibid., 70–3, 76.
35 Ibid., 76.
36 Kirsch and Holmes, 'The Rome Conference,' 4.
37 David Scheffer, 'The United States and the International Criminal Court,' *American Journal of International Law*, 93 (2001): 18.
38 David Scheffer, 'U.S. Ambassador on Security Council and the Prosecutor,' *International Criminal Court Monitor*, special ed., 1996, 4, 10.
39 William Lietzau, 'International Criminal Law after Rome: Concerns from a U.S. Military Perspective,' *Law and Contemporary Problems*, 119 (2001): 120–1, 123.
40 Cited in John Bolton, 'The United States and the International Criminal Court,' address to the Federalist Society on February 14, 2004, Washington, D.C., http://www.stage.amicc.org/docs/Bolton11_14_02.pdf (accessed August 3, 2010).
41 King and Theofrastous, 'From Nuremberg to Rome,' 82, citing Helle Bering, 'The Rest of the World's Court,' *Washington Times*, July 30, 1998, A23.
42 Scheffer, 'A Negotiator's Perspective,' 8–9; Lietzau, 'International Criminal Law after Rome,' 121–2.
43 Axworthy, *Navigating a New World*, 203; Charles A. Smith and Heather M. Smith, 'Embedded Realpolitik: Reevaluating United States' Opposition to the International Criminal Court,' in Steven C. Roach, ed., *Governance, Order, and the International Criminal Court: Between Realpolitik and a Cosmopolitan Court* (Oxford: Oxford University Press 2009), 29–53.
44 Scheffer, 'U.S. Ambassador on Security Council,' 4, 10; Deitelhoff, 'The Discursive Process,' 33, 50, 59.

45 Scheffer, 'The United States and the International Criminal Court,' 12, 19.
46 Fanny Benedetti and John L. Washburn, 'Drafting the International
    Criminal Court Treaty: Two Years to Rome and an Afterword on the Rome
    Diplomatic Conference,' *Global Governance*, 5 (1999): 27–8.
47 Pace and Schense, 'The Role of Non-Governmental Organizations,' 120.
48 Schabas, *The International Criminal Court*, 18; Kirsch and Robinson, 'Reach-
    ing Agreement,' 70.
49 Confidential e-mail correspondence with an LMG delegate.
50 Robinson, 'Case Study,' 173.
51 Washburn, 'The Negotiation of the Rome Statute,' 374.
52 Robinson, 'The Canadian Perspective,' 13.
53 See Roy S. Lee et al., eds., *The International Criminal Court: The Making of
    the Rome Statute: Issues, Negotiations, Results* (The Hague: Kluwer Law
    International 1999), 92 (Canadian informal proposal on crimes against
    humanity); 207 (Canadian, American, and Argentinian co-drafting of text
    for working group on defences); 215–15 (Canadian and American compro-
    mise proposal on national law); 284–5 (Canada coordinating formalized
    informal consultations to find consensus on protection of national-security
    information); 379 (joint proposal by Canada, US, and others on qualifica-
    tions).
54 Axworthy, *Navigating a New World*, 204.
55 The description of events in this paragraph is drawn from Kirsch and Hol-
    mes, 'The Negotiating Process'; Washburn, 'The Negotiation of the Rome
    Statute'; and Lawrence Weschler, 'Exceptional Cases in Rome: The United
    States and the Struggle for an ICC,' in Sewall and Kaysen, eds., *The United
    States and the International Criminal Court*, 85–114.
56 Benedetti and Washburn, 'Drafting the International Criminal Court
    Treaty,' 29.
57 Washburn, 'The Negotiation of the Rome Statute,' 373–4; Benedetti and
    Washburn, 'Drafting the International Criminal Court Treaty,' 29.
58 Washburn, 'The Negotiation of the Rome Statute,' 361, 373 (citing inter-
    views by the author with members of the U.S. delegation, other U.S.
    officials, and other delegates).
59 Axworthy, *Navigating a New World*, 204.
60 Scheffer, 'A Negotiator's Perspective,' 89.
61 Axworthy, *Navigating a New World*, 204.
62 Washburn, 'The Negotiation of the Rome Statute,' 374.
63 Sheffer, 'The United States and the International Criminal Court,' 12, 15.
64 See generally, Robinson, 'The Canadian Perspective,' 8.
65 Kirsch and Robinson, 'Reaching Agreement,' 77.

66 Weschler, 'Exceptional Cases,' 88, 108.
67 Statement by Gonzalez Galvez, 7th Plenary Meeting, June 18, 1998, UN Doc. A/CONF.183/SR.7.
68 Statement by Gonzalez Galvez, 9th Plenary Meeting, July 17, 1998, UN Doc. A/CONF.183/SR.9.
69 This should not be confused with the pre-Rome Preparatory Committee, which we have also referred to as PrepCom.
70 This paragraph draws from Philippe Kirsch and Valerie Oosterveld, 'The Post-Rome Conference Preparatory Commission,' in Cassese, Gaeta, and Jones, eds., *The Rome Statute*, particularly 99–101.
71 See Scheffer, 'The United States and the International Criminal Court,' 19; Ruth Wedgwood, 'The Irresolution of Rome,' *Law and Contemporary Problems*, 64 (2001): 193, 199–200.
72 Scheffer, 'The Negotiator's Perspective,' 8.
73 President William J. Clinton, Statement on the Rome Treaty on the International Criminal Court, December 31, 2000, 37 (1), Weekly Compilation of Presidential Documents 4 (2001), http://www.fdsys.gpo.gov/fdsys/pkg/WCPD-2001-01-08/pdf/WCPD-2001-01-08-Pg4.pdf (accessed August 4, 2010).
74 Press Release, United States Congress, Statement of Senator Jesse Helms (December 31, 2000), cited in Wedgwood, 'The Irresolution of Rome,' 196.
75 Confirmation Hearing of General Colin L. Powell as secretary of state, Senate Foreign Relations Committee, January 17, 2001, S. HRG. 107–14, http://www.frwebgate.access.gpo.gov/cgi-bin/getdoc.cgi?dbname=107_senate_hearings&docid=f:71536.pdf (accessed August 1, 2010).
76 Remarks of John Bolton, under-secretary for arms control and international security and head of the administration's ICC team, to the Senate Foreign Relations Committee, July 23, 1998, http://www.iccnow.org/documents/Bolton%20Quotes_ICC.pdf (accessed August 4, 2010).
77 Axworthy, *Navigating a New World*, 205.
78 Department of Foreign Affairs and International Trade (DFAIT), 'Canada and the Court,' http://www.international.gc.ca/court-cour/icc-canada-cpi.aspx?lang=eng&menu_id=62&menu=R (accessed August 1, 2010).
79 See Robert Hage, 'Implementing the Rome Statute: Canada's Experience,' in Roy S. Lee, ed., *States' Responses to Issues Arising from the ICC Statute: Constitutional, Sovereignty, Judicial Cooperation and Criminal law* (Ardsley, N.Y.: Transnational Publishers 2008), 47.
80 DFAIT, 'Implementing the Rome Statute,' http://www.international.gc.ca/court-cour/statute-rome-statut.aspx?lang=eng&menu_id=71&menu=R (accessed August 1, 2010).
81 DFAIT, 'Canada's Support for International Accountability and Rule of

Law,' http://www.international.gc.ca./court-cour/accountability-imputa-bilite.aspx (accessed August 1, 2010).

82 Elisa Gutiérrez, 'México ante la Corte Penal Internacional,' *Revista de la Facultad de Derecho y Ciencias Políticas*, Universidad Pontificia Bolivariana, Medellín, Colombia, ISSN 0120–3886, no. 104, 2006, 16, http://www.upb.edu.co/pls/portal/docs/PAGE/GP_NOTICIAS/PG_NOTI_ARCHIVOS/mexico.pdf (accessed April 13, 2010).

83 See Socorro Flores Liera, 'Ratification of the Statute of the International Criminal Court by Mexico,' in Lee, ed., *States' Responses*, 275.

84 Press release, Secretaria de Relaciones Exteriores, 'México y la Corte Penal Internacional,' http:/www.participaciosocial.sre.gob.mx/docs/ligas_de_interes/publicaciones/cpi/boletin03_cpiosc.pdf (accessed April 13, 2010).

85 Mauricio Ibarra, ed., 'Memoria del Foro Internacional: La Soberanía de los Estados y La Corte Penal Internacional,' Comisión Nacional de los Derechos Humanos, Mexico City, 2002, 75.

86 Kai Ambos et al., eds., *Temas actuales del derecho Penal Internacional: Contribuciones de América Latina, Alemania y España*, (Montevideo, Uruguay: Konrad-Adenauer-Stiftung 2005), 48.

87 Constitución Política de los Estados Unidos Mexicanos,' *Última Reforma*, April 27, 2010, http://www.cddhcu.gob.mx/LeyesBiblio/pdf/1.pdf (accessed May 14, 2010). Our translation.

88 Remarks of Marc Grossman, under-secretary for political affairs, United States, Department of State, to the Center for Strategic and International Studies, May 6, 2002, http://www.2001-2009.state.gov/p/us/rm/9949.htm (accessed August 1, 2010).

89 Aly Mokhtar, 'The Fine Art of Arm-Twisting: The US, Resolution 1422 and Security Council Deferral Power under the Rome Statue,' *International Criminal Law Review*, 3 (2003): 295.

90 Ibid.

91 Eric M. Meyer, 'International Law: The Compatibility of the Rome Statute of the International Criminal Court with the U.S. Bilateral Immunity Agreements Included in the American Servicemembers' Protection Act,' *Oklahoma Law Review*, 58 (2005): 97.

92 'Proposed Text of Article 98 Agreements with the United States,' July 2002, http://www.amicc.org/docs/98template.pdf (accessed August 4, 2010).

93 Statement by Gerard Van Bohemen, New Zealand Ministry of Foreign Affairs and Trade, to the United Nations General Assembly, 62nd Plenary Session, *Report of the International Criminal Court*, November 8, 2007, http://www.iccnow.org/documents/New_Zealand_(CANZ).pdf (accessed December 1, 2008).

94 Coalition for the International Criminal Court (CICC), 'Countries Opposed to Signing a US Bilateral Immunity Agreement: US Aid Lost in FY04 &FY05 and Threatened in FY06,' http://www.iccnow.org/documents/CountriesOpposedBIA_final_11Dec06_final.pdf (accessed August 1, 2010).

95 Human Rights Watch, *Bilateral Immunity Agreements* (New York: HRW, June 20, 2003, http://www.hrw.org/campaigns/icc/docs/bilateralagreements.pdf (accessed August 4, 2010).

96 Quotation from a speech by Jorge Eduardo Navarrete to Transparency International in January 2003, Human Rights Watch, *Bilateral Immunity Agreements* (New York: HRW, June 20, 2003), http://www.hrw.org/campaigns/icc/docs/bilateralagreements.pdf (accessed August 4, 2010).

97 Golzar Kheiltash, 'From Mexico to Yemen: Counterintuitive US BIA Policy Expands,' Citizens for Global Solutions, http://www.globalsolutions.org/programs/law_justice/icc/bias/BIA_Commentary.pdf (accessed August 4, 2010). We found it impossible to confirm this figure. The $13.4 million in Economic Support Funds that Mexico received in 2005 fell to $9 million in 2006, a loss of just $4.5 million.

98 CICC, 'Status of US Bilateral Immunity Agreements (BIAs),' http://www.iccnow.org/documents/CICCFS_BIAstatus_current.pdf (accessed August 1, 2010).

99 Cited in Citizens for Global Solutions, 'Unintended Consequences of the US Bilateral Immunity Agreement Policy,' 2008, http://www.globalsolutions.org/issues/analysis_unintended_consequences_u_s_bilateral_immunity_ agreement_policy (accessed August 4, 2010).

100 Ibid.

101 Roger Pardo-Maurer, deputy assistant secretary of defense for Western hemisphere affairs, quoted in Jackson Diehl, 'A Losing Latin Policy: Are We about to Punish Democratic Allies?' *Washington Post*, March 10, 2006, http://www.washingtonpost.com/wp-dyn/content/article/2006/03/09/AR2006030902194.html (accessed August 4, 2010).

102 CICC, 'Status of US Bilateral Immunity Agreements.'

103 President George W. Bush, 'Memorandum for the Secretary of State,' October 2, 2006, http://www.amicc.org/docs/Bush%20ASPA%20Memo%202%20October%202006.pdf (accessed August 4, 2010); President George W. Bush, 'Memorandum for the Secretary of State,' November 2, 2006, http://www.amicc.org/docs/White%20House%20Memo%2022%20November%202006.pdf (accessed August 4, 2010); President George W. Bush, 'Memorandum for the Secretary of State,' January 2, 2009, http://www.amicc.org/docs/White%20House%20Memo%2016%20January%202009.pdf (accessed August 4, 2010).

104 Lee Feinstein and Tod Lindberg, *United States Interest in the International Criminal Court* (Washington: Brookings Institution 2009), 53.
105 Ibid., 58–9, 95.
106 For a description of these efforts, see Benjamin N. Schiff, *Building the International Criminal Court* (New York: Cambridge University Press 2008), 227–33.
107 Ibid., 229.
108 UN Secretary-General, 'Report of the International Commission of Inquiry on Darfur to the United Nations,' January 25, 2010, http://www.un.org/News/dh/sudan/com_inq_darfur.pdf (accessed August 3, 2010).
109 Schiff, *Building the International Criminal Court*, 230.
110 Ibid.
111 Weschler, 'Exceptional Cases,' 95.
112 See 'Grant U.S. Aid Listed by Country, Just the Facts,' http://www.justf.org/All_Grants_Country (accessed August 6, 2010).

9. Offsetting the US Embargo of Revolutionary Cuba

1 This chapter was researched by Ariana Lopes Morey with the help of Haidy Durán Gil. It has profited from the expert commentaries of ex-ambassadors Lorenzo Vignal (Mexico) and John Graham (Canada), Ana Covarrubias (Colegio de México), and Carlo Dade (FOCAL, Ottawa).
2 Translation by Foreign Broadcast Information Service. Presented in Latin American Network Information Centre, 'Castro Speech Database.' Castro and Echeverria transcript is available at http://www.lanic.utexas.edu/project/castro/db/1987/19870822.html (accessed June 12, 2011).
3 Brian Bow, *Canadian-American Public Policy: "When in Rome": Comparing Canadian and Mexican Strategies for Influencing Policy Outcomes in the United States* (Orono, Maine: Canadian-American Center 2006), 12–13.
4 Mexico, Political Constitution of the United Mexican States, Article 89, X, in *Mexican Constitution as of 2002*, trans. Ron Pamachena, Historical Text Archive, http://www.historicaltextarchive.com/sections.php?op=viewarticle&artid=93#T3C3 (accessed January 15, 2011).
5 For an exploration of the domestic factors that shaped Mexico's Cuba policy, see Olga Pellicer de Brody, *México y la revolución cubana* (Mexico City: Centro de Estudios Internacionales, El Colegio de México, 1972); and Arthur K. Smith, Jr, 'Mexico and the Cuban Revolution: Foreign Policy-Making in Mexico under President Adolfo Lopez Mateos (1958–1964)' (PhD thesis, Cornell University, 1970).

6 Ana Covarrubias Velasco, 'La política mexicana hacía Cuba a principios de siglo: de la no intervención a la protección de los derechos humanos,' *Revista Foro Internacional*, 43, no. 3 (2003): 628.

7 Mario Ojeda, *Alcances y límites de la política exterior de México* (Mexico City: El Colegio de México 2006), 60.

8 Smith, Jr, 'Mexico and the Cuban Revolution,' 71–2.

9 Manuel Tello, *México: una posición internacional* (Mexico City: Joaquín Mortiz 1972), 147.

10 Ibid., 70.

11 See quote by Emilio Sánchez Piedras, president of the Permanent Committee of Congress, in Smith, Jr, 'Mexico and the Cuban Revolution,' 71.

12 Pellicer de Brody, *México y la revolución cubana*, 33–4.

13 Smith, Jr, 'Mexico and the Cuban Revolution,' 95.

14 Inter-American Conference for the Maintenance of Continental Peace and Security, Inter-American Treaty of Reciprocal Assistance (Rio Treaty), Article 6, http://www.state. gov/p/wha/rls/70681.htm (accessed January 15, 2011).

15 Smith, Jr, *Mexico and the Cuban Revolution*, 149.

16 Pellicer de Brody, *México y la revolución cubana*, 29.

17 Soft-liner countries included Brazil, Argentina, Chile, Bolivia, and Ecuador. See Smith, Jr, 'Mexico and the Cuban Revolution.'

18 Gordon Connell-Smith, *The Inter-American System* (London: Oxford University Press 1966), 177.

19 Smith, Jr, 'Mexico and the Cuban Revolution.'

20 Pellicer de Brody, *México y la revolución cubana*, 44–5.

21 Ibid., 45

22 Ojeda, *Alcances y límites*, 69–71.

23 Connell-Smith, *The Inter-American System*, 177.

24 Yoram Shapira, 'La política exterior de México bajo el régimen de Echeverría: retrospectiva,' *Revista Foro Internacional*, 19, no. 1 (1978): 74.

25 'Joint Communiqué following the State Visit to Peru, July 17, 1974,' Manuel Tello, *La política exterior de México (1970–1974)* (Mexico City: Fondo de Cultura Económica 1975), 233.

26 Kate Doyle, 'The Nixon Tapes: Secret Recordings from the Nixon White House on Luis Echeverría and Much Much More,' August 18, 2003, *The National Security Archive* (Washington, D.C.: George Washington University, 18 August 2003), http://www.gwu.edu/~nsarchiv/NSAEBB/ NSAEBB95/ (accessed April 27, 2008).

27 Interview with Lorenzo Vignal, February 5, 2010, Mexico City, and confirmed by former Canadian ambassador John Graham, November 23, 2010.

28 Kate Doyle, 'Double Dealing: Mexico's Foreign Policy toward Cuba,' *National Security Archive* (Washington, D.C.: George Washington University, March 3, 2008), http://www.gwu.edu/~nsarchiv /NSAEBB/ NSAEBB83/index.htm (accessed January 15, 2011).

29 Doyle, 'The Nixon Tapes.'

30 Atlantic Council of the United States, *International Perspectives on U.S.-Cuban Relations* (Washington: August 1998), 3.

31 Ibid., 24.

32 Velasco, 'La política mexicana,' 630.

33 Ley de Protección al Comercio y la Inversión de Normas Extranjeras que Contravengan el Derecho Internacional, http://www.diputados.gob.mx/ LeyesBiblio/pdf/63.pdf (accessed April 25, 2009).

34 Peter Kornbluh and William LeoGrande, 'La Habana-Washington: México, mediador oficioso,' *Proceso*, 11 (2009): 46–49.

35 Interview with Phillip Brenner, American University, Washington D.C., April 21, 2009.

36 Kornbluh and LeoGrande, 'La Habana-Washington,' 47.

37 Speech in Managua, Nicaragua, February 21, 1982. Transcribed in Bruce Michael Bagley, Roberto Alvarez, and Katherine J. Hagedorn, eds., *Contadora and the Central American Peace Process: Selected Documents* (Boulder, Colo., and London: Westview Press 1985), 101

38 Hal Klepak, 'From Reasonable Steadiness to "from Crisis to Crisis": Mexico-Cuba Relations in the Post-Cold War Era,' in Michele Zebich-Knos and Heather Nicol, eds., *Foreign Policy toward Cuba: Isolation or Engagement?* (New York: Lexington Books 2005), 93.

39 FSLN, www.fsln-nicaragua.com (accessed June 9, 2010).

40 Interview with Lorenzo Vignal, February 5, 2010, Mexico City.

41 Carlos Salinas de Gortari, *Mexico: The Politics and Policy of Modernization* (Barcelona: Plaza and Janés Editores 2002), 241–56. See also Kornbluh and LeoGrande, 'La Habana-Washington,' 48–9.

42 Canada's constructive engagement came to an end in 2009, when Prime Minister Stephen Harper's remarks at the Port of Spain summit were construed by Havana as anti-Cuban.

43 John M. Kirk, 'Back in Business: Canada-Cuba Relations after 50 Years' (Ottawa: FOCAL, Canadian Foundation for the Americas, 1995), 9.

44 John M. Kirk and Peter McKenna, *Canada-Cuba Relations: The Other Good Neighbor Policy* (Gainesville: University Press of Florida 1997), 40.

45 Ibid.

46 Lana Wylie, 'Isolate or Engage? Divergent Approaches to Foreign Policy toward Cuba,' in Zebich-Knos and Nicol, eds.; *Foreign Policy toward Cuba*, 16.

47 Sahadeo Basdeo, 'Helms-Burton Controversy: An Issue in Canada-US Foreign Relations,' in *Canada, the US and Cuba: Helms-Burton and Its Aftermath* (Kingston, Ont.: Centre for International Relations, Queen's University, 1999), 10. See also Kirk and McKenna, *Canada-Cuba Relations*, 63.

48 Letter to the authors from former Canadian ambassador John Graham, November 23, 2010.

49 Kirk, 'Back in Business,' 10.

50 Ibid., 24.

51 Archibald R.M. Ritter, 'Canadian-Cuban Economic Relations: Past, Present, and Prospective,' in Robert Wright and Lana Wylie, eds., *Our Place in the Sun: Canada and Cuba in the Castro Era* (Toronto: University of Toronto Press 2009), 250.

52 Kirk and McKenna, *Canada-Cuba Relations*, 89–90.

53 Basdeo, 'Helms-Burton Controversy,' 5.

54 United Nations, Economic Commission for Latin America and the Caribbean (ECLAC), 'Canada's Trade and Investment with Latin America and the Caribbean,' January 29, 2003 (Washington, D.C.: UN 2003), 2, http://www.eclac.cl/publicaciones/xml/0/11960/lclwasl61.pdf (accessed February 24, 2009).

55 Atlantic Council, *International Perspectives*, 3.

56 U.S.-Cuba Trade and Economic Council, *Foreign Investment and Cuba*, March 20, 1999, http://www.cubatrade.org/foreign.html (accessed February 22, 2009).

57 Ritter, 'Canadian-Cuban Economic Relations,' 251.

58 Ibid., 256.

59 Kirk and McKenna, *Canada-Cuba Relations*, 45

60 See interview with John Noaln, Jr, who participated in arranging the exchange for the Kennedy administration, in 'Legends in the Law: A Conversation with John E. Nolan Jr.,' District of Columbia Bar, 2009, http://www.dcbar.org/for_lawyers/resources/legends_in_the_law/nolan.cfm (accessed April 30, 2009); and Kirk and McKenna, *Canada-Cuba Relations*, 47.

61 Kirk and McKenna, *Canada-Cuba Relations*, 53–4.

62 Robert Wright, *Three Nights in Havana* (Toronto: Harper Collins 2007).

63 Sahadeo Basdeo and Ian Hesketh, 'Canada, Cuba, and Constructive Engagement: Political Dissidents and Human Rights,' in Sahadeo Basdeo and Heather N. Nicol, eds., *Canada, the United States, and Cuba: An Evolving Relationship* (Boulder, Colo.: North-South Center Press 2002), 29.

64 Peter McKenna and John M. Kirk, 'Canada-Cuba Relations: Old Wine in New Bottles?' in Zebich-Knos and Nicol, eds., *Foreign Policy toward Cuba*, 70.

65 Wylie, 'Isolate or Engage?' 10.
66 Basdeo and Hesketh, 'Canada, Cuba, and Constructive Engagement,' 29.
67 Peter McKenna and John M. Kirk, '"Sleeping with an Elephant": The Impact of the United States on Canada-Cuba Relations,' in Morris Morley and Chris McGillion, eds., *Cuba, the United States, and the Post-Cold War World* (Gainesville: University Press of Florida 2005), 161.
68 Ibid.
69 Ibid., 162.
70 Ibid., 167.
71 Interview with Phillip Brenner, American University (Washington, D.C.), April 21, 2009.
72 Patrick Jude Haney and Walt Vanderbush, *The Cuban Embargo* (Pittsburgh: University of Pittsburgh Press 2005), 114.
73 Basdeo and Hesketh, 'Canada, Cuba, and Constructive Engagement,' 32.
74 Quote from Jeff Sallot, 'Ottawa Condemns Bill on Libya, Iran,' *Globe and Mail*, July 25, 1996, A9, as cited in McKenna and Kirk, '"Sleeping with an Elephant,"' 163.
75 McKenna and Kirk, '"Sleeping with an Elephant,"' 164.
76 Basdeo and Hesketh, 'Canada, Cuba, and Constructive Engagement,' 32.
77 Ibid., 32–3.
78 Ibid., 33.
79 Interview with Lorenzo Vignal, 5 February 2009, Mexico City.
80 President Nixon in conversation with President Echeverría in June 1972. Transcribed in Doyle, 'The Nixon Tapes.'
81 de Gortari, *Mexico: the Politics and Policy of Modernization*, 102.
82 Kirk and McKenna, *Canada-Cuba Relations*, 51.
83 Ibid., 49.
84 Declarations made before the Subcommittee on Latin American Affairs of the Committee of Foreign Affairs of the House of Representatives, February 13, 1963. Quoted in Ojeda, *Alcances y límites*, 49.
85 Telephone interview with Cresencio Arcos, ex-US ambassador to Honduras, Washington, D.C., March 12, 2008.
86 McKenna and Kirk, '"Sleeping with an Elephant,"' 154. See also Radio Havana Cuba, April 28, 1998, http://www.radiohc.org/Distributions/Radio_Havana_English/.1998/98_apr/rhc-eng-04.28.98 (accessed April 24, 2009).
87 Jan Knippers Black, 'The United States-Cuba Standoff: A Double Con?' in Zebich-Knos and Nicol, eds., *Foreign Policy toward Cuba*, 63.
88 Ibid., 61.
89 Paul Lewis, 'Cuba Is Elected to the U.N. Security Council,' *New York Times*,

October 19, 1989, http://www.nytimes.com/1989/10/19/world/cuba-is-elected-to-the-un-security-council.html (accessed April 25, 2009).

90 'Profile: Non-Aligned Movement,' BBC News, January 7, 2009, http://www.news.bbc.co.uk/2/hi/2798187.stm (accessed April 25, 2009).

91 Duncan Campbell, '638 Ways to Kill Castro,' *The Guardian*, August 3, 2006, http://www.guardian.co.uk/world/2006/aug/03/cuba.duncancampbell2 (accessed April 23, 2009).

Conclusion to the Book

1 Robert O. Keohane and Joseph S. Nye, Jr, *Power and Interdependence* 4th ed. (New York: Longman 2011).

Epilogue to the Trilogy

1 Brian Bow, *The Politics of Linkage: Power, Interdependence, and Ideas in Canada-US Relations* (Toronto: University of Toronto Press 2010), 4–6.

2 Earl H. Fry, *Lament for America: Decline of a Superpower, Plan for Renewal* (Toronto: University of Toronto Press 2010).

3 Ted Magder, 'Franchising the Candy Store: Split-Run Magazines and a New International Regime for Trade in Culture,' *Canadian-American Public Policy*, 34 (April 1998).

4 Blayne Haggart, 'North American Digital Copyright, Regional Governance and Potential for Variation' (PhD thesis, Carleton University, 2011).

5 Bow, *The Politics of Linkage*, 2–3.

6 Monica Gattinger and Geoffrey Hale, 'Borders and Bridges: Canada's Policy Relations in North America,' in Gattinger and Hale, eds., *Borders and Bridges: Canada's Policy Relations in North America* (Toronto: Oxford University Press 2010), 11.

7 Within the vast, Europe-centred literature on regionalism, two contributions stand out. First, Andrew Howell – 'Explaining the Resurgence of Regionalism in World Politics,' *Review of International Studies*, 21 (1995): 331–58 – presented the optimistic view that globalization was taking place through the establishment of regions. Ten years later, Björn Hettne – 'Beyond the "New" Regionalism,' *New Political Economy*, 10, no. 4 (2005): 543–71 – reviewed the criteria for defining the still-proliferating phenomenon.

8 Colin Robertson, 'Now for the Hard Part: Renewing the Canadian-American Partnership,' Strategic Studies Working Group Paper (Toronto: Canadian International Council, 2001); Daniel Schwanen, 'Beyond the

Border and Back to the Future: Seizing the Opportunity to Enhance Canadian and US Economic Growth and Security' (Toronto: C.D. Howe Institute, forthcoming).

9 Christopher Sands, 'The Canada Gambit: Will It Revive North America?' (Washington, D.C.: Hudson Institute 2011).

10 Communication from Stephen Blank to the authors, June 28, 2011.

11 Geoffrey E. Hale, '"In the Pipeline" or "Over a Barrel"? Assessing Canadian Efforts to Manage US Canadian Energy Interdependence,' *Canadian-American Public Policy*, 76 (February 2011): 25.

12 Peter Katzenstein, *A World of Regions: Asia and Europe in the American Imperium* (New York: Cornell University Press 2005), 25–6.

13 Robert A. Pastor, *The North American Idea: A Vision of a Continental Future* (New York: Oxford University Press 2011), 97.

Acknowledgments

This book is the product of much more brainpower than came from our own two heads. From its genesis through its gestation and on to its maturation and production, the project would have been impossible without the collegial support from younger and older researchers not just in the three countries of North America but overseas as well.

Genesis and Gestation

The genesis of *Dependent America?* stretches back over fifteen years to the many hands and long labours that produced its two predecessor volumes whose specific debts are acknowledged on pages 497–502 of *Uncle Sam and Us* and pages 557–63 of *Does North America Exist?*

The actual idea of reversing the direction of causality in most North American research and assessing the impact of Canada and Mexico on the United States occurred to Stephen Clarkson in 2005 while working with his students on the latter book's continental governance problematic, but it was not until the 2006–7 academic year that he actively recruited half a dozen top undergraduates – including Matto Mildenberger – to start helping him clear away the brush. By the fall of 2007, Clarkson and Mildenberger had developed a partial draft for consideration that year in a graduate seminar. For 2008–9 a second, expanded draft was available for another stimulating academic workshop, the result of which was a number of draft chapters that we could then start pulling up to a professional level.

So our first debt of thanks goes to these BA and MA students who worked on a wide range of issues, sometimes casting light, occasionally spreading darkness, but always provoking our own thinking and helping the analysis evolve. Most directly involved were: on the economy (chapter 1), Derek Carnegie, Nadiya Sultan, and Ian Swain; on energy (2), Héloïse Apestéguy-Reux, Anu Carena Harder, and Sarah Yun; on labour (3), Charles Belanger; on the military (4), Gabriel De Roche, Erin Fitzgerald, Tim Klodt, and Sara Mojtehedzadeh; on border security (5), Gabriel De Roche, Mike Lawrence, Jim Mylonas, and Sarah Ryman; on narcotics (6), Mike Lawrence, Gilleen Witkowski, Gabriel De Roche, and Harry Skinner; on trade and investment agreements (7), Denitza Koev and Robert Whillans; and on the International Criminal Court (8), Paul Jarvey and Artiom Komarov. Much more research goes into a book that seems to come out the other end. Even if their work could not be used, we are grateful for the stimulus we received from Mike Lawrence on theoretical issues; from Daniel Yoo and the hip-hop artist Professor D on North American cultural power; from Anila Akram on our study's normative implications; from May Jeong and Jonathan Sas on the Montreal and the Kyoto environmental protocols; and from Stephen Brown-Okruhlik on international financial relations. Special thanks to Brian Kolenda for bringing his expertise as a young international lawyer to rescue our chapter on the ICC and to Ariana Lopes-Morey for her mastery of the Cuba dossier (9).

We organized conferences for some of these students with their counterparts in Waterloo at the Centre for International Governance Innovation in 2008 and 2009 when we profited from comments by professors from the University of Waterloo and Wilfrid Laurier University including Alistair Edgar, Patricia Goff, Eric Helleiner, Ian Rowlands, Daniel Schwanen, and Debora Van Nijnatten.

Maturation

Trinational research cannot be executed only from one's home base. As Canadians, we needed access to academic colleagues, government officials, think-tank analysts, and informed citizens in the United States and Mexico. Financing to take Clarkson's undergraduate students to the two capitals for a week's work to finish their research came from the deans of the Faculty of Arts and Science at the University of Toronto, Sinervo Pekka and Meric Gertler, through their Student Experience Fund – to Washington in 2007, 2008, and 2009 and to Mexico City in 2008.

United States

We and our students profited immeasurably from interviewing individual experts at a number of Washington's institutions, specifically at the Woodrow Wilson Center for International Scholars: its inimitable director, Lee Hamilton; the very helpful directors of its Canada (David Biette) and Mexico (Andrew Selee) institutes; plus Geoffrey Dabelko, Robert Donnelly, Kent Hughes, Kathryn Lavelle, and Robert Litwak; at the Canadian Embassy: Ambassador Michael Wilson, Kevin Adams, Kelly Anderson, Alec Attfield, Allen R. Brown, Paul Connors, Susan Harper, Colonel D. Craig Hilton, Bruce Levy, Lynn McDonald, Kevin O'Shea, Tristan Sangret, Carolyn Strauss, Kathleen Tolan, Jason Tolleand, and Brenda Willis; at American University: Philip Brenner, Ernesto Céspedes, Daniel Hernández, David Hunter, William LeoGrande, James T. McHugh, Robert Pastor, Anthony Quainton, Arnold Trebach, and Paul Wapner; at the Brookings Institution: Pietro S. Nivola; at the Canadian-American Business Council: Scotty Greenwood; at the CATO Institute: Ted Galen Carpenter and Daniel Griswold; at the Center for International Policy: Adam Isacson; at the Center for Strategic and International Studies: Edward Chow, Robert Ebel, George Fauriol, Sarah O. Ladislaw, General Dwight Mason, Armand Peschard-Sverdrup, David L. Pumphrey, General Victor Renuart, Christopher Sands, and Sidney Weintraub; at the Congressional Research Service: Carl Ek, Steve Clarke, Colleen Cook, Ian Ferguson, Rebecca Rush, Angeles Villereal, and Liana Sun Wyler; at the Council on Foreign Relations: Edward Alden; at the Drug Policy Alliance: Bill Piper; at the Economic Policy Institute: Robert E. Scott; at the Energy Policy Research Foundation: Lucan Pugliaresi; at Georgetown University: John Bailey, Marc Busch, Bruce Everett, and Barbara Kotschwar; at George Washington University: Henry R. Nau and Graciela Kaminksy; at Green Strategies: Roger Ballentine; at the *Globe and Mail*'s Washington Bureau: John Ibbitson; at the Hudson Institute: Christopher Sands; at the Institute for Policy Studies: Sanho Tree; at Inter-American Dialogue: Michael Shifter; at the International Monetary Fund: Jonathan Fried; at Law Enforcement against Prohibition: Howard J. Wooldrige; at the Migration Policy Institute: Susan Ginsburg, Deborah Myers, and Marc Rosenblum; at the Motion Picture Association of America: Michael O'Leary; at the National Commission on Energy Policy: Nathaniel Gorence; at National Defence University: John Cope and David King; at the Office of the

US Trade Representative: Everett Eissenstat; at the Petersen Institute for International Economics: Jeffrey Schott and Gary Clyde Hufbauer; at the Pew Center on Global Climate Change: Eileen Klaussen; at the Pew Hispanic Center: Rakesh Kochhar; at the Johns Hopkins School for Advanced International Studies: Scott Barrett, Charles Doran, and Tamara Woroby; at the University of Maryland, College Park: Peter Morici; at the US Department of Agriculture: Steven Zahniser; at the US Department of Defense: Bill Ellis, James McFadden, and Colonel Don Olds; at the US Department of Energy: Rhiannon Davis, Andrea Lockwood, and Gary Ward; at the US Department of State: Robert Allison; at the US Federal Energy Regulatory Commission: Jeffrey Wright; at the World Bank: Jeff Chelsky; at the World Resources Institute: Hillary McMahon; plus the sui generis independent energy-policy expert, Joseph Duckert.

Mexico

It is impossible to see Mexico from Toronto. A standard research grant from the Social Sciences and Humanities Research Council of Canada made extensive stays in Mexico during the winters of 2008, 2009, and 2010 possible for consulting with experts, presenting lectures for discussion, and participating in conferences.

In Mexico City the following made themselves available for consultations or discussions: at the Centro de Investigación y Docencia Económicas: Jorge Chabat, Jorge Schiavon, and Rafael Velázquez Flores; at the Colegio de Defensa Nacional: General Juan Alfredo Oropeza Garnica; at the Colegio de Mexico: Ana Covarrubias Velasco and Guillermo Palacios y Olivares; at the Instituto Tecnológico Autónomo de México: Athanasios Hristoulas; at the Secretaría de Economía: Juan Carlos Baker Pineda, Beatriz Leycegui, Hugo Perezcano, and Roberto Zapata Barradas; at the Secretaría de Energía: Leonardo Beltrán; at the Secretaría de Relaciones Exteriores: Rodrigo Bustamante Riva Palacio, Hilda Dávila Chávez, Roberto Dondisch Glowinski, Alejandro Estivill Castro, Alberto Fierro Garza, Rodolfo Godínez Rosales, Gerónimo Guttierez Fernandez, Jesús Gutiérrez Castro, Reyna Martínez López, David Renato Nájera Rivas, the late and much lamented Carlos Rico, Enrique Rojo Stein, Eduardo Sosa Cuevas, and Reyna Torres Mendivil; at the Senate: Eloy Cantú Segovia, senator for the state of Nuevo León; at the Universidad Iberoamericana: Imtiaz Hussain; and at the Universidad Nacional Autónoma de México (UNAM): Alejandro Álvarez

Bejar, Ana Maria Aragones, Raúl Benitez Menaud, Maria Teresa Guttiérez Haces, and Nora Lina Montes. Other Mexicans who contributed their knowledge and expertise are Leticia Calderón Chelius, Eduardo Nivon Bola, Luz Maria de la Mora, Guillermo Velasco, and former ambassador Lorenzo Vignal.

Although Mexico's US embassy is located on Washington's Pennsylvania Avenue, it was Mexican territory for us. Thanks to the initiative of Carlos Pujalte, Mexico's consul general in Toronto, briefing visits were scheduled at the embassy where we and our students profited from the insights of Ernesto Cespedes, Carlos Felix Corona, Fernando González Saiffe, Mauricio Ibarra, Antonio Ortiz Mena, Manuel Suarez-Mier, Julián Ventura, and others.

Stephen Clarkson also profited from comments received when presenting papers, giving lectures, or holding seminars on this research at the Centro de Relaciones Internacionales, Universidad Autónoma de Querétaro, February 7, 2008; the University of Havana: Canadian Studies University Network of Cuba's Conference on Canada's Approach to Latin America, February 19, 2008; the Centro de Estudios Demográficos, Urbanos y Ambientales (CEDUA), Seminario Interdisciplinario sobre Estudios Ambientales y del Desarrollo Sustentable, Colegio de México, February 25, 2008; the Departamento de Relaciones Internacionales, Facultad de Ciencias Políticas (UNAM), February 27, 2008; the Instituto para Investigaciones Económicas (UNAM) workshop on energy insecurity in North America, February 12, 2009; the Colegio de México, February 20, 2009; the Instituto Tecnológico de Monterrey (Santa Fe), February 23, 2009; the Centro para Investigaciones sobre América del Norte (UNAM), February 24, 2009; and the Departamento de Ciencias Políticas, Colegio de la Frontera Norte, Tijuana, March 13, 2008.

Book launches in Mexico for *Does North America Exist?* generated commentaries at the Instituto Tecnológico de Monterrey (Ciudad de México) by Teresina Gutiérrez Haces, Carlos Rico, Andrés Rozental, and Isabel Studer, February 23, 2009, and at the Instituto para Investigaciones Económicas (UNAM) by Alejandro Álvarez Bejar, Sarahí Ángeles, Raúl Benítez Menaud, María Esther Ceceña, and Teresina Gutiérrez Haces, February 27, 2009.

Canada

Similar opportunities for getting feedback to our developing analysis were made available in Canada at McGill University, March 5, 2009; Ryerson University, October 1, 2009; the Intergovernmental Community of Practice, Government of Ontario, November 24, 2009; the Faculty of Law, University of New Brunswick, March 18, 2010; the Canada-United States Law Institute, University of Western Ontario: Distinguished Lecture, November 22, 2010; the Department of Political Studies, Queen's University, November 24, 2010; and the Université de Montréal, November 25, 2010. It is another learning experience to engage interested citizens in one's findings, and opportunities for these kinds of exchange were most productive in chapters of the Canadian International Council in Vancouver, the Lakehead, Waterloo, Toronto, and Montreal.

Political economy is an inherently interdisciplinary undertaking, so it was a joy for Clarkson to have the opportunity, thanks initially to a virtual professorship granted by the late and much lamented Law Commission of Canada, to enter into a long partnership with the environmental law scholar Stepan Wood, which resulted in our publishing in 2010 *A Perilous Imbalance: The Globalization of Canadian Law and Governance* with UBC Press. Not only did this collaboration consolidate the legal-theory substance behind Clarkson's notion of supra- and external constitutions, it broadened his understanding when he had the opportunity with Stepan Wood to present the book's findings to other legal scholars at: the Environmental Law Group and the IUCN Academy of Environmental Law, Faculty of Law, University of Ottawa, March 24, 2010; the Department of Justice, Government of Canada, Ottawa, March 24, 2010; Innis College, University of Toronto, March 25, 2010; the Political Science Department, University of Waterloo, March 29, 2010; the Centre for International Governance Innovation, Waterloo, March 29, 2010; Osgoode Hall Law School, York University, April 7, 2010; le Centre de Recherche en Droit Public, Faculté de Droit, Université de Montréal, March 30, 2010; and the Munk Centre, University of Toronto, October 20, 2010.

North America

Participating with colleagues as they generate their own books on North America has been a continuing stimulation for our thinking. Clarkson is particularly grateful in this regard to the invitations received by the following colleagues to contribute papers and join in conferences that ultimately generated their own publications: Ricardo Grinspun and Yasmine Shamsie, eds., *Whose Canada? Continental Integration, Fortress North America, and the Corporate Agenda* (McGill-Queen's, 2007); Jean Daudelin and Daniel Schwanen, eds., *Canada among Nations 2007* (McGill-Queen's, 2008); Louis Pauly and William Coleman, eds., *Global Ordering: Institutions and Autonomy in a Changing World* (UBC Press, 2008); Daniel Drache, ed., *Big Picture Realities: Canada and Mexico at the Crossroads* (Wilfrid Laurier University Press, 2008); Burkhard Eberlein and Bruce Doern, eds., *Governing the Energy Challenge* (University of Toronto Press, 2009); Jon Fossum, 'Transnational Governance, Deliberative Supranationalism, and Constitutionalism,' for the RECON WP 9 Conference on Global Transnationalisation and Democratisation Compared, European University Institute, May 16–17, 2008; Maria Teresa Gutiérrez Haces, 'North American Linkages: NAFTA's Legacy,' Instituto para Investigaciones Económicas (UNAM), March 5, 2008; Isidro Morales, 'National Solutions to Transborder Problems? The Challenges for Building Cross-Border Governance Practices in Post-NAFTA North America,' Escuela de Graduados en Administración Pública y Política Pública, Instituto Tecnológico de Monterrey (Monterrey), March 11, 2008; Isabel Studer: to celebrate the publication of the *Revista Mexicana de Política Exterior*'s special number on North America, Instituto Tecnológico de Monterrey (Ciudad de México), February 23, 2010; and Jeffrey Ayres and Laura MacDonald: Conference on 'North America in Question: Regional Integration in an Era of Political Economic Turbulence,' Atlanta, Ga., March 3–4, 2010.

It was also productive to draft chapters that triggered engagement with anonymous peer reviewers for their books: Burkhard Eberlein and Bruce Doern, eds., *Governing the Energy Challenge: Canada and Germany in a Multilevel Regional and Global Context* (University of Toronto Press, 2009); Jeffrey Ayres and Laura Macdonald, eds., *Contentious Politics in North America: National Protest and Transnational Collaboration under Continental Integration* (Palgrave Macmillan, 2009); Henrik Enderlein, Sonja Wälti, and Michael Zürn, eds., *Handbook on Multi-Level Governance* (Edward Elgar, 2011); and Christoph Herrmann, ed., *European Yearbook of International Economic Law* (2010).

We also profited from collegial responses when presenting earlier iterations of our analysis at the following academic conferences: ACSUS, 19th Biennial Conference, Toronto, November 18, 2007; a workshop on 'North American Perspectives on Border Security' organized by ACSUS, the North American Center for Transborder Studies at Arizona State University, and the Border Policy Research Institute at Western Washington, San Diego State University, January 12, 2008; ACSUS, 20th Biennial Conference, San Diego, California, November 21, 2009; the American Political Science Association, 2009 Annual Meeting, Toronto, Ontario, September 3, 2009; and the Canadian Political Science Association, 82nd Annual Conference, June 2, 2010.

When outside the continental limits of Canada, the United States, and Mexico, one's perspective on North America can develop a broader perspective. Clarkson has benefited in this regard from being able to present his work and have it scrutinized at the Department of Political Science, University of Munich, June 16, 2009; the Center for Advanced Studies, University of Munich, June 18, 2009; the University of Havana's biannual conference of the Asociación cubana de estudios canadienses, February 14, 2010; the Instituto Tecnológico de Monterrey (Ciudad de México), February 23, 2010; the Kolleg-Forschergruppe on 'The Transformative Power of Europe' in the Otto Suhr Institute for Political Science, Free University, May 10, 2010; the Political Science Department, University of Freiburg, July 22, 2010; and the Nordic Association for Canadian Studies, May 18, 2010.

To put our understanding of North America into a global perspective and generate a comparative analysis of it as a world region, it was extremely useful to have been able to make a lecture and research trip to India thanks to the support of the Department of Foreign Affairs and International Trade (DFAIT), the close cooperation of Bernard Francis, Simon Cridland, and Stewart Beck at the Canadian High Commission in Delhi, and the organizational capacities of the Shastri Indo-Canadian Institute which organized encounters at: Jamia Millia Islamia University, Delhi, January 18, 2011; Banares Hindu University, Varanasi, January 22, 2011; School of Management, Indian Institute of Technology (Bombay), Mumbai, January 27, 2011; University of Mumbai, January 27, 2000; SNDT Women's University, Mumbai, January 28, 2011; School of Management, University of Pondicherry, February 2, 2011; University of Madras, February 4, 2011; and Jawaharlal Nehru University, February 25, 2011.

Support from DFAIT also made possible Dr Alberto Gago's organizing a trip to Argentina where Clarkson could engage with the evolution of regionalism and North America's fragmented interaction with Latin America by giving talks to the Consejo Argentino de Relaciones Internacionales (Argentine Council on Foreign Relations), April 8, 2011, and the Facultad de Ciencias Políticas y Sociales, Universidad Nacional de Cuyo, April 11 and 12, 2011, and leading a graduate/faculty workshop at the Facultad de Ciencias Políticas y Sociales, Universidad Nacional de San Juan, April 13, 14, and 15, 2011.

Clarkson's Mexican research for *Does North America Exist?* was greatly facilitated by the excellent research assistance provided by Blanca Martínez López, who continued to help when called upon during the first years of this project. In the winter of 2010, her friend and colleague Haidy Durán Gil proved an outstanding successor. Her prime task was to arrange the review by appropriate experts of the Mexican content of the manuscript's nine chapters. As a former official in the Secretaría de Economía, she was able to organize interviews with senior government officials. As a highly capable researcher herself, she worked on each chapter to sharpen and deepen the Mexican side of its analysis.

It was only fitting that Matto Mildenberger, who had helped overcome the many obstacles requiring resolution for *Does North America Exist?* became Stephen Clarkson's co-author for this book. As a brilliant undergraduate in 2006–7, he had researched the US-Canada-Mexico labour-migration issue. While pursuing his MA he assisted in mentoring the other students whom Clarkson recruited over the next two years for this project. He crafted and administered the funding applications that enabled us to take our students to Washington and Mexico City, where he helped chaperone them in their interviewing. As a young colleague he collaborated in the revisions of every draft, taking particular charge of the data collection and analysis in chapters 1, 2, and 3 and ensuring the accuracy and accessibility of the manuscript's many references. But beyond the drafting work we did together, his overarching contribution was as a stimulating intellectual colleague, who discussed every idea during the long time it took to bring this project from inception to completion.

Production

At the University of Toronto Press, the publication process has been smooth and supportive. Daniel Quinlan has proven to be an excellent editor who perceptively reads and comments on the manuscripts he receives. He found two readers who helped crystallized conceptual issues with which we were struggling and so pushed us to raise the manuscript to a decidedly higher level, a quest that was greatly helped by Salvator Cusimano and Matt Zerker in the academic year 2010–11.

Meanwhile, we also asked a number of colleagues in Canada, the United States, and Mexico to review the chapter fitting their expertise.

These in-house peer reviewers' contributions are noted in each chapter's first reference. We would also like to express our gratitude at the very end of this effort to Curtis Fahey – for his rapid and insightful copy editing. But even he could not save us from whatever errors of fact and interpretation may still lurk in and between the lines – defects that remain our own responsibility.

Stephen Clarkson, University of Toronto
Matto Mildenberger, Yale University
August 2011

Index

OTHER PUBLICATIONS BY STEPHEN CLARKSON

Monographs

Does North America Exist? Governing the Continent after NAFTA and 9/11 (2008)

The Big Red Machine: How the Liberal Party Dominates Canadian Politics (2005)

Uncle Sam and Us: Globalization, Neoconservatism, and the Canadian State (2002)

Trudeau and Our Times. Volume 2: The Heroic Delusion (1994), trans. as *Trudeau: L'illusion héroique* (1995) (with Christina McCall)

Trudeau and Our Times. Volume 1: The Magnificent Obsession, trans. as *Trudeau: l'homme, l'utopie, l'histoire* (1990) (with Christina McCall)

Canada and the Reagan Challenge: Crisis in the Canadian-American Relationship (1982)

The Soviet Theory of Development: India and the Third World in Marxist-Leninist Scholarship (1978)

City Lib: Parties and Reform (1972)

L'analyse soviétique des problèmes indiens du sous-développement (1955–64) (1971)

Books Edited

My Life as a Dame: The Personal and the Political in the Writings of Christina McCall (2008)

Governing under Stress: Middle Powers and the Challenge of Globalization (2004) (with Marjorie Griffin Cohen)

Visions 2020: Fifty Canadians in Search of a Future (1970)

An Independent Foreign Policy for Canada? (1968)